TANGMERE

Following the partial destruction by German bombs of the officers' mess at RAF Tangmere in
March 1941, the mess was temporarily removed to Shopwyke House, a mile distant.
It is depicted here in the summer of 1942; note the presence of the USAAF officer.

Detail from oil on canvas by Olive Snell, courtesy of Lord Zetland and the RAF Museum.

TANGMERE

**Famous Royal Air Force Fighter Station
An Authorised History**

Reginald Byron
and
David Coxon

GRUB STREET
in association with
TANGMERE MILITARY AVIATION MUSEUM

First published in 2013 by
Grub Street Publishing
4 Rainham Close,
London
SW11 6SS

Reprinted 2014

Cover design by Sarah Driver
Book design by Roy Platten, Eclipse – roy.eclipse@btopenworld.com

Printed and bound by the Berforts Group, UK

Set in a sans serif typeface designed by Sussex artist Eric Gill in 1928
and widely used by Crown departments and the Royal Air Force from
the 1930s to the present day.

Contents

Prologue

This book traces the history of the Royal Air Force fighter station at Tangmere, near Chichester, West Sussex, from its beginnings in the First World War until its closure in 1970.

In its time, it was one of the best known and strategically most important fighter stations in the British Isles. Its original purpose was to defend a wedge-shaped sector of southeast England from Beachy Head and the city of Brighton in the east to the commercial port of Southampton in the west, with the naval base at Portsmouth in-between, extending north across the South Downs into Surrey and the southwestern outskirts of London. The station became well known in the 1920s and 1930s for the highly-polished air displays given at the RAF Air Pageants at Hendon by the pilots and aircraft of its resident squadrons, 1 and 43.

On the outbreak of the Second World War, 1 Squadron was the first RAF fighter squadron to be sent to France with the British Expeditionary Force, its ground echelon departing the day after war was declared, to be followed by 16 Hurricanes on 8 September 1939. With the fall of France in May 1940, Tangmere's squadrons found themselves in the front line, covering the withdrawal of the BEF and defending two of Britain's principal south coast ports and her shipping in the English Channel against the predations of the Luftwaffe, now flying from French airfields as close as only 70 miles away. During the Battle of Britain from July through October 1940 and the Blitz on London and other cities that followed, Tangmere was one of the main fighter stations to engage the Luftwaffe's attempt to destroy Britain's defences and break her will to fight. Tangmere's Hurricane and Spitfire pilots of 43, 601, 145, 602, 213, and 607 Squadrons gave as good accounts of themselves as any of 'the few', as Winston Churchill described them, upon whom the defence of the nation so vitally depended during that summer and autumn.

For the next three years, Tangmere continued to defend southern England against enemy attack, and turned increasingly to an offensive role making intruder sorties into German-occupied France, seeking out enemy aircraft and attacking Luftwaffe airfields and other vital infrastructural targets such as radar installations, railway junctions and power stations, and so gradually turn the tables by putting the enemy on the defensive. The tactical way forward was led by Wing Commander Douglas Bader and his fighter squadrons based at Tangmere, Westhampnett, and Merston in the spring and summer of 1941. Later, in August 1942, Tangmere was one of the chief jumping-off points for the fighter squadrons providing air cover for Operation Jubilee, the combined raid on Dieppe, directly across the Channel, the biggest aerial operation thus far in the history of warfare. Tangmere also served as a forward base during these years for 161 Squadron, whose Lysanders, landing in farmers' fields at night, inserted and retrieved secret agents operating with the Resistance deep inside occupied France. During 1942, 1943, and 1944, Tangmere's Spitfires, Typhoons, and Mustangs continued to harass the enemy across the Channel with increasing accuracy, ferocity, and persistence.

From March to June 1944, fighter squadrons from all over the country again massed at Tangmere and its neighbouring airfields, some built especially for the purpose, in preparation for Britain's part in Operation Overlord, covering the D-Day landings on Gold, Juno, and Sword beaches. The Tangmere Sector operations room, the nearest sector control room to the battle area, was a vital link in the command-and-control system of the RAF's Second Tactical Air Force and the combined (with the USAAF's Ninth Air Force) Allied Expeditionary Air Force; so important was it that in April its readiness to undertake this task was personally inspected by General Dwight D. Eisenhower, the Supreme Commander of the Allied Expeditionary Forces in Europe. No sooner had the massed squadrons begun to relocate to forward airfields in France following the invasion on 6 June than a new menace appeared, the retaliatory launch of V1 flying bombs aimed at London. Tangmere's remaining squadrons, and those on defensive duties at nearby stations, shot down hundreds of them before they could reach their targets.

As the V1 attacks diminished and the Allied armies pushed on into Germany, the station, now far away from the battlefront, took on a new lease of life with the arrival of the Central Fighter Establishment (CFE) in January 1945. The CFE's work was concerned with the testing and evaluation of new developments in tactical air warfare. The Fighter Leaders' Schools, operated under the CFE's aegis, brought together pilots from all over Britain, the Commonwealth, and other Allied countries to train them in the use of the most up-to-date equipment, weapons, and fighter tactics and prepare them to take command of squadrons and wings. The war in Europe ended in May, but the very real prospect of another D-Day in the Far East, an Allied invasion of the Japanese Home Islands, gave renewed urgency to the CFE's task.

Following VJ Day and the end of the Second World War, Tangmere once again settled down to a peace-time routine, for a while at least. The High Speed Flight, formed to make an attempt on the World Air Speed Record, came to Tangmere in the summer of 1946 and successfully achieved its aim. The same high-speed course was used once more in 1953 by the Hawker Aircraft Company, whose chief test pilot Neville Duke set another new World Air Speed Record. In the meantime, it had become clear that a new era had been ushered in: the Cold War. The threat of aerial attack was now from the east, rather than from the south across the Channel; Tangmere was no longer well positioned as an interceptor station. By the end of 1958, Fighter Command had withdrawn its last squadron. The aerodrome was used by Signals Command for another six years or so, during which Canberra and Varsity aircraft were sent up on daily flights to calibrate air-defence radars and navigational aids, and for a time a helicopter was maintained on stand-by for air-sea rescue duties. RAF Tangmere then served as a home to various non-flying units of Transport Command until the aerodrome was decommissioned in 1970.

Along the way, our story of RAF Tangmere touches upon several other aerodromes in the neighbourhood which were, in one way or another, connected with Tangmere: these include Westhampnett (now known as Goodwood), Merston, Ford, Shoreham, Friston, and Thorney Island. The first two, Westhampnett and Merston, were 'satellites' of Tangmere, or overspill airfields under Tangmere's immediate control, that were brought into use during 1940-41.

Ford was an independent RAF station from late 1940 until it was handed back to the Royal Navy in August 1945. Tangmere and Ford were built at the same time, 1917-18, and for the same purpose, as 'acceptance parks' for Handley Page bombers that were to be used in France by the Air Service of the American Expeditionary Forces during the First World War, but the war ended before the plan could be completely carried through. During the Second World War, the functions of the two aerodromes were once again intimately intertwined: Tangmere was predominantly a day-fighter station, and Ford maintained mainly night fighters; their roles in the air defence of the sector were complementary and interdependent. In January 1945, Ford officially became a satellite of RAF Tangmere to accommodate the Central Fighter Establishment's Night Wing, while the Day Wing was maintained at Tangmere itself.

Shoreham, a pre-war civil airfield, was for a brief period during 1944 formally transferred to RAF Tangmere as a satellite station in the run-up to D-Day and some weeks following. Friston, a former emergency landing ground (ELG) that was improved to accommodate fighter squadrons in the build-up to Operation Overlord, was similarly parented by Tangmere from April 1944 to May 1945, and again from February to April 1946. Thorney Island, a nearby Coastal Command base, was occasionally used temporarily to accommodate Tangmere's experimental Fighter Interception Unit in 1940-41 and Tangmere Sector fighter squadrons during Operation Jubilee in August 1942 and again around D-Day in 1944. Also included in the story of RAF Tangmere are the advanced landing grounds (ALGs) that at various times came under the Tangmere Sector command structure. There were seven ALGs in Sussex and one in Surrey, temporary airfields built mainly to accommodate the fighter squadrons that were to be deployed across the Channel with the Second Tactical Air Force in support of Operation Overlord in June 1944. Four were nearby and had close connections with Tangmere, which acted as their 'mother' station. These were Apuldram, Bognor, Funtington, and Selsey. The others, Chailey, Coolham, Deanland, and Horne, were farther away and had less to do with Tangmere apart from the period immediately before and after D-Day.

The foundations of this story are the official diaries, or Operations Record Books (ORBs), of the stations and squadrons (each kept their own) now preserved in the National Archives at Kew, London. Each book is made up of sheets of RAF Form 540, ledger-size printed forms specifically designed for the purpose of reporting events in a standard format. For Tangmere, there is a month-by-month account of the main events on the station from June 1925 to the end of its life, excepting the months of January and February and August to December 1945, which have been lost. Ford's ORB is complete, from its first day as an RAF station to its last. Well over 1,000 pages of these records have been consulted in the writing of this book, as well as other documents written at the time by those who were there or whose duty it was to make an accurate account of events more-or-less as they happened. Full details of the ORBs and other documents we have consulted are listed in the References at the end of this book. Generally speaking, it has been our intention to be guided by the ORBs. We follow the Tangmere ORB quite closely, and quote from it frequently.

The records are not without their problems for historical researchers, however. The style of reporting and level of detail changed over the years, and much depended on the personal propensities of the officers responsible for keeping the ORBs. Completing the Form 540 pages could be either taken as a serious task, or as a routine administrative chore dashed off in perfunctory fashion by someone with little patience for such things. The ORB pages were usually prepared at the end of the month. They could be vague about the details of events in the preceding four weeks if the officer responsible did not make proper notes at the time and relied upon memory to fill in the blanks. Other officers gave much more precise details, and clearly drew upon carefully kept diary notes of the preceding weeks' events which were cross-checked against flying control logs, departmental returns, and pilots' combat reports giving details of their sorties. The month's summary could vary in length from one sheet of Form 540 to seven, eight, ten or more. From the 1930s, the forms were normally typed rather than written in longhand. Errors such as reversed figures can sometimes be seen in the ORBs that were probably introduced by the typist and were not caught by the officer who appended his signature; perhaps a minor matter then, but a more important one now if, say, '59 Lancasters' was typed when '95 Lancasters' was intended, or vice-versa. Nevertheless, despite their varying level of detail and occasional errors and omissions, the ORBs are the most trustworthy records available to us since they were written at the time (and so have the advantage of contemporaneity) by people who were there.

Problems of reliability arise even more acutely with recent oral interview material, or autobiographical reminiscences written long after the event, or with books and articles that do not make it clear where their information comes from. We have tried to check the details given in much-later sources, where we have used them, against the official documents made at the time and where discrepancies occur we have given greater weight to the official documents. Two examples of such discrepancies can be given here: it is something of a legend at Tangmere that the labour of German prisoners-of-war was used in the construction of the aerodrome during the First World War; it may have been, and this idea has found its way into print, but we have been unable to verify this with any official documentary evidence made at the time and so we have not accepted this as fact and repeated it in this book as if it were.

A second example is the strafing of Field Marshal Erwin Rommel's staff car in Normandy on 17 July 1944, with which there is a Tangmere connection. Charley Fox, who may have been the man responsible and was interviewed on several occasions about the incident later in life, for nearly 60 years was firmly convinced that his wingman on the sortie in question was his close friend Steve Randall, with whom he normally flew. The Fox-Randall story has been repeated many times and is even the subject of a children's book. Yet the squadron's ORB, consulted only in 2003, showed Fox's wingman to have been someone else; Randall had not flown on that sortie at all. Charley had misremembered this vital fact, which meant that the man who actually flew with Fox on that occasion, Edward L. Prizer, was not during his lifetime given credit for firing at the car along with Fox. Both Prizer's flying log book (which came to light in 2011) and the details of the squadron's sorties flown that day as given in the squadron ORB confirm that he, and not Steve Randall, was Charley's wingman when together they attacked a vehicle at a time and place that might well have meant that it could have been, and probably was, Erwin Rommel's staff car.

A number of people have helped to make this book a reality, to whom we owe our thanks. Quite independently of the efforts that were being made to establish a museum on the aerodrome at Tangmere in the decade following its closure, Mr Charles Townsend, who lived at Church Farm House, Tangmere, had begun to do some research on the early history of the aerodrome. Mr Townsend was a retired civil engineer with a lively curiosity and interest in the past; he had, for example, surmised the existence, rightly as it turned out, of medieval frescoes on the walls of Tangmere's St Andrew's Church underneath centuries' worth of distemper and white paint. His research into the history of the village, and of the aerodrome, involved many hours patiently examining the Goodwood estate papers and official records in the National Archives at Kew, as well as corresponding with dozens of people and Crown departments to find out where further pieces of information might be garnered. Most of his papers were later deposited in the West Sussex Record Office at Chichester; some found their way into the archives of the Tangmere Military Aviation Museum. We have used some of the documents located by Mr Townsend in the writing of Chapter 1 of this book, and the investigative trail he left has helped us to find many other pieces of historical evidence about the aerodrome that were not accessible to him when he was doing his research in the early 1980s.

For the use of the extracts from published and unpublished works that appear in this book, we thank Mrs Gwendoline Duke, Mrs Daphne Olley, Mrs Diana Richey, and the families of H. R. Allen, James Beedle, Sir Robin Hooper, Jeremy Howard-Williams, Edward Prizer, Sir Frederick Rosier, Sir Anthony Selway, Peter Townsend, and Stanley Vincent; publishers Crécy, Grub Street, Pen and Sword, Random House, the University Press of Kansas, and the Aviation Bookshop (proprietors of the Beaumont editions of James Beedle's *43 Squadron*); the editors of the *Military History Journal;* Air Commodore Graham Pitchfork MBE for his permission to use an extract from his book *Shot Down and in the Drink*, and Michael Shaw for allowing us to quote from his book, *Twice Vertical: The History of No. 1 Squadron, Royal Air Force*.

We should like particularly to thank seven of our museum colleagues: David Burleigh MBE, who compiled the appendices, a painstaking task involving much detective work; Marion Cover, who patiently transcribed the station ORB for the month of June 1944; Caroline Byron, Valerie Cuthbert, and Simon Godfrey, who combed through our archives for useful materials; Pete Pitman, who helped to locate some of the photographs; and Group Captain David Baron OBE, who carefully corrected a full draft of the manuscript. We were also helped by the staff of the Royal Air Force Museum, the National Archives, the West Sussex Record Office, the Imperial War Museum, and the United States Air Force Historical Research Office, all of whom responded generously to our queries and supplied us with materials that we have used in this book. Finally, and most importantly, we should like to express our indebtedness to the Council of the Tangmere Military Aviation Museum Trust Company. Without the Council's support, this project would not have been possible.

In a story as complex as this, involving so many facts, figures, events, and people, the authors have had to be selective about what has been included in this book and what has been left out in order to keep it to a manageable length, and there are bound to be errors and omissions that have escaped us despite repeated re-readings. The responsibility for any infelicities rests entirely with us, as the authors. If you, as a reader, notice anything that ought to be mentioned or corrected in a future edition, please let us know.

1

Air Defence of Great Britain
1916 – 1938

The village of Tangmere, whose recorded history can be traced back to the seventh century, lies a mile south of the Roman road of Stane Street, linking London with Chichester. The Domesday Book of the eleventh century records Tangmere as having a population of about 120 souls and a Saxon church. By 1341, the Manor of Tangmere had been granted by King Edward II to the Archbishop of Canterbury. Following the Reformation its ownership passed back and forth between Crown, church, and nobility until it was acquired by Charles Lennox (1735-1806), the third Duke of Richmond. It remained part of the family's extensive Goodwood estates until 1935, when the Manor of Tangmere was broken up and parts of it were sold to cover the death duties on the estate of the eighth Duke.

The origin of what was later to become the Royal Air Force aerodrome at Tangmere was a chance forced landing in a large open field just to the south of the village, thought to be part of Church Farm tenanted by Mr George Bayley, in November 1916. Lieutenant Geoffrey Dorman of the Royal Flying Corps was piloting an FE2B pusher biplane when it developed engine trouble on a flight from Shoreham to Gosport. He put his aeroplane down in the field apparently without damage, and in his report on the incident offered his opinion that the open field and those round about would make a good landing ground, by which we can presume that he meant that the fields were level, firm, and well-drained without boggy patches, ditches, trees, or other obstacles, and had favourable prevailing breezes for taking off and landing. His report appears to have had an immediate effect at higher levels.

The Goodwood estate papers include a letter dated December 1916, only a month or so later, from HM Comptroller of Lands, War Office, sent to Mr R. Hussey Freke, the Duke of Richmond's land agent, referring to the proposed establishment of an aerodrome at Tangmere. Ten months later, by September 1917, 200 acres of land, including a substantial part of Church Farm, had been compulsorily requisitioned from the Goodwood estate under the Defence of the Realm Regulations (1914), along with parts of East Hampnett Farm tenanted by Mr C. W. Atkey, and other adjoining parcels of land. By that time, a temporary two-foot-gauge railway line had been laid from the London, Brighton and South Coast's goods sidings at Drayton, a mile distant, to convey wagonloads of sand, gravel, and other building materials to the airfield site and extensive ground works were in progress.

The first evidence of the occupation of the aerodrome in the Goodwood papers is contained in a letter dated 24 March 1918, sent to Mr Freke, the Duke's land agent, from Captain A. Broomer, adjutant of 92 Squadron, who gave his address as Tangmere Station, Royal Flying Corps. A letter of April 12th from Mr Freke complains of damage to the chimney of one of the Duke's cottages at Boxgrove, clipped by an aeroplane of 93 Squadron making a forced landing. We know from another source, a letter written by an RFC pilot named Bogart Rogers, that 91 Squadron had arrived at Tangmere a month earlier on 15 March 1918, followed by 92 on the 17th, and Rogers's own squadron, 93, a day or two later.

Despite appearances, however, it was not a Royal Flying Corps aerodrome. While it was initially occupied by the RFC's 91, 92, and 93 Squadrons from March 1918, the RFC was merely a temporary tenant, using the aerodrome for training purposes until the Air Service of the American Expeditionary Forces was ready to move in.

On its entry into the First World War on 6 April 1917, the United States was ill-prepared to contribute to the air war in Europe. In 1914, the Aviation Section of the US Army Signal Corps had a complement of only 28 officers and 166 other ranks; by 1917 this had risen to a little over 100 officers and 1,000 other ranks, but there were no pilots with combat experience, and no combat-worthy aircraft that could be deployed in France with the American Expeditionary Forces. By September 1917, plans had been drawn up for the Air Service to be expanded to 260 front-line fighter and bomber squadrons, and the United States sought arrangements with Britain, Canada, and France to train the pilots and to supply the aeroplanes and overseas aerodromes that the new American expeditionary squadrons would need.

An agreement was signed between the American and British governments in January 1918 to equip 30 night-bombing squadrons with an initial order of 310 Handley Page 0/400 two-engined bombers – or, more precisely, the finished airframe parts and engines of 310 bombers – to be built under licence in the United States, then shipped to Britain for assembly. A disused cotton mill at Oldham, Lancashire, and some adjoining fields were to be prepared for the assembly and testing of the new American bombers. At the same time, suitable sites for five ASAEF aerodromes (initially referred to as 'acceptance parks') along the Sussex coast, within easy reach by the bombers of airfields on the French side of the Channel, were identified at Ford Junction, Tangmere, Rustington, Southbourne, and Goring-by-Sea. Work had already begun to build aerodromes on the first two of these sites when the responsibility for their completion was taken over by the Americans. The American government sub-contracted most of the construction work on these projects to the British government, and agreed to pay the cost of materials and labour plus a fixed percentage in overheads.

The plan called for the first three American night-bombing squadrons to be equipped and trained at the five ASAEF aerodromes in Sussex and transferred to airfields in France by 1 September 1918. A series of setbacks and delays owing to manufacturing difficulties, labour shortages and logistical problems meant that the programme soon fell behind schedule. By November 1918, the American-made parts for only 107 of the 310 Handley Page bombers and only 50 of the 350 hp Liberty 12-N engines that were intended to power them had arrived in Britain. When the Armistice came into force on 11 November, the first ten aircraft were still being fitted out in the factory at Oldham, and only two of the five ASAEF aerodromes, Tangmere and Ford Junction, were sufficiently well advanced in their construction to be declared operational before the war came to an end. A start had been made on the American aerodromes at Rustington and Southbourne, but little or nothing had been accomplished at Goring-by-Sea.

Following the Armistice, in December 1918 Lieutenant Colonel W. H. Shutan, officer in charge of the Construction Division of the Air Service, American Expeditionary Forces, submitted a final report on the work done under his command, which included responsibility for the five Handley Page aerodromes. Tangmere, like Ford, was one of the closest to completion when the Armistice was declared because the land had been acquired and work had already started on the construction of an aerodrome. Colonel Shutan mentions this, and goes on to describe what building works were done at Tangmere while under American administration, which included the construction of 'three aeroplane sheds about 180' long and 200' wide', (that is, three sets of double Belfast-truss General Service hangars) 'being similar in every way to those erected for the British Air Force' and 'the whole of the designs and work [for these hangars being] carried out under the supervision of the Administration of Works & Buildings, Air Ministry'.

In addition to the buildings that had been planned originally by the RFC, the ASAEF specified a 'shed for the housing of four Handley Page machines, with extended wings' and 'in order that the depreciation of the machines should be minimised as much as possible ... the system which was adopted was to heat the air by passing it through steam-heated coils and passing this hot air into the building by means of electric fans'. 'The technical and regimental buildings were constructed in a similar matter to the [General Service] aeroplane sheds, viz. of concrete floors, brick walls, timber roof trusses.' Mention is made also of a self-contained water system whose source was a bore-hole, an elevated main tank, and an auxiliary electric booster pump for the fire mains. Power sufficient to supply all the station's needs, including 'the whole of the camp with electric light', the fire-main pump, and other equipment was provided by a plant consisting of 'two oil-engines fitted with electric dynamos'; and a self-contained drainage and sewage treatment system was constructed to prevent contamination of the soil. Central petrol storage tanks, with distribution points at several places on the aerodrome, are also mentioned. 'With respect to the regimental buildings, provision for complete washing, cooking and bathing, and sufficient accommodation was provided to allow everyone in the camp to have a hot bath at least once a week.'

The Air Ministry's Aerodrome Board, in one of their first quarterly surveys following the establishment of the Royal Air Force in April 1918, described Tangmere as 'a Training Depot Station (Three Unit) for American Units, Handley Page Training' and gives an inventory of the facilities of the station as at 1 August 1918. Under 'Technical Buildings' are listed six aeroplane sheds each 170' x 100' (the three pairs of double Belfast-truss hangars referred to in Col. Shutan's report), a Handley Page shed measuring 330' x 90' (also mentioned by Col. Shutan) and an Aeroplane Repair Shed 'with Plane Stores' which was a single Belfast-truss hangar of 170' x 100' that Col. Shutan omitted to mention. The Air Ministry inventory goes on to list two motor transport sheds; seven workshop buildings; technical, fuel, oil and ammunition stores; six instructional huts; three unit commanders' offices; a power house; and a guard house. Messes and quarters for officers, sergeants, men, and a women's hostel are also listed. Messing and quarters at Tangmere were originally planned by the RFC for 170 officers, 48 NCOs, 370 men, and 284 women, but it is not clear whether the women's living quarters were actually constructed to this extent by the Americans since so far as is known the ASAEF had very few, if any, women in its service living on overseas stations. At the time the Aerodrome Board inventory was made, 1 August 1918, the permanent hangarage was about half finished (portable Bessoneau hangars were still being used by the RAF training units who had been present on the station since March), but the technical and living quarters buildings had been completed and were ready for occupation.

Tangmere officially opened as an ASAEF station on 1 August 1918. As the American airmen arrived, the RAF's 91 and 93 training squadrons moved out to make space for them. No. 92 (T) Squadron remained at Tangmere to train the Americans on a variety of aircraft types. Coincidentally, or perhaps not, these three RAF training squadrons were made up of mostly American and Canadian volunteers. Over 300 Americans are thought to have joined the RFC or RAF during the First World War, most of whom, following training, were randomly assigned to whatever squadrons needed replacement pilots. Some of them, like John Donaldson of the RAF's 32 Squadron, who had joined the RFC in 1916 and transferred to the Air Service of the AEF after the entry of the United States into the war, remained attached at his request to an RAF squadron until the Armistice. Even after April 1917, Americans continued to join the RFC or RAF rather than the ASAEF because – by virtue of Britain's much longer experience of aerial warfare – the training was better organised, it was better equipped, and the prospects of seeing early action on the Western Front were greater.

One of the Americans in the RAF who passed through Tangmere was Bogart Rogers, whose collected letters – a number of them written at Tangmere – were published in 1996 under the title, *A Yankee Ace in the RAF*. On 20 March 1918, he wrote:

We've been working all morning putting up [Bessoneau] hangars as the camp is only about half finished. The hangars come with a pile of girders, several rolls of canvas, and a box of bolts and metal fittings. Getting them together is like working out a jig-saw puzzle. However when they are up they make fine, large sheds.

We have a fine large mess hall with lounging rooms and electric lights and our quarters aren't at all bad. But both are only about half finished, and the plaster is still damp.

The aerodrome is large and level as a tennis court and covered with turf like any front lawn. It's situated in a very pretty part of Sussex, about five miles from the Channel and mid way between Portsmouth and Bristol [presumably Rogers meant to write Brighton]. The nearest town of any size is Chichester which is about four miles away. Tangmere is merely a hamlet situated back of the camp.

Rogers says that there were 'any number' of different types of aircraft on the station 'ranging from tiny scouts to enormous bombers'. He describes the daily training routine: three or four hours of flying from 06.30 to 13.00 three days a week, and from 12.00 until dark on the other three days. Within two weeks of his arrival at Tangmere, he was flying single-seat SE5As, one of the standard front-line fighters of the time.

By May, Rogers had been assigned to 32 Squadron, stationed in France. His new squadron included eleven other Americans, five of whom were ASAEF pilots on attachment and six – like Rogers himself – RAF volunteers, plus fourteen Canadians. Of the Americans, John Donaldson, Alvin Callender, Frank Hale and Bogart Rogers became 'aces', credited with shooting down five or more enemy aircraft. This proportion of Americans in 32 Squadron was fairly typical: in 1917-18, about one-third of the pilots in RFC and RAF front-line squadrons were Americans or Canadians.

Between August and November, the ASAEF airmen at Tangmere flew BE2Es, DH4s, DH9As, Farman F50s, British-built 0/400s and other aircraft, often landing at the other nearly finished and now likewise ASAEF-manned Handley Page aerodrome at Ford Junction. Ford had also opened in August, with the 92nd Aero Squadron (not to be confused with the RAF's 92 (T) Squadron at Tangmere) taking up residence. On 15 September an advanced training school was established at Ford for the ASAEF's Night Bombardment Section, where 28 officers and 70 other ranks were under instruction in night navigation by radio direction. On completion of the course, the squadron would be transferred to France.

As it turned out, none of these airmen had completed their night bombardment training at Ford, and none of the ASAEF's own 0/400 bombers had been delivered by the factory at Oldham when the Armistice came into force on 11 November. One set of parts produced by the National Aircraft Factory No. 1 at Croydon for 0/400 F.5349, an RAF machine, was, however, being assembled at Ford as a training exercise for the American engineers and aircrew pending the arrival of the ASAEF's own aeroplanes. A contingent of US Army Signal Corps official photographers visited Ford Junction aerodrome in October 1918 and took a number of photographs of this 0/400 and of the American airmen present on the station. Six days after the Armistice, the ASAEF ground staff and aircrew of the 92nd Aero Squadron at Ford moved to Tangmere along with their aeroplanes, but very soon thereafter the ASAEF personnel began to pack up and by 21 December the 92nd Aero Squadron had been disbanded and the American airmen had left for home. No evidence has come to light of the presence of ASAEF airmen at Tangmere into January 1919, although a few administrative staff might have remained for a time to make arrangements for the disposition of American-owned supplies and equipment.

For the rest of 1919 Tangmere aerodrome was used by the RAF, presumably with the permission of the Americans, who still owned it, as a demobilisation and training depot. There is evidence, for example, that a cadre of 16 officers and men of 41 Squadron, who had flown SE5As in France, were resident on the station from 7 February until October, when they moved to Croydon. No. 61 Training Squadron was also present until the end of the year and elements of 14, 32, 82, 84, 92, 148, and 207 Squadrons were known to have been on the station for varying periods; there may have been others of which there are no surviving records. At the end of 1919, following an inventory of its buildings, fixtures, and facilities, the aerodrome was vacated and put up for disposal.

The Goodwood estate papers include two letters dated 5 July and 5 August 1921 in the correspondence between the Disposals and Liquidation Commission (who were charged with arranging the return of property requisitioned by the Crown during the First World War and negotiating compensation for its use); and Mr Freke, the Goodwood land agent; and Messrs Stride, estate agents acting for the Duke of Richmond.

From Mr Freke to Messrs Stride:
> . . . His Grace is willing to accept £60 per acre for the 39¼ acres of land (subject to measurement) upon which the aerodrome buildings stand, the sale being subject to tithe apportionment and the land being substantially fenced.

From the Disposals and Liquidation Commission to Messrs Stride:
> I am now instructed on behalf of the United States government to proceed with the proposed purchase, namely the Duke of Richmond's land, about 39¼ acres, @ £60 per acre, and Mr Reynold's [sic] land, approximately 10 acres, for £700.

The American government had paid the British government £256,000 to construct and equip the aerodrome buildings and other facilities at Tangmere, and may have hoped to realise a better return on their investment by buying the land on which the buildings stood. If so, it proved to be an overly optimistic decision, as they failed to find a buyer in the months that followed. Papers in the National Archives at Kew dated 1923 (AIR 2/240) and correspondence in the Goodwood estate letter book refer to the purchase of these 49¼ acres of land and the aerodrome buildings for £18,000 from the American government by the Crown when it was decided, in that year, to reactivate the station as a part of the RAF's expansion of Home Defences. An Air Ministry confidential minute noted that the buildings were 'in a very fair state of repair' and 'a saving of roughly £80,000 to £90,000' would be effected by utilising this station instead of building on a new site.

The Steel-Bartholomew Committee of 1922 had been set the task of devising a plan to counter the threat to national security posed by a French air force many times greater in size than the RAF. The British defences of 1914-18 had been drastically reduced from about 850 serviceable aircraft at the time of the Armistice. By 1921, at its lowest point, only five RAF squadrons remained on Home strength – one fighter squadron and four army co-operation squadrons, none of which was assigned to the defence of

London, and comprising, altogether, about 40 operational aircraft – compared with a serviceable strength of roughly 600 French aircraft across the Channel. Although the prospect of an aerial attack by the French was regarded as extremely remote, it was felt politically unacceptable that there should be such a great disparity in strength between the French and British air forces, as was the virtual absence of credible British ground-based anti-aircraft defences. Accordingly, the responsibility for the Air Defence of Great Britain (ADGB) was transferred from the War Department to the Air Ministry, and prime ministerial approval was given for the number of fighter squadrons and stations, along with observation posts, anti-aircraft batteries, searchlights, and their personnel (now placed under RAF control), to be expanded with immediate effect.

Tangmere, because of its strategic position and its already substantially finished facilities, seems to have been one of the first aerodromes to benefit from this new policy. Before the year 1923 was out, the American-owned land and buildings at Tangmere had been purchased by the Crown. An additional 130¼ acres of land that had been taken over by the War Department on a temporary basis during the First World War for use as the aerodrome's landing ground (including 86¼ acres of Church Farm in the tenancy of Mr Bayley, and 44 acres in the Parish of Boxgrove in the tenancy of Messrs J. W. Blunden and Sons) were sold by the Duke of Richmond to the Crown for £7,616 and the former tenants compensated for their losses. Renewed work began on the station, putting up new accommodation blocks; renovating the seven Belfast-truss General Service hangars, the Handley Page shed, and other infrastructural facilities that had been built in 1917-18; and restoring and improving the landing ground.

On 1 June 1925, Tangmere was re-opened as a military aerodrome, this time under the aegis of the Royal Air Force, but for nearly a year-and-a-half was used as an aircraft storage depot pending the arrival of new fighter aircraft and the officers and men to fly and maintain them, as well as all the other personnel and equipment needed to bring the new station into operation. During the 1920s, with most of its squadrons tied down on peace-keeping duties in the Middle East and the Northwest Frontier, the RAF's resources were fully stretched and it took time to assemble cadres of experienced men to form these new, additional ADGB fighter squadrons and to recruit and train pilots, riggers, fitters, general duties airmen, and medical, administrative, and domestic staff.

The first entry in the Operations Record Book for RAF Tangmere as an ADGB station was made on 23 November 1926, recording the arrival of the new station commander, Wing Commander John Tyssen MC, who had formerly commanded 36 and 58 Squadrons on the Western Front and 20 Squadron on the Northwest Frontier. Three weeks later, three flights of Gloster Gamecocks of 43 Squadron commanded by Squadron Leader A. F. Brooke arrived from Henlow along with their headquarters staff.

Three months later, in March 1927, they were joined by a nucleus of 1 Squadron officers, recently returned from Iraq, initially under the temporary command of Flight Lieutenant F. L. Luxmoore DFC. Soon after his arrival, Frank Luxmoore's application to stand down from general duties and go on the half-pay list was accepted. Over the following years, the gazette pages of *Flight* magazine mention his name as pursuing a colourful variety of aviation interests, which included racing as a private entrant in the King's Cup and other air races in the late 1920s; establishing (along with others) Portsmouth, Southsea and Isle of Wight Aviation, which provided scheduled services with a fleet of Airspeed Couriers between Ryde and Portsmouth, Southampton, and Bournemouth in the late 1930s; and later (in the 1940s) his best-known accomplishment, designing the Aerocar, a twin-boom aircraft accommodating its passengers in a low-slung gondola.

For a brief period following Frank Luxmoore's departure and before the arrival in 1928 of a permanent commanding officer, 1 Squadron was commanded by its senior flight commander, Flight Lieutenant S. F. Vincent AFC. In his autobiography, *Flying Fever*, Stanley Vincent describes his memories of the station:

> Tangmere was an extremely pleasant station, near Chichester and the south coast and Goodwood golf course. It was a sunny part of England and often had beautiful clear weather while the rest of the country, just across the South Downs, was under low cloud. Taking full advantage of this we were able to do a lot of flying. We had a new married quarter and pleasant neighbours so life was good.
>
> On days when there were large banks of cumulus clouds we played a game, in 'A' Flight, of follow-my-leader, round, over, under and through valleys but never actually inside the cloud. The idea was for

the leader to lose his followers; it really did teach quick reactions necessary for a fighter pilot. The leader would dive through a gap and promptly climb vertically up beyond the cloud, over the top and a diving turn after and so on. It got increasingly difficult for the followers and usually No. 4 would get flung out on the whip-lash effect. Then a reformation – No. 2 would lead and No. 1 then tagged on the end and so on. It was exhilarating.

One of my lasting impressions of flying came from a trip at Tangmere; night-flying in a Siskin at a time when it was completely clouded over at about 2,000 feet, and very dark and dreary. I climbed up into the cloud, as by this time we had the necessary instruments and after about another 1,000 feet suddenly came out into a clear sky with an almost full moon. The effect of this sudden change was staggering; mile after mile of almost flat but dimpled white 'eiderdown' below and a dome of clear sky with myriads of stars and the moon above. I sang with joy, and it was perhaps lucky that it was pre-radio telephony so that other aircraft or ground stations could not hear. After too short a time I had to come back to murky reality by descending well to the south of the aerodrome so that I would not fly into the Downs.

Twice, during my three years there, the squadron won the inter-squadron annual gunnery competition for which we did our air-to-ground and air-to-air (towed-target) firing at Sutton Bridge on the Wash. We spent three weeks there carrying out the various practices and competitions daily. I was the individual winner the first year and was second the following. On the last occasion we had to fly back to Tangmere on Friday the 13th with a formation of thirteen aircraft, which I led in spite of an adverse weather report and low clouds with rain showers. Several pilots were apprehensive, so I related my Friday the 13th experiences in France. By squeezing through the 'Shoreham Gap' [referred to by others as the 'Arundel Gap'] in the Downs, we all duly arrived.

A disconcerting incident did occur when we were practising for one of the Hendon displays. With 43 Squadron, who shared Tangmere with us, and 25 Squadron from Hawkinge, we were to carry out wing manoeuvres including aerobatics of a fairly mild but showy type. One exercise entailed the wing in line astern, diving down in succession followed by a climb into a half-loop with a half-roll off the top, so that the line snaked back over itself. This was a reasonably safe manoeuvre as the climb into the half-loop would take the leader and those following well above those still diving at a fairly gentle angle, and the half-roll would take them slightly out of line to those following.

Eustace Grenfell, leading our squadron which led the whole wing, was over-anxious that when he pulled over he would be well above those down the line. So as he started his half-loop, he kept going up and up before pulling over at the top. Leading the second flight of three, I was No. 4 in line close behind No. 3 of the leading flight. When I got into the vertical position, the other two ahead were still going vertically themselves, straining to follow No. 1 and I realised that he himself would not be able to carry out his half-roll, and would be bound to lose too much speed and fall out of it to the danger of all below. No. 2, also realising this, pulled over with his half-loop, but already having lost speed did a sloppy twist; No. 3, overtaking him, hit his tail with his propeller. I could see all this happening in front of me and decided to complete my half-loop and half-roll while I had full control, so over I went, thus avoiding what was happening above.

Those behind followed me according to plan, so I found myself leading a long line of Siskins which I proceeded to re-form into squadrons by signals, and break up the party.

Grenfell, 'waffling' out of the top of his half-loop, came out at 90 degrees to that desired entirely on his own. No. 3, with a smashed propeller, was fortunately over the aerodrome and so could shut off his engine and landed successfully. No. 2, having lost part of his tailplane, contemplated taking to his parachute, but realising he could maintain level flight, climbed to a safe height for parachuting to find out if there was sufficient control to attempt landing. Finding the minimum safe speed that he could use down to ground level, he very ably brought his damaged aeroplane down to a successful landing. Grenfell then decided he would not try to lead the formation, and it fell upon 'old Joe' and I led from then on.

Indeed, Vincent found himself leading quite a lot of the time during Grenfell's tenure as CO of 1 Squadron. As senior flight commander, it was left to Vincent to run the squadron's day-to-day affairs when the CO was otherwise engaged. Seemingly, Grenfell was otherwise engaged a good deal of the time, mainly with his sailing dinghy, which he kept at Itchenor on Chichester Harbour (he was even known to have capsized his boat with the CO of 43 Squadron – Squadron Leader Cyril Lowe MC DFC, the great rugby player – crewing for him, while Stanley Vincent and his 43 Squadron opposite number looked after the business of the squadrons in their absence).

If anyone could be called 'an airman's airman', Vincent would be at the top table. After his tour on the Western Front, he was posted to the School of Special Flying at Gosport in the last year of the Great War to teach flying instructors the arts of tactical air warfare, for which he was awarded one of the first AFCs to be gazetted. Later, at Croydon with 24 Squadron, he taught HRH Prince Albert, Duke of York (later King George VI) to fly, as well as on one occasion informally instructing his elder brother the Prince of Wales. Winston Churchill, then Minister of War and Air Minister, being the sort of man he was, thought that in order to know more about the latter post he should learn to fly. Major Jack Scott, who had done great service in the First War, initially took the task upon himself but not being the finest pilot succeeded only in crashing the aircraft, breaking his legs, with Mr Churchill – who fortunately remained unscathed – in the rear seat. Thereafter Stanley Vincent looked after Mr Churchill's instruction.

Vincent was extremely lucky to have had his excellent flying and teaching skills recognised by his superiors and to have remained on the active list when so many of his colleagues holding regular commissions were ordered to choose between half-pay or be severed altogether from the service during the retrenchments suffered by the RAF from 1919 to the mid-1920s; even those who remained, like Vincent, were truly tested by being made through force of circumstance to stay at the same rank and pay grade for years on end. Their reward was borne of their love of flying; a married man by 1928, Vincent was delighted to be posted as a senior flight commander at Tangmere, where the couple's first child was born. His legacy to Tangmere was a poplar grove planted under his supervision to the southwest of the officers' mess while he was president of it in 1930. The grove came to be known as 'Vincent's Folly', which in the fullness of time he returned to inspect in 1948, along with the station and its squadrons, as air vice-marshal (AVM) and air officer commanding (AOC) 11 Group.

No. 1 Squadron was fully equipped by November 1927 and from this date until the beginning of the Second World War, together with 43, made Tangmere the envy of all who wished to serve on an RAF fighter station. Tangmere's primary role in the Fighting Area, ADGB, was to protect the port of Southampton and the naval base at Portsmouth. During the summer, a tropical routine was operated at the station; flying starting at 07.30 hours when the first sections would take off, the flying continuing until the station was stood down at 13.00 hours. Lunch followed, after which the squadron personnel were released for the remainder of the day to enjoy the local delights, such as playing golf at nearby Goodwood. After dinner, pubs such as the Old Ship at Bosham, the Red Lion at Pagham and the Unicorn in The Hornet, Chichester, were frequented by the squadrons. The Metropole and Hippodrome in Brighton, down the coast, were also favourite entertainment spots for aircrew and airmen alike. No wonder then, that in the depressed days of the late 1920s and early 1930s the RAF was referred to as the 'best flying club on earth' and its pilots envied by all.

Mark Selway, then a young pilot officer just out of Cranwell on his first posting, recalled those days:

Tangmere turned out to be one of the finest stations a young man could ever wish to go to. It was situated a little way from Bognor, a little way from Chichester and to its east it had Arundel. Then there was Littlehampton and Hove and then Brighton, and to its west, having passed through Havant, you came across Portsmouth and after that Southampton. All the way along this coastline was our happy hunting ground in the evenings. An ancient car full of penniless pilot officers would go off, if you had the money, and do a little pub crawling, and we got to know all the most delightful pubs along the South Downs.

Well, I was posted to 'A' Flight of 1 Squadron and with me came Freddie Wightman, and Teddy Corbally. No. 43 Squadron was the 'other' squadron, great rivals of ours. We had supercharged Siskins; Armstrong-Whitworth Siskins equipped with Armstrong Siddeley 385 hp engines. No. 43 Squadron's aircraft had the unsupercharged engines. When we met in friendly combat on our daily flying exercises 43 Squadron always had the better of us lower down, but if we could catch them a little bit higher, at perhaps 10 or 15,000 feet, our superchargers gave us the edge and we could, by a process of twirling and twisting, usually get the better of them.

My commanding officer was Squadron Leader Eustace Grenfell, who terrified the wits out of us. He was a very surly looking, plain officer with a distinguished war record. He had a DFC, MC, and an AFC, and he was a brilliant pilot. But he was most unattractive, poor man, and well known to the whole of the air force as being so. We all went for an interview, the four of us, and Tommy Hope also came with us. Tommy was a short-service officer. The interview didn't last very long. All that Grenfell said was "I've got quite enough pilots, I really don't want any more. I didn't ask for you to come here and I don't know why they've sent you. But while you are here you had better behave yourselves, and", he added, "if I catch any of you low flying I'll have you flogged."

We came out of the interview rather dazed and asked each other on our way back to the flight office: "Could it be so?" In the advanced year of 1929 could it be that a commanding officer had the powers to flog his officers? We didn't think so, but it was, to say the least of it, rather a surprising introduction to our first squadron.

But all this was compensated for by the three flight commanders. My own was Stanley Vincent, an awfully nice chap. He was an 'old man', at least 35, because he was wearing World War ribbons, including an AFC. He was a brilliant pilot and we learned more from him about what the Royal Air Force was all about than we had during the many long months at Cranwell.

The reason why these two squadrons were situated at Tangmere, which was very near the south coast, was that we were designated as 'Interceptor' squadrons. Our task was to intercept enemy aircraft coming over to attack England, and it is strange to reflect that the only enemy we could possibly envisage, or think about doing such a thing, was France and so we were always thinking about intercepting aircraft coming from that country. We used to carry out 'battle flight climbs' to 20,000 feet. A duty battle flight climb was done almost every week and it was done either in formation, with others, or solo. We had to do this climb as rapidly as possible so as to get used to it.

Now we had no oxygen in those days; oxygen wasn't fitted, and so you were inclined to feel a little faint at 20,000 feet or higher and to behave, well, not quite in your normal manner. Later on of course this became known as 'anoxia' or lack of oxygen. So up we climbed, dressed in long leather flying boots which you pulled on, rather like salmon fishing boots and a romantic sort of leather coat with sleeves and a collar which you strapped round yourself, and a helmet. There was no radio of course or any means of communicating with other aircraft, or indeed to the ground. That was one of the operational training tasks we had to do and the only other one was the ordinary task of learning how to fly and operate our aircraft. There were aerobatics, formation flying, cross-country flying, navigation and that was all we had to do in order to qualify as a member of the squadron, and be able to meet enemy aircraft in combat.

And then there was 'cloud flying'. Great fun of course; the only instruments we had were the air speed indicator, the altimeter that had a needle which merely told you very roughly if you were going up or coming down, and what approximate height you were at. Then there was a thing like a carpenter's spirit level, only slightly curved, fixed to the instrument panel in front of you which told you whether your wings were level. Very rudimentary, and to become a good cloud flyer with just these three instruments you needed concentration of a high order. Then there was 'diving on ground targets'. We had a target at the edge of the airfield and we used to dive on it and take photographs through the guns with a camera gun. Instead of firing bullets you just pressed the same trigger and you took a picture.

'Pin-pointing' was of course flying with a map on your knee and identifying a particular point to which you flew and on return you reported what you had seen. Also there was 'interception'. This was a most hit-and-miss affair and consisted of flying off and looking to see whether you could spot and intercept another Siskin which had arranged to fly in towards the airfield at the same time.

There was the convenience of what was called the Arundel Gap. Tangmere was situated just south of the South Downs and its proximity to the sea gave it a great deal more good weather than they got to the north of the Downs. Very often there was low cloud and rain to the north and when you were returning from that direction and getting lower and lower with the clouds just above you and the tree tops just underneath there came a point when the Downs rose into the clouds and you had to do something about it. Either go back to where you had come from, or turn to the left or right and sneak along until you reached the railway that went to Arundel. You then followed this railway line at rooftop height and you would go through the Arundel Gap. You would appear on the other side and even if the weather wasn't any better you knew at least that the ground was flat and you could set a course which would bring you right to Tangmere. We used the Arundel Gap constantly and as far as I know it is still found very useful to those who haven't any radio, or who prefer to keep the ground in sight!

I began to get rather busier in January with cross-country flights around London over which I see the weather was often very thick. And again to Portsmouth with a formation. And then 'Air Fighting' with Simonds and Reber-Percy, both of the 'other' squadron. Any time you met any of them – and you knew them by the black and white chequerboard design on the sides of the fuselage – you offered battle and the offer was always promptly taken up. This was an exercise which kept you alert and watchful and it also strengthened the arm muscles with all the pulling into ever tighter and tighter turns in order to get into the vital position behind your opponent.

In the spring of 1929, 25 Squadron also equipped with Siskins but based at Kenley, Surrey, joined 1 and 43 to form the 3 (Fighter) Wing. At the Hendon Air Pageant in the summer of that year, 27 Siskins of the three squadrons performed together as a wing and drew great acclaim from fellow professionals and the public. During the early 1930s, squadrons would fly off for the annual air firing practice camp, usually conducted at Sutton Bridge, near the Wash. Tangmere's 1 and 43 Squadrons were no exception and their pilots would compete with each other and the other RAF fighter squadrons for the highly prestigious Sir Philip Sassoon Flight Attack Trophy. Usually one of the Tangmere squadrons would carry off the trophy, in spite of summer flying only taking place during the mornings!

In May 1931, 43 Squadron changed their Siskins for the new

Hawker Fury. No. 1 Squadron, much to their dismay, had to wait for the new fighter aircraft until the following year. The Fury was a most attractive aeroplane which had, for a biplane, very clean lines and proved to be the RAF's first fighter aircraft capable of exceeding a speed of 200 mph. The aircraft had a service ceiling of 29,500 feet and a range of 270 miles.

The spring of 1932 was typical of life on the station in the early 1930s. Both Tangmere squadrons would be seen working up for the annual Hendon Air Pageant, the RAF's shop window to the British public. No. 43 would be found practising their 'roped show' (three squadron Furies performing an air display tied together), and No. 1 would be seen practising combined aerobatics with three Furies.

Over the next few years, first one Tangmere squadron and then the other would win honours at the annual air pageants, air defence exercises and gunnery camps. A proof of the high standing held by these squadrons in the 1930s was that many of those coming to the end of their initial flying or ground trade training would apply to be posted to 1 or 43 Squadron. Another sign of Tangmere's pre-eminence as a fighter station during the 1930s was that the newly-formed RAF auxiliary squadrons would vie with each other for the privilege of holding their summer camp on the station.

Both Mark Selway, who wrote these words, and his friend and rival Teddy Corbally cut their teeth as young pilots at Tangmere; Fred Rosier came along a little later. All three later rose to air rank: both Mark Selway and Fred Rosier to air marshal and in their turn Knights Commander of the Bath and ADC to the Queen, and Teddy Corbally to air vice-marshal. They were just three of the many young pilot officers who passed through Tangmere in those years. What appeared good fun for overgrown schoolboys was in fact a very serious business: constant practice instilled methodical preparation, discipline, wariness, opportunism, selflessness, and unthinking reactions in the air, all qualities that would come into their own when the country found itself at war once more. By then, these young pilot officers, amongst many others who had learnt their craft in the late 1920s and into the mid-1930s, had themselves become squadron leaders, wing commanders, and group captains whose many hours of disciplined formation flying and mock combat in the leisured years between the wars would prove an invaluable asset to a beleaguered nation in instilling the most essential practical skills of air-fighting and survival into the hastily-trained 20-year-olds who met the enemy in the skies over Britain in the summer of 1940.

Between them, the young pilots of 1 and 43 Squadrons flew tens of thousands of hours in close formation flying and in mock combat at Tangmere. Although there were forced landings and accidents on take-off and landing, as might be expected, only four mid-air collisions involving eight pilots are recorded in the squadron ORBs over the twelve years from 1926 to the end of 1937, with five pilots parachuting to safety and only three deaths, a remarkably low statistic compared with those which followed the introduction of heavier and faster aeroplanes and the greatly accelerated training programmes that were to follow during the war years.

From 1929 to 1937, the attractions of the south coast and the renown of Tangmere's fighter squadrons (and its officers' mess) made it a popular choice for the summer camps of the Auxiliary Air Force (AAF), who competed for the privilege of spending two weeks under canvas at the station. Formed by Order in Council in 1925 as a part of the new arrangements for the Air Defence of Great Britain, the AAF was intended to provide a corps of civilian pilots trained and equipped to RAF standards who were willing to devote their weekends and summer holidays to flying and would be called up to full-time duty should a national emergency arise. The AAF got off to a slow start, as the formation of squadrons was a completely voluntary effort and those who participated were expected to devote a good deal of their time, without pay, and to cover the cost of their uniforms, mess bills, and other expenses. It was not an attractive proposition for men who did not have independent means or well-paid jobs, or who were married or in mid-career. From the very beginning, the AAF squadrons were self-selecting: one had to 'fit in' at the mess table, and this usually meant having a public school background and the right social connections. No wonder, then, that a few of these squadrons, such as 601 (County of London), which was called 'The Millionaires' Squadron', gained reputations as exclusive flying clubs for bankers, stockbrokers, and the sons of wealthy parents. However, the majority of AAF squadrons, especially those formed from the mid-1930s as the clouds of war began to form, were not made up of privileged young men but much more ordinary chaps who wanted to fly, and to contribute to their country's defence as their fathers and uncles had done in the First World War.

Four auxiliary squadrons were regular visitors to Tangmere during the summers of the 1930s, 500 (County of Kent), 503 (County of Lincoln), 600 (City of London), and 604 (County of Middlesex). Others included 602 (City of Glasgow), 603 (City of Edinburgh), 605 (County of Warwick), 607 (County of Durham), 608 (County of York, later North Riding), and 612 (County of Aberdeen). The AAF squadrons, by the early 1930s all equipped with Westland Wapiti bombers, spent their time at Tangmere practising offensive and defensive tactics against ground targets and the fighter-interceptors of Tangmere's regular squadrons. Many of these AAF squadrons would return to Tangmere following the outbreak of war.

It was the end of May 1931 when 43 Squadron was re-equipped with new aircraft, the Hawker Fury, which had arrived in ones and twos throughout the month. No. 1 Squadron was expected to receive them shortly after. In addition to the Furies, which were equipped only for day flying, 1 and 43 Squadrons each had two Hawker Demon two-seat fighters for night flying equipped with instrument panel lighting and wing-tip and tail lights. The Demons were capable of 185 mph and, like the Furies, were powered by Rolls-Royce Kestrel engines.

In June 1934, 'C' Flight of 1 Squadron, consisting of five Fury aircraft with their riggers, fitters, and pilots, departed for a tour of Canada as a part of the Canadian Centenary celebrations. The aircraft, dismantled, were sent by sea, reassembled, and during July gave aerobatic flying displays at Ottawa, Montreal, and Quebec, along with other places, to great popular acclaim. The detachment was commanded by Tangmere's station commander, Wing Commander G. C. Pirie MC DFC, later Air Chief Marshal Sir George Pirie KCB, who was for a time inspector-general of the RAF.

A year later, in 1935, 1 and 43 Squadrons were two of the thirty-seven squadrons drawn up on parade at Mildenhall for inspection by King George V to celebrate his Silver Jubilee. This was also the year that Mussolini's Italian air force bombed and used poison gas in Abyssinia. This news finally stirred the British government into action and an improvised force was sent to Egypt to protect the Suez Canal. Within months, Adolf Hitler's Luftwaffe was beginning to flex its muscles, and before long would be deploying its Condor Legion in support of Franco's fascist army in Spain. This was the period when many of the RAF's best pilots, those in Tangmere's squadrons being no exception, were withdrawn to form the nucleus of new squadrons. The clouds of war were gathering, and the expansion of the RAF had begun.

One of these new boys of 1935 was Peter Townsend, who in 1944 would be appointed equerry to King George VI. Townsend's first posting as a young pilot officer was to 1 Squadron at RAF Tangmere. In his autobiography, *Time and Chance*, he wrote:

A keen and sometimes reckless rivalry united rather than opposed 1 and its sister squadron, 43. Both flew the nimble, silver, streamlined, Fury biplane. The Fury was sensual, thrilling, like a lovely girl, perfect in looks and manners; slim, graceful, tender to the feel. She responded tactfully, generously to every demand and was never spiteful, as some aeroplanes – and girls – can be. Though feminine charm cannot be measured in terms of bust, waist and hips only, I give the Fury's basic data: she was driven by a Rolls-Royce Kestrel motor ... Her speed was just over 200 mph and she was armed with two Vickers machine guns which, by means of an interrupter gear, fired through a two-bladed wooden propeller. The gun-breeches projected into the cockpit, so that, when the guns fired, they splattered you with oil and gave you a rather heroic look.

Beside the right-hand gun hung a neat little tool-bag, whose most precious tool was specified as a 'plug, clearing, Vickers'. When a split cartridge jammed a gun, you gripped the stick between your legs, and with your Fury careering half out of control across the sky, fumbled in your tool bag, extracted the 'plug, clearing, Vickers' and stuck it into the breech of the jammed gun, wriggling it to and fro to clear the cartridge.

Our planes were proudly caparisoned with the squadron markings on the top wing and fuselage – flaming red triangles (as the press called them) for 1 Squadron and black chequer-boards for 43. If war came we would ride forth in our colours like knights of old to joust with the enemy. But not for a moment did the possibility of war occur to us, nor that we were potential killers. The public, admiring our cavortings in the sky, called us intrepid birdmen, dicing with death. We liked that; it made us laugh.

The airfield at Tangmere was a broad meadow. The slender spire of Chichester Cathedral pointed the way there; another landmark, more rustic, was the old windmill on the Downs to the north. In summertime the wheels of our Furies swished through the long grass as we landed; soon after my arrival they took a second crop of hay off the airfield and a herd of sheep was set to graze the herb. Slothful sheep and flying Furies were not meant to co-exist; both they and we had some alarming moments.

Aircraft hangars, with their massive bulk, do not normally fit easily into the rustic scene. Ours did, with their wooden beams and uprights and their gently curving roofs. German prisoners of war built them in 1917, and German airmen were later to demolish them with their bombs. Meanwhile life at Tangmere was peaceful, pastoral. I loved the place; it was my home from home.

Fighting Area (our command) possessed but thirteen fighter squadrons to defend Britain. (There were 52 when the Battle of Britain began in 1940.) We flew off to lunch with friends at other fighter stations or away for the week-end, our suitcase squeezed into the space where the oxygen bottle and the radio set were normally housed – or simply strapped on to the lower wing. The latter method was ruled out after a pilot – his name, ironically, was Angel – killed himself while diving low over his girl-friend's house to say hullo. With the added resistance of the suitcase, Angel's wings simply folded.

Three of Fighting Area's squadrons, ourselves, 43 and 25, were designated 'Interceptor Squadrons'. We were the elite troops, the first to be thrown against the enemy in the event of an attack, climbing steeply and rapidly to intercept the first waves of bombers. Just how we were to find them, nobody knew. Radio communication and direction-finding were still in the folkloric stage, as witness our pleasantly bucolic call-signs and the exercises we performed to perfect our positioning technique. We were 'Waxwing'; 43 were 'Wagtail'; the ground station was 'Woodpecker', always crying out for the position of his feathered friends so that, after some delay, he could pass them a new interception course. By which time the enemy would be several miles away.

Waxwing and Wagtail pilots knew their sector like the back of their hand – naturally, since our pin-pointing exercises sent us off in search of objects as small as duck-ponds, water-troughs and odd-shaped telegraph poles. The Old Man of Cerne Abbas provided the acid test. A huge figure cut out of a chalk hill in Roman times, he was hard to spot. To prove you had done so, you had only to mention a striking detail: the Old Man sported an erected phallus several yards long.

Radio 'homing' was available, but fighter pilots more often trusted their own instincts rather than the uncertain technique of the ground station. Our favoured method was to 'Bradshaw' (so called after the railway time-table); you followed roads and railway lines, flying low enough, when necessary, to read the name-boards of the stations.

At Tangmere, the black ball indicating 'no flying' was automatically hoisted when clouds covered the Downs. If the weather clamped down while you were north of the Downs, the standard approach to Tangmere was to fly 'on the deck' down the London-Arundel railway, through the Arundel Gap (in the hills), turn right to Barnham Junction and there, right again and count sixty. Unfailingly, Tangmere then loomed out of the murk. But our make-shift methods of navigation and interception, while always remaining part of a fighter-pilot's repertoire, were soon to be replaced by scientific ones. Some way from Tangmere, at Polegate, huge lattice masts were being erected – sinister sentinels in a forbidden zone. They were an unmentionable secret. Their name was radar.

We carefully preserved a non-professional atmosphere in the mess. Talking shop was *mal vu* and a fine was imposed on pilots 'shooting a line' with gestures which went above shoulder-level. The 'Line-book' recorded exceptional claims, of which the best-known RAF classic went: 'There I was, on my back, in a cloud, with nothing on the clock.' We made fun of danger, of death even, and took care to prevent our profession from turning us into professional bores. We were not the army, nor the navy. We had precious few traditions and we knew it. We just lived, sometimes all too briefly, for the joy of living.

By late 1935, 43 Squadron had been cut down to a mere cadre and 1

Squadron had been reduced to only fifteen pilots. At the Hendon Air Pageant of 1936, No. 1 participated as immaculately as ever but 43 was so under strength that for the first time since 1929 the squadron could not attend and never flew at Hendon again. However, by the middle of 1936 the RAF's expansion scheme was beginning to produce new pilots, the best being posted to Tangmere's squadrons. In May 1936, newly qualified as a commissioned pilot of 'above average' flying ability, 20-year-old Fred Rosier arrived at Tangmere, posted to 43 Squadron, along with his great friend Pilot Officer P. R. 'Johnnie' Walker, who was posted to 1 Squadron at the same time. From Sir Frederick Rosier's autobiography:

I spent the next three years at what was affectionately known as 'Tanglebury' with what was without doubt one of the finest squadrons in the RAF. At that time 43 Squadron held both the trophy for gunnery and the Sassoon trophy for the annual pin-pointing competition. The first two of these years were carefree when I felt that I belonged to one of the most exclusive flying clubs in the world. The third was the year we exchanged our Furies for Hurricanes and prepared for a war that seemed inevitable. 43 Squadron had two flights, each with six Furies, powered by a 580 hp Rolls-Royce Kestrel V-12 supercharged, water-cooled engine. I was posted to 'B' Flight, commanded by Flight Lieutenant J. W. C. 'Hank' More who was an exceptional pilot, and also a world-class squash player. 'A' Flight was commanded by Flight Lieutenant R. I. G. MacDougall who was also the acting squadron commander. My first flight in a Fury from Tangmere was on 13 May 1936.

A little bit about the daily routine: the batman I shared with another officer would awaken me with a cup of tea at 7.00 am, the curtains would be drawn, the bath filled, my clothes for the day laid out, and my shoes polished. After breakfast I would go down to the flight office and we would then fly two or three times a day. The summer routine was to rise at 6.00 am and to work until 1.00 pm, leaving the afternoon free for sports and for sailing at West Wittering and Itchenor.

My log book for June 1936 lists some of the training carried out that month as: 'Camera-gun attacks on other aircraft, instrument flying, formation flying, cross-country flights, pin-pointing, slow flying and spinning, message-bag dropping, battle climb to 25,000 feet with full war load and high altitude flying.'

The food in the mess was excellent. My pay as a pilot officer was about £18 a month; out of this my mess dues covering subscriptions, food and drink came to £8 and my tailor's bill to £2, leaving about £8 spending money. This sounds very little but £1 could buy over forty pints of beer or twenty-three packets of cigarettes. For £5 I could have a good night out in London and return with some change.

In March 1937, two new squadrons, 72 and 87 (Fighter), equipped with Gloster Gladiators, were formed at Tangmere along with 233 equipped with General Reconnaissance (GR) Anson aircraft. In May, Flight Lieutenant E. M. 'Teddy' Donaldson, a flight commander in 1 Squadron at RAF Tangmere, was given the assignment of organising a squadron aerobatic team for the summer. Donaldson was to lead a team of four Hawker Fury aircraft and after a week of practice Flying Officer H. E. C. 'Tops' Boxer and Pilot Officers Johnny Walker and Prosser Hanks were selected to join him. In this coronation year of King George VI, the Air Pageant at Hendon was attended for the first time by a ruling monarch. Donaldson's young pilots were the stars of the show and won a rare standing ovation from the crowd.

After further practice and following an aerobatic competition against other crack RAF squadrons held at Northolt, 1 Squadron was delighted to hear that they had been selected to represent the RAF at the International Aviation Meeting at Zürich in July. This was the first time that the Air Ministry had authorised an RAF unit to represent Britain at a major international meeting on the Continent. The Fury aircraft selected for the competition were given a thorough overall at Tangmere with the help of Rolls-Royce and Hawker representatives. Before leaving for Zürich, Donaldson insisted on constant practice whatever the weather. Tops Boxer flew in the No. 2 position on Donaldson's starboard wing, while Johnny Walker held a similar No. 3 position to port. Hanks flew line astern on his leader in the new and controversial 'box' position.

The team arrived at Zürich's Dübendorf airfield on 25 July, just in time for a practice before the show opened on the following day and for the first time saw the Luftwaffe's new monoplane fighter, the Me109, close up.

Throughout the week the team competed against Europe's finest aerobatic teams. As the week progressed towards the climax on the final Sunday, it was noticeable that their rivals were becoming increasingly daring in an effort to compete with the 1 Squadron team. On the Saturday, the Furies of No. 1 took equal honours with the Italian team and all was set for the final day.

When Sunday dawned it was apparent that the weather had taken a turn for the worse with many thunderstorms building up close to the airfield. Donaldson's team took off in a huge cloudburst but somehow he managed to thread the team in and out of the bad weather, looping and rolling when he found the opportunity. In spite of the difficulties, the team managed to complete the entire sequence and landed to tumultuous applause. The rest of the day's programme was abandoned and Donaldson's team were pronounced the winners. The team returned to Tangmere the next day to be greeted with a tremendous reception.

From December 1937 until June 1938 the station was commanded by Group Captain Keith Park MC DFC AFC, later AOC 11 Group during the Battle of Britain. In June 1938, a civil air display was held at Gatwick. This proved to be one of the last of the Fury aerobatic displays to be seen by the British public. The diplomatic situation in Europe was becoming extremely serious and preparation for war rapidly increased.

At Tangmere another building programme started with the construction of new workshops, motor transport buildings, more barrack blocks, and accommodation quarters. The airfield was increased in size by extending its boundaries to the east. The airfield now had a maximum landing run of 4,500 feet and was surrounded by an asphalt-surfaced perimeter track. No. 217, another GR Anson squadron, replaced 72 and 87, the two newly-formed fighter squadrons.

The Munich Crisis in September 1938 resulted in air raid shelters being hurriedly built around the camp and slit trenches dug near the squadron dispersals. Hangars were camouflaged and the squadrons' Furies and Demons were painted dark green and brown – the sleek silver aircraft with their bright squadron markings had gone forever. The Furies were hastily converted for night flying by the addition of cockpit and navigation lights improvised from bicycle and motor-car parts. Soon after, the Furies began to be replaced by Hawker Hurricanes, 1 Squadron being equipped in October and 43 a month later. Working-up on these new fighter aircraft began immediately in preparation for the coming conflict, which now appeared inevitable.

Meanwhile, momentous developments were taking place in the technology of air defence. As Britain's relations with Germany became increasingly strained, it was generally understood that if war should break out, then the primary weapon to be used against Britain would be the bomber, as it had in the First War, but bigger, faster, capable of flying much higher, and immensely more destructive. Air exercises conducted in the summer of 1934 had made it clear that London was wide open to enemy bomber attack, despite the searchlights, anti-aircraft gun batteries and additional fighter stations introduced under the ADGB arrangements of 1923-24. Greatly strengthened air defences were needed. This prompted Air Marshal Sir Robert Brooke-Popham, air officer commander-in-chief of ADGB, to authorise the setting-up of the Committee for the Scientific Survey of Air Defence under Sir Henry Tizard to consider how far developments in science and technology could be applied to the problem.

Robert Watson-Watt, who was then superintendent of the Radio Department of the National Physics Laboratory at Teddington, was asked to investigate the possibility of a 'death ray' capable of incapacitating the engines and crew of an enemy aircraft. Watson-Watt demonstrated that it was not possible to generate a radio signal with enough power to bring down an aeroplane, but suggested that the use of radio waves, and reflected radio waves, might detect enemy aircraft and give early warning of their approach long before they could be detected by acoustical or optical devices. He documented these ideas in his famous memorandum of 1935. The Air Ministry was impressed and sanctioned further research. Initial experiments showed that detection on short waves was possible, and practical tests using relatively low-powered prototype equipment succeeded in detecting a Handley Page Heyford bomber at a range of eight miles.

Bawdsey Manor in Suffolk was requisitioned as a research station, and Watson-Watt then gathered together a team of physicists and radio engineers to develop further the capabilities of radio location, or radar at it later became known. Watson-Watt proposed a succession of thirteen 'Chain Home' (CH) stations to be built along the east and south coasts to form a continuous defensive screen that would be capable of detecting enemy aircraft approaching Britain and pass their range, bearing and height on to the RAF who could scramble aircraft to meet them; once in the air, the fighters could be vectored by radio telephony directly to an enemy formation. The potential value of these developments and proposals was immediately recognised at the highest levels; a million pounds was allocated to the project forthwith. So great was the urgency that the first steps in the establishment of the Chain Home system, specifications for the commercial manufacture of the transmitters and receiving equipment – much more powerful than the early prototype equipment, capable of detection at ranges of up to 200 miles – had been drawn up by the end of 1936.

In January 1937, the RAF's Radio Direction Finding (RDF) training school was established at Bawdsey Manor and the first Chain Home radar station was developed on the site and was fully functional by May 1937. Others were to follow during 1938 and 1939. So secret were these installations that when war broke out, and it now seemed only a matter of time until it did, their true function would remain unknown not only to the Germans, but to most of the British public. Official reference to these installations as Radio Direction Finding or RDF stations was intentionally misleading, suggesting that the function of these installations was merely to transmit homing signals or radio beacons as aids to aerial navigation, whereas their true primary function was to detect and track enemy aircraft approaching the British Isles from the Continent and not (at least initially) to help friendly aircraft find their way.

By 1937 an Airborne RDF group had been formed at Bawdsey Manor in order to investigate the possibilities of installing radio location equipment (soon to be called AI, for airborne interception) in aeroplanes for fighter defence at night or in poor visibility. Little progress had so far been made by the RAF in night flying beyond sending up day interceptors in the dark to acclimatise the pilots and to exercise searchlight batteries. At that time there was no runway lighting for 24-hour operation at RAF aerodromes. Radios, too, were inadequate, hampering effective ground control. Jeremy Howard-Williams, who flew night-fighter operations with 604 Squadron for 30 months before being posted to the Fighter Interception Unit at Ford in August 1943, later wrote:

This sorry state of affairs continued right through to the Air Ministry fighter specifications of the 1930s which finalised the Spitfire and the

Hurricane (in particular, F.37/34 and F.1 0/35). In his book *Duel in the Dark*, Peter Townsend records his dismay in October 1940 at being ordered to prepare his squadron for specialised night-fighter work; he complains that there was 'practically nothing about the Hurricane which could remotely qualify it as a true night fighter'. He goes on to list some of its drawbacks: the cockpit lighting was poor, the compass badly sited, there was no AI, the exhausts weren't screened from ahead, and the various control knobs and levers were set too closely together to allow secure operation in the dark when wearing the bulky flying gear needed for warmth in a cockpit which was all right on a sunny day but was not heated for night work (the RAF had to wait for the Mosquito before it was recognised that it might actually be more efficient rather than decadent to be warm at 25,000 feet); Townsend could also have mentioned the Hurricane's poor endurance for night work.

So ... the boffins [at Bawdsey] were looking well ahead of the Air Staff .... By the summer of 1937 the first crude AI equipment was flying in an Anson; it only gave range, and two years were to elapse before a suitable system of switching between aerials would give indication of azimuth and elevation.

In the Chain Home stations, Britain would soon have a fully operational electronic early warning system that was to prove of inestimable value. It tipped the balance of advantage in Britain's favour, and without it the result of the coming conflict would have been very different. But putting radar in an aeroplane and developing effective control and reporting systems presented enormous technical challenges. Reliable radar-directed night fighting remained, for the time being, out of reach.

2
Clouds of War become a Storm
1939 – 1940

By February 1939, the re-equipment of both 1 and 43 Squadrons with Hawker Hurricanes had been completed. Most of the officers and men at Tangmere had grown fond of the open-cockpit Furies and, obsolescent as they had become, were sorry to see them go. A few – like Fred Rosier's K5674 – would be passed on to the South African air force, but most would be dismantled for parts or scrapped. The Furies were the perfect machines for the thrilling aerobatics that Tangmere's squadrons had become famous for performing at air displays, but as warplanes they were capable of only a little over 200 mph and were armed with just two antiquated Vickers Mk IV .303 machine guns firing through the propeller. In May 1939, the station was once again open to the public on Empire Air Day and for most of the visitors it would be the first time they would have seen an eight-gun Hawker Hurricane close up and heard the distinctive sound of a Rolls-Royce Merlin engine passing overhead at more than 300 mph; in those days, a speed that no one would yet have experienced as a passenger in either a military or civil aircraft. It was also the last time the station would be open to the public until Tangmere's first 'At Home' Day during the Battle of Britain Week celebrations in September 1953.

As 1939 wore on, the tempo of preparation for war gradually increased. Experienced pilots, fitters, and administrative staff of both resident squadrons continued to be posted elsewhere to form the cadres of officers and NCOs bringing new squadrons into being, or re-forming those disbanded previously, with reservists and newly-trained recruits taking their places at Tangmere. Getting the squadrons up to field-force strength and full readiness was a constant preoccupation for the station and squadron commanders and their adjutants.

Nearby, at Poling, near Littlehampton, and at Ventnor on the Isle of Wight, Chain Home radar stations had been, or were being completed and going operational, as was the Filter Room at Stanmore which collected the information by dedicated telephone lines from the CH stations, relayed it to 11 Group headquarters at Uxbridge, and then to the sector fighter stations to decide which squadrons should be scrambled to make the interceptions. Tangmere's closest two Chain Home stations, like all, had fixed aerials oriented to detect aircraft approaching the coast from the Continent but could not track them inland. Once enemy aircraft had crossed the coast, observation and listening posts would still be relied upon to track them for some months to come.

No Hendon Air Display was held in 1939. Everyone in the RAF anxiously awaited the outcome of the political negotiations between Britain and Germany, which were not going well. Mobilisation came on 5 August; those on leave were recalled, and those reservists who had not yet voluntarily reported for duty (as some had done) were called up. The air exercises involving Tangmere's squadrons during the summer with the French l'Armée de l'Air and other RAF squadrons were abbreviated, as no one wanted to deplete the strength of their home stations for any longer than was absolutely necessary. Tension was growing; everyone was apprehensive but as prepared as they could be.

On 25 August, Tangmere's general reconnaissance squadron, 217, equipped with Ansons, was posted to Warmwell. On the 30th, 1 Squadron received orders for a special advance party and 16 Hurricanes to be prepared to move off at one-hour's notice for France, the total party not to exceed 100 personnel and 30 tons of stores for two weeks' supply. On 2 September, Germany invaded Poland. The next day, as expected, war was declared on Germany. No. 605 (County of Warwick) Squadron, AAF, arrived from Castle Bromwich for duty with six Hurricanes and ten Gladiators to replace No. 1, whose departure was imminent. The auxiliaries of 605 were keen but not yet fully operational, having just received their first Hurricanes and not yet having completed their conversion to them. The following day, the 4th, 1 Squadron's ground party departed by rail for an 'undisclosed destination', which everyone knew to be France. Four days days later, sixteen pilots and their aircraft took off for France followed over the next couple of weeks by the rest of the squadron's personnel, spares and tools, and field equipment. No. 1 Squadron was the first RAF fighter squadron to be deployed in France, and would be one of the last to leave.

Paul Richey was one of those sixteen pilots. In his autobiography, *Fighter Pilot*, first published anonymously in 1941, he wrote:

> We took off in sections of three, joining up, after a brief individual beat-up, into flights of six in sections-astern, then went into aircraft-line-astern. Down to Beachy Head for a last look at the cliffs of England, then we turned out across the sea. As we did so Peter Townsend's voice came over the R/T from Tangmere: "Goodbye and good luck from 43 Squadron!"
>
> There was not a cloud in the sky, scarcely a breath of wind on the sea, and the heat in the cockpits was almost unbearable, as we had on all our gear – full uniform, overalls, web equipment, revolver, gas mask slung, and Mae West. Only the almost complete absence of shipping in the Channel brought home to us the fact that there must be a war on somewhere. After about thirty minutes Dieppe appeared through the heat haze and we turned down the coast towards Le Havre.
>
> Our airfield at Havre lay north-west of the town on the edge of 400-foot cliffs. It was new and spacious, with an unfinished hangar on one side. On the other side, surrounded by trees, was a long, low building that turned out to be a convent that had been commandeered to billet us. The squadron closed in, broke up into flights of six, then sections of three and, after appropriately saluting the town, came in to land individually. We taxied in to a welcome from our troops: 1 Squadron had arrived in France, the first of the British fighter squadrons to do so.

From then on, little other than ordinary daily routine occurred at Tangmere for nearly eight months. The 'Phoney War' dragged on without much to report in the station or squadron ORBs. Until the fall of the Low Countries and France, the main threat of air attack was along the east coast of Britain, within range of Luftwaffe bombers based in Germany, not along the south coast. No. 43 Squadron, along with other regular fighter squadrons from stations in southern England, was sent north; initially to Acklington, 20 miles north of Newcastle-upon-Tyne, in the middle of November to reinforce 13 Group and remained in northern England and in Scotland until returning once again to 11 Group and Tangmere at the end of May. The station ORB notes no events of much significance apart from the arrival for duty of 501 (County of Gloucester) Squadron, AAF, in November 1939 to replace 43, and the arrival in December of 601 (County of London) Squadron, AAF, to replace 605 Squadron who were moved to Scotland in February.

April saw the formation of an experimental Fighter Interception Unit (FIU) at Tangmere, initially with four Blenheims equipped with an early form of airborne interception radar which, it was hoped, would enable them to 'see in the dark' and hence operate as night interceptors. This was experimental work in conjunction with Bawdsey Manor. The idea was that when a CH station picked up a possible intruder, an AI-equipped Blenheim night fighter would be vectored toward the target by CH radar and then, when within 1,000 yards or so, use its on-board short-range AI radar to identify the target and close in on it. While still experimental, the unit went operational at the end of May, attempting to intercept enemy intruders operating under the cover of darkness. The work was of keen interest at the highest levels: on 9 June, a visit to it would be made by Captain Harold Balfour, under secretary of state for air; Sir Henry Tizard, scientific adviser to the chief of the Air Staff; and Robert Watson-Watt, scientific adviser on telecommunications to the Air Ministry. Watson-Watt would make further visits to FIU at Tangmere, fine-tuning the apparatus and operating procedures, but it was not until the introduction of ground controlled interception (GCI) radar at the end of 1940 and beginning of 1941 that AI-equipped night fighters would begin to have many operational successes; until then, only about a dozen enemy aircraft would be intercepted by night fighters, most of these by visual means in strong moonlight.

The 'Phoney War' came to an abrupt end on 10 May 1940, when Germany launched an invasion of France and the Low Countries. Within a week the Netherlands had fallen to the Germans and by the 20th of the month Panzer divisions had reached Amiens and effectively trapped the BEF, which now made for Dunkirk. The front line of battle had suddenly moved onto Tangmere's doorstep, just 70 miles – 20 minutes' flying time – across the Channel, and momentous events immediately began to unfold.

On the 10th, 501 Squadron left Tangmere for France. On the same day, 145 Squadron, not yet fully operational, arrived from Filton to take its place, and two flights of 601 Squadron, at that moment the only operational squadron remaining on the station, were detailed to proceed to Hawkinge for a sweep over Holland and Belgium, their first proper war patrol in the Hurricanes to which they had recently converted. They were back at Tangmere that evening not having sighted any enemy aircraft, and did the same the next day. On the 12th and 13th they flew to Manston and Hawkinge again, but remained on standby and saw no operations.

No. 1 Squadron, which had been in France with the BEF since the beginning of September and whose operations thus far had consisted of defensive patrols and only occasional contact with a Luftwaffe that until now seemed reluctant to engage, suddenly found itself in the thick of battle as *Blitzkrieg* was unleashed. On 10 May, 1 Squadron was at Vassincourt in the Meuse département in Lorraine, 200 kilometres east of Paris. From the squadron ORB:

10.5.40

It has come. Today, for us, war broke out and there was ceaseless activity. 'A' patrol consisting of F/L Walker, F/O M. H. Brown, F/O Kilmartin, P/O Richey and Sgt Soper accounted for a Dornier 215 near Longuyon. [The] bombers' objectives appeared to be [the] railhead and station nearby. Later in the morning F/Lts Hanks and Lewis brought down a Dornier 17. P/O Mould and F/O Drake each destroyed an Me110 but P/O Mould's machine was shot about but managed to reach the aerodrome where his aircraft passed out. Meanwhile at Neuville droves of Dorniers were passing overhead at regular intervals and orders were received to take every machine that was flyable into the air and circle madly round the aerodrome. One Hurricane had no guns. F/O Salmon departed by car to pick up F/L Walker and F/O Lorimer and at mid-day the squadron moved to Berry-au-Bac near Reims. Half an hour after arriving at the new aerodrome, the Boche came over and left their visiting cards in the form of 14 anti-personnel bombs. Unfortunately three French labourers and three horses were killed. The operations tent was immediately removed to a more salubrious point. This proved to be a wise precaution.

11.5.40

Meanwhile, at Neuville, a rear party of approx. 100 men had been left in case the squadron was ordered to return. At Berry-au-Bac the morning was uneventful, but in the afternoon two patrols were out and considerable embarrassment was caused by the Huns. 'B' Flight were first, and northeast of Rethel at 17,000 feet ran into a flock of Me110s. A general melee resulted and three enemy aircraft may definitely be claimed. One managed to force-land west of Chémery and two prisoners were taken by the French. Later in the afternoon, 'A' Flight took off and at 19.15 hours over Mézières at 7,000 ft contacted about 40 enemy bombers escorted by 15 MEs. 'A' Flight attacked the escorts, the bombers turning north and a good time resulted. Questioning pilots immediately after combat it has been found extremely difficult to obtain concise information as to what actually happened, as most pilots after aerobating themselves into a stupor were still pressing imaginary buttons and pulling plugs an hour or so after landing. The wreckage of eight Me110s and one Hurricane were found. F/O Richey commenced a long series of parachute jumps. In passing it is as well to place on record the gratitude of the squadron as a whole at the unfailing kindness and ready welcome accorded us by Madame Jean at the Hotel Metz, Bar-le-Duc. It was a home from home for all of us for many months. May the misfortunes of war pass her by.

12.5.40

The rear party at Neuville moved en masse to Berry-au-Bac. The CO, S/L Halahan, led a patrol over Maastricht on the border of Belgium and Holland, and the flight had much excitement in combat with various types of enemy aircraft. S/L Halahan destroyed an Me109 and an Arado, but being hit in the engine force-landed successfully wheels up. F/O Lewis got an Me109 but was himself on fire and leapt nimbly overboard and landed safely by parachute minus one eyebrow. Kilmartin collected an He112. The CO had a grandstand seat after landing and witnessed a battle royal between French and German tanks and remarked that the Belgian troops were running faster than the refugees. F/O Lewis aroused doubts in the minds of the simple locals and was slung in the 'cooler' for an hour or so. He was later released and sped on his way back to the squadron in a French car.

13.5.40

At this time the most fantastic rumours were circulating and no one seemed to know the true position of the German forces. Bombing raids were now of frequent occurrence and many people who had been wearing spurs to keep their feet from slipping on their desks moved about with some alacrity. Wing headquarters retired in a cloud of dust to the cellar due to a bomb dropping on the [railway] station opposite. 'B' Flight destroyed an He111 (F/L Hanks) which landed in the same field as an Me110 brought down on the 11th. F/O Lorimer force-landed at St Loup-Terrier. In an earlier engagement, Mould, Clisby and Goodman accounted for three He111s and two Me110s. F/O Clisby landed beside one of the machines shot down and chased the startled crew all over the countryside, waving a revolver. He wanted their autographs!

'B' Flight tackled a shower of 15 Me110s. F/L Hanks washed out two, Lewis, Mould and Boot one each, but in the fracas Hanks got a shell in the gravity tank, caught fire and went into a cluster of spins, but landed safely. Due to being bathed in glycol, F/L Hanks arrived with eyes like poached eggs. Unfortunately, Clisby and Lorimer were shot down in this engagement and have since been posted as missing. Both these pilots had put up an extraordinarily stout show to date and their loss is a heavy blow to the squadron.

'A' Flight carried out a patrol over Sedan which was then in German hands. It was intended to be a cover patrol, but they were fully occupied in saving themselves due to the unwelcome attentions of squads of Me109s. Before they came home, Kilmartin accounted for two, Soper one, and F/O Brown one Me109 and one Ju87. Sgt Clowes, also, an Me109 and a Ju87, F/O Stratton a Ju87, and F/O Palmer an Me109. Meanwhile F/O Salmon had gone by road to Mézières to fly back a Hurricane, force-landed there by F/O Richey. Salmon and his men arrived in the midst of a large-scale raid on Mézières and spent an hour clawing earth whilst the Huns methodically blasted the place out of all recognition. During the lull, a dash was made for the aerodrome where it was found that the maintenance party had spent their time dashing in all directions pursued by delighted Dornier 215s. The lorry was written off, and while we were congratulating ourselves on having seen the last of them, eight Dorniers came down and proceeded to shoot up the remaining French machines. Everyone embraced Mother Earth whilst the Huns played havoc up and drown the 'drome. They made a Teutonically thorough job of it, even to putting a burst of fire in the unfortunate Hurricane. In the end, our Hurricane was the only machine not on fire. During all this time, the French ground personnel scattered in all directions.

For the next five weeks 1 Squadron patrolled, attacked, withdrew and withdrew again as the Wehrmacht steam-rollered their way through northern France. Between 10 and 19 May the squadron claimed at least 86 victories at the cost of 17 Hurricanes, two pilots killed, one captured, and two seriously wounded. From then until 1 Squadron's return to Tangmere on 18 June, together with 73 Squadron, the very last RAF fighter squadrons to leave France, no further losses were suffered, although claims for 16 more enemy aircraft were submitted to bring the squadron's total since the outbreak of war to at least 125 (17 of which remained unconfirmed). In a one-of-a-kind block award, ten Distinguished Flying Crosses and three Distinguished Flying Medals were awarded by King George VI to the pilots of the squadron for their extraordinarily spirited and tenacious actions in the Battle of France. The thirteen recipients were Squadron Leader P. J. H. Halahan; Flight Lieutenants P. R. Walker, P. P. Hanks, and M. H. Brown; Flying Officers J. I. Kilmartin, L. R. Clisby (posthumous), P. H. M. Richey, P. Mould, and C. D. Palmer; Pilot Officer W. H. Stratton; Flight Sergeant Pilot F. J. Soper; and Sergeant Pilots A. V. Clowes and G. F. Berry.

Meanwhile, back at Tangmere, on 16 May orders were received for one flight of 601 Squadron to proceed to France via Manston; once at their destination, Merville, the flight was divided between two flights of 3 Squadron. Flight Lieutenant Sir Archibald Hope, and Flying Officers Cleaver and Rowley to 'B' Flight, and Flying Officers Clyde, Robinson, and Branch to 'A' Flight. On the same day, 238 Squadron was re-formed at Tangmere with Spitfires but, as the Spits were needed elsewhere, soon changed them for

Hurricanes. The next day, 17 May, 145 Squadron was hurriedly declared operational and on the 18th and 19th sections of 145 and 601 flew sorties as a composite squadron, patrolling the beaches and covering the BEF, accounting for a total of 11 or 12 enemy aircraft claimed shot down for the loss of three pilots posted missing. 'A' Flight of 601 Squadron returned to Tangmere from France on the 22nd, followed by an order for the squadron to proceed to Middle Wallop on the 31st. That evening, 14 Hurricanes of 43 Squadron under Squadron Leader George Lott DFC landed at Tangmere, returning home after an absence of more than six months.

The next morning, 1 June 1940 at 06.00 hours, 43 Squadron was detailed to patrol and protect shipping coming out of Dunkirk in company with 145 Squadron and rendezvous with two other fighter squadrons from Hawkinge as a part of Operation Dynamo, intended to give continuous dawn-to-dusk air cover to the evacuation from the beaches. The patrol was without incident, and after refuelling at Manston a second patrol in company with 145 took off at 11.00 hours. Jimmy Beedle, in his book, *No. 43 (F) Squadron: The Fighting Cocks*, describes what happened next:

At 11.25 hours 145 Squadron detached itself to attack enemy bombers approaching shipping. 43 Squadron remained on the patrol line Calais-Dunkirk. Approaching Dunkirk, Me109s were seen coming in head on 'in large numbers'. At the same time Me110s broke through the cloud away to the west. There was a total of about 60 enemy aircraft. 43 Squadron had nine Hurricanes, dispersed in three sections. They were:

Blue: 1. S/L Lott 2. F/O Woods-Scawen 3. F/O Wilkinson
Red: 1. F/L Simpson 2. F/O Edmonds 3. Sgt Ottewill
Black: 1. F/O Carswell 2. Sgt Hallowes 3. Sgt Gough

Thereafter the story can be told only through the reports of the individual pilots, for the fight was essentially one of individual battles with no time or opportunity for cohesive action.

'For five to ten minutes', wrote Squadron Leader Lott, 'I found myself concentrating on avoiding action as one 109 after another appeared in rear of me. Eventually two 110s approached from the starboard bow and I turned in towards them hard and got a 45 degree deflection burst at one at under 100 yards. This a/c now went into a steep dive which enabled me to give a five-seconds' steady burst from dead astern. Heavy black smoke appeared from both engines as soon as the burst was begun. I did not follow as I considered I had followed a straight course for long enough and being on my own I set course for home when I picked up Blue 3 *en route*.' Blue 3 (F/O Wilkinson) had been involved with two 109s which he had fired on and hit. One had disappeared diving vertically into cloud at 3,000 feet, the other attacked head-on, had disappeared. The other member of Blue Section, Tony Woods-Scawen, was 'returning to Tangmere alone, having left earlier than the rest of our pilots'. Having engaged one of several attacking 109s he had 'knocked pieces off his trailing edge port wing during two bursts of five seconds' when a hit in the radiator followed by a 'deluge of glycol inside the cockpit' compelled him to retire.

Red 1, flying at 50 feet, had a more eventful crossing of the Channel. Pursued for 15 miles by a 109 which 'I was unable to attack as my windscreen was covered in oil, I evaded his attack and fire by turning and skidding', reported John Simpson. He had had marked success. One 109 had been shot into the sea in flames after a single three-second burst, after which, following a dog fight, he had got onto the tail of another and seen it dive, one wing aflame, into the ground three miles east of Dunkirk.

F/O Edmonds (Red 2) had been equally successful. Two short bursts at two 109s had no observed effect, both aircraft half rolling and diving vertically away and an attack on a third was frustrated by a 110 which attacked from the port quarter, hit the Hurricane and compelled it to break away. He then sighted a 109 attacking another Hurricane. Turning, he successfully got behind the enemy and a five-second burst caused it to break up completely. Finally, a 110 diving away after an attack by another Hurricane received all his remaining ammunition and it went down completely on fire. This last contact, like those of the next two pilots, took place ten miles inland, for the German aircraft were tending to retire towards their own lines so that the area of combat drifted towards the east.

Sgt Peter Ottewill (Red 3) who had once in a jocular moment

dubbed himself 'The Black Ace' (and was not allowed to forget it) now began to justify his title. His report is of interest not only for his achievements but for the pertinent comments made on the performance of the Hurricane relative to his opponents.

'In the dog fight that ensued I managed to get onto the tail of one of the 109s almost immediately. He had, I am sure, no suspicion of my presence for I closed to about 100 yards and fired two two-second bursts. The E/A [enemy aircraft] exploded and descended like a ball of fire. I managed to get onto the tail of two other 109s who immediately half rolled, but I was able to follow and overhaul each of them easily. Although I fired two short bursts at each no damage was observed. On pulling out of the second dive another 109 passed me across my line of sight and I gave him a long burst of six seconds at about 60 degree deflection and the E/A spun into the sea with smoke pouring from the engine. By this time most of the E/A were flying fast towards the German lines over Dunkirk, and the fighting was taking place just over the land. I climbed up towards a large number of Me110s who were sitting above the scene of the fighting and occasionally diving in when they saw a "lame duck". I singled out one of the 110s, farther back from the rest and alone. Unfortunately he saw me coming and climbed away from me easily although I was climbing at full throttle in fine pitch, and with the automatic boost cut-out pulled.

'As it was obviously hopeless to follow him I dived away and very luckily found myself almost right on the tail of another 110 flying southwest over Dunkirk. I opened fire at 250 yards and gave a five-second burst closing to 150 yards. The E/A dived violently with the starboard engine spurting black smoke and flames. I did not see it crash or make a landfall as I noticed another aircraft immediately behind me which I took to be an enemy (but almost certainly F/O Edmonds) and on pressing my firing button to give the last of my ammunition to the 110, I discovered I was out of ammunition. I did a very tight right hand turn, half rolled and dived vertically from 8,000 feet to 1,500 feet at full throttle, when I pulled out and returned to base at sea level. There was no sign of the aircraft which had been on my tail after this manoeuvre which showed me as doing 450 mph on ASI [air speed indicator] and broke the underpanelling in pulling out. Although it caused me to black out it was by no means uncomfortable. My aircraft sustained no hits and showed marked superiority over the enemy in manoeuvrability.'

Of the remaining section F/O Carswell was in the sea, Sgt Gough had died, and Sgt Jim Hallowes was collecting the best bag of the squadron's day.

He got onto the tail of a 109 which was about to attack another Hurricane. The 109 looped and rolled off the top. 'This brought it into my line of sight; I closed to 150 yards and opened fire. The E/A burst into flames almost immediately and dived into the sea. I maintained height of approximately 10,000 feet and endeavoured to remain in cloud base. The mainplane of a 109 and several other pieces fell out of the cloud in front of my machine.' Two 109s, diving from cloud, were chased to 7,000 feet, and fire opened at 30 to 45 degree deflection. One rolled but while on its back caught fire and one mainplane came off – it went into the sea or on the edge of the coast. A passing encounter with another 109 was inconclusive but soon after four Me110s were seen diving through cloud. Selecting one a little behind the others two short bursts were delivered from below and behind. 'The whole tail fell off this machine which dived into the sea. I then saw one Hurricane shot down in flames by another Hurricane. I tried to get the attacker's number but broke to attack another 109. [The] E/A tried evasive tactics, half rolling as I opened fire and then fled inland. I followed for fifteen miles, getting in several short bursts. Pieces were falling off the E/A when my ammunition gave out and I last saw it diving steeply to the ground. I did not follow the machine down to see if it crashed but returned to Manston.'

The tally for the day was seven Me109s and two Me110s destroyed and six more damaged, three so badly that they might as well have been destroyed; and on 43 Squadron's side, two aircraft and one pilot lost, two Hurricanes damaged, and one pilot wounded. Given the odds of seven or eight to one, it was an impressive result. But the squadron's pleasure in its success was short-lived. Six days later, on 7 June, again in company with 601, 43 Squadron sent up ten Hurricanes to carry out an offensive patrol from Le Tréport to Aumale. 43 Squadron's aircraft were jumped by Me109s; in the melee, two Me109s were shot down and the composite formation broke up; 601 and 43 were on different radio frequencies and once they lost visual contact they were out of touch.

When they landed at Rouen (Boos) to regroup as ordered, there were only six 43 Squadron pilots. Rowland, Edmonds, Wilkinson, and Hallowes were missing. It was later learned that Rowland and Hallowes had been shot down but were all right. Sergeant Buck's Hurricane burst a tyre on landing at Rouen, where there were no spares. Of the ten 601 Squadron Hurricanes, only five landed at Rouen; one had turned back unserviceable for Tangmere, and another had landed in the wrong place and turned up a little later, but three were unaccounted for. The remaining Hurricanes were ordered to refuel and re-arm; three 601 Hurricanes and all five of 43's were sent up again to patrol along the line of the Somme, sighting a formation of enemy bombers but encountering heavy anti-aircraft fire and coming under attack by large formations of Me109s and Me110s. Three of 43's five remaining Hurricanes were shot down, but all three pilots (Ayling, Ottewill, and Woods-Scawen) survived and later got back to England.

At Tangmere, only two of the ten 43 Squadron Hurricanes which had taken off that morning returned: those of Squadron Leader Lott and Flight Lieutenant Simpson. They were accompanied by one 601 Squadron Hurricane, the other 601 pilots having returned to Middle Wallop where they were temporarily stationed. Sergeant Buck was still stuck at Rouen. That evening, George Lott received an order from Fighter Command to take 43 Squadron into the air again next morning with six Hurricanes. He explained why he could not comply. The squadron was stood down for a fortnight to bring it up to strength again. Together, 43 and 601 Squadrons lost four pilots and seven aircraft that day, with only two Me109s and one Me110 to show for it.

On 17 June 1940, the French government laid down arms and the last of the BEF was evacuated. No. 1 Squadron was among them. From the squadron ORB:

17.6.40

During the night there had been a terrific thunderstorm and most people awoke in the morning rather damp but spirits were still high. Arrangements were still being made for the move to La Rochelle but at midday orders were given for all but about 16 ground staff to move to La Rochelle for embarcation; the remainder were to stay on the aerodrome and eventually leave by Bombay when the last of the BEF had been evacuated. The journey to La Rochelle was made without incident of note and at 19.00 hours the party of two officers and 42 men embarked with about 2,000 other troops on two colliers, one of which was still half-loaded with coal. At midnight the strange vessels moved off from the quay side whilst German aircraft flew overhead, and we said goodbye to La Belle France after nine-and-a-half months from the day of landing.

18.6.40

The aircraft left St Nazaire aerodrome, for England, at 11.45 hours, arriving at Tangmere at 13.30 hours. In the meanwhile the ground staff had arrived at Plymouth, and the squadron was posted to Northolt.

No. 1 Squadron's remaining Hurricanes touched down at Tangmere, but their pilots stayed for only a day. The pilots who had been the mainstay at Vassincourt when the German invasion began, including Walker, Hanks, Kilmartin, Stratton, Palmer, Mould, Lewis, and Squadron Leader Halahan had been rotated back to England on 24 May, to be replaced by new pilots under Squadron Leader D. A. Pemberton. During its sojourn in France, the squadron had covered nearly 1,000 kilometres zig-zagging across the country, moving from one airfield or improvised landing ground to another as the Wehrmacht advanced. The last days were a headlong retreat: most of the squadron's baggage and spares were lost or abandoned and crippled aircraft which in normal circumstances could have been easily repaired had to be set alight to deny them to the enemy. No. 1 Squadron's personnel arrived in England with little more than they could carry in a kitbag, knapsack, or their pockets. Gone, too, were the operational records relating to the squadron's time in France; the ORB entries quoted above were reconstructed from verbal accounts in the weeks following its return.

No. 601 Squadron got back to Tangmere on 16 June after two weeks' duty at Middle Wallop. Four days later, the newly-reformed 238 Squadron left Tangmere. Together with 43 and 145 Squadrons, 601 flew interceptions and sector patrols, three, four or five per day for each pilot, two days on and one day off, remaining at readiness, watching and waiting, occasionally engaging enemy raiders attacking ports and shipping in the Channel. With the fall of France, von Rundstedt's army was now in control of the entire western European coastline from the Arctic Circle to the Pyrenees, and Göring had ostentatiously stationed hundreds of aircraft on Dutch, Belgian, and French airfields – an aerial armada much greater than the whole of the RAF – in readiness for Operation Seelöwe, the invasion of Britain. Hitler was biding his time, making no particular secret of his moves, confident that the overwhelming odds would bring Mr Churchill to the negotiating table. For much of June and the whole of July, while Hitler waited for the British government to bow to the inevitable, he avoided antagonising the British public with bombing raids on centres of population that might result in large numbers of civilian casualties; the Luftwaffe was confined mainly to reconnaissance flights and raids on ports and shipping. But the pause served only to strengthen British resolve, and gave precious time to build more aircraft, train more pilots, make more .303 ammunition, searchlights, anti-aircraft shells, Anderson shelters, gas masks, morphine, and sandbags; to organise local Air Raid Precautions committees, ambulance crews, Local Defence Volunteers, Observer Corps posts, and women's armed services auxiliaries; and make arrangements to evacuate children from crowded urban areas to safety in the countryside if need be.

Nos. 43, 145, and 601 Squadrons would remain at Tangmere for the next six or seven weeks. No. 145 Squadron moved to the newly-opened Westhampnett satellite aerodrome, two miles northwest of Tangmere, on 31 July. Eric Marsden, then an engine fitter with 145 Squadron, recalled those weeks:

Within ten days of my arrival at Tangmere, somewhere about 20 May, events in France and the Low Countries had created such pressure on fighter defence that the squadron was declared operational, and began patrolling over the retreating BEF, or rather, beyond them, trying to cut down the numbers of enemy aircraft which were strafing the retreating forces. For a while our pilots were able to land at forward landing grounds at the end of the first sortie of the day, returning to Tangmere late in the evening after a day of up to six or seven sorties against or in search of enemy aircraft. Our pilots were dog tired, and tended to crawl into their beds straight after debriefing. We got stuck in immediately to service and DI (daily inspection) the kites ready for the morrow, working as long as necessary on repairs where needed; badly shot-up kites were taken out of service, and the flight's spare kites brought into use – whenever we had them. It was a matter of pride to have the maximum number of serviceable aircraft since this showed up on the squadron strength board at group, and poor serviceability reflected badly on everyone in the squadron. As the retreat continued, forward landing grounds continued to be lost, so the squadron sent a detachment to Manston to act as a forward servicing party with our aircraft operating from there during the day, although there were still squadrons operating from France.

With the completion of the evacuation from Dunkirk, and the last withdrawals from further south in France, there was a short lull during which time 'Boydy' [Flight Lieutenant Adrian Hope Boyd, 'B' Flight commander] began to sharpen us up in the business of what came to be known as a 'scramble' – getting sections of aircraft, held at readiness, into the air as quickly as possible. We began to learn to live in one of three states: readiness, stand by (with a time attached, from immediate stand-by, to 15 or 30 minutes) to released, or stood-down. At readiness, everyone, from pilots to general duties chaps, was on tenterhooks, waiting for the signal for furious activity. In the other two states we were free to work like blazes on any unserviceable aircraft on the flight line. Only when the kites were in the air could we sit still – if we could, since a loudspeaker above the pilots' crew-room door allowed us to hear RT between our own squadron pilots in the air, sometimes a facility of dubious advantage. Hearing someone you like, in deep trouble, can be quite distressing.

Having analysed the flight tracks of enemy aircraft from the known airfields in France, with regard to targets in England, and taking account of the performance of the Merlin III Hurricane, with the DH variable-pitch prop, along with the reaction time of Fighter Control, which depended upon the RDF chain along the coast, Boydy came to the conclusion that the maximum time allowable for a possibly successful scramble was two minutes. Our first attempts to achieve this were pretty poor – perhaps of intent, since Boydy had the pilots run from the crew-room with seat-pack 'chutes clipped in place, to climb into the kites, and then start up.

I have since thought that this was a deliberate ploy, to overcome the long-held belief in the sanctity of the parachute at that time. Regulations for the care and maintenance of parachutes in the RAF of those days were perhaps even more stringent than for aircraft, and each 'chute had its own log book, just like the aircraft. Every 'chute had to be unpacked at regular intervals, and aired and checked for humidity in an air-conditioned parachute store, repacked by trained packers, and issued on a signature. They tended to be objects almost of awe to some aircrew, and were handled carefully. Others simply slung them in a corner until required, and regarded them as more of a nuisance than of value. Nevertheless, there was a general belief that the seat-type pilot parachute should be sat upon only by the pilot, in flight, to reduce the possibility of the fabric sticking and failing to open properly if needed, due to perspiration or humidity caused by the warmth and moisture from the body. Anyway, the pilots soon got fed up with waddling along carrying 22¾ lbs. of parachute clipped to their posteriors, and we experimented with various positions where the 'chute might best be set to await the arrival of the pilot in a scramble. It had already been decided that the kites would be started up by the ground crew, and we now had the somewhat dubious advantage of sitting for hours in an aluminium bucket seat, front edge biting into the underside of the thighs, awaiting a signal to start our machines.

Boydy had a general duties chap as a duty phone operator, sitting in the crew-room, with the job of switching on a large electric bell, fitted outside the crew-room door, in the event of a scramble call. His own aircraft, usually 'K' (being the first letter in the second half of the alphabet, for 'B' Flight) sat immediately in front of the crew-room, so that the bell, the general duties chap, and the crew-room door could be seen in the rear-view mirror. Not until the parachute was kept in the aircraft's bucket seat, with all harness straps laid out over the cockpit edge, so that the pilot could be strapped into the kite, with engine warm and running, could we achieve the two minutes or less, with a deal of team-work by the mechanic and rigger. Despite the different trades, most pairs would take turns in the cockpit, the second member sitting on the starter trolley by the starboard wing tip, ready to press the button of the trolley-acc on signal from the mechanic in the cockpit, who could then press the aircraft's starter button to spin the engine. Immediately the engine fired up, the mechanic on the trolley-acc had to run in to the nose of the kite, beside the leading edge of the wing, unplug the heavy-duty starter cable, and fasten the flap covering the electrical socket: a screwdriver job, often in a worn slot. Retrieving the cable, and pulling the heavy trolley-acc clear of the kite, he then had to run to the trailing edge of the starboard wing, reach into the open bay in the fuselage behind the pilot, and turn on the oxygen supply, replacing and fastening the fairing panel, about three feet by two feet, in the blast of the prop. From there he ran to the starboard front of the kite, to be in view of the pilot, until the mechanic who had been strapping the pilot in place jumped down to the port front, to take the chocks away signal when the pilot was ready – often this was done with both mechanics by the leading edge already tailing on to the chock ropes to pull clear without any waste of time.

Whilst sitting at readiness a nice balance had to be maintained between keeping the engine warm enough for an immediate take-off, and running the engine occasionally to keep it warm without using so much fuel as to impair the available flight time, as well as to avoid the possibility of oiling up those two horrible plugs in the two rearmost cylinders. This system of starting for scrambles had a big advantage in that the people who were most used to starting the kites, the ground crews, were there to do it, instead of sometimes anxious or even nervous pilots who pumped the throttles too much, or over-primed, with disastrous results.

After a sortie it was customary to make a circuit of the field before landing, and our pilots soon developed a time-saving trick of their own on the first pass: they flew low over their own parking place and ground crew to show us on the ground whether or not the guns had been fired. As every plastic modeller knows, the gun ports were covered with fabric (when we had the time) and were red doped, so that the sight of tattered, blackened fabric was a signal for a quick dash to collect four pairs of ammo tanks. On the Hurricane, re-arming was intended to be by quick-change ready-loaded tanks, rather than by tediously feeding individual belts into separate containers.

As part of our preparation for the mass attacks which we all expected following the fall of France, Boydy had the squadron's sergeant armourer run an instruction course on re-arming the Hurricane. This included the general duties chaps whose normal jobs were running the petrol bowser and similar work. This left our trained armourers free to run down the lines of aircraft using their cleaning rods on fired guns, and concentrating on loading the Brownings correctly, fastening the breeches, and cocking the guns by hauling the breech blocks back by means of a piece of looped cable with a wooden toggle handle. The guns could not be cocked mechanically in the air, so if this were not done, the pilot would take off unarmed. Since we were short of petrol bowsers, refuelling was the chief source of delay, which meant that the mechanic and rigger on each kite had time to speed up the turn-round by taking part in other essential jobs.

Changing the oxygen bottle was technically the instrument basher's job, but there were not enough of them to cope under these circumstances, so whilst it became officially a rigger's job, we engine mechanics would also muck in. By these means, we eventually got our flight from 'down' to 'up' in eight minutes, a creditable time even by today's standards and, I imagine, a time impossible for a Spitfire squadron at that date. Speaking for myself, I became so conditioned by the sound of the scramble bell that for years I jumped and looked round for something to do whenever I heard an electric bell.

I suppose it was somewhere about the end of June that we received orders to repaint the undersides of our kites in the new 'sky' colour, specified as a mixture of so many parts matt white, so many parts an unremembered blue, and so many parts yellow, with the aim of producing a somewhat duck-egg blue. However, here again, stores played their usual part – not enough of the right blue, not enough of the right yellow, so we had to use what we could get. In addition, we were painting aircraft which were black on one wing, and white the other. This, together with the fact that the paint was being mixed in limited quantities (fixed by the sizes of the containers we had available), resulted in a flight line where the kites varied in colour from a strongish light blue to a distinct duck-egg green, and mostly with a darker port wing, where the black showed through. Some of the kites coming in as replacements from the MUs [maintenance units] and repair units had been painted over the old black and silver underside scheme and showed different again. It was quite a long time before we achieved anything like a uniformity of colour.

June and July were marked by a continuous flying effort, a steady drain on our original set of pilots, the introduction of the Rotol 35-degree variable pitch, constant speed airscrew; Polish, RN, and Australian pilot replacements; and two technical sources of controversy: a new harmonising arrangement for the guns, and the 'Big Wing Theory' [A massed formation of fighters intended to intimidate the enemy]. The Jablo-bladed Rotol props were regarded as the best thing since sliced bread, giving better climb and better engine control; in fact the edge they gave over the DH VP was regarded by many pilots as the difference between success and failure – and the difference between being a pilot and an old pilot. As to the harmonising, we saw our drivers and armourers with the pattern boards for the new and the old systems, and to most of us ground crew the patterns on both appeared to be irregular, random arrangements, so that we wondered what was the purpose of these curious scatters of aiming points. The harmonising distance was changed as a result of the analysis of ciné camera results which showed that most pilots were opening fire far too early. Boydy had already shown his preferred range by nudging a Heinkel's rudder with his spinner when he opened fire – unfortunately it also put 'K' out of action for several hours, because the engine and hydraulic oil from the EA sprayed back all over the Hurricane so that it took two of us some hours to clean it down with petrol and paraffin. Boydy's pleasure in his victory was also somewhat marred by the complete ruination of a good uniform. He'd taken off in tunic and slacks, not the new battledress, and without coveralls or flying jacket, and when his screen blacked out with oil, he had to pull his cockpit hatch back and stick his head out, without goggles, to get back to the station with his own prop blowing the oil off the front cowlings back into the cockpit.

The He111 came down at Selsey, nearby, and the fin and rudder were brought back to the flight and set up by the wall of the crew-room as a trophy. I remember that we all remarked on the excellence of the paint finish, which seemed to be superior to that on our kites. A maker's plate from this He111, which I kept for many years, showed that this particular aircraft had been built – if I remember correctly – in 1936, and, bullet holes apart, I remember that we remarked on how little sign of weathering the fin showed; in fact the fin and rudder looked like new.

The 'Big Wing' idea cut right across Boydy's thoughts on the right way to tackle the interception problem. He gave a talk to the whole flight on the subject, and we gathered that Park, CO of 11 Group, was not impressed either. But, we were told, Leigh-Mallory had bent ears in important places, and it had to be tried out. So, one day, instead of the squadron taking off and vanishing rapidly into the blue, we were treated to the sight of circling Hurris, waiting for other squadrons to form up, until finally, 120 aircraft formed a huge wing and set off to do battle. It took 11 minutes to form up. Unfortunately, by the time they got to where the battle was supposed to be, it was somewhere else, and Boyd (for one) came down in a fairly evil temper at the wasted effort. It was the only time to my knowledge that the Tangmere squadrons were involved in that approach up to the time we went north on rest in the middle of August. Perhaps not very effective, as interceptors, but what a sight: 120 Merlins droning, and all those Hurris in one great mass!

In July a party of us were told off to crew for some Spits which were due to come in to Tangmere; these turned out to be a detachment of 602 City of Glasgow Squadron, who were going to get

Top left: American Air Service personnel pose for the photographer with their dual-control Airco DH.9A bearing the name 'Florence' and the insignia of the 92nd Aero Squadron, at Ford Junction in October 1918. Note the officer's Pershing tunic and silver pilot's wings. *Official US Army Signal Corps photograph.*

Top right: ASAEF 92nd Aero Squadron at Ford Junction aerodrome, 25 October 1918. First Lieutenant A. W. Bevin is the pilot of this French-built Farman F.50 twin-engined night bomber being prepared for a photographic flight; note the observer's camera-mount on cockpit side. Canvas Bessoneau hangars in the background. *Official US Army Signal Corps photograph.*

Above left: Handley Page 0/400 night bomber in one of the new Belfast-truss hangars at Ford Junction, October 1918. This example is an RAF machine, whose parts were produced at Croydon, being assembled as a training exercise for ASAEF engineers and airmen pending the arrival of their own licence-built 0/400s. *Imperial War Museum Q66102.*

Above right: A dozen Gloster Gamecocks of 23 Squadron lined up for inspection, Henlow, 1926. No. 43 Squadron moved from Henlow to Tangmere in November; their Gamecocks were identical apart from black-and-white chequerboard markings. Armstrong-Whitworth Siskin II-IAs replaced 43's Gamecocks in June 1928.

Left: A Handley Page 0/400 with Liberty engines in American national markings taken at an airfield in the USA. The roundel is white at the centre, followed by red and blue, and was in official use between January 1918 and May 1919. The aeroplane was probably built in early 1919 from parts originally destined for the ASAEF's night-bombing squadrons, for which Tangmere had been intended as a training depot, and gives a good impression of how Tangmere's ASAEF 0/400s would have looked had the war continued for another six months.

Above: No. 1 Squadron Inter-Unit Tug-of-War Champions, Tangmere, 1928. Squadron Leader Eustace Grenfell MC DFC AFC is seated in the middle. *Museum Collection.*

Left: Armstrong-Whitworth Siskin J8895 in one of the three double hangars, built in 1918, at Tangmere. Note the wooden Belfast-type roof trusses. This photo also shows clearly the unequal size of the upper and lower wings, hence the Siskin's description as a sesquiplane design having a lower plane of about half the area of the upper.

Below left: Tangmere, 1930. In the centre, front row, is Squadron Leader Cyril Lowe MC DFC, 43 Squadron's commanding officer. On the extreme right, front row, is Flying Officer Eugene Esmonde, who rejoined the armed forces on the outbreak of war. On 12 February 1942, as a lieutenant commander, Fleet Air Arm, he volunteered to lead a flight of Swordfish torpedo-bombers in a gallant but hopeless daylight attack on the heavily-defended German battle cruisers *Gneisenau*, *Scharnhorst* and *Prinz Eugen* as they escaped from Brest. Esmonde was awarded an immediate but posthumous Victoria Cross. *Museum Collection.*

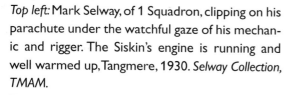

Top left: Mark Selway, of 1 Squadron, clipping on his parachute under the watchful gaze of his mechanic and rigger. The Siskin's engine is running and well warmed up, Tangmere, 1930. *Selway Collection, TMAM.*

Top right: Hawker Furies of 'C' Flight, 43 Squadron, on an affiliation visit from Tangmere to 604 (County of Middlesex) Squadron Auxiliary Air Force at Hendon, 17 April 1932. *Museum Collection.*

Above left: RAF Tangmere from the air, August 1933, as photographed from a Westland Wapiti two-seat day bomber of 604 (County of Middlesex) Squadron, AAF. No. 604, based at Hendon, is visiting Tangmere for its two-week summer camp. On the ground are more Wapitis belonging to 600 (City of London) Squadron, AAF, also based at Hendon, which was present on the station during the same fortnight that year. In the foreground is the Handley Page shed, and to its left is tented accommodation for the AAF squadrons visiting the station. *Museum Collection.*

Middle right: No. 1 Squadron Fury K2881 at Tangmere, 1937. This was one of the aircraft flown in the RAF Air Pageant at Hendon and at the International Aviation Meetings at Zürich that year. *Hodkinson Collection, TMAM.*

Above right: No. 1 Squadron from Tangmere was the first fighter squadron to be sent to France with the Advanced Air Striking Force (AASF) in September 1939. The *mairie* at Neuville-sur-Ornain, in the background, served as the mess until April 1940. *Left to right:* W. Drake, L. R. Clisby, L. Lorimer, P. P. Hanks, P. W. O. Mould, Squadron Leader P. J. H. Halahan, J. F. Demozay (French interpreter), P. R. Walker, D. M. Brown (medical officer), P. H. M. Richey, I. J. Kilmartin, W. H. Stratton, and C. D. Palmer. *Imperial War Museum C1293.*

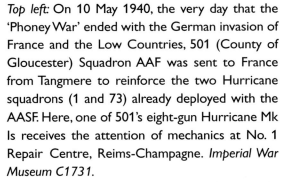

Museum HU72440.

Top left: On 10 May 1940, the very day that the 'Phoney War' ended with the German invasion of France and the Low Countries, 501 (County of Gloucester) Squadron AAF was sent to France from Tangmere to reinforce the two Hurricane squadrons (1 and 73) already deployed with the AASF. Here, one of 501's eight-gun Hurricane Mk Is receives the attention of mechanics at No. 1 Repair Centre, Reims-Champagne. Imperial War Museum C1731.

Top right: Due to heightened security, photographs of Tangmere during the Battle of Britain are virtually nonexistent, and press photography was strictly controlled by the Censorship Bureau of the Ministry of Information. Some morale-boosting photographs such as downed enemy aircraft were, however, allowed. This Heinkel He111 crashed at East Beach, Selsey, on 11 July 1940, shot down by Pilot Officers Wakeham and Lord Shuttleworth of 145 Squadron based at Westhampnett. Later in the Battle, on 8 August, both pilots crashed into the Channel south of the Isle of Wight and were posted missing. Imperial War

Above left: Tangmere's nearest Chain Home radar station at Poling, near Arundel, was the target of a concerted attack by Ju87 Stuka dive-bombers on 18 August 1940. LACW Avis Hearn, who stuck to her post as a telephonist passing the details of the attack to Fighter Command even as the station was being blown apart, was awarded the Military Medal for her selfless devotion to duty that day. Poling is pictured here in 1945; before the bombing, there had been four 360-foot steel transmitter towers rather than three. Imperial War Museum CH15173.

Above right: Flight Lieutenant W. H. 'Willie' Rhodes-Moorhouse of 601 (County of London) Squadron AAF accompanied by his wife Amalia (whose brother, Dick Demetriadi, also of 601, had been killed on 11 August) and his mother Linda. Willie's father, W. B. Rhodes-Moorhouse, was the first RFC pilot to be awarded the Victoria Cross, posthumously, for a gallant bombing raid on 26 August 1914. This photograph, taken in London on the occasion of the award of Willie's DFC, was published in The Aeroplane magazine, 13 September 1940. Ironically, by then, Willie was dead also, having been killed in action on 6 September.

clued up in readiness to be our replacements when we pulled out for 'rest' for our pilots. Happily, we were free of this duty within two or three days. Westhampnett being declared fit for occupancy and operations, we were taken there by lorry, with all our personal gear, kit bags and all, and dumped unceremoniously in the corner of a large field, containing, as far as we could see, three unfinished Nissen huts and little else. Approaching the hut allotted to us, we got evidence of the curious mentality of the administration staff: the huts had been built with a door and two windows in each end, and the windows, metal framed, were glazed, and had then had the glass painted black for black-out purposes, which was of little relevance, since there were no light bulbs supplied, nor was the electricity connected up. There was no furniture of any kind, and the concrete floors were just set, but not yet dry. It was no good thinking of our new, comfortable barrack blocks at Tangmere; a certain rapidity of action was required, and a few of us made tracks for the pile of aircraft servicing stores which we had unloaded, and grabbed the rigging mats which Hurri squadrons still carried for use on the older fabric-bashed wing types. Rigging mats are rather like the tambour shutters of a roll-top desk, about 30" wide, slats about 1½" x ½", and backed with about a ⅜" thickness of felt. Laid on two long timbers snitched from the fence or hedgerow, set on bricks, they made excellent beds. As for those unlucky enough not to think of this expedient, they spread groundsheets and blankets on the damp concrete, and spent the first few nights in horrid discomfort, with the chore of hanging blankets to dry every morning, from the considerable condensation which developed under their 'beds' during the night.

Our washing facilities were two boards laid along the existing farm horse-trough about four hundred yards along the field – about where the tunnel is under what is now the Goodwood motor circuit. The dining hall, at first shared by all ranks, was an open-sided wagon shed, in which an acute sense of geography was well worthwhile to avoid being the recipient of any of the rain of swallow and swift droppings from the ancient timbers above, not that there was much opportunity to make meals a social occasion; like most things, including our days off, we did everything at a run, so that 'scoff' became a truly accurate name for our food. The NAAFI [Navy, Army and Air Force Institutes], we discovered eventually, was a marquee on the eastern side of the field, nearer to the 'A' Flight dispositions, with a few trestle tables and folding benches, and an atmosphere of dampness and gloom. Few of us used it much, even given the opportunity. Luckily we soon had regular daily visits from either a NAAFI or a WVS [Women's Voluntary Service] van dispensing the inevitable tea and wads (wads were buns or cakes), and even occasionally chocolate and cigarettes.

The tempo of the air war steadily increased in late July and early August. Our pilots were getting distinctly frayed around the edges, and I know that one or two considered themselves as 'written off' already – it didn't affect their attitude to flying and fighting, but they had no hope of survival for themselves. It was a grievous time for us, for we could do little to help. We couldn't take their places, though most of us would have given anything for the chance. It might not be incorrect to say that our respect and liking for our pilots almost became love at this time – and we had to watch them – indeed help them to take off to go and die in ones and twos, until the core of experienced, battle-trained men became dangerously small. We had 'good' days, like the one on which the squadron claimed, I think, 21 victories, 11 going to our flight. Whatever may have happened as a result of analysis of records and claims, and consequent adjustment of scores, our blokes honestly thought they'd knocked down that many EAs, and we were credited with them and given a day's rest by no less than Sir Archibald Sinclair himself, who came down to see us, accompanied by a news film unit, who took shots of wholly unreal 'squadron scrambles': all aircraft in neat vics of three, dressing by the right, etc., all nice and tidy, nothing like the chaos of the real thing, when the kites belted off straight from their dispersal point, regardless of wind direction, and formed up in the air.

This was the period of the heavy attacks on the Channel convoys, and Boyd, by now considerably decorated, and I think a squadron leader, was prevailed upon to make a broadcast on the BBC describing these attacks and the resulting battles as our fighters attempted to drive off the enemy. Perhaps he read a script prepared by BBC or Ministry of Information script writers, for in that broadcast he mentions his canopy and goggles being damaged and lost as a result of a passing bullet – an incident which was a part of his being shot down a day or two later by cross-fire from a Spit when both he and the Spit pilot opened up on a Dornier 17, SO-K having been hit in a series of vital places: Pesco pump (instruments), main engine oil compound relief valve, glycol header tank, air compressor, as well as shattering his special canopy. By the time he got back to Westhampnett he was half blinded by oil and glycol, the kite was streaming trails of white glycol vapour and oil smoke, and seemed likely to brew up at any time. His undercart was U/S so he belly-landed along the edge of the field by the flight line, and promptly hopped out, yelling for a screwdriver, with which he jumped back into the kite, to salvage the clock as a souvenir of his first crash.

At any rate, he was quite apologetic for the embellishments to his story when we congratulated him on his broadcast. The truth was that we very rarely saw a kite with bullet holes. I imagine that those pilots who got in front of unfriendly guns were those who came back by train; certainly, up to the time of the Spitfire incident, we'd had no serious damage to any of ours. I don't know to what extent this may have been the experience of other units, but it was true of 'B' Flight, 145 Squadron. This account of the convoy attack, broadcast, and then printed in 'authoritative' reference works, is just one example of the way in which 'history' becomes slightly bent away from actuality; in this case quite a minor incident, but sometimes involving displacement of events through a fair period of time, especially at a time when the keeping of diaries might be frowned upon. Even the official squadron diaries are not immune to these influences, sometimes being doctored to preserve reputations.

By the end of the second week of August we could no longer put up a full squadron on readiness, and our pilots were pretty well worn out; the people running Fighter Command must have had remarkable powers of judgement in this matter, using each squadron to its limit before taking it out of the line for rest. We were moved up to Drem, near Edinboro'; the lucky ones amongst us flew up in a Sparrow from the transport squadron at Finningley: kit bags, tool boxes, the lot. We had to wait hours for our take-off, because of repeated Condition

Reds: the sky above was criss-crossed with contrails, and Me110s were being chased all over Sussex, though we didn't even see the one reported as passing overhead – it was ducking from cloud to cloud, and being chased by one of our kites.

Adlertag, 13 August, marked the launch of the Luftwaffe's large-scale attacks on the British mainland, and is nowadays generally considered to mark the start of the Battle of Britain. But for Tangmere's squadrons it had begun five days earlier. The first phase of the Battle consisted mainly of protecting British ships passing through the English Channel, for which Tangmere's squadrons were ideally placed. 145 Squadron's ORB tells the story:

8.8.40

Weather. Fine. The squadron engaged with very large formations of Ju87s and Me109s at 09.00 hours. This engagement developed into numerous dogfights and in the end the squadron's bag was six Ju87s and three Me109s destroyed and others damaged. P/O L. A. Sears and Sgt E. Baker failed to return. At 12.45 hours, Blue section engaged some 10 enemy aircraft, 25 miles south of the Isle of Wight; in this action three Me110s and one Me109 were shot down. Blue section suffered no losses. At 16.10 hours, the squadron was heavily engaged with more than 100 enemy aircraft over a convoy, south of the Isle of Wight. In this combat six Ju87s and two Me110s were destroyed. P/O E. C. J. Wakeham, P/O Lord Shuttleworth, and Sub-Lieut F. A. Smith RN failed to return.

No. 43 Squadron lost two pilots in the same action, and 601 none. On the 9th and 10th, there were no scrambles and no enemy aircraft were encountered by Tangmere's patrols, but on the 11th and 12th the Luftwaffe was back again in force. Again, from the 145 Squadron ORB:

11.8.40

Weather: Fine all day. The squadron engaged very large numbers (about 150-200) Me109s and Me110s south of Swanage at about 10.30 hours. In the face of these numbers the combat took the form of a succession of dogfights. The squadron's bag was three Me110s and two Me109s destroyed, and two Me110s and one Me109 damaged. F/O G. R. Branch and F/O A. Ostowicz failed to return. Squadron Leader J. R. A. Peel force-landed in the Isle of Wight and sustained an injured wrist, and P/O A. N. C. Weir was forced down, without serious injury, near Chistchurch.

12.8.40

Weather: Fine all day. The aircraft of the squadron engaged large numbers of enemy aircraft (chiefly Ju88s and Me110s) in the Isle of Wight area at 12.25 hours. The squadron total was one Ju88 confirmed, two Ju88 unconfirmed, one Me110 unconfirmed, and one Do17 probably destroyed. F/L Pankratz, P/O J. M. Harrison, and Sgt Kwiecinski failed to return.

No. 145 Squadron had lost ten pilots, killed or missing, in three days of fighting, and was now taken out of the line. No. 601 had lost four on the 11th, 1 Squadron (on two days' detachment to Tangmere) had lost one pilot on the 11th, 43 had lost two on the 8th and would lose another pilot on the 14th. How many enemy aircraft Tangmere's squadrons actually destroyed in these early weeks of intensive air fighting – soon to become as known as the beginning of the Battle of Britain – is uncertain. The squadrons were often mixed up in combat and there was a good deal of double-counting. The only certainty is that despite being heavily outnumbered the RAF's pilots gave at least as good as they got.

No. 145 Squadron, exhausted and depleted, left Tangmere on 15 August 1940, to be replaced at Westhampnett by Spitfire-equipped 602 (City of Glasgow) Squadron, AAF, which had arrived two days earlier and now moved into 145's former accommodation huts. On that day, Prime Minister Winston Churchill was at Fighter Command Headquarters, Bentley Priory, with Air Marshal Hugh Dowding, AOC-in-C of Fighter Command, observing the progress of the enemy bombing raids. This was the fifth day of the Luftwaffe's concentrated aerial assault on the RAF's 11 Group airfields. By the end of this day, another 75 German aircraft had been shot down – a real blow to the previously invincible German air force. The Luftwaffe always referred to this day as 'Black Thursday'. For their part, Fighter Command had lost 30 aircraft with 17 pilots killed. At last, the tide seemed to be turning, at least for the moment. Churchill, on leaving Dowding's HQ that evening, described it as: 'One of the greatest days of history'.

Despite the setbacks of the previous day, the Luftwaffe returned to the attack on Friday, 16 August. At about eleven o'clock in the morning, after the early mist had cleared, three small enemy raids were seen to be approaching Kent. Believing the raids to be a feint, the AOC 11 Group, Air Vice-Marshal Keith Park, committed only a few fighters to meet the raids. Two *staffeln* (the German equivalent of squadrons) of Junkers Ju88 bombers broke through and successfully bombed West Malling, one of 11 Group's important sector stations protecting London.

Shortly after noon, the Chain Home stations detected three large enemy formations heading for the Thames estuary. This time, Park scrambled over 80 fighters to intercept and many of the bombers were turned back. About the same time, to the south of London, about 250 enemy aircraft managed to cross the coast unopposed between Brighton and Folkestone. When the defending Hurricanes and Spitfires reached them they were split up into small formations which dropped bombs on Farnborough and the London docks where 66 civilians were killed. Two Junkers Ju88s managed to penetrate as far as Brize Norton aerodrome, Oxfordshire, where in a short but very accurate raid, two hangars full of Oxford training aircraft were bombed and 46 aircraft destroyed. At noon a third large build-up of enemy aircraft was picked up by the Chain Home stations setting course towards the English coast from Cherbourg. Between 12.30 hours and 12.45 hours eight fighter squadrons were scrambled to meet the threat. This enemy force of about 150 aircraft comprised a large formation of Ju87 (Stuka) dive-bombers and escorting Me109 fighters.

When the Stukas reached the Nab Tower, east of the Isle of Wight, the leading aircraft fired off signal flares and the force split into three groups; a small number peeled off to attack the Ventnor Chain Home station, a second lot set course towards Portsmouth, where later they attacked Gosport, and the largest group headed for RAF Tangmere. The Hurricanes of Tangmere's 43 and 601 Squadrons were scrambled to meet the enemy force head-on over the Solent. No. 43 Squadron's intelligence officer, Flying Officer Cridland, quoted in Frank Carey's autobiography, reported what happened to the squadron:

Eleven squadron Hurricanes flown by Squadron Leader Badger, Carey,

Woods-Scawen, Gray, Lane, Hallowes, Gorrie, Upton, du Vivier, van den Hove and Noble took off at 12.45 hours and intercepted 50 to 100 Ju87s travelling north off Beachy Head [curiously, this statement does not agree with other sources which say that this enemy formation crossed the coast 50 miles to the west at Nab Tower] at 12.55. The squadron was at 12,000 feet and enemy aircraft were at 14,000 feet in flights of five [or] seven, in close vics, the vics stepped up. A head-on No. 5 attack was made at once; some turned straight back to France, and jettisoned their bombs and the leading enemy aircraft was shot down by Squadron Leader Badger, who was leading the squadron as Green 1 and two people baled out. There were escorting Me109s at 17,000 feet but they took little part in the engagement: some of the pilots never saw them at all. The squadron then returned and attacked from astern whereupon the combat developed into individual affairs and lasted approximately eight minutes. Some of the enemy aircraft made no attempts at evasion while others made use of their slow-speed manoeuvrability by making short steep climbing turns and tight turns – at least one [Hurricane] pilot made use of his flaps to counteract this.

Frank Carey, then a pilot officer, summed up his part in the action in his autobiography:

This was the first time that Tangmere itself was attacked – with considerable success too. We met the raid head-on over Selsey Bill. Due to our positioning, we were only able to fire on about the second wave, leaving the leaders more or less undisturbed in their bombing. However, we were very lucky that our head-on attack so demoralised the Ju87s that they, and the successive waves behind them, broke up. Some dropped their bombs into the sea in an effort to get away.

No. 43 Squadron did not have it all their own way: Woods-Scawen was slightly wounded and had to crash-land at Parkhurst on the Isle of Wight, and Hamilton Upton had to make a forced landing on the beach at Selsey.

Tangmere's 601 Squadron, led by Flight Lieutenant Sir Archibald Hope, having been scrambled at 12.25 hours, was initially ordered to patrol over the base but was soon vectored towards Bembridge on the Isle of Wight and instructed to climb to 20,000 feet. Between Tangmere and the Isle of Wight they saw the Stukas below them. Hope ignored the controller's instructions to maintain height because of the fighters above and turned to attack the Stukas, now dive-bombing Tangmere. In the following engagements, the squadron shot down three Stukas as they turned south to make their escape. One Stuka was shot down by Flying Officer Carl Davis, the bomber crash-landing at Bowley Farm, South Mundham; both crew members died. Another Stuka crashed by the roadside in Selsey and another was shot down over Pagham.

Early in 601's engagements with the Stukas, an American volunteer, Pilot Officer William 'Billy' Fiske was hit by one of the dive-bombers' rear gunners. Streaming glycol and on fire, he managed to crash-land his Hurricane back on Tangmere aerodrome just as the Stukas began their dive-bombing attack. Fiske's aircraft came to a stop against the western boundary fence. Having earlier been warned of the Hurricane returning with its pilot injured, Dr Courtney Willey, the only medical officer present in the Station Headquarters, ordered the two nursing orderlies, Corporal George Jones and AC2 Cyril Faulkner, to take the ambulance to collect the wounded pilot. Despite the bombs dropping around them, Jones and Faulkner extracted the badly hurt Fiske from his cockpit and brought him to the sick quarters.

Meanwhile, Dr Willey, on hearing the station tannoy warning, "Take cover! Take cover! Stukas sighted coming towards Tangmere! Take cover!", moved his twelve patients into a bomb-proof shelter. Shortly after the bombing started, the sick quarters received a direct hit and Dr Willey was buried up to his waist when the chimney breast collapsed. Ignoring his injuries, he set up an emergency sick bay and carried on treating the seriously wounded. When Billy Fiske arrived by ambulance, Dr Willey climbed into it and found the pilot conscious but badly burnt from the waist down. Fiske was given a shot of morphine and, twenty minutes later, after the aerodrome roads had been cleared of rubble, he was rushed to the Royal West Sussex Hospital in Chichester. For their actions that day, Jones and Faulkner were awarded the Military Medal and Dr Willey was awarded the Military Cross. Pilot Officer Billy Fiske died of his injuries the following day. He was buried in the churchyard of Boxgrove Priory on the afternoon of 20 August, four days after he was shot down.

At Tangmere's satellite aerodrome, Westhampnett, the recently arrived 602 Squadron with its Spitfire Mk Is and commanded by Squadron Leader Sandy Johnstone, was scrambled just before 13.00 hours and ordered by Tangmere's sector controller, David Lloyd, to orbit the base at 2,000 feet. However, once airborne the Spitfire pilots could see formations of Ju87 Stuka dive-bombers approaching Tangmere from the south. Findlay Boyd, a 602 Squadron flight commander, once airborne saw a Stuka pulling up after dropping its bombs on Tangmere. He quickly shot the bomber down. The other members of the squadron clawed their way into the air in an attempt to reach the escorting Messerschmitts above. This they successfully accomplished with Johnstone, Urie and Webb all reporting, after landing, claims of enemy aircraft destroyed.

The German attack was not only fought in the air. Second Lieutenant E. P. Griffin of the Royal Engineers Construction Company based at RAF Tangmere, on hearing the air raid warning, went to his battle position and with his Lewis machine gun shot down a Messerschmitt Me110. The aircraft crashed three-quarters of a mile from the aerodrome, killing the three members of its crew. A few days later his colleagues presented him with a cartoon entitled, 'The Glorious 16th of August 1940'.

The Stuka attack on Tangmere aerodrome had started at 13.00 hours and lasted only 20 minutes. The bombing was extremely accurate with no bombs dropped outside the aerodrome perimeter. In that time, the Luftwaffe destroyed or damaged beyond repair (with the exception of one), all the pre-war hangars, the station workshops, stores and the water pumping station. The officers' mess, the y-service hut and many other buildings were also badly damaged and auxiliary systems such as the station tannoy, power, water and sanitation were put out of action. Five Blenheims, including those flown by the Fighter Interception Unit, seven Hurricanes, and a Magister were destroyed on the ground and other aircraft damaged. Some 40 vehicles were also destroyed in the raid.

The Luftwaffe did not escape unscathed; the returning fighters claimed 25 enemy aircraft destroyed, including two Me110s, five Me109s and eight Stuka bombers with a further seven Stukas damaged. However, the real tragedy for Tangmere on that day was the death of ten RAF personnel (all but one were later buried in Tangmere's St Andrew's churchyard) and three civilians. A further 20 persons were injured. One of the civilians who died was Henry Ayling, a civilian builder; he was killed when the slit trench he was sheltering in received a direct hit from a Stuka bomb. He is buried in Chichester Cemetery. His wife never remarried.

Leading Aircraftman Maurice Haffenden was an engine fitter with 43 Squadron and later described the day's events in a letter to his relations:

> [At] lunchtime at 1 pm the loudspeakers, with a greater urgency than before, suddenly appealed, "Take cover! Take cover!" Within three minutes of that warning I saw the first of the Junkers coming straight down on the 'drome in a vertical dive. The leader was within 2,000 feet of the ground — long wing span — fixed undercarriage — single engine — and then w-h-e-e-e-z .... I went head-first down a manhole as the first bomb landed on the cookhouse. For seven minutes their 1,000-pounders were scoring direct hits and everything was swept away by machine-gun bullets. I never believed such desolation and destruction to be possible. Everything is wrecked — the hangars, the stores, the hospital, the armoury, the cookhouse, the canteen — well, everything.
>
> By special permission a Lyon's ice cream fellow is allowed in the 'drome. He always stands just outside the cookhouse on the square. He was last seen standing there guarding his tricycle but now at the same spot is a bomb crater thirty feet deep. But there were quite a few casualties. In the early evening they still were sorting out the bloody remnants of flesh and bones and tied them in sheets.

Joyce Fryer still clearly remembers 16 August 1940. She was on school holiday that bright sunny day and was living with her grandmother Pat Collins in Tangmere village. Her father was on Ford aerodrome, helping to construct the runways and her grandfather was in nearby Aldingbourne where he worked in a nursery. When the air raid warning siren sounded at lunchtime she and her grandmother rushed to the dugout her grandfather had built in the garden. Her grandmother took with her a cooking pan of boiled rice and some golden syrup. Joyce remembers the screams of the Stukas as they dived on the aerodrome and the sound of the bombs exploding. When the 'all-clear' sounded they emerged safe from their shelter and could clearly see the smoke rising from the RAF station down the road.

Following the raid, the Hurricanes landed between the craters and were quickly refuelled and re-armed. On the aerodrome, flags were placed to mark unexploded bombs and the clear-up work began. In the afternoon soldiers from nearby bases were drafted in to fill in the craters and to clear the rubble. That evening, Sandy Johnstone observed:

> I drove over [from Westhampnett] to Tangmere in the evening and found the place in utter shambles, with wisps of smoke still rising from the shattered buildings. Little knots of people were wandering about with dazed looks on their faces, obviously deeply affected by the events of the day. I eventually tracked down the station commander [Group Captain Jack Boret] standing on the lawn in front of the officers' mess with a parrot sitting on his shoulder. Jack was covered with grime and the wretched bird was screeching its imitation of a Stuka at the height of the attack! The once-immaculate grass was littered with personal belongings which had been blasted from the wing which had received a direct hit. Shirts, towels, socks and a portable gramophone – a little private world for all to see …Rubble was everywhere and all three hangars had been wrecked.

Jack Boret later ordered that the following entry on the day's events should be made in the station's Operations Record Book, giving special recognition to the fact that the station remained fully operational throughout the day: 'The depressing situation was dealt with in an orderly manner and it was considered that the traditions of the RAF were upheld by all ranks. In conclusion, it must be considered that the major attack launched on this station by the enemy, was a victory for the RAF.'

On 16 August 1940, Churchill was again watching the outcome of the enemy air raids, this time with Air Vice-Marshal Keith Park at 11 Group Headquarters at RAF Uxbridge. On leaving that evening, he was heard to say, 'Never in the field of human conflict was so much owed by so many to so few' – the very words he used in the famous speech he made on the Battle of Britain in the House of Commons four days later. Despite these stirringly patriotic words, Churchill knew that it was not over yet. Seventy-eight RAF pilots had been killed (18 from Tangmere, including Billy Fiske, who would die the next day) and another 27 were badly injured and lost to the RAF's strength in the last eight days of air fighting; more than half were seasoned men whose places would have to be taken by newly-trained pilots, more vulnerable because they lacked combat experience. In fact, at that moment victory was a long way off if ever it were to be achieved.

Friday the 17th was relatively quiet; the Luftwaffe sent up no big formations that day. The following day they came again in force. A large flight of enemy aircraft was reported approaching from the south and southeast shortly after 14.00 hours apparently heading straight for Tangmere. Initially it was thought that their intention was to finish off RAF Tangmere and the other fighter stations of 11 Group, and the south coast sector controllers ordered every available fighter into the air to protect these airfields. This turned out to be a miscalculation, which put Tangmere's Hurricanes and Spitfires in the wrong places. The Luftwaffe's targets were not the 11 Group aerodromes. About ten miles off the coast, the formation broke up into four groups, each of 20 to 30 Stuka dive-bombers, and proceeded to attack four separate targets: the Chain Home station at Poling, the naval air stations at Ford and Gosport, and the Coastal Command airfield at Thorney Island. Three of the four groups of Ju87s succeeded in reaching their targets without opposition and accurately dropped their bombs before Tangmere's fighters could get into position to engage them.

At Ford Naval Air Station, only six Lewis guns of First World War vintage were manned when the Stukas attacked. Bombs rained down on huts, hangars, buildings and aircraft drawn up together for maintenance. The airfield's petrol and oil tanks and storage compounds were hit, causing huge fires. Twenty-eight people were killed and 75 wounded. Fourteen parked aircraft were destroyed and a further 26 aircraft were damaged. Two hangars, the motor transport sheds, two stores buildings, the ratings' and petty officers' canteens and numerous accommodation buildings were also destroyed. The station was a scene of utter ruin and remained out of action for a month. It was put back into limited operation only in mid-September, not – as previously – as a Fleet Air Arm station but as an RAF airfield to accommodate 23 Squadron's Blenheim night fighters and, later, the Fighter Interception Unit, which had been bombed out of Tangmere on the 16th and temporarily removed to Shoreham. Ford aerodrome, while in formal terms for the rest of the war an independent RAF station that kept its own ORB, in many ways operated as a satellite to RAF Tangmere and was often described as such by its personnel until the summer of 1945, when the airfield was returned to the Royal Navy and its remaining RAF squadrons and staff transferred to Tangmere.

The CH station at Poling was badly damaged and was not restored to full-time watch for more than a week, during which time mobile units were deployed nearby to maintain radar coverage. At Gosport, five aircraft on the ground were lost and five damaged. Several buildings were wrecked and two hangars damaged, but there were no casualties. Successful interceptions by 43 and 601 Squadron Hurricanes disrupted the raid against Thorney Island, and three of the attacking Ju87s were shot down. Nonetheless, two hangars and two buildings were wrecked, three aircraft were destroyed on the ground, and five civilian workers were injured when a 50 kg bomb landed on their shelter.

The Stukas reached most of their targets without opposition, but once they had dropped their bombs, it was a different story. According to the 602 Squadron ORB, a loose group of about 60, which included those that had attacked Ford, began to withdraw to the south accompanied by their escorting Me109s. As they did so, 602's Spitfires caught up with them, downed seven Ju87s and damaged another, but were bounced by the 109s. Flight Lieutenant Dunlop Urie was wounded but made it back to a safe landing at Westhampnett. Flying Officer Ian Ferguson was also wounded and nearly electrocuted by hitting high tension cables at Merston. Sergeant Basil Whall force-landed on the beach near Middleton-on-Sea. Five of 602's aircraft were written off that day, although no pilots were lost.

Tangmere's squadrons, 601 and 43, shot down eight Ju87s and one Me109 and damaged another eight Ju87s and two Me109s. Two pilots of 601, Guy and Hawkings, were killed. Frank Carey of 43 Squadron caught a bullet in the knee and crashed-landed his shot-up Hurricane in a field, but was back on duty a month later. LACW Avis Hearn (later Avis Parsons), who stuck to her post as a telephonist passing the details of the attack to Fighter Command even as the Poling Chain Home station was being blown apart by Luftwaffe bombs, was awarded the Military Medal for her selfless devotion to duty that day. The Luftwaffe had inflicted some damage, but at great cost. The Stukas, 100 mph slower than the Hurricanes and Spitfires, had not previously been opposed by such large and effectively organised forces of fast, monoplane interceptors and the result was disastrous for the Luftwaffe. No Ju87s came the next day and they would not be deployed against

Tangmere again.

The 19th was quiet by comparison. Although no one could have known it at the time, Tangmere's moment of gravest threat from the Luftwaffe had passed; the aerodrome would not be the target of another massed attack, and would not be bombed again even by a lone raider, for nearly six months. Its squadrons would, however, continue to fly sector patrols and be scrambled by Fighter Command to intercept enemy aircraft on their way to targets elsewhere. The only enemy aircraft sighted in the sector on the 19th was a lone Ju88, which 'B' Flight of 602 Squadron engaged and destroyed at the cost of Pilot Officer Moody's Spitfire which was set alight by gunfire and forced him to bale out, safely, for the second time in two days. What remained of the Fighter Interception Unit at Tangmere was moved to Shoreham Airport for the time being, and 17 Squadron arrived from Debden to relieve 601 Squadron.

On Sunday the 25th, 17 Squadron was scrambled to intercept a formation heading for RAF Warmwell. They were engaged off Portsmouth; five Me110s and one Me109 were shot down, three of the Me110s by Flying Officer Count Manfred Czernin, for the grave loss of 17 Squadron's commanding officer, Squadron Leader Cedric Williams, who was killed in the same action. Only seven bombers got through to their target at Warmwell, hitting two hangars and the station sick quarters. Raids on the Isle of Wight and Portsmouth, on the 25th, resulted in the loss of one Hurricane from 43 Squadron and two 602 Squadron Spitfires; although two of the pilots were wounded, all three parachuted to safety.

The month ended with more losses. On the 30th, the Luftwaffe launched one of their largest aerial assaults so far; wave after wave of bombers and fighters attacked airfields in Kent and Surrey, with eleven smaller formations coming in over the south and southeast to carry out diversionary raids on Birmingham, Sheffield, Norwich, Colchester, Southampton, Bristol, and Cardiff. The RAF sent up more than 1,000 sorties to meet the enemy; for half an hour either side of midday, twelve Hurricanes of 43 Squadron were in action over Kent and Sussex, during which Sergeant Dennis Noble was hit and his aeroplane went down with him still in it at Woodhouse Road, Hove. Later the same day, nine of 43 Squadron's fighters engaged enemy aircraft again over Kent. Squadron Leader Badger was forced to bale out; he had the bad luck to come down in trees and never recovered, dying of internal injuries nine months later.

Caesar Hull took over as 43 Squadron's commander. On the last day of the month, two of Tangmere's pilots crash-landed following damage to their aircraft during interceptions, Sergeant Steward of 17 Squadron at Maidstone and Sergeant Elcombe of 602 Squadron at Dungeness; both were unhurt and made their way back to Tangmere. At the beginning of September, 601 Squadron returned from Debden and No. 17, its temporary replacement, returned there. According to Jimmy Beedle, in the following week, September 7th:

As 4 pm approached the radar plots received at Bentley Priory made it obvious that something extraordinary was building up across the Channel and soon the vanguard of the biggest raid to date was crossing the coast on a 20-mile front stepped up from 14,000 to 23,000 feet; 'a tidal wave a mile-and-a-half high and covering 800 square miles' was one description of it. 11 Group scrambled eleven squadrons and called the other ten to readiness at the same time as they alerted the neighbouring 10 and 12 Groups.

The enemy force, 350 bombers and 600-plus fighters came in two waves some 30 minutes or so apart. Initially the airborne squadrons, deployed to defend the airfields and aircraft factories which experience during the past two weeks pointed out as being the probable targets, were not best disposed to meet the main thrust which headed straight for London, so that part of it reached the capital unmolested.

During this stage 43 were still on the ground at readiness. Earlier during the quiet of mid-afternoon the sector controller had indicated the possibility of releasing the squadron before dusk – it was their turn for an evening off. But as the first part of the attacking aerial armada turned for home, harried all the way, the second wave showed up on the plotting tables and at 16.35 nine aircraft of 43 were scrambled. Ordered to fly on varying vectors they finally sighted, crossing the coast near Folkestone at 18,000 feet, a formation of 25 Dornier Do17 bombers with a ring of fighters circling 500 feet above and others behind stepped up to 25,000 feet. Following some miles behind were two similar groups of escorted Dorniers.

With no other friendly fighters in view, Caesar [Hull] led his nine Hurricanes towards the front group, climbing until he was 1,500 feet above the bombers, with Kilmartin and his rearmost section of three another 2,000 feet higher still. Telling Kilmartin to keep the fighters off, Caesar peeled off to the left and dived down. 'We heard his throaty chuckle as he told us to sail in and smash 'em', and those were the last words anybody ever heard from him. Sergeant Hurry, No. 2 in his section, was the last to see him. 'He went in astern of a Dornier and I pulled out to make a synchronised beam attack. I raked the bomber from one end to the other and broke down and under. When I turned to come in again there was no sign of anybody else.'

At 17.50, Flt Lt Kilmartin taxied into dispersal at Tangmere, took off his flying helmet, said just two words to Flt Sgt Parker, "My God", turned and went into the dispersal hut. Van den Hove, Sgt Hurry and Sgt Barrow came back a little later and Sgts Mills and Jefferys phoned in from Detling where they had landed to refuel, but Caesar, Dick Reynell and Sgt Deller were all missing. Deller had baled out unhurt near Ashford. Dick Reynell had baled out too, seconds before his Hurricane blew up in mid-air over Blackheath but something had gone wrong with his parachute and he had died on hitting the ground. Caesar was found ten miles away from his comrade at Purley, still in his aeroplane, itself so badly damaged by fire that it was identified only from the serial numbers on the guns.

Tony Woods-Scawen, too, had been lost five days earlier, shot down by an Me109 over Ashford. No. 43 Squadron, on continuous operations at Tangmere without a break since the end of May (apart from a week on temporary duty at Northolt in July) was stood down the next day. It had done more than its share, had suffered more than its share, and none could have done more than the 'Fighting Cocks'.

Their place was taken by 607 (County of Durham) Squadron, AAF. In the meantime, 601 Squadron would suffer the grievous loss of Willie Rhodes-Moorhouse and Carl Davis, both old pre-war squadron hands and both shot down in flames over Kent on Friday, 6 September. Willie, whose father had won a posthumous VC in the Great War – the first to be awarded for gallantry in the air – had been awarded a DFC only a few weeks earlier. His 21-year-old brother-in-law, Dick Demetriadi, also of 601, had been killed in August. Willie's mother Linda had lost her husband in 1914, and now her only child; Amalia Demetriadi, Willie's wife, had lost both her brother and her husband in less than a month. Carl Davis's DFC had been gazetted the previous week, and his promotion to flight lieutenant had come through three days earlier; Carl was married to Sir Archibald Hope's sister Anne, and Archie Hope to Carl's sister Ruth. 601 Squadron would be stood down from operations at the end of the month, to be replaced by 213 Squadron.

9 September was a baptism of fire for 607 Squadron. On the day after they arrived at Tangmere to replace 43, in the late afternoon 607 were scrambled, sending up 12 Hurricanes to intercept a large formation of 60 or 70 Luftwaffe bombers and their escorting fighters over Surrey. A leading echelon of He111s and Do17s with high-cover Me109 escorts were just to the east of Guildford heading towards Weybridge and Brooklands. 607's Hurricanes lined up on the bombers and went in before the escorts could get down at them. The bomber formation broke up in confusion and the German raid was aborted. The cost to 607 Squadron was three pilots killed, and the loss of three more Hurricanes whose pilots baled out or crash-landed but survived.

That evening, the people of London would be subjected to the heaviest Luftwaffe bombardment since the war began. Two-hundred-and-fifty Luftwaffe bombers dropped high explosive and incendiary bombs in the centre of the city; huge fires burnt round St Paul's Cathedral, Ludgate Hill, the Guildhall, the Bank, the docks, and the crowded streets of the East End. Four hundred people, nearly all civilians, were killed and another 1,400 made homeless. Although no one knew it at the time, this was to be the first day of a 57-day Luftwaffe onslaught on London that later became known as 'The Blitz', and signalled a change in the strategy of the German High Command. It marked the end of their attempts to knock out military, infrastructural and industrial targets such as shipping, ports, railway junctions, radar stations, airfields, and aircraft factories; from now on, the object was to hit the civilian population indiscriminately, and to bomb them into surrender.

From Tangmere's point of view, the battle went on much as before for another three or four weeks. The station's squadrons – now 213, 602, and 607 – took to the air on a continuous rota of patrols whether or not enemy formations were reported in the vicinity, looking for lone raiders and reconnaissance aircraft, or standing at readiness to scramble when enemy formations approached Tangmere's sector or Tangmere's squadrons were ordered to reinforce the defences in other sectors such as Middle Wallop, Northolt, Kenley, Biggin Hill, North Weald, and Debden. With the benefit of hindsight, we now look back upon 15 September – celebrated as Battle of Britain Day – as the pivotal moment when the tide turned in Britain's favour. But for Tangmere's squadrons, it was just another day in a long-drawn-out battle of attrition; nothing especially unusual about it was noted in the Operations Record Books. On the 15th, the Luftwaffe came again in force, as they had before. Around 150 Dorniers and Heinkels, with Me109 escorts, approached London over northern Kent shortly after 2 pm. They were met by 170 RAF fighters, including Hurricanes of 213 Squadron stationed at Tangmere. One of 213's pilots, Sergeant G. D. Bushell, described what he saw – perhaps, understandably enough, with a bit of embellishment – in a letter he wrote the next day, 16 September 1940:

> I must write you in some detail of the most spectacular engagement I have ever seen, which took place yesterday with such success for the RAF and particularly for our group – a sector of SE area containing several squadrons – which altogether accounted for 116 aircraft shot down and 13 seriously damaged with 30 more probables.
>
> It was early afternoon when the 'phone rang and the squadron was ordered to patrol a point about 50 miles south of London at 20,000 feet. We took off and climbed through a layer of cloud 10/10 thick (this means it was so complete that no part of the earth could be seen at all, once we had passed through and got above it).
>
> We were just reaching the patrol area and were being ordered by wireless to keep a sharp look out to the south, when we first saw the object of our journey – a black mass approaching from that direction, at our height, and about nine miles away. We turned due south, and fingering our gun buttons, flew straight at them head on, at our maximum speed; as we rapidly closed, one could see the nature of this huge formation – they were flying twelve abreast, each twelve stepped up a few feet higher than the one preceding it, and there were about ten steps of them, so that looking from the front, the whole looked like one massive box, rather longer than it was wide, coming straight at us and growing larger and larger every second. They were in perfect and compact formation, and it was an awe-inspiring if

terrifying sight.

Suddenly, the front of this box lit up with flame after flame as if someone were flashing mirrors in the sun, and an instant later we were in a hail of shells and machine-gun bullets. We persisted on our course, and half a second later, we were ploughing through them like a hot knife through butter, firing as we went. Never have I seen or imagined the resultant confusion.

In that second the whole formation was so routed and ruined that no two German aircraft were left in the company of one another; Dornier 17s fell away to the left and right like so many skittles, the first three steps jettisoned their bombs and scattered in all directions, the steps of the formation split up, wheeled round and flew back on their tracks dropping their bombs and twisting and turning in a vain effort to avoid our fighters who were after them like greyhounds.

Having passed clean through the centre of this formation now routed, I turned about and observed a few stragglers going in varied directions, some were engaged by Hurricanes and were dropping out of the sky in flames. I saw one going on by itself in the direction of London, and chased it at full speed, the rear gunner opened fire on me, which I at once returned, this was the signal for the release of all bombs immediately, and a turn back for home. I beat him on the inside of the turn and silenced the rear gunner with a broadside burst, the enemy aircraft then dropped out of sight into the thick cloud layer at 10,000 feet; with no bombs he was harmless, and must have flown off home in the cloud layer for I did not see him again.

I pulled the nose of my machine up, and found myself almost beneath another straggler (heading for London), the rear gunner opened fire on me and I saw his tracer bullets miss my starboard wing by several feet. I returned the fire, and instantly the bomb hatches opened and a load of bombs fell just in front of my aircraft. I closed the range to 50 yards and silenced the rear gunner. I raked the machine from nose to tail with my fire and suddenly it plunged into the clouds in a vertical dive.

I looked around and observed German fighters high above being engaged by Spitfires. I had wondered why they had not pounced down on our tails when we engaged the bombers; the answer was being enacted in front of my eyes. My ammunition was all gone, so I dived down through the clouds and saw the Do 17 I had hit crash into a wood, explode and catch fire – and something else I saw which gratified me more than I can say; I was flying over open country, and every field for miles around was plastered with bursting bombs and the smoke of same – bombs that had been meant for London.

Even as I watched, half a dozen landed in a wood and some more in a pond, clouds of smoke were coming from every place, and burning wreckage everywhere indicated the fate of what had a few minutes earlier been a crack formation of the German air force. The way these aircraft, over a hundred of them, were scattered by our head-on attack, is something I shall never forget. If only Londoners could have seen that spectacle. If only it could have been filmed. But I think a film would have failed – people would have said it was a fake – impossible. I believe the numbers in the papers speak for themselves of the success of 15 September.

We lost a number of Hurricanes, but numbers I may not mention. This, however, is beyond censorship – ALL the pilots of those machines are alive to-day; some in hospital I grant you, but only one, through the loss of an arm, will never fly again.

You must forgive me for 'blowing our own trumpet' but I should be criminally guilty to hide from my friends all of this wonderful engagement, this spectacle which was so sadly hidden from the ground by the layer of cloud.

The inauspicious beginning of 607 Squadron's tour of duty at Tangmere continued with a run of extraordinarily bad luck. In addition to the three pilots and six Hurricanes lost on 9 September, within a month they would lose another five pilots and twelve Hurricanes. On one day, 1 October, six 607 Squadron Hurricanes were shot down near Swanage: two pilots were killed, and four crash-landed their damaged aircraft without serious injury; in the following week two 607 Hurricanes collided near Slindon resulting in the death of one of the pilots and the destruction of both aircraft. Fighter Command ordered the withdrawal of 607 Squadron two days later, and replaced them with 145 Squadron who now returned, once more, to Tangmere after having spent eight weeks with 13 Group in Scotland.

Between 15 September – the height of the Battle – and the end of October, when the Luftwaffe's attacks tailed off as winter approached, 145 Squadron lost two pilots killed and six Hurricanes, 602 Squadron lost two pilots and seven Spitfires, and 213 Squadron lost one pilot and three Hurricanes. During November and December there were no combat losses among Tangmere's squadrons. No. 213 Squadron left Tangmere for a well-earned rest at the end of November after three months in the front line. On 8 December, 602 Squadron was released and transferred to Prestwick after nearly four months at Tangmere.

Three fresh squadrons, 302 (Polish), 219, and 610 (County of Chester) spent Christmas 1940 at Tangmere, along with 145 Squadron, the last of the Battle of Britain squadrons remaining on the station. No. 302 Squadron had come from Northolt, where the station had been under the command of Group Captain Stanley Vincent. There, the squadron had earned a reputation for their practice of making fearless, highly-effective head-on attacks against enemy bomber formations at closing speeds of 500 mph or more. This was not then a recommended textbook tactic in either the RAF or the Luftwaffe, but would later be used in increasing desperation by the Germans against British bombers when the tide of war turned.

Group Captain J. A. Boret MC AFC, Tangmere's station commander, was awarded the CBE in the New Year's Honours List, 1941. He accepted the honour on behalf of all those who had served at RAF Tangmere in 1940. Among them were fifty-seven pilots who took off from Tangmere's fields in their Hurricanes and Spitfires to meet the enemy from July through October but did not return.

Pilot Officer D. G. Ashton, 266 Squadron, 12.8.40
Pilot Officer R. Atkinson, 213 Squadron, 17.10.40
Squadron Leader J. V. C. Badger DFC, 43 Squadron, 30.8.40
died of injuries 30.6.41
Sergeant Pilot E. D. Baker, 145 Squadron, 8.8.40
Flight Lieutenant C. E. Bowen, 607 Squadron, 1.10.40
Flying Officer G. R. Branch EGM (GC), 145 Squadron, 11.8.40
Sergeant Pilot N. Brumby, 607 Squadron, 1.10.40

Sergeant Pilot J. A. Buck, 43 Squadron, 19.7.40
Flying Officer W. H. Coverley, 602 Squadron, 7.9.40
Pilot Officer J. Cruttenden, 43 Squadron, 8.8.40
Pilot Officer J. A. J. Davey, 1 Squadron, 11.8.40
Flight Lieutenant C. R. Davis DFC, 601 Squadron, 6.9.40
Pilot Officer R. S. Demetriadi, 601 Squadron, 11.8.40
Wing Commander J. S. Dewar, 213 Squadron, 12.9.40
Pilot Officer W. G. Dickie, 601 Squadron, 11.8.40
Flying Officer I. B. Difford, 607 Squadron, 7.10.40
Pilot Officer G. J. Drake, 607 Squadron, 9.9.40
Sergeant Pilot D. W. Elcombe, 602 Squadron, 26.10.40
Pilot Officer W. M. L. Fiske, 601 Squadron, 16.8.40
died of injuries 17.8.40
Pilot Officer J. Gillan, 601 Squadron, 11.8.40
Flight Lieutenant W. E. Gore DFC, 607 Squadron, 28.9.40
Sergeant Pilot L. N. Guy, 601 Squadron, 18.8.40
Pilot Officer J. H. Harrison, 145 Squadron, 12.8.40
Sergeant Pilot R. P. Hawkings, 601 Squadron, 18.8.40
Flying Officer J. F. J. Haworth, 43 Squadron, 20.7.40
Squadron Leader C. B. Hull DFC, 43 Squadron, 7.9.40
Pilot Officer R. R. Hutley, 213 Squadron, 29.10.40
Flight Lieutenant M. M. Irving, 607 Squadron, 28.9.40
Pilot Officer A. R. I. G. Jottard, 145 Squadron, 27.10.40
Sub-Lieutenant I. H. Kestin, RN, 145 Squadron, 1.8.40
Sergeant Pilot J. Kwiecinski, 145 Squadron, 12.8.40
Sergeant Pilot J. Lansdell, 607 Squadron, 17.9.40
Pilot Officer J. D. Lenahan, 607 Squadron, 9.9.40
Pilot Officer P. C. Lindsey, 601 Squadron, 26.7.40
Pilot Officer R. A. de Mancha, 43 Squadron, 21.7.40
Sergeant Pilot H. F. Montgomery, 43 Squadron, 14.8.40
Pilot Officer H. W. Moody, 602 Squadron, 7.9.40
Sergeant Pilot D. Noble, 43 Squadron, 30.8.40
Pilot Officer J. R. S. Oelofse, 43 Squadron, 8.8.40
Flying Officer A. Ostowicz, 145 Squadron, 11.8.40
Flight Lieutenant W. Pankratz, 145 Squadron, 12.8.40
Pilot Officer S. B. Parnall, 607 Squadron, 9.9.40

Flight Lieutenant R. C. Reynell, 43 Squadron, 7.9.40

Flight Lieutenant W. H. Rhodes-Moorhouse DFC, 601 Squadron, 6.9.40

Flight Lieutenant L. H. Schwind, 213 Squadron, 27.9.40

Pilot Officer L. A. Sears, 145 Squadron, 8.8.40

Pilot Officer Lord R. U. P. Shuttleworth, 145 Squadron, 8.8.40

Sub-Lieutenant F. A. Smith, RN, 145 Squadron, 8.8.40

Pilot Officer J. L. Smithers, 601 Squadron, 11.8.40

Sergeant Pilot M. H. Sprague, 602 Squadron, 11.9.40

Sergeant Pilot J. V. Wadham, 145 Squadron, 12.10.40

Pilot Officer E. C. J. Wakeham DFC, 145 Squadron, 8.8.40

Sergeant Pilot B. E. P. Whall DFM, 602 Squadron, 7.10.40
died of injuries 8.10.40

Squadron Leader C. W. Williams, 17 Squadron, 25.8.40

Sergeant Pilot A. Wojcicki, 213 Squadron, 11.9.40

Pilot Officer C. A. Woods-Scawen DFC, 43 Squadron, 2.9.40

3
Harassing the Enemy
1941 – 1943

New Year's Day 1941 was frosty and foggy, with low cloud. The conditions were judged unsuitable over occupied France for night-intruder patrols. The weather improved the next day and as darkness fell the first of six Blenheim Mk IF night fighters of 23 Squadron took off from Ford, crossing the Channel to patrol their assigned sectors, looking for enemy aircraft in the Lille, Beauvais, and Abbeville areas. One of the Blenheims intercepted an He111 over Verneuil and shot it down. On the next night, six Blenheims again carried out offensive patrols in the same sectors. One Blenheim, YP-X, with its crew of three, Squadron Leader Coleman, Flight Sergeant Mathews, and Sergeant Macrory, failed to return. The last RDF plot of their aircraft was in the vicinity of Dieppe. The entry for that day in 23 Squadron's ORB notes that a message of condolence was received from the AOC 11 Group, Air Vice-Marshal Trafford Leigh-Mallory.

On 8 January, Leigh-Mallory visited Tangmere. He stayed the night at Chichester, and the following morning inspected the squadrons at their dispersals before proceeding to Westhampnett and thence to Durrington, between Goring-by-Sea and Worthing, to see the new, top-secret GCI radar station that had been in operation for less than a month and was still experimental. The original RDF stations used separate, fixed antennae for transmitting and receiving which were placed to detect enemy aircraft approaching the coast from seaward; once they had crossed the coast, they could not be tracked inland by the CH stations and the Observer Corps then took over. This system was much more successful than the enemy had reckoned with during their daylight raids from July through October 1940, but once the Luftwaffe's tactics changed to night bombardment, observers on the ground were handicapped by the darkness and the accuracy of the information they provided could not be relied upon to the same extent.

The need for a more versatile system of detection was an urgent priority. Developments in transmitter switchgear allowed the suppression of the transmitter pulse such that a single aerial could be used for both transmission and reception. The aerial could be made more compact, it could be made to rotate giving it a 360-degree sweep, and the now-familiar plan position indicator with the home point at its centre soon followed. This work continued at Bawdsey Manor through the summer and into the autumn of 1940. By December, three experimental GCI (ground control intercept) installations had been hurriedly completed at Durrington, Sopley (near Christchurch, Hants), and Sturminster Marshall, Dorset. They proved successful, and a further twelve mobile units were ordered for immediate use. By the spring of 1941, GCI would be an operational reality. It would be used to direct searchlights onto intruders, and more effectively to guide interceptor night fighters to their targets.

The Luftwaffe's change of tactics in the autumn of 1940 to night-bombing raids on Britain's cities and towns gave Fighter Command's day-fighter squadrons some breathing space and enabled them to make up for their recent losses and deficiencies in personnel and equipment. At the end of 1940 there were 1,200 fighter pilots. By the summer of 1941 this number had increased to approximately 1,600. Fighter aircraft, particularly Spitfires, were now pouring off the assembly lines, mainly due to the building of a new Vickers-Armstrong shadow factory at Castle Bromwich, near Birmingham, which greatly increased production rates. The Spitfire had proved itself more nimble in air-to-air combat than the Hurricane, and in its improved marks would soon come to be the RAF's preferred single-seat interceptor despite being less rugged and more expensive to build. An increasing number of front-line Home Defence squadrons, including those stationed at Tangmere, re-equipped with Spitfires during 1941; eventually, the Hurricanes would be relegated to other less critical roles.

The leadership of both Fighter Command and 11 Group had changed at the end of 1940 and was responsible for the development of new tactics. Sir Hugh Dowding, thought at the time to be exhausted and too defensive-minded, was replaced by a more charismatic and confident figure, William Sholto Douglas. Keith Park, AOC 11 Group during the Battle of Britain, was replaced by Trafford Leigh-Mallory who had been AOC 12 Group during the Battle. Leigh-Mallory, persuaded by one of his 12 Group squadron commanders, Douglas Bader, favoured the 'Big Wing' concept. A wing of at least three squadrons (most fighter stations' entire resources) would form up in a body overhead and attack the German formations. 12 Group was based to the north of London and was able, on occasions, to achieve the formation of a wing of fighters. The results were mixed when this was attempted, and Park claimed that this focus, by 12 Group, on the time-consuming formation of wings resulted at times in their inability to provide support when it was sorely needed to augment the hard-pressed squadrons of 11 Group defending the southern approaches to London.

With these changes of leadership, a new policy was set out: 'leaning into France', meaning a change from purely defensive tactics to making offensive sweeps. Such sweeps had begun in late 1940 with small numbers of single-seat fighters (up to four aircraft) crossing the Channel, with the aim of provoking the Luftwaffe into aerial combat. In order to carry out these missions (known as 'Rhubarbs') the raiding aircraft required low cloud cover protection to achieve surprise. The Rhubarb sorties were not successful; the enemy did not come up to fight and the raids were mainly ignored by the Luftwaffe. They were also costly. Too many experienced pilots were lost in the poor weather that the tactic depended upon; and baling out over the sea all too often led to a loss of consciousness within a matter of minutes due to hypothermia, and subsequent death by drowning.

In January 1941 a new type of operation was introduced to entice the Luftwaffe into battle. Fighter sweeps were now conducted by five squadrons flying as a wing. The Luftwaffe again refused to take the bait and stayed on the ground. It was then decided that a small group of light bombers, usually Blenheims of 2 Group, Bomber Command, should be added to the raiding force. These operations, known as 'Circuses', succeeded in attracting enemy fighter opposition because they were mounted against specific strategic and military targets such as radar installations, railway marshalling yards, power stations, and enemy airfields. Circuses were planned at Fighter Command level. In a Circus the bombers were escorted by wings of fighter aircraft providing high and close cover, the formation being known as a Beehive. Other wings would be directed by Fighter Command to provide top cover for the Beehive and target support whilst the Beehive was over the target area, and withdrawal support as the Beehive left the target. The tactic provoked German retaliation. From the station ORB:

12.3.41

Tangmere bombed and machine gunned between 21.04 hours and 22.15 hours by a single enemy aircraft flying at approximately 2,500 feet. Thirteen bombs of small calibre were dropped and one 500 lb in the course of the attacks, which were made at approximately ¼ hour intervals. The following casualties were sustained:- Killed, two service personnel, two civilians. Injured, three service personnel, one civilian. Some damage was caused to buildings, and the east wing of the officers' mess partially destroyed. Bofors and machine-gun posts opened fire during the attacks.

13.3.41

Tangmere again bombed, at 23.15 hours by a single hostile machine from approximately 4,000 feet, and 12 small-calibre bombs were dropped. All ground defences were in action in the course of the attack. The casualties sustained were as follows:- One airman fatally injured, and three others wounded. A number of MT vehicles were severely damaged and several buildings received slight damage as a result of this attack.

15/16.3.41

Tangmere bombed at 23.45 hours on 15 March, 1941, and at 00.45 hours on 16 March, 1941, by one enemy aircraft on each occasion from a height of approximately 12,000 feet. Twenty-four bombs were dropped in the course of the first attack, outside the aerodrome, including a number of anti-personnel bombs. In the second attack approximately 14 bombs were dropped, including five delayed-action bombs, these falling in one stick near the centre runway and one off the aerodrome resulting in damage being caused to four Spitfires of 145 Squadron, of which only one was repairable at unit. The only casualty sustained was one airman, who received slight injuries in the second raid. Damage was caused to MF/DF and HF Transmitting aerial system, and minor damage to the HF Transmitting building, and two channels of VHF and Post Office cabling were severed.

20.3.41
Approximately twelve bombs were dropped to the west of the aerodrome, between the station and the Aldingbourne MF/DF building, at approximately 22.30 hours.

28.3.41
As a result of hostile bombing it was decided to disperse still further and some 400 airmen were moved to the Race Course, Goodwood.

10.4.41
At 05.55 hours today three bombs were dropped. Casualties:- five airmen killed, 14 wounded. Roads cleared by 11.00 hours. Watch office – delayed-action bomb outside – alternative WO arranged in stores trailer. No. 8 Barrack Block almost completely destroyed by a direct hit from HE bomb. No. 5 Barrack Block seriously damaged. Link Trainer Room damaged by bomb which passed clean through two opposite side walls without exploding, having ricochetted off the road outside. This is believed to be the bomb which is lying unexploded just outside the watch office.

5.5.41
At 00.15 hours this morning, after a night of some enemy activity in the vicinity, one small bomb was dropped and exploded just outside No. 2 Officers' Married Quarters, the front rooms of which were damaged and rendered uninhabitable. There were no casualties.

12.5.41
At 00.05 hours a large number of incendiary bombs were dropped on Tangmere by low-flying enemy aircraft, and this form of low attack was continued intermittently until 02.40 hours. Some 23 HE bombs of various calibres were dropped on the aerodrome and main site and the Drem lighting was put out of action. A stick of 15 bombs was dropped across the south side of the aerodrome, rendering it unserviceable: A Magister aircraft was burnt out; the east wing of

the sergeants' mess was completely destroyed; Barrack Block No. 4 was severely damaged, and the works and buildings offices were shattered.

At 01.45 three small HE bombs were dropped on the north side of Westhampnett aerodrome.

In all these raids, not one casualty was sustained, thereby justifying the policy of dispersal, and at Westhampnett the damage was made good by 08.30 hours. At Tangmere, the aerodrome craters were filled and the debris on the Main Site cleared from the roadways by 21.00 hours. No. 4 Works Flight and the Army Military Pioneer Corps from Middleton rendered conspicuous service and enabled the clearing-up programme to be carried out expeditiously.

17.5.41

The officers' mess was transferred from Tangmere to Shopwyke House today, and the sergeants' mess moved into the officers' mess, Tangmere.

8.7.41

Enemy aircraft, believed to be Ju88s, attacked Tangmere aerodrome between 01.55 and 02.15 hours today, and dropped 29 HE and six AP bombs. Of these, seven HE fell around the watch office and the remainder on the aerodrome. The old hangar behind the watch office was hit by incendiaries, which pierced the roof and fell on the cement floor, and a fire was started in the offices adjacent to the hangar, which was extinguished promptly. There were no casualties which vindicated the policy of wide dispersal practised on this station. All personnel behaved in an exemplary manner, and the willing and courageous assistance of the Tangmere company, 'B' Company, 70th Btn, Royal Sussex Regiment, was particularly noticeable. A great many incendiary bombs, probably more than 200, were dropped but were promptly extinguished. The aerodrome was completely serviceable by 20.30 hours.

The conditions at the squadrons' dispersals round the aerodrome were primitive and uncomfortable, and became very unpleasant during the winter of 1940-41. Photographs depicting pilots sitting pleasantly relaxed in deck chairs in the sunshine outside the officers' mess awaiting the scramble bell were the stuff of patriotic publicity. The reality was much more likely to be wet, cold, and muddy, with long tedious hours spent in cramped dispersal huts waiting for calls to action that did not materialise. At Westhampnett, the airfield was particularly prone to waterlogging; the wheels of parked aircraft sank into the mud and had constantly to be moved by their ground crews to keep them from getting bogged down to their axles, and aircraft servicing was done in the open in the wind, rain, and snow. At times the landing ground and perimeter tracks at Westhampnett were rendered completely unusable, as during December 1940 and into January 1941 when snowfalls further added to the surface-water problem and turned the most heavily-trafficked tracks into deep muddy ruts.

Airfield construction crews moved in to lay concrete perimeter tracks and hard-standings, and erected several Blister hangars at Westhampnett. Some improvement was effected, but the waterlogging of the landing ground itself remained a persistent problem despite repeated attempts to cure it and to some extent remains so to this day. At Merston, one-and-a-half miles to the southwest of the main aerodrome, plans to bring a second satellite airfield into operation were delayed by the wintry weather and the diversion of resources to Westhampnett to keep it functioning. Not until April 1941 was Merston ready for occupation, coincidentally by 145 Squadron. They had been the first squadron to use Westhampnett in July-August 1940, and had once again to contend with the problems of sorting out the myriad details of getting a new aerodrome fully into operation and made as habitable, if not as comfortable, as the spartan conditions allowed.

On 18 March 1941, Wing Commander Douglas Bader arrived at Tangmere as wing commander (flying), a new post in Fighter Command. On arrival he found that the Tangmere Wing consisted of 145 Squadron commanded by Squadron Leader Jack Leather and 616 (South Yorkshire) Squadron led by Squadron Leader H. F. 'Billy' Burton and at Westhampnett, 610 (County of Chester) Squadron under Squadron Leader John Ellis. All three squadrons were equipped with Spitfire IIAs and IIBs. With the improving spring weather and to protect the squadrons from night bombing raids on RAF Tangmere, 145 Squadron was moved to Merston, now re-opened. 616 Squadron also moved from Tangmere to Westhampnett to join 610. In the middle of April,

Squadron Leader Paddy Woodhouse took over 610 from John Ellis and Squadron Leader Stan Turner, a Canadian who had fought with Bader on 242 Squadron in the Battle of Britain at Duxford, took over 145 Squadron. Also in April, Group Captain A. B. 'Woody' Woodhall arrived at Tangmere as station commander and chief controller, a post he had held at Duxford when Bader was there. Woodhall was known for inspiring confidence in the squadrons he was controlling with his unhurried and confident manner on the radio and for allowing the leader in the air to make his own decisions after giving him the necessary information.

As he had done at Duxford during the Battle of Britain, Bader chose to mainly fly with only one of the wing's squadrons, 616. In his section within the squadron he flew with two pilots that made their names later in the war: Flying Officer 'Cocky' Dundas and Pilot Officer 'Johnnie' Johnson. Dundas later became the RAF's youngest group captain and Johnson the RAF's highest-scoring fighter pilot. In early June 1941 Ken Holden, a flight commander in 616 Squadron, was promoted to squadron leader and took over 610 Squadron, and Bader's team for the summer's operations was complete. It was about this time, in early summer, that a notice appeared on 616's 'A' Flight notice board: 'Bader's Bus Company – daily tickets to the Continent – Return tickets only!' 'Bus Company' may have had something to do with the wing's radio call sign, 'Green Line Bus'.

On taking over the wing, Bader ordered that all squadron operations within the wing should be flown in 'Finger Four' with sections of four aircraft flying in such a way as to cover each other. When covering a Circus, the Tangmere Wing would normally operate with the three squadrons flying at different levels and depending on the time of day the wing would cross the French coast at a point where it was best advantaged with regard to the sun. In a morning operation they would aim to cross in both directions near the French town of Gravelines and in the afternoon near the port of Boulogne.

By June 1941 the Circuses, usually conducted twice a day, were well under way. A typical day for the wing was 25 June 1941 when it covered Circus 22 between noon and 13.00 hours. On crossing the French coast contact was made with 30-plus Me109s near Gravelines. In the ensuing battle 610 Squadron claimed one Me109 destroyed and one a probable. Bader, flying with 616 Squadron, claimed one Me109 destroyed and one shared with his number two, Sergeant Jeff West. Other claims by 616 Squadron were two enemy aircraft as probables and two damaged. On the same day between 15.45 and 17.40 hours the Tangmere Wing flew cover for Circus 23. About 15 miles inland from the French coast, Bader was warned of 12 Me109s approaching from the east. Wing Commander Max Aitken (who as a squadron leader had commanded 601 Squadron at Tangmere), on this occasion flying with 610 Squadron, destroyed one and Sergeant Raine of the same squadron damaged another. Squadron Leader Holden, CO of 610, also damaged an Me109. No. 145 Squadron claimed two enemy aircraft destroyed and two damaged, one of which had been attacked by their Squadron Leader Stan Turner. No. 616 Squadron was not so lucky on this operation with two sergeant pilots shot down and killed. Another sergeant pilot, Bob Morton, was lucky to reach Hawkinge after his Spitfire had been severely damaged when jumped by two Me109s. On the other hand, Bader attacked a group of four Me109s with his No. 2 in the Boulogne area and managed to destroy one, his victim being Oberleutnant Heinz Gottlob of I/JG 26. Gottlob managed to bale out but was so badly wounded that he never flew again.

During July and early August 1941 the Circus operations continued and the Tangmere Wing's Spitfire IIs were replaced with cannon-armed Spitfire Vs with their more powerful Merlin 45 engines which gave the aircraft a top speed of 360 mph at 25,000 feet. On 28 July there was a major change to Bader's team: 145 Squadron was replaced by another experienced squadron, No. 41, led by Squadron Leader Donald Finlay. Four days later Finlay was promoted to acting wing commander and Squadron Leader L. M. 'Elmer' Gaunce, a Canadian, took over the squadron.

On 9 August 1941 the Tangmere Wing was ordered to provide target support for Circus 68, a bombing raid on Gosnay, near St Omer. Bader took off as normal with 616 Squadron with Jeff West as his No. 2; his normal wingman, Sergeant Alan Smith, was unavailable. Nos. 616 and 610 Squadrons set course, but 41 Squadron failed to join up. As the two squadrons crossed the French coast at 28,000 feet, Me109s were seen to port and below. No. 616 Squadron attacked, covered by 610 above, but were bounced by other Me109s before 610 could intervene. In the ensuing close engagements (Johnson said later that it was on that day he came closest to having a mid-air collision), Flight Lieutenant 'Buck' Casson, 616's 'B' Flight commander, was shot down and Wing Commander Bader's Spitfire also went down. Exactly what happened to Bader remains a mystery to this day. Bader maintained that he had a mid-air collision with an Me109. The Germans said differently: JG 26's Kommodore, Oberst Adolf Galland, claimed that Bader had been deliberately shot down by one of his own pilots. Naturally, Bader never accepted this theory. Another more plausible explanation is that Bader was inadvertently shot down by 'friendly fire' from one of his wing's Spitfires in the chaotic aerial battle that day.

After a struggle to get out of his cockpit and leaving one of his metal legs behind, Bader parachuted to safety near St Omer. Buck Casson survived a crash landing near Marquise, just short of the French coast. On 14 August the German authorities notified the British via the Red Cross that Bader and Casson had been taken prisoner. Group Captain Woodhall broadcast the welcome news over the Tangmere station tannoy. The Germans offered free passage for an RAF aircraft to deliver a replacement leg to Bader at Galland's JG26 airfield at Audembert. The British did not take up this offer but dropped a leg by parachute from a Blenheim several days later during a routine Circus operation to Longuenesse.

The Tangmere Wing claimed 22 Me109s destroyed, ten probables and eight damaged on the Circus 68 operation of 9 August for a loss of five Spitfires destroyed, including those of Bader and Casson, and two damaged. According to Luftwaffe records, however, only two Me109s were destroyed on that day. The first operation conducted by the Tangmere Wing after losing Bader was led by Wing Commander Don Finlay. He was succeeded by Paddy Woodhouse, who had commanded 610 Squadron, on 14 August. Two weeks later, 610 left Westhampnett for Leconfield, to be replaced by 129 Squadron. What Leigh-Mallory referred to as 'the season' ended on 30 September 1941. The results for Fighter Command were disappointing. Between the middle of June and the beginning of September, Fighter Command had lost 194 pilots in these cross-Channel operations. In the same period the German losses of fighter aircraft based in France and the Low Countries was 128. As the Germans were fighting over territory that they controlled, many of their pilots who survived after being shot down were able to return to the fight. The RAF's pilots, however, were likely either to be taken prisoner if they baled out or crash-landed in France, or be lost by drowning if they took to their parachutes over the sea or ditched in the Channel. On 6 October, Billy Burton's 616 Squadron left to be replaced by 65 Squadron. With the departure of 616, the last of the original Tangmere Wing squadrons, the story of Bader's Bus Company came to an end.

Meanwhile, at Ford, 23 Squadron had converted from their Blenheim IF night fighters to the night-intruder version of the Douglas DB7 in March 1941. As a light bomber, it was called the Boston by the RAF. As a night fighter, with a reduced bomb load and additional forward-firing guns, it was called the Havoc. The Havocs were much faster than the Blenheims, with a top speed to 340 mph as compared with the Blenheims' 260 mph, as well as having more fighter-like flying qualities. The squadron had been very active since December 1940 in seeking out enemy bombers at night near their home bases in German-occupied France, Belgium, and Holland. In March, 23 Squadron detached two of their Havocs to operate from Tangmere. Some RAF Havocs would later be fitted with AI radar. Others had their armament removed and were additionally fitted with a 2,700-million-candlepower searchlight in the nose; vectored by GCI radar, these unarmed 'Turbinlite' Havocs were intended to find enemy bombers operating under the cover of darkness, close in using their AI radar and then use the searchlight to illuminate targets for their accompanying fighters to shoot down. The searchlight was powered by lead-acid batteries mounted in the bomb bay, which supplied enough current for about two minutes of operation. Operational formations consisted of one Turbinlite Havoc and six Hurricanes. Since the regular squadrons often stood down for the night, it was sometimes a problem getting a flight of Hurricanes readied for these night sorties. Eventually, the Turbinlite detachment at Tangmere was augmented by its own, dedicated flight of night-fighter Hurricanes which were used only for these operations.

On 2 July 1941, a little over a year since it had come back from France, 1 Squadron returned to its ancestral home at Tangmere. Equipped with Hurricane IIs, it was assigned to the night defence of Portsmouth and Southampton. The squadron embarked on a very intensive night interception work-up. Much of the time was spent in developing new interception techniques with the Turbinlite Havocs of 1455 (Fighter) Flight, later to be redesignated 534 Squadron, a new unit formed at Tangmere on 7 July 1941 and which would remain on the station until January 1943. During August 1941, 1 Squadron's Hurricane Mk IIs were replaced with Mk IICs. These aircraft were armed with four 20-mm Hispano cannon in place of the Browning machine guns and had the provision to carry two bombs beneath the wings. In November the squadron was declared fully operational as a defensive night-fighter unit but because of the reduced German bomber activity over southern England was soon reassigned as a night-intruder unit to make offensive patrols over France.

On 1 November 1941 Squadron Leader James MacLachlan DFC took over command of 1 Squadron. He was already an experienced fighter pilot with six victories to his name in the Battle of Britain and two more in Malta. In Malta he had been shot down and badly wounded in February 1941, losing his left arm below the elbow. On his return to England he had been fitted with an artificial arm especially designed to operate the controls of a Hurricane. On his arrival at Tangmere, MacLachlan set to work training up 1 Squadron for night-intruder operations which continued through the winter of 1941-42.

January 1942 was a month of poor weather which limited flying and hampered operations. Tangmere's squadrons made only seven offensive sorties during the month, and neither lost any of their own aircraft nor downed any of the enemy's. It was the first time since June 1940, when France had fallen to the Germans and Tangmere had suddenly found itself in the front line of defence, that the monthly scoreboard of victories and losses had remained blank. The bad weather continued into February. The station ORB for the 12th, however, has the following entry:

In extremely bad weather, 41 and 129 Squadrons, together with five Hurricanes of 1 Squadron, took part in the action against the *Scharnhorst*, *Gneisenau*, and *Prinz Eugen* off the Belgian coast and claim one Me109F damaged by 129 Squadron, one Me109F damaged by 41 Squadron, three Me109F destroyed by 41 Squadron. Our losses were two pilots from 1 Squadron (one since reported prisoner-of-war) and one pilot each from 41 and 129 Squadrons.

That afternoon, as the pilots of the Spitfires and Hurricanes of Tangmere's 1, 41, and 129 Squadrons engaged the swarms of Me109s escorting the escaping German battle cruisers as they headed north, they might have heard the news before taking off or while they were refuelling at Manston that Lieutenant Commander Eugene Esmonde, leading a squadron of Swordfish torpedo-bombers, had valiantly attempted to sink the battle cruisers earlier that day off the French coast. Eugene Esmonde had been commissioned as a pilot officer in the RAF in 1928, and had served at Tangmere. He was as much one of 'Tangmere's Own' as anyone. Mark Selway, who was at Tangmere at the same time as Esmonde, remembered him from 1930 and what he did on that day in February 1942:

> He was dark and small and very quiet and turned out to be a very nice chap and we were glad to have him as a messmate. He joined 43 Squadron and used to come out with us on all our parties.
>
> When Eugene Esmonde's short-service career in the Royal Air Force came to an end he became a pilot with Imperial Airways and when the war started he was a full captain, qualified on several types. He immediately joined the navy and in 1941 he was commanding a squadron of Swordfish torpedo bombers in the Fleet Air Arm. It was during that command that he and his squadron played a vital part in the locating and sinking of the German battleship *Bismarck* and after the action Esmonde was awarded the DSO.
>
> But in February 1942 came the famous 'break out' of the *Gneisenau*, *Scharnhorst* and *Prinz Eugen* from Brest. These three Nazi capital ships were commerce raiders with a great nuisance value in the Atlantic and other oceans and part of their function was to keep the Royal Navy busy stopping them from doing great damage to our vital convoys. One of these ships alone would have been able to sink a fifty-ship convoy in a matter of hours. At this stage in the war they had retired to the German-occupied port of Brest where they were bombed at regular intervals by the RAF. The RN and the RAF kept them under surveillance and substantial forces were available in case they should break out towards our vital shipping routes. But Hitler had other plans and wanted them back in Kiel. He did not want to risk sending them back round the usual route via Iceland where they would have to fight and possibly suffer the same fate as the *Bismarck*. So he decided on a Channel dash and made secret arrangements which unfortunately led our intelligence services to believe he would leave Brest at such time to let the ships go through the narrow part of the Channel in hours of darkness. This would to some extent protect the ships from large-scale daylight attack.

Our own plans were designed to assemble suitable forces so as to make a night attack on the ships and Esmonde's Swordfishes were to be stationed at Manston in Kent. Esmonde had agreed that it would be possible for his squadron to make night attacks on these ships when they would not have the Luftwaffe to contend with. Defending fighters could not attack targets which were only 50 feet off the water in the dark. Owing to the great care and secrecy with which the German navy had made their plans, it came as a shock when the first reports came in to say that the ships had made their breakout during the night of 12 February and were already up the Channel as far as Cherbourg. Unless we could bring them to battle in a matter of hours they would escape and the chance to destroy this menace would be gone.

Such was the disarray that the British were in at this short notice that no forces were available except Esmonde's Swordfishes and one squadron of fighters supplied by the RAF. Esmonde got the news at Manston and was asked whether in view of his volunteering to attack by night this also meant that he would attempt a daylight attack with no proper defence against the very large force of Luftwaffe fighters that were continuously circling the ships. Those who were at Manston said afterwards that Esmonde's face seemed drained of blood and turned a grey colour. A naval officer said afterwards that it was like talking to a man already dead. The odds were enormous and it was left to the unfortunate Esmonde to make a decision.

To his undying credit and also that of his six crews he said he would go. The result is history. He led his squadron at 50 feet into a hurricane of fire from the three ships, the attendant destroyers and from a protecting wing of German fighters. Esmonde's squadron was smashed to pieces and shot down into the sea. Three survivors were picked up later and reported what they had seen. Esmonde was awarded an immediate but posthumous Victoria Cross and all the survivors were highly decorated.

There have been many VCs in the past hundred years but I doubt whether any have occasioned such mental torture as this. Esmonde must have known that the Royal Navy, the Admiralty, the British public – especially Winston Churchill – were all awaiting the outcome. He was asked to make a cold-blooded decision to commit suicide, he and his crews. And he said he would go. England expected that Esmonde would do his duty. He did.

At Tangmere, after the winter's working-up, the first night-intruder operation occurred on 1 April 1942, when Squadron Leader MacLachlan and Flight Lieutenant Karel Kuttelwascher took off at 22.15 hours for a three-hour night-intruder sortie. The CO returned to Tangmere with nothing to report; Kuttelwascher, on the other hand, found a Ju88 taking off from Melun airfield, followed it into the circuit and shot it down. On 16 April Kuttelwascher shot down a Do217 at St André, MacLachlan again being out of luck. However, on the following night MacLachlan destroyed a Dornier at St André, damaging another. On the same night Kuttelwascher flew to Boos airfield, near Rouen, and shot down a Do217. As he was observing this aircraft crashing he was attacked by a Ju88. The German night fighter missed his target and was shot down by Kuttelwascher. On 30 April, Kuttelwascher ventured further into Brittany and destroyed a Do217 taking off from Rennes. His night's work was not over; on the flight back to Tangmere he caught and shot down an He111 into the sea near Dinard. On 3 May, MacLachlan destroyed a Dornier preparing to land at Dinard and then an He111 turning onto final approach at the same airfield. On the following night, Kuttelwascher destroyed three He111s by joining the circuit at St André and shooting down the three Heinkels before the airfield defences realised what was happening.

On 16 May 1942 both MacLachlan's and Kuttelwascher's achievements were recognised: MacLachlan was awarded the DSO and Kuttelwascher the DFC. On 4 June both MacLachlan and Kuttelwascher added to their scores when the CO destroyed two Dorniers at St André. An hour later, Kuttelwascher destroyed a Heinkel and another Dornier at the same airfield. On 22 June St André was again the target when Kuttelwascher shot down a Ju88. On 2 July he succeeded again at St André when he destroyed two Dorniers. On 8 July, 1 Squadron was moved to Acklington for a rest. In three months the squadron had destroyed 22 enemy aircraft and damaged a further 13 more. Of those destroyed, five were attributed to MacLachlan and 15 to Kuttelwascher.

While these intruder operations continued, it was evident from early July that something big was brewing, although no one yet knew what it was. The station Operations Record Book notes a build-up of forces and a highly unusual number of squadron movements during the month which everyone must have noticed despite attempts to keep them secret: within a week, 66, 118, and 501 Squadrons arrived, left a few days later, and returned on a date that was not recorded; 232, 416, and 1 Squadrons left and No. 43 arrived to join 23, 129, 131, 141, 340 (Free French) and 412 (Canadian) who were being accommodated on the station and at Westhampnett and Merston. At the end of the month, 129 Squadron moved to Thorney Island as a lodger unit under Tangmere's command, and 340 left for Hornchurch, vacating Westhampnett for the use of the US Army Air Force, whose 31st Pursuit Group took over the airfield on 30 July; the next day, Westhampnett became an American station under the operational control of RAF Tangmere. No. 141 Squadron was moved to Ford on 10 August. Eight days later the nature of the anticipated big operation was revealed. The following notation was made in the station ORB on 18 August 1942:

> During the afternoon a conference was held in the intelligence hut, at which the AOC of 11 Group, Air Vice-Marshal Leigh-Mallory presided. Also present were the SASO, Air Commodore Harcourt-Smith, Group Captain C. H. Appleton [Tangmere's station commander], the wing commander flying and the officers commanding and flight commanders of 3, 32, 41, 43, 66, 87, 118, 129, 130, 131, 164, 175, 245, 253, 412 (Canadian), 501 and 309 (USA) Squadrons of Fighter Command, and 88 and 107 Squadrons of Bomber Command. The AOC outlined Operation Jubilee, a combined operation which was to take place over Dieppe, and stressed the important role the RAF would have to play. At the conclusion of the conference the Hurricane Close Support Squadrons – 174 and 175 Hurricane Bombers, and 3, 32, 43, 87 245 and 253 Hurricane Fighter Squadrons – were briefed by Group Captain Appleton and other senior officers on the station. Later the squadron commanders and flight commanders of the Spitfire squadrons – 41, 66, 118, 129, 130, 131, 309, 412 and 501 Squadrons – were similarly briefed.

Some weeks earlier, the British Combined Chiefs of Staff, encouraged by the daring commando raid on St Nazaire in March 1942, had drawn up plans for a similar, but far more ambitious seaborne raid on a French port. Air cover for this raid was essential and accordingly the target had to be within the limited combat radius of Spitfires and Hurricanes flying from southern England. The small numbers of troopships and landing craft available at the time precluded any attempt at a full-scale invasion. However, combined operations considered that a 'reconnaissance in force' to test the mettle of the German defences and to discover what resistance would have to be met to seize a seaport were both worthwhile objectives. It was also seen as a means of enticing the Luftwaffe up to fight. They had been reluctant throughout 1942 to challenge the sorties the RAF had been flying over northern France.

The small French seaport town and peace-time holiday resort of Dieppe was selected as the target as it lay only 70 nautical miles across the Channel, was within easy range of RAF day fighters and represented a reasonable sea crossing for the invading forces which could be transported there and back within a day's sailing. By early August 1942, all the pieces of the elaborate plan were complete. Operation Jubilee was planned for 18 August 1942 and called for the landing of approximately 6,000 troops, the majority being Canadian. The RAF was responsible for providing air cover throughout the day, close support during the assault on the port and beaches, and tactical reconnaissance and close support during the withdrawal. Air Vice-Marshal Leigh-Mallory was designated commander for the operation and for one day an unprecedented number of squadrons would be under his direct control. It was decided that the air operation would be controlled from 11 Group's operations room at RAF Uxbridge. Fifty Spitfire squadrons, including three from the USAAF's 31st Fighter Group, were assigned to the general protection of the assault forces over Dieppe and the surrounding area and would vary in strength from two to six squadrons patrolling Dieppe according to the phase of the operation.

The two most vulnerable phases, the landing and the withdrawal, would warrant maximum fighter cover. Of the Spitfire squadrons, only five were equipped with the new Spitfire Mk IX or the high-altitude Mk VI, the remainder being equipped with the Mk Vb, acknowledged as being inferior to the Fw190A-3, the standard fighter of the Luftwaffe in northern France at this point in the war. The bombing and strafing attacks on selected targets, including the well-defended heavy-calibre gun batteries protecting the port, would be conducted by six Hurricane Mk II cannon-armed night-intruder squadrons and two specialised fighter-bomber units. Bostons of 418 (RCAF) Squadron would also give bombing support during the opening phases while it was still dark. Opposing the Allied air forces were the battle-hardened and experienced Luftwaffe fighter groups JG2 and JG26; each had about 125 Fw190s and Me109s at their disposal. Included in these two groups were two *staffeln* (squadrons) of Fw190A-2 *Jabo* fighter-bombers.

On 17 August, the weather worsened and it was decided to postpone the operation for 24 hours. At Tangmere and its satellite airfields Westhampnett and Merston, the resident squadrons were reinforced by other squadrons with 87 Squadron's night-intruder Hurricane IICs joining 43 Squadron, similarly equipped. The Spitfire Vs of 41 Squadron and the Ibsley Wing (66, 118 and 501 Squadrons) also arrived at Tangmere and 412 (RCAF) Squadron flew in from Merston, leaving 131 Squadron at the satellite airfield. Westhampnett's contribution was the recently arrived 309th Fighter Squadron's Spitfire Vs of the United States Army Air Force. Leigh-Mallory sent a signal to all participating units which concluded with the following words:

> The safety of the expedition from the onslaught of the enemy air force rests in your hands. The responsibility is great, but I am confident that every pilot will do his damndest to destroy any enemy aircraft that may attempt to attack our ships or our fighting men – Good luck to you all.

On 19 August, the day of the operation, 43 Squadron was the first to take off, led by Squadron Leader Daniel le Roy du Vivier; its 12 Hurricanes departed Tangmere in the dark at 04.25 hours and flew across the Channel to attack gun positions on the beaches and buildings immediately to the west of Dieppe harbour. Jimmy Beedle takes up the story:

> At ten minutes to five, 12 Hurricanes [of 43 Squadron], cannons and machine-guns blazing, went in, line abreast against gun positions on the beaches and in the buildings to the west of the harbour entrance at Dieppe. First into attack though they were, the Hurricanes found the defences alerted after a smoke-laying mission made a few minutes earlier by Boston medium bombers. Intense and accurate flak poured

up and, during that initial run-in, seven of the Hurricanes were struck, of which only du Vivier's with a cannon shell through a non-vital part of his starboard wing could be classified as negligibly damaged. 'B' Flight especially suffered severely, five of their six aircraft being hard hit. Hank Wik, a flight sergeant from Canada, his engine dead, could do no more than glide over the houses of the town to crash in the fields beyond. P/O Snell, a little more fortunate, managed to claw his way upward to 2,000 feet before rolling over and abandoning his burning aircraft above a tank-landing ship which picked him out of the water, dried his clothes and set him to earn his keep for the rest of the day by operating the machine-gun on the port side of the bridge. (He claimed to have shot at two Fw190s but to have missed by a mile.) Of four other sorely smitten Hurricanes that turned back for base one carried a pilot who had felt the whole aircraft shake at the same time as he heard a loud bang but did not discover the cause, a pram-sized hole in the fuselage behind the radio, until he reached Tangmere.

F/O Turkington made a most creditable touch-down with the elevators partly missing and wholly shredded, and P/O Trenchard-Smith of Australia earned for himself the enduring name of 'Tailless Ted' after returning to the owners a Hurricane on which the top half of the fin and the rudder had vanished and the remnants of the latter hung to the rudder post only by the bottom hinge and the control cables. But F/L Lister outperformed the field and turned in the supreme exposition of all. Hit over the target twice, his port wing was a shambles; the panels above the cannons blown off; a four-foot square hole in the trailing edge took in the aileron up to its inboard hinge and the outermost cannon wrenched from its by no means slender mounting was askew, damaging the front spar and buckling the leading edge. But the Hurricane kept flying though cautious experiment on the way back established that 190 IAS was the minimum speed at which level flight could be maintained and the damage visible from the cockpit was patently sufficient to make Lister realise that he dare not lower the flaps.

So it was that those who at dispersal watched the return of the squadron in ones and twos suddenly saw an all-black Hurricane come boring out of the mist, flying above the main runway so fast that it might have been an early morning beat-up born of exuberance except that the pilot was obviously trying to make contact with the ground by repeatedly jerking the nose downwards, losing a few feet each time he did so. The early morning mist had not fully dispersed so that the south-west areas of the 'drome were still lost to view and the Hurricane was still making its quick stabbing dabs at the ground when it vanished into the haze. A solitary voice, recognising the aircraft, said "Christ, that's Freddie", but no one else spoke. There followed an anguished silence of waiting for the sickening whoomph of exploding fuel tanks; but there came no sound save the drone of other airborne squadrons as, unseen in the distant haze, the Hurricane brought its pilot safely to rest.

Sensing rather than sighting the fast-approaching boundary fence, Lister drove onto the deck with 210 on the clock, and the Hurricane took it. Most aeroplanes of that period, hitting the ground at such speeds, would simply have disintegrated; others, dug in the nose, flipped over on to their backs and crushed the skulls of their unfortunate occupants. The Hurricane, possessed of no such venomous streak, just kept going straight and level, ripping open the green turf beside the runway and spewing out the brown clods to either side until, with the radiator wrenched away, it slid to a halt close to the boundary fence and the sunken road beyond. The air intake had gone, the propeller blades were all sheared at the roots, the spinner was stove in, the bottom cowlings torn. The wheel bay and cannon muzzles were packed with hard-driven earth, and the port wing was a scarcely cohesive jumble of twisted metal and torn skin. But from out of it stepped, quite unhurt though a little stunned by his good fortune, one very valuable flight commander. Returning with du Vivier to dispersal he arrived with the flourish "Freddy lives to fly again" which he did three more times that day, at the end of which he had won a DFC. No bad effort after that kind of landing, and no slight recommendation for the Hurricane either.

No. 43 Squadron sustained the loss of, or damage to, seven aircraft in their first attack, but none of their pilots were seriously hurt. By 07.50, the squadron was back in the air making a second sortie in their twelve hurriedly patched-up or replacement Hurricanes looking for ten E-boats reported to be sailing out of Boulogne. Despite a long search, none were found and 43 was back at Tangmere by 09.20 hours. Later that morning the Spitfires of 41 Squadron provided top cover for the Canadians of 412 Squadron patrolling over the assault ships and 43 Squadron returned for its third sortie with another Hurricane squadron again to search for E-boats. None were found. Gun positions southeast of Dieppe were also attacked by 87 Squadron Hurricanes covered by the Spitfires of 41, 412, and 501 Squadrons.

In the early afternoon, 43 Squadron, escorted by 66 Squadron Spitfires, flew their fourth and last sortie over the beaches, harbour and town in an attempt to silence the gun batteries that were causing havoc to the withdrawing troops. This time the Luftwaffe Fw190s attacked the squadron but only Sergeant Bierer's Hurricane was damaged. Later in the afternoon 41, 118, and 501 covered the returning ships. In the battle over the ships, two Do217s were shot down for the loss of two Spitfires, including that of 41's CO Squadron Leader Hyde.

For their part in the raid, the USAAF was to provide cover throughout the day, to attack enemy coastal batteries and defences and to lay a smokescreen over the eastern headland during the assault and withdrawal. This American contribution included the B-17 Flying Fortresses of the 97th Bombardment Group (the first USAAF B-17 bombardment group to go operational in the Second World War) based at High Wycombe, which during the morning successfully attacked the JG26 airfield at Abbeville-Drucat, bombing with commendable accuracy from 16,000 feet.

At Westhampnett the Americans of the 309th Fighter Squadron were called to readiness at 03.45 hours. By 08.50 the squadron's twelve Spitfires were at their rendezvous point with the RAF's 130 and 131 Squadrons over the invasion ships. The Americans soon encountered a dozen Fw190s in their assigned sector and during the ensuing engagement, Lieutenant Samuel Junkin found himself in a one-to-one dogfight with an Fw190, which he managed to shoot down before he was subsequently attacked by a second Fw190. Wounded in the shoulder by cannon fire, he momentarily passed out, but regained consciousness just above the sea. He climbed to 1,000 feet to bale out but had to free a jammed cockpit hood before he could escape his Spitfire. Rescued by an RAF air-sea rescue launch, he was transferred to a ship that had picked up Lieutenant Collins, who had been shot down in the same engagement. Sam Junkin's victory was the first by a USAAF Eighth Air Force fighter pilot.

For their second sortie of the day, just before midday, the 309th flew with the RAF's 81 and 131 Squadrons escorting Boston bombers attacking gun positions. They met with little opposition. The 309th flew top cover for their third mission of the day when Captain Thorsen and Lieutenants Biggard and Payne engaged a flight of German bombers attacking ships below and succeeded in damaging a Dornier 217. Despite these successes, the 309th otherwise fared badly during the day's engagements. Five of their twelve pilots were lost. The Americans' eagerness to see action was no substitute for the wisdom of experience in their first encounter with the aggressive defence put up by battle-tried Luftwaffe pilots.

Merston's 131 Squadron, whilst providing low-level cover over the ships, destroyed an Fw190 in the morning. During a top cover mission in the early afternoon, two Do217s were destroyed and another damaged. An evening scramble sortie from Merston resulted in the destruction of a Ju88 and damage to two Do217s near Selsey Bill. One of the squadron's Spitfires was damaged but was able to crash-land near Selsey. The pilot survived. Tangmere's aircraft had been tested to the full on 19 August. However, the squadrons involved suffered losses; an example being the three squadrons of the Ibsley Wing which lost eight aircraft with three pilots killed.

As night fell on Operation Jubilee, over 2,600 sorties had been flown by the 68 squadrons of the combined Allied air force. Nearly 850 sorties – approximately one-third of the Allied total – were flown by the fighter squadrons controlled by RAF Tangmere's operations room. The raid had been the largest and most complex aerial operation thus far in the history of warfare, and Tangmere had played a major part in it. Despite the casualties (88 Spitfires and Hurricanes lost), Fighter Command had carried out all the tasks with which it had been entrusted within its limited resources. The Luftwaffe, if not held at bay, had been checked. Although the Dieppe Raid proved to be very costly on the ground, the air cover was judged to be highly effective and much was learnt about the organisation of large-scale aerial operations that was to be of value later in the war.

The next day, most of the squadrons that had gathered at Tangmere for Operation Jubilee returned to their home stations. The USAAF's 309th Fighter Squadron remained at Westhampnett, and on the 20th conducted the very first American escort mission for USAAF B-17 Flying Fortresses, three days after the first B-17 sortie had been flown over Axis-occupied territory. That first B-17 mission, flown from High Wycombe on 17 May, successfully attacked the marshalling yards at Rouen-Sotteville and was escorted by RAF Spitfires. The pilot in the left-hand seat of the lead aircraft was Major Paul Tibbets, who would be remembered as the captain of the *Enola Gay*, the B-29 which dropped the first atomic bomb on Hiroshima.

On 22 August, the 307th Fighter Squadron, which had been stationed elsewhere, arrived at Merston and on 29 August the 308th arrived at Westhampnett. All three squadrons of the 31st Fighter Group were now together for the first time since leaving the States, and the reason for this soon became apparent. On a visit from General Carl Spaatz, the commander of the Eighth Air Force, the 31st Fighter Group were told of their impending reassignment to the Twelfth Air Force to cover Operation Torch, the Allied invasion of North Africa. In the meantime, the group continued to work up as an autonomous unit. The last sortie that all three squadrons flew together as a group was a diversionary operation for Circus 221 on 2 October. Then they began to pack up, handing over their Spitfires to other USAAF units.

A week later, the 49th Fighter Squadron of the USAAF's 14th Fighter Group, equipped with Lockheed P-38 Lightnings which they had flown across the Atlantic in July as a part of Operation Bolero, took up residence at Westhampnett. The P-38 pilots flew their share of standing defensive patrols along with Tangmere's RAF squadrons and made their first operational sortie into enemy-occupied territory on 15 October, escorting RAF Bostons to Le Havre on a Circus, but saw no enemy aircraft. A week later they received a call to escort USAAF B-17s, but again saw no opposition. A Rhubarb over occupied France in company with RAF Spitfires was the 14th's third and final operational sortie from Tangmere. Two weeks later, at the end of the month, the 14th Fighter Group and their Lightnings were transferred to the Twelfth Air Force in the Mediterranean Theatre. Thereafter, Westhampnett reverted to its former status and RAF squadrons immediately moved back in. Merston, however, had remained vacant following the departure of the USAAF's 307th on 11 October. The previous winter, Merston had been rendered unserviceable for three months because of waterlogging. It was now closed to allow the Airfield Construction Wing to extend the main SW-NE runway, to try to improve the drainage, and to lay additional Sommerfeld tracking; it did not re-open until April.

The beginning of 1943 brought a distinct change in Allied fighter tactics. The Germans had suffered severe setbacks at Stalingrad and in North Africa and the USAAF's Eighth Air Force was building up its strategic bomber force in East Anglia. These B-17 and B-24 heavy bombardment groups were now ready to begin large-scale daylight bombing raids into enemy-occupied Europe. 1943 therefore saw a change in objectives for the Allied air forces. Instead of Circuses escorting a small number of light or medium bombers to lure enemy fighters into action, the support of large-scale raids by heavy bombers became the principal mission of RAF Fighter Command. 'Ramrods' or bomber escort sorties gradually replaced Circuses.

By April 1943 the RAF's day-fighter force comprised 69 squadrons, the majority of them equipped with Spitfire Mk Vs, a variant that was proving inferior to the German Fw190 and latest mark of Me109. The Tangmere Wing in January 1943 comprised 485 Squadron of the Royal New Zealand Air Force and the RAF's 610 Squadron, both equipped with Spitfire Vbs. By this point, the RAF's wings had been reduced from three to two squadrons. When 485 Squadron arrived at Westhampnett, they were led by Squadron Leader Stan Grant and then from the end of March by Squadron Leader R.W. Baker. In the spring of 1943 the New Zealand squadron escorted bomber missions into France and carried out patrols against the hit-and-run German fighter raids on the English south coast towns. Occasionally other sorties were carried out such as weather reconnaissance missions across the Channel and protection of air-sea rescue operations.

Another New Zealand squadron, 486, had arrived at Tangmere on 30 October 1942 equipped with Hawker Typhoon IBs. For the first five months of the squadron's stay their Typhoons were used as low-level interceptors to patrol against the hit-and-run raids being made by Luftwaffe Fw190s and Me109s along the English Channel coast. Normally flying in pairs, they proved successful against these raids with four enemy aircraft destroyed by the end of March 1943. No. 486 Squadron was joined in March 1943 by another Typhoon squadron, the RAF's 197, which had formed the previous December at Drem, East Lothian. No. 197's first operational sorties from Tangmere consisted mainly of defensive standing patrols some five miles from the coast between Beachy Head and the Needles; these hourly patrols were flown from dawn until dusk.

From April the number of these raids diminished and shortly after Squadron

Leader Desmond Scott took over the command of 486 Squadron they were allowed to turn to offensive operations across the Channel into northern France. Within two weeks after commencing these operations, the squadron had claimed two Fw190s destroyed, another probably destroyed and a fourth damaged. On offensive missions Scott normally took eight aircraft (four loose pairs) for sweeps across the Channel. He would attempt to seek out early morning E-boat flotilla movements in the Baie de La Seine. Such sorties, known as 'Roadsteads' (low-level missions against shipping), were not without their danger as the E-boats returning to their bases were often protected by flak ships.

During the summer of 1943, RAF fighter-bombers were increasingly used to attack enemy airfields and 197 became a 'Bombphoon' squadron with their aircraft converted to carry a 250 lb bomb under each wing. It was not unusual for the two Tangmere Typhoon squadrons to operate as a wing with 197 Squadron carrying out a bombing mission and 486 Squadron escorting. For such missions the take-off procedure was the same, with aircraft from the lead squadron lining up on the runway. The wing leader and his No. 2 would then depart followed by the remainder of the squadron taking off in pairs. The wing leader, once airborne, would remain at low level, flying a relatively slow wide circuit of the airfield. Each following pair of the two squadrons would, once airborne, cut corners to join up rapidly in formation in their respective positions. Within one complete circuit of the airfield the wing would be formed.

In addition to such sorties the Typhoons were engaged in protecting search and rescue missions. In one such sortie, in July 1943, 486 Squadron sighted and then flew protection over a downed Wellington bomber crew whilst an air-sea rescue Hudson dropped an airborne lifeboat. The protecting Typhoons were attacked by 15 Fw190s. The Typhoons claimed two destroyed and two probables without loss to themselves. In appreciation of the part the squadron played in their rescue the bomber crew presented 486 Squadron with an autographed yellow skull cap and the lifeboat's centreboard which became the squadron's scoreboard. Another interesting event occurred on 18 July 1943, when 486 escorted two Mustangs, one flown by Squadron Leader James MacLachlan on a daylight intruder sortie. The escorting 486 Typhoons, as ordered, broke away on crossing the French coast and shortly after MacLachlan was shot down by ground fire and killed.

In September another Typhoon squadron, 183, joined 486 and 197 and Squadron Leader Scott was promoted to wing commander and put in charge of the Tangmere Typhoon Wing. With the formation of the Typhoon Wing came a new role for 486 and 183 Squadrons: fighter-bombing. In this, the two squadrons quickly joined 197 Squadron in becoming proficient at medium- and low-level bombing. In medium-level bombing, the target area was approached at 6,000 feet and after diving the bombs would be released at between 3,000 and 2,000 feet. Low-level bombing was far more dangerous and after much experimentation using concrete practice bombs the wing perfected the technique of approaching the target at nought feet, then climbing just before the target to 400 feet before releasing the bomb. This ensured the bomb was released at the correct angle, thereby reducing the risk of it bouncing and exploding under the attacking Typhoon. The end of the year saw the Tangmere Typhoon Wing continuing to take the fight to the enemy with further Ramrods escorting Mitchells and Marauders to disrupt the building of 'special construction' sites of unknown purpose which were later revealed to be V1 rocket launching ramps and their supply depots.

Escorted bomber formations often attracted enemy opposition. A typical encounter occurred in April 1943 when Tangmere's Spitfire Wing with other squadrons was instructed to escort Lockheed Venturas bombing the Abbeville marshalling yards. The Luftwaffe responded with about 40 Fw190s and Me109s. In the ensuing battle, 485 Squadron claimed three German fighters destroyed for the loss of two Spitfires. A change in the composition of the Tangmere Spitfire Wing occurred in June 1943 when 610 Squadron left Westhampnett and 485 departed for Biggin Hill to re-equip with Spitfire Mk IXs. They were replaced for a few weeks by 501 and 167 Squadrons until the arrival on 21 June of 41 Squadron and a week later, 91 Squadron. Both these squadrons were equipped with Spitfire Mk XIIs. This Spitfire variant was essentially a standard Mk Vc airframe modified to take a Rolls-Royce Griffon III engine. This aircraft, armed with two 20-mm cannon and four .303 machine guns, was designed as a low level fighter with clipped wings to increase manoeuvrability.

The new Spitfire Wing, led by Wing Commander Rhys Thomas, carried out their first mission on 29 June, escorting USAAF B-17s to Le Mans. During July the wing was assigned to further Ramrods escorting B-17s, Marauders, Mitchells and Typhoons to targets in France. In August the focus of the Ramrods was on enemy airfields, and the wing participated in raids on St Omer, Tricqueville, Poix, Lille, Bernay, and Abbeville. August also saw Wing Commander Ray Harries taking over control of the Tangmere Wing. The constant bombing of enemy airfields brought increased enemy fighter opposition during September which led to more opportunities for the escorting Spitfire XIIs of the Tangmere Wing. They destroyed 28 aircraft that month. The beginning of October was hectic. From the station ORB:

1.10.43
The month started with a Rhubarb on road and rail targets over the Airal/Lisieux area by 197 Squadron, during which a transformer and flak tower were damaged. The same squadron also undertook a Roadstead in the Étretat/Cap de la Hague area.

2.10.43
Nos. 41 and 91 Squadrons acted as close escort to the 1st box of 36 Marauders in Part I of Ramrod 256, bombing St Omer/Longueness area. A Roadstead was undertaken by 486 Squadron over Cherbourg/Le Havre area.

3.10.43
197 and 486 Squadrons acted as withdrawal cover in Part I of Ramrod 259 covering the Vire area, and during this operation one Typhoon of 486 Squadron was destroyed. 41 and 91 Squadrons acted as escort cover in Part I of Ramrod 259 over Beauvais. 197 Squadron took part in an air-sea rescue escort to a Walrus; dinghy located 12-15 miles NE of Barfleur. 486 Squadron was also out on an air-sea rescue, and found bomber crew 20-30 miles S. of St Catherine's Point. On this same day 41 and 91 Squadrons acted as withdrawal cover in Part III of Ramrod 258. During this operation F/S Gray was lost and his Spitfire XII.

Several enemy aircraft crossed in with a stream of our bombers returning between Brighton and Hastings. RAF Station Ford was machine gunned and anti-personnel Butterfly bombs were dropped. Ford was unserviceable for the remainder of the night and all aircraft had to be landed at Tangmere.

4.10.43

Air-sea rescue operation continued for Typhoon pilot (F/S Sheddan of 486 Squadron) who baled out in V20 square yesterday. 197 with W/C Scott spotted dinghy in 15 minutes. Walrus arrived later with Typhoon escort and picked up pilot, but in landing on sea damaged a float. Sea had become too choppy for landing. High-speed launches went out later and picked up pilot from dinghy and also Walrus crew. The damaged Walrus was sunk on the spot and by 15.00 hours the operation was concluded and F/S Sheddan in Portsmouth Hospital.

Medium and heavy bombers such as Marauders, Stirlings, Halifaxes, Wellingtons, Bostons, Liberators, Mitchells, Fortresses, and Lancasters on their way back from missions were putting down at Tangmere almost every day, shot up, with engine failures, or with injured men aboard.

After 4 October the weather conditions deteriorated and restricted operations to Rhubarbs for the next couple of weeks. Later in the month the weather improved and the Ramrod missions resumed. On 28 October the wing had a very successful day. Whilst escorting Ramrod 263, nine enemy aircraft were destroyed for no loss to the wing. By November, however, the constant bombing of the German-occupied airfields in northern France resulted in their abandonment by the Luftwaffe and this meant fewer opportunities for the Tangmere Spitfires. In fact during the last month of 1943 the Tangmere Spitfire Wing was not opposed by the Luftwaffe despite their having the capacity to do so.

As well as its primary mission, supporting its fighter squadrons, RAF Tangmere served an important secondary function, acting as the forward base for 161 Special Duties Squadron, Bomber Command. This squadron's task was to support covert operations in Axis-occupied countries by supplying resistance groups and individual agents who were working with the Allies, enabling them to collect vital intelligence and to inflict damage to the enemy's war effort through espionage and sabotage. No. 161 Squadron used a variety of aircraft, including Whitleys, Halifaxes, Stirlings, and Wellingtons to drop supplies and agents by parachute into enemy-occupied territory. While agents could be 'inserted' by parachute, they could not be 'extracted' or brought back in the same way. Westland Lysanders, single-engined aircraft with the ability to take off and land in a short distance, and twin-engined Lockheed Hudsons were used for this purpose. No. 161 Squadron's home station was RAF Tempsford, Bedfordshire. From the end of February 1942, RAF Tangmere was used as a forward base, convenient for its proximity to France which enabled its Lysanders, in particular, to leave British airspace with rested pilots and full fuel tanks and hence reach further into France on operations that often took eight or nine hours. 'A' Flight of 161 Squadron regularly arrived at Tangmere and remained, ready for operations, during the 'moon periods', seven days before until seven days after the full moon.

The operations centre for 161 Squadron at RAF Tangmere was Tangmere Cottage. It was ideally situated outside the camp across the road from the station's entrance and screened by a tall hedge. Arriving agents were brought to the cottage's back door out of sight of the road. At first, only the upper floor of the cottage was used by the squadron for accommodating pilots and their passengers, the reception room downstairs being used by the station's Roman Catholic priest. As the work of the squadron increased, the priest was found alternative accommodation and the main ground floor room was used for operational flight planning and as a mess room, with sleeping quarters upstairs. During the war, a valued trophy was kept on one of the cottage's internal walls. This trophy was the personal flag of the German governor of Caen which had been 'liberated' from a flagpole by a French youth and flown back on one of the squadron's missions.

By far the greatest number of these clandestine operations conducted from Tangmere was undertaken by Lysanders. The Lysander had originally been designed for army co-operation work. With its short take-off and landing capabilities (250 yards landing, 310 yards take-off), extraordinarily low minimum speed (54 mph), large wheels and sturdy fixed undercarriage, the Lysander was ideally suited for getting in and out of small, rough landing grounds and farmers' fields. Westland was awarded the contract to modify Lysander Mk IIIs into dedicated 'special duties' aircraft. All armament was removed and the normal variable-pitch propeller was replaced by a constant-speed three-bladed version. A 150-gallon permanently fixed fuel tank was added under the fuselage which increased the aircraft's range from 600 miles to about 1,000 miles with an endurance of 10 hours' flying. The normal gunner's compartment was modified considerably. The canopy was replaced with a one-piece unit that slid rearwards on rails to allow quick entry and exit. A ladder was permanently fitted to the port side to allow ease of access and the floor was lengthened and strengthened. The bulky radio was replaced with a much smaller one and a rearward facing two-seater bench for the passengers was installed with a locker underneath. A shelf was built at the rear of the compartment which could also serve as a seat.

The operations, carried out during moonlight periods, called for an exceptional degree of skill and courage on the part of the pilot. Daphne Olley, who joined the WAAF and qualified as a radio operator at the end of 1941, arrived at Tangmere in 1942. She remembers:

I was posted to Tangmere, which was part of 11 Group Fighter Command. We had Hurricanes, Typhoons, Spitfires, etc. Also, 161 Squadron aircrew would appear for operations sometimes, usually around full moon. They were nicknamed the 'Moon Men'. They went on clandestine missions over enemy territory, using Lysanders or sometimes Hudsons.

My first job as a trained RT operator was at Flying Control. We sat in small, sound-proof cubicles with a little hatch through into the control room. We had to log every word that was said over the RT from ground-to-air and air-to-air. We wrote in longhand but there were many signs and abbreviations for well-used phrases, i.e., 'w/co' meant 'will comply'.

It seemed that the aircrew had no idea that their conversation was being logged because on one occasion the controller sent two pilots into my cubicle to watch and listen. They stood behind me reading as I wrote and I was very nervous at first but was soon too busy to worry about them. When the action was over they looked very embarrassed and said they didn't know we were listening in.

Of course the language was pretty blue at times so we just wrote 'Polish' instead. We had a Polish squadron stationed with us at the time so that was OK. The logs were sometimes taken away for enquiries; for instance, who saw someone go down – where and when – and also who was to be credited with a 'kill' when two pilots made the same claim. It was all very exciting and often very sad. I remember one of our girls being in tears because she had to listen and log a pilot saying the Lord's Prayer as he went down. You never forget those things.

After some time at Flying Control, I was sent to the Homer Direction Finding Station. The Homer was in a field outside the airfield and in a line with the runway. We had to cycle around the perimeter and out into the country to reach it and at night it was very lonely and quite creepy.

The aerial was just under the roof and was reached by a ladder through the ceiling. In the room below were a receiver and a large calibrated wheel. There was also an open phone line to Flying Control. This was used by the clerk to pass on the vector or course to the controller. He in turn passed the vector to the pilot. There were also four Sten guns and ammunition, which we hadn't a clue how to use. Also an electric wall heater on which we used to heat cans of beans and make toast.

This radio channel was only used for planes needing help, Mayday calls etc., and also by 161 Squadron pilots coming home from drops or pick-ups in enemy territory. Any plane in trouble would tune into this channel, and we would bring them in. Sometimes we would see the damaged planes on the airfield as we went off duty and wonder how they had made it home.

We were not allowed to open the door to anyone except the officer with the password. However, on one occasion, when we had brought home a New Zealand crew, there was a knock at the door and, before I could stop her, my clerk had unlocked the door. In came three very drunken airmen wanting to thank us. Fortunately we were stood down; otherwise the noise would have been heard at Flying Control. We had great difficulty getting them out and the next morning we realised that the tyre marks of their jeep showed up in the light covering of snow. We had to run around and scuff out the marks before the next crew came on duty or it was seen from the air. As we cycled back to our billet we saw the jeep pranged in a ditch. I thought what a wasted effort it was to bring them in only so that they could end up in a ditch. I heard afterwards that they were not badly hurt but I guess they were in trouble over the smashed jeep.

We used to feel very apprehensive when we cycled around the perimeter and saw the black Lysanders standing at dispersal. We knew we were in for a bad night. On one occasion we had a call from

Control to tell us to be on our toes. That had not happened before, although we always knew when the Moon Men arrived that something big was afoot. After listening in for several hours I suddenly heard the hiss of a transmitter. The pilot would transmit for a few seconds every two minutes – no longer in case the Germans were also using their DF. I managed to get a bearing but it was very difficult to tell whether I had him on a magnetic or a reciprocal bearing. For instance, suppose I had him on 360 degrees north, I would also pick him up on 180 degrees south. If I gave him the wrong bearing I could send him away instead of bringing him home.

To decide which bearing was correct, I had to press down a large wooden plate above the wheel which I was rotating. When I had the sound as clear as possible I would press the plate down with my thumbs and if the sound decreased I had the right bearing. It was very difficult at times to tell the difference and this was one of those times.

I took the plunge and passed on the vector to the controller. I was surprised when I didn't hear him pass it on to the pilot. I still could only hear the hiss as the RT was turned on. Suddenly the worried-looking clerk said the controller wanted to speak to me and handed me the phone. I was panic-stricken as this was unheard-of, and I felt even worse when he called me an idiot and a few other choice things. I said I could only report what I was hearing and he said it could not be the plane they were waiting for.

I knew someone was out there so I carried on taking bearings and passing them on and suddenly I heard a voice and a call-sign. When I passed it on, Control came to life and eventually we heard the plane fly overhead. We were then ordered to stand down. By that time I was a nervous wreck. Soon afterwards the phone rang and the clerk said, "He wants to speak to the girl with the golden voice", and she handed me the phone. It was the controller, full of apologies and praise. What a night that was!

No. 161 Squadron pilots operating into France often had to fly 300 or 400 miles over enemy territory, navigating by dead reckoning, using a map in one hand and flying the aircraft with the other one. The pilot then had to find the landing field where he had to land, transfer his passengers and finally take off and fly back to Tangmere. This was a difficult enough task during daylight let alone at night in enemy territory. The route was checked during the flight with the aid of a small light, called a 'wander light' that illuminated a specially-prepared fold-out map. In order to prepare the map prior to the mission, strips were cut out of a half-million map (1:500,000) so that the track to be flown was in the middle with about 50 miles displayed either side of the track. The map was then folded so that it could be held in one hand showing two panels along the route. The last two panels were on a map of twice the scale (1:250,000) to give more detail around the landing field. Before departure from Tangmere, the maps were marked up with the latest intelligence on flak defences and 'gen' cards were written showing the basic navigation details for each leg, the compass heading and distance to the next turning point. On the 'gen' cards were also written the Morse code letters to be flashed by beacons on the night of the operation. The cards were normally stuck down on a part of the map that would not be needed, normally the blank English Channel area.

Near to the landing field the pilot would look for the identification Morse code signal flashed by torch light by the ground party. If the identification code was incorrect the landing would not be attempted. Following exchange of recognition signals, lights would appear on the ground showing an inverted letter 'L' with the landing run being marked by two torch lights for width and three for length. The pilot would then fly parallel with the long leg of the 'L', noting the heading on the aircraft's compass, and would then turn 180 degrees on to the downwind leg at about 500 feet above the ground throttling back to reduce speed to 100 mph. Following the turn on to final approach, the pilot would aim to cross the edge of the landing field at 70 mph with slats out and flaps down. After landing the aircraft would be U-turned and taxied back to the reception party where another U-turn would be made to line up the aircraft ready for take-off following the exchange of passengers. Time on the ground would be kept to a minimum; usually less than five minutes elapsed between landing and take-off for the return flight to Tangmere.

On the night of 27-28 February 1942, Flight Lieutenant A. M. 'Sticky' Murphy, piloting a Lysander, carried out 161 Squadron's first pick-up operation. Everything went according to plan, unlike an earlier sortie flown by Murphy when he was serving with 138 Squadron. On that occasion he had landed in a field in Belgium and come under fire from German troops lying in ambush. Although wounded in the neck and losing blood, he nonetheless succeeded in flying his Lysander back to Tangmere. In March 1942, Murphy was promoted to squadron leader and took command of 'A' (Lysander) Flight. His next mission to France was rather unusual, as it was the only occasion in which an Avro Anson – borrowed from a training unit – was used for a pick-up operation. It was needed because four passengers were to be collected from a field near Issoudun, and the Lysander's normal passenger load was only two. Although visibility was poor, which made visual navigation difficult, Murphy eventually reached the landing zone. 'Landing completed without trouble and the four passengers embarked very rapidly', he later reported. One of these passengers was Squadron Leader John 'Whippy' Nesbitt-Dufort, a Lysander Special Duty pilot of 138 Squadron who had crashed near Issoudun on 28 January during a forced landing. The aircraft fell into Vichy hands, but the driver towing it away 'accidentally' stalled his vehicle on a railway level-crossing; the aircraft was hit by a train and completely destroyed. After a month in hiding with the resistance, Nesbitt-Dufort was relieved to be rescued.

Despite the operational dangers, 161 Squadron's casualties were not especially heavy, a fact attributable largely to the high standards of navigation and airmanship of its pilots and aircrew. The Lysander pilots were required to have flying skills of the highest order, and most had previously been fighter or bomber pilots with operational experience. Enemy action was an ever-present threat, with the Special Duty aircraft being vulnerable to enemy flak and night fighters when in the air, and to small-arms fire when landing in France. It was not uncommon that Lysanders returned to Tangmere riddled with bullet holes made by the rifles of Vichy and German patrols who had reached the scene just as the aircraft were taking off. So well-practised were the Special Duties pilots and reception committees that it was to be nearly two years before the squadron's first enemy-fire casualties were to occur. In the early hours of 11 December 1943, a Lysander piloted by Flying Officer J. R. G. 'Jimmy' Bathgate was shot down near La Ville-aux-Bois-lès-Pontavert; Bathgate and his two passengers – French agents – were killed.

Bad weather, especially when it involved fog or ice, was another serious hazard. On one disastrous night, 16-17 December 1943, two Lysanders were lost while trying to land at Tangmere in fog on their return from a Special

Intelligence Service operation to collect four French agents. Flight Lieutenant J. M. 'McB' McBride's aircraft crashed short of the runway, the aircraft burst into flames and McBride was killed, although his two passengers were rescued. Stephen Hankey, the pilot of the second Lysander, took the decision to divert to Ford aerodrome but crashed into a hillside in the thick fog; there were no survivors among the three aboard.

Night-time operations, even in full moonlight, brought their own hazards: on 16-17 April 1943, Flight Lieutenant John Bridger's Lysander hit an unseen high-tension cable when attempting to land on a field south of Clermont-Ferrand. The blinding flash temporarily dazzled him, but he kept control of the aircraft and landed to disembark his passengers. One of the main tyres had burst and Bridger decided to puncture the other with a shot from his revolver in order to make his take-off easier. Fortunately the wheel rims did not dig into the ground and he was able to return safely to base.

Sometimes aircraft were damaged in landing on unsuitable fields and were unable to take off. In September 1942, Flight Lieutenant W. G. Lockhart's Lysander went into a ditch on the landing ground and had to be abandoned. Lockhart set the aircraft on fire to prevent it falling into enemy hands and took to his heels, successfully evading capture although the two French agents who were awaiting extraction were caught after fleeing the landing ground and imprisoned.

The landing grounds were sometimes found to be too soft to take the weight of an aircraft (although they may have seemed firm enough when walked upon). Guy Lockhart's Lysander was stuck in the mud in a field near Saumur for a nerve-racking seventeen minutes in March 1942 before he was able to take off with his two passengers. On two occasions pilots were forced to abandon their aircraft. The first instance of this occurred in April 1942, when Pilot Officer John Mott's Lysander got stuck in the mud when landing near Issoudun at Le Fay, a small airfield west of Ségry (Indre). Mott tried to destroy the aircraft but did not succeed in making it burn; he was caught by Vichy troops, but the Belgian MI9 agent with him managed to get away. The Lysander was recovered and was put on display in the museum of captured aircraft at Nanterre near Paris where it remained until it was destroyed in 1944. The experience of Flight Lieutenant Robin Hooper on 16-17 November 1943 was even more dramatic, as recounted in Hugh Verity's book *We Landed by Moonlight*:

After two unsuccessful attempts I got down off a very tight low circuit (even for a Lizzie!) dropping in rather fast and rather late through the mist. I soon realised that the ground was very soft indeed – softer than it had been on 'Oriel' a few nights before when I had landed and, to their great disgust, ordered the others not to do so. At first, when I braked, the wheels just locked and slid; but very soon it was a question of using quite a lot of throttle to keep moving, and it seemed best to keep moving at all costs. Turning was all but impossible since the wheels dug into deep grooves. Finally we managed to turn 90 degrees to port and there stuck. The aircraft was immovable even with +6 boost, so I told the passengers to get out and got down myself to inspect. We were bogged to spat-level; the ground appeared to be a wet, soggy water-meadow. The reception committee came running up: I organised them to push and we attempted some more +6 boost without the slightest effect except perhaps to settle the wheels a little more firmly in their ruts. 'Georges', the operator (a Belgian agent, Jean Depraetere) was in a great state of nerves and it was Albert, his second-in-command, (who had been failed on the Lizzie course for over-impetuosity), who really took charge.

At this point someone suggested getting some bullocks from the nearest farm; after a certain amount of fuss this was agreed and a small well-armed party set off to collect bullocks, spades and some planks or brushwood (my idea, as far as I remember). The rest of us continued to dig trenches in front of the wheels with the idea of making a kind of inclined plane up which they could be pulled. About 20 minutes later an odd procession loomed up out of the mist; two very large bullocks, trailing clanking chains, the farmer, his wife, his two daughters and the three chaps from the reception committee. The farmer shook me warmly by the hand, asked me when the British were going to land in France, and got to work. He hitched the bullocks (Fridolin and Julot by name) to the legs of the undercarriage, and we all heaved. Nothing whatever happened. Two more (anonymous) bullocks were fetched; we continued to dig, but the best result we ever got was to pivot one wheel round the other. This of course had no effect beyond making a large hole round the stationary wheel which stuck even more firmly. This must have gone on for about two hours. Why we weren't arrested ten times over I have no idea, except that the nearest Boche was at least 10 miles away and the local gendarmerie had more sense than to poke their nose into things which were no concern of theirs. Finally, we realised that it was getting late and that we had not a hope of digging the aircraft out. We decided to abandon the struggle.

Robin Hooper decided to burn the aircraft and go into hiding with the resistance. He was picked up by Wing Commander Bob Hodges a month later.

No. 161 Squadron's 'A' (Lysander) Flight, now under Squadron Leader Hugh Verity's command, had a very busy year in 1943 flying 116 missions into France, of which 81 were successful. The majority of the operations were carried out by three pilots, Verity himself and Flying Officers McCairns and Vaughan-Fowler. Hugh Verity made 29 successful Lysander pick-ups during his time as commanding officer. On one sortie, he was south of the River Loire when he encountered impenetrable fog over his landing ground, forcing him to abort the mission. This was especially unfortunate because he was to land Jean Moulin, the co-ordinator of General de Gaulle's resistance networks in southern France. Having decided to return to Tangmere, he found the airfield also blanketed in fog. Believing his wheels to be just above the runway, Verity cut the throttle; but he was thirty feet too high, and the Lysander smashed into the ground. Miraculously, it did not catch fire. Always the complete gentleman, Verity apologised profusely in French; Moulin responded in kind, thanking his pilot for "a very agreeable flight".

When it became necessary to pick up more than three or four passengers in one sortie, the two-engined Lockheed Hudson was used by 161 Squadron. This aircraft could carry up to ten 'Joes', or passengers, whose names were never known to the aircrew in case they should have to abandon their aircraft and be captured by the enemy. The Hudson's crew was made up of a pilot, a navigator and a wireless operator/air gunner. The flarepath used on the ground had to be 100 metres longer than that required for the Lysander and was marked by torch lights at 150-metre intervals. Although the navigation to the destination was much easier with a dedicated navigator, the landing compared with a Lysander operation was more difficult. The

Hudson was three times heavier than the Lysander and the approach speed had therefore to be faster. However, the load carried by one Hudson would have needed three Lysanders. The first Hudson operation took place on the night of 13-14 February 1943 when Wing Commander P. C. Pickard (who had developed the flight operating procedures for the Hudson sorties) flew five agents into France, landed them, and took off again returning to England while the unsuspecting Germans and Vichy slept.

As 1943 drew to a close, the outlook was very different from what it had been at the beginning of 1941. The RAF were no longer on the defensive but had gradually built up their strength, with pilots pouring in from the Commonwealth Air Training programme; the Arnold Scheme and the British Flying Training Schools in Canada and the USA; and new, faster, and more heavily-armed aircraft rolling off the production lines in their hundreds, then thousands. The air offensive had been decisively taken by the Bader Wing in the spring and summer of 1941 and, with the Americans' military and industrial power fully committed since the beginning of 1942, had gathered strength to the point that by the end of 1943 the tables had well and truly turned.

The enemy's military, industrial, and transport infrastructure within reach of Tangmere's Typhoon fighter-bomber squadrons was being put under unremitting pressure by their attacks and those by the Allied medium and heavy bombers that Tangmere's Spitfires were now escorting to their targets almost daily, deeper and deeper into enemy-occupied territory. Night fighters, directed by GCI radar and carrying their own airborne radar, were making greater numbers of successful interceptions and gradually denying the enemy the cover of darkness. The organisation and supply of subversion and sabotage from within occupied Europe were also being made increasingly effective, materially assisted by 161 Squadron's Lysander flights from RAF Tangmere. At the end of 1943, Hitler had lost North Africa, the Wehrmacht was being pushed back to Poland's pre-1939 eastern border by the Allied-supplied Russians, the Allies had taken half of Italy and its government had switched sides, and Hitler's fragile alliances with weak client states in the Balkans and on the Black Sea were crumbling.

4

Operation Overlord and the Second Tactical Air Force 1944

On the morning of the fifth we got up to find our aircraft painted with white and black stripes. The day is near. No flying today. After supper we packed our sleeping tents and equipment which was being sent to the invasion departure point. Tension is mounting high. The group captain was scheduled to speak at eleven. We had a short crap game then broke up as the mess tent filled with fellows from both wings. Outside it was cloudy, cool, with a full moon. Talk ran rampant among the boys squatted on the ground. G/C McBrien entered and the clamour ceased. An army major produced a blackboard. There it was! A picture of the French coast and the whole plan of attack drawn on it. D-Day was in the morning. He talked for an hour. Our sector was to provide the air cover for the greatest invasion in history. Silent faces watched as the tactics and strategy unfolded. And then it was over. Our boys piled in trucks and went to intelligence for briefing. There was a cold breeze outside now, at one in the morning. We talked and joked a lot. It all felt great. After briefing we rushed to our huts where we were now sleeping and jumped into bed. Two hours of restless sleep then we were wakened at three, rushed to the mess tent with that hangover feeling that comes from interrupted rest, and had breakfast. Down at dispersal we waited around 'till eight when our boys took off on their first sweep. Those of us remaining sat conjecturing at what it was going to be like, but the intensity of the event fell away and it seemed like any other day. The boys returned and we all rushed out to meet them. They said they saw almost nothing -- and were very disappointed at having run into no Hun aircraft at all. The expected big air battle over the beach just hadn't come off and we were annoyed at the cowardice of the Jerries.

After a meal at three in the afternoon we sat around till six, then my turn came. I took off with the squadron. There was low broken cloud, blue clear spaces and a bright sun shining through occasionally. We cross the coast, flying low over the water, passed the Isle of Wight and headed out to sea. Through the haze below we saw masses of ships going in all directions. They were everywhere below during the sixty-mile crossing. Then the French coast was ahead. Much smoke and haze but surprisingly inactive. The coast towns seemed untouched from above. For half an hour we patrolled, watching constantly, friendly aircraft were everywhere. Then over the RT: "Huns, six o'clock above." We turned sharply and climbed. At 14,000 we were above them -- in to attack. The CO led my section of four. They broke around to our tails. We pulled into them and chased them down towards the clouds. For what seemed an hour we dodged after them through the broken cumulus but the weather was on their side and they escaped. We returned, had supper. Tired as hell. Another bunch took off at 9.30 but I was among the bed-bound. Now it's eleven and we're sitting around the huts. We'll be up at three again tomorrow. Jerry should be out in numbers. I've finally arrived at my highest aspiration and am ready for a great lot of fun. The army's success depends on us.

Edward L. Prizer, 412 (RCAF) Squadron, Tangmere, 6 June 1944

The top-level planning for Operation Overlord had begun in 1942, and by the middle of the year more than 70 sites for additional airfields had been identified in southern England. Their purpose would be three-fold: first, to provide bases for the large number of fighter squadrons that would be needed to establish air superiority and give air cover to the army as the invasion proceeded. Second, to act as temporary staging-posts for those squadrons that were intended to move to airfields across the Channel immediately the invasion troops and advance airfield construction parties had secured and prepared the ground for fighter operations at the battlefront. And third, to be available as emergency landing grounds for damaged or fuel-short aircraft returning from sorties over enemy-occupied territory. Not all 70 sites would be built upon. The need would be for rudimentary airfields that would require only basic facilities for day-only operations and would consist of runways, refuelling and re-arming points, hard-standings for the aircraft, and little else. The belief was that the ALGs would not be used during the winter months and therefore accommodation for personnel under canvas and in requisitioned nearby houses would suffice. Nothing was to be permanent. The ALGs, it was thought, would be used only for a few weeks or months and would be returned to agricultural use when they were no longer needed.

The specification of the ALGs included a main runway of 4,800 feet in length with a secondary runway of 4,200 feet. When necessary, a reduction of 200 feet was accepted providing the longest runway was east-west (the direction of the prevailing wind). The construction of the ALGs was carried out by specialised RAF and Royal Engineers forward airfield construction units, the first of which was formed in the summer of 1942. These groups would go on to construct temporary airfields on the Continent, immediately to be followed by Servicing Commando Units, in support of the Allied armies as they fought their way across Europe.

The aim was to complete the ALGs by March 1943 and work on grading and clearing the sites quickly got under way following the formation of the construction groups. Trees had to be felled to provide adequate clearance on either side of the runway strips and on the approaches to the runways. Due to the poor winter weather of 1942-43 many of the ALGs were not completed until the early summer of 1943. The material used for the runways was usually Sommerfeld Track, a steel netting construction held rigid by steel bars and rods and secured in position by angled pickets. The intensive operations that began in the summer of 1943 identified problem

Above: Spitfire Mk IIA P7753 of 616 (South Yorkshire) Squadron AAF at Tangmere, 1941. No. 616 was one of the Tangmere Wing squadrons that developed daylight-intruder tactics, making offensive sorties over enemy-occupied France to seek out and engage Luftwaffe aircraft. Wing Commander Douglas Bader normally flew with this squadron. He was shot down during one such intruder sortie, Circus 38, on 9 August 1941.

Below: The telegram sent by the Germans via North Foreland Radio on 13 August 1941, conveying the information that Douglas Bader had been taken prisoner on the 9th and that his right prosthetic leg had been lost. *Museum Collection.*

---

harges to pay

........s.   d.

RECEIVED

POST ✠ OFFICE
TELEGRAM

Prefix.   Time handed in.   Office of Origin and Service Instructions.   Words.

4   m   **4**   (Confirmation copy)

FFU   FFU

B   To

No.

OFFICE STAMP

(postmark: NORTH FORELAND 13 AU 41 RADIO)

m

Northforelandradio de FFU

Wing Commander Douglas Bader am 9.8.41 in gefangenschaft geraten.
Beifallschirmabsprung prothese des rechten beines verloren.
Bader erbittet schnellste uebersendung neuer prothese.
Abwurf mit fallschirm von deutsher seite freigestellt.
Tag und uhr zeit des abwurfes auf funk weg uebermittelnat ~~abwurffunn~~ abwurfort
wird dann von hier bezeichnet.
Abwurfflugzeug hat freies geleit.

For free repetition of doubtful words telephone " TELEGRAMS ENQUIRY " or call, with this form at office of delivery. Other enquiries should be accompanied by this form and, if possible, the envelope.

bling them to attack enemy airfields in occupied Europe well beyond the reach of Tangmere's single-seaters. Ford continued to specialise in night-fighter and night-intruder operations until its return to the Royal Navy in August 1945. *Imperial War Museum CH4048.*

Middle: Eight pilots of 43 Squadron pause for a group portrait in 1941. Flight Lieutenant Daniel le Roy du Vivier is fourth from right. A year later, du Vivier would become squadron commander and lead 43 in the Dieppe Raid from Tangmere. The squadron was on the top line for 12 hours continuously that day, made four complete squadron trips to Dieppe – a total of 48 individual sorties – and sustained no losses. *Coffey Collection, TMAM.*

Left: No. 1455 (Turbinlite) Flight, pictured at Tangmere in July 1942. In September, the flight would be redesignated as 534 Squadron. A standard Douglas DB7 Boston is shown here, presumably for security reasons; most of its DB7s were Havocs fitted with Turbinlite equipment in the nose and bomb bay. The CO, Squadron Leader G. O. Budd DFC, seated with the squadron's mascot at his feet, shot down three He111s within the space of eight minutes on the night of 10-11 April 1941 while flying a Beaufighter with 604 (County of Middlesex) Squadron AAF, then based at Middle Wallop. Note the presence of the US-AAF liaison officer. *Museum Collection.*

Top: YP-P, 'Evelyn', a Douglas Havoc I of 23 Squadron, is readied for a low-level night-intruder sortie at Ford on 28 November 1941. The Havocs were equal to Hurricane MkIICs in speed (340 mph) but had greater range and firepower, ena-

Above: Spitfire V of the USAAF's 308th Fighter Squadron, 31st Fighter Group, 1942. The concrete hard-standing, blister hangar, and flat landscape suggest that it could have been pictured at Tangmere rather than at Westhampnett, where the squadron was stationed from late August to the end of September. The 31st then went on to North Africa and Italy, but continued to fly successive marks of Spitfires until they converted to P-51Ds in March-April 1944. By then, the 31st's Spitfires had destroyed 194 enemy aircraft. *Museum Collection.*

Middle: No. 118 Squadron pilots and their adjutant (in peaked cap) between sorties at one of Tangmere's dispersals during Operation Jubilee, the Dieppe Raid, on 18 August 1942, the biggest aerial operation thus far in the history of warfare. The air cover was judged to have been highly effective, and the lessons learnt from it were incorporated into the planning for Operation Overlord.

Right: A press photo of Squadron Leader Denis Crowley-Milling's Typhoon being bombed up in June 1943. No. 181 Squadron pioneered the use of 'Bombphoons' beginning in September 1942 at Tangmere; in a ground-attack role against targets across the Channel, they proved very successful. This photo, clearly showing the Typhoon's arma-

ment, was classified by the Censorship Bureau of the Ministry of Information as too sensitive for publication at the time. *Imperial War Museum HU87560.*

Left: Ground staff at work on a Spitfire Mk V of 610 (County of Chester) Squadron AAF at Westhampnett, 11 April 1943. No. 610 was then on its second posting to Westhampnett; two years earlier, it had been part of the Bader Wing. In the summer of 1944, the squadron would return to the Tangmere Sector for a third time, flying Griffon-engined Spitfire XIVs from Friston (then a satellite of RAF Tangmere) on V1 interception duties. *Imperial War Museum CH9248*.

Below: Lysander pilots of 161 (Special Duties) Squadron at Tangmere, 1943. Left to right: Robin Hooper, Mac McCairns, Peter Vaughan-Fowler, Hugh Verity, Bunny Rymills, Stephen Hankey. Together, these pilots (and others of the squadron) made hundreds of sorties deep into German-occupied France, navigating by moonlight, landing in farmers' fields, picking up and delivering intelligence agents and mail. Their return flights lasted up to 7 hours. *Verity Collection, TMAM*.

Above: The men of 41 and 91 Squadrons photographed while posing for another photographer. These two squadrons were resident at Tangmere from October 1943 to February 1944. Both were equipped with Spitfire XIIs and flew defensive patrols against the Luftwaffe's Fw190s making low-level tip-and-run raids along the south coast, as well as flying shipping reconnaissance sorties and bomber escort missions. Note the new control tower nearing completion in the background. *Coffey Collection, TMAM.*

Right: General Dwight D. Eisenhower, seen here being spoken to by ACM Sir Trafford Leigh-Mallory, is entertained by Tangmere's officers at the Ship Hotel, Chichester, 21 April 1944. The Supreme Commander of the Allied Expeditionary Forces in Europe was on a tour of inspection of the preparations for Operation Overlord, including the Tangmere Sector operations room at Bishop Otter College, opened in February, which would be a vital link in the D-Day command and control system. *Coffey Collection, TMAM.*

Above: Armourers of 609 (West Riding) Squadron AAF at Thorney Island loading three-inch rocket projectiles. For nine weeks before D-Day and two weeks beyond, five Typhoon squadrons under Tangmere's command were accommodated temporarily at this Coastal Command base. Their duty was to soften up targets across the Channel in advance of the landings and to provide ground-attack support for the invasion troops until forward airfields in Normandy had become established. *Imperial War Museum CH13345.*

Below: Apuldram, a temporary advanced landing ground near Chichester, was home to six Czech and Polish Spitfire squadrons from April to July 1944. Personnel accommodation was under canvas or in requisitioned buildings nearby. Here, two Mk IXs of 312 (Czech) Squadron are receiving attention, seen from within one of the four Extra Over Blister hangars on the site. By the end of November, the hangars and runway tracking had been removed and the land returned to agriculture. *Imperial War Museum CH18720.*

Above: Group Captain A. G. ('Sailor') Malan briefs officers of 145 (French) Wing, Second Tactical Air Force, at Merston on the morning of D-Day. To Malan's right is Lieutenant Raoul Duval; to his left is Commandant C. Martell in flying kit. Wing Commander W.V. ('Bill') Crawford-Compton is standing at right, pipe in hand. The wing was made up of three Free French squadrons, 329, 340, and 341, flying Spitfires in support of 2 Group light and medium bombers. They moved to France on 19 August 1944. *Imperial War Museum CL29.*

of 133 Wing, 2TAF, were its first occupants. In the foreground a Mustang Mk III of 129 Squadron is armed with 250 lb bombs which were used to attack enemy positions on the beachheads and beyond as the invasion proceeded. *Imperial War Museum MH6845.*

Right: Situated six miles southwest of Horsham, Coolham was one of Tangmere Sector's more outlying advanced landing grounds and had a lifespan of just three months, from April through June 1944. Three Mustang squadrons

Above: From D-Day until mid-August, 21 temporary airfields were laid in the British and Canadian invasion zones in Normandy fully employing 17,000 airfield construction and servicing personnel. Most were at least 1,000 yards long by 100 yards wide and used square mesh steel tracking, as shown here. As these forward airfields were completed, the 2TAF fighter wings massed in Sussex and Kent were transferred across the Channel to maintain close air support to the ground forces as they advanced inland. *Imperial War Museum CL710*

Left: Airfield B2 at Bazenville was built by the Royal Engineers 16th Airfield Construction Group together with the RAF's 3201 and 3209 Servicing Commandos who started work just after midnight after D-Day. It was completed on 13 June. Two days later, three RCAF squadrons of 144 Wing commanded by Wing Commander J. E. ('Johnny') Johnson took off from Ford to be deployed here, the first 2TAF unit to be based on the Continent and to operate from France after D-Day. *Imperial War Museum CL162.*

areas where Sommerfeld Track was not suitable and in these areas Square Mesh Track (SMT), a three-inch square mesh, was often used.

Typical of the ALGs being built across southern England was Apuldram. In February 1943 construction began on the site to the south of Chichester. Two runways were constructed at Manor Farm, the longest running NE-SW towards the village of Birdham. A subsidiary NW-SE runway was constructed to the NE of the site giving a runway plan resembling a crucifix. The runways were laid with the metal track which allowed the grass to grow between the steel mesh. This allowed the farmers to graze their animals on the airfield when it was not in use. Some buildings were erected, but in the main tented accommodation was provided for pilots and ground crew. Nearby cottages were requisitioned and field kitchens set up. The building of the subsidiary NW-SE runway required a road to be sealed off and a house to be demolished.

On 2 June 1943, three squadrons (175, 181, and 182) of Hawker Typhoons arrived under the command of Acting Wing Commander Denis Crowley-Milling, who had served at Tangmere in 1941 under Douglas Bader. The crews quickly settled in, erecting their accommodation tents. They were at Apuldram for a month, initially carrying out practice sorties in the local area which included testing the metal runways when bombed-up with two 500 lb bombs. Ten days after arriving, the squadrons carried out their first offensive operation over enemy territory when they attacked Abbeville aerodrome. Between mid-June and the end of the month, Apuldram's Typhoons continued to attack targets in France but not without loss or incident. On 19 June, Pilot Officer Cockburn (a speedway motorcycle rider before the war) failed to return after he was seen attacking a railway train. On 23 June the squadrons were bombed-up for another attack on Abbeville aerodrome, an escort being provided by the Tangmere Typhoons of 486 (RNZAF) Squadron. The bombing was successful despite an attempted interruption by Fw190s, two of which were shot down by the Kiwi Typhoons.

The aircraft at Apuldram were having continuing problems using the metal runways and often became bogged down in soft ground after leaving the tracking. A serious accident occurred when a 175 Squadron pilot crashed into a ditch and the aircraft turned upside down. He was trapped for some hours until a heavy crane was brought over from Tangmere to release him from his cockpit. On 30 June an interesting event occurred when an American B-17 four-engined bomber aircraft was seen orbiting over the airfield. The aircraft made an approach from the Chichester direction over Donnington and Stockbridge and made a safe landing. One of the crew was the actor Clark Gable. He had joined the USAAF after the death of his actress wife Carole Lombard in an aircraft crash. Gable had arrived in the UK in April 1943 and joined the 508th Bomb Squadron flying from US Base 110, Polebrook, Northamptonshire. Acting as a cameraman, he was making a recruiting film and flew five missions in total, including the one that ended in the emergency landing at Apuldram. It is said that, to the delight of the local female population, he attended local dances in Chichester before the B-17 departed after being repaired.

After the Typhoons left, the airfield reverted to stand-by status and by the end of the year all flying on the airfield had ceased, enabling the construction teams to return. The drainage problems experienced during the previous summer months were tackled and four half-hooped-shaped Extra Over Blister hangars were erected to provide some protection from the weather for aircraft maintenance and repairs. Also, extra metal track was laid for aircraft hard-standings.

On 1 April 1944, three Czech squadrons (310, 312, and 313) arrived with their clipped-wing Spitfire LF (low flying) Mk IXB aircraft. That evening the airfield servicing echelon arrived by road and Apuldram was once again operational. To provide anti-aircraft protection, 2804 Squadron RAF Regiment set up camp in the field by Apuldram Church. They quickly installed Bofors gun positions. Bombs for the aircraft arrived by road and were stored in a bomb dump near the airfield. Living accommodation mainly continued to be under canvas with the officers' mess located in a barn. Temporary HQ buildings were brought in by road and set up. Apuldram's complement had now reached nearly 2,000, necessitating some officers being billeted in houses in Chichester. During April, the weather turned worse and although operational capability was not affected, the domestic site turned into a sea of mud. Additional off-duty attractions included a camp cinema (entry prices: one shilling for officers, sixpence for NCOs and fourpence for other ranks) and 'Harry's Café' set up on a large barge moored on the harbour side at Dell Quay.

The Czech squadrons were tasked up to D-Day with a variety of missions including Noball attacks (bombing V1 flying bomb launch sites), bomber escort duties and offensive patrols. As the offensive operations built up during the late spring of 1944, Apuldram's squadrons suffered inevitable losses. In early May, funerals were held for three Czech pilots who had been killed in flying accidents. The funeral service was held at St Richard's Roman Catholic Church, Chichester, followed by the burials at Chichester's Portfield Cemetery, 2804 Squadron RAF Regiment providing the bearer and firing parties. In mid-May one of 312 Squadron's pilots was killed when his aircraft collided after landing with the one behind as he vacated the runway. The last day of May was particularly sad for the Czechs when four pilots were lost whilst attacking targets in the St Malo area, including the CO of one of the squadrons.

By the end of 1943, Fighter Command had ceased to exist. It had been replaced by two new entities: the Second Tactical Air Force (2TAF) and Air Defence Great Britain (ADGB). The function of 2TAF was to establish and maintain air superiority in support of the Allied armies before, during, and after the planned invasion; and to provide the ground forces with air cover and ground-attack support all the way to Berlin and beyond as required. The idea of 2TAF was to bring together under unified command the forces required to accomplish this. The flying units were an amalgamation of the Army Co-operation Command; 2 Group, Bomber Command; and those RAF, RCAF, RNZAF, RAAF, Free French, Belgian, Dutch, Norwegian, Czech, and Polish fighter squadrons under the aegis of the RAF that were chosen for tactical deployment across the Channel. 2TAF would be combined with the USAAF's Ninth Air Force as the Allied Expeditionary Air Force (AEAF) under the overall command of Air Chief Marshal Sir Trafford Leigh-Mallory.

A new level of on-the-ground organisation was created in the RAF: the 'Airfield'. One of the first to be formed was 124 Airfield at Merston in October 1943. It was, apparently, a dry run to see exactly what was needed to make a fully functioning RAF station – albeit a temporary one – completely independent, self-contained, and mobile. Squadrons were reduced to just the CO, his adjutant, a couple of dozen commissioned and NCO pilots, and 18 or 20 aircraft. They were to be complemented by numbered Airfield Servicing Echelons supporting all the squadrons of the airfield rather than any squadron in particular; RAF Regiment rifle and light anti-aircraft units; and administrative, meteorological, flying control, armaments, communications, transport, stores, catering, police, chaplaincy, and medical staff who were to hold themselves and their equipment in readiness to move as a unit by sea or air to new locations at the front on a couple of hours' notice.

It is important to keep in mind that 'Airfield', as a unit of 2TAF's organisation, referred to the people and the equipment needed to do the job, and not to the station or landing-ground itself. Thus, for example, when 124 Airfield moved from Merston to Hurn in April 1944 it continued to be 124 Airfield, now located at Hurn. Its place at Merston was taken by 145 Airfield. The use of the word 'Airfield' to describe these units caused so much confusion that in May it was replaced by the term 'Wing'. Most 2TAF wings had three squadrons usually flying the same type of aircraft and often collaborating on operations, but a 'squadron' was no longer the same as it had been, since it did not have its own riggers and fitters, tools and spares; and a wing now included many other people and wide array of equipment that would have been a part of a station's establishment before the formation of 2TAF.

No. 11 Group of the now-defunct Fighter Command continued to exist inasmuch as the boundaries of the Tangmere Sector remained largely unchanged and still defined the area covered by its sector operations room and the zone of its primary responsibility for air defence. The Second Tactical Air Force was broken down into four additional groups: 2 Group, previously 2 Group of Bomber Command, which contained all the RAF's remaining light-medium bombers still operating from the UK, mostly Bostons and Mitchells; 83 and 84 Groups; and 85 (Base) Group. Both 83 and 84 Groups comprised wings of fighters, fighter-bombers, photo-reconnaissance, and artillery-spotting aircraft – Spitfires, Typhoons, Mustangs, and Austers – to support the planned invasion and the advance of the armies on Berlin. 83 Group was intended to support the British Second Army, although it had not yet been revealed where the army would land, while 84 Group would support the Canadian First Army. 85 (Base) Group included, amongst other types of aircraft, four wings of radar-equipped Mosquito night fighters to supplement the day fighters of 83 and 84 Groups.

As one of the RAF's main sector control stations on the front line on the eve of the invasion, Tangmere had an enormously important and enormously complex role to play in Operation Overlord. The new sector operations room, opened on 15 February 1944, was located at Chichester in the galleried main hall of Bishop Otter College, a women's teacher-training college whose buildings had been requisitioned for WAAF accommodation in 1942. Tangmere's sector operations room had control of wings belonging to all four groups of 2TAF: Nos. 2, 83, 84, and 85 as well as defensive ADGB squadrons. Most of the British air power to be thrown at the enemy over the beaches on D-Day – fifteen of the eighteen day-fighter wings and half the night-fighter strength of 2TAF – would be coordinated and controlled by Tangmere. Its men and women would bear a huge weight of responsibility for the success or failure of the air cover component of the invasion. Six weeks before D-Day, no one was left in any doubt about this after a visit to inspect the preparedness of the station and its operations room was made by the Supreme Commander of the Allied Expeditionary Forces in Europe, General Dwight D. Eisenhower, his deputy commander Air Chief Marshal Sir Arthur Tedder, AEAF commander Air Chief Marshal Sir Trafford Leigh-Mallory, and 2TAF commander Air Marshal Sir Arthur Coningham.

Just to the west of the Tangmere Sector, units of the USAAF's Ninth Air Force (9thAF) had taken over ten RAF airfields in the Middle Wallop Sector: Beaulieu, Stoney Cross, Andover, Chilbolton, Thruxton, Holmsley South, Ibsley, Warmwell, Middle Wallop and Christchurch as well as ALGs at Lymington, Winkton, and Bisterne. Initially these stations were used for P-47 Thunderbolt and P-38 Lightning fighters. Apart from some photo-reconnaissance F-6 Mustangs based at Middle Wallop, nearly all of the USAAF's long-range, high-altitude P-51 Mustang squadrons were based elsewhere and remained attached to the Eighth Air Force, mainly flying bomber escort missions for B-17 Fortresses and B-24 Liberators. The tasks of the low-level fighter and fighter-bomber squadrons of the 9thAF in the Middle Wallop Sector were to achieve air superiority and soften up targets across the Channel in preparation for covering the landings of divisions of the US First Army on the westernmost invasion beaches. The P-47 and P-38 squadrons would then move to temporary forward airfields following their army's planned advance into Germany, paralleling the preparations being made by the RAF in the Tangmere Sector for the eastern part of Normandy. Once the 9thAF fighter squadrons had relocated across the Channel, four of the USAAF's airfields in the Middle Wallop Sector would continue to be used until mid-August by B-26 Marauders flying tactical bombing missions in support of the Allies' advance through France. 2TAF and 9thAF aircraft would be passing frequently through each other's airspace along the south coast, and effective coordination between the two sector control centres would be vital. Interestingly, while there were clashes and disputes between the senior Allied commanders and a great deal of political manoeuvring at higher levels (for example, Leigh-Mallory, nominal commander-in-chief of AEAF, was to be sidelined just before D-Day and effectively played no further part in Operation Overlord), the quality of communication and coordination at the local level between the 9thAF and 2TAF operations staff and controllers was excellent in the run-up to D-Day, and would remain so throughout the Battle of Normandy.

In the Tangmere Sector, during the spring of 1944, Spitfire, Typhoon, and Mustang squadrons, servicing echelons, and other personnel and equipment gradually moved in from other parts of the country and worked up as wings in preparation for relocation across the Channel when the time came. Ramrods, Roadsteads, Rodeos, Rangers, and Noball sorties were being flown continuously, weather permitting, as were standing defensive patrols. The 9thAF and other RAF fighter units were doing the same next door in the Middle Wallop Sector. The Luftwaffe was now putting up relatively little opposition under this unremitting onslaught and the frequency and ferocity of their attacks on the British mainland had declined markedly: a mass raid on London by about 70 Luftwaffe aircraft passing over Selsey on 24 March was a now-unusual occurrence. Within the Tangmere Sector, the running totals at the end of April since hostilities began in September 1939 were 811 enemy aircraft destroyed, 245 probably destroyed, and 432 damaged. Fifty-three Luftwaffe aircraft were destroyed by Tangmere Sector squadrons, including Ford's night fighters, in the air and on the ground in the first four months of 1944.

During the first seven days in May, the squadrons of the Tangmere Sector – and by the end of the month there would be around 40 of them at RAF Tangmere, Westhampnett, Merston, Ford, Thorney Island, Shoreham, Friston, and the ALGs – were busy on escort duties, dive-bombing Ramrods, Roadsteads, and Rodeos while at the same time working up as wings. A rota of assignments was devised to give all the wings more-or-less equal time in the air on training and operations, since apart from the occasional 'big show' there were now too many squadrons for them all to be doing operational sorties every day, or even every second or third day, however eager their pilots may have been to see action. From the beginning of the month, the enemy appeared to be more active on the ground than usual, probably because they believed the Allied invasion to be imminent as the summer approached. The accumulation of forces in southern England, which had gathered greatly increased momentum from April, could not be completely hidden from the enemy; the real question was where the Allies would land. Allied disinformation, carefully leaked to the enemy, pointed towards Pas de Calais. The Germans took the bait, and began moving men and materiel by road, rail, barges and coastwise shipping, providing numerous targets of opportunity for the Allied air forces.

On 3 May, a section of 127 Wing on air-sea rescue patrol was instrumental in saving a pilot who had baled out over the Channel at 21.00 hours. They located the pilot, dropped him a dinghy, and dropped flame floats enabling a Sea Otter to pick him up. Unable to take off safely in the gathering darkness, the pilot of the Sea Otter reported that he was going to taxi to shore. The Canadians in their Spitfires orbitted over the Sea Otter until they were ordered to return to base. The next day, 345 (Free French) Squadron returning from a sortie spotted an RN motor torpedo boat on fire in the Channel; a section of its Spitfires patrolled over it until the crew were picked up. Another section of 345 Squadron orbitted a Mitchell when it came down in the sea not far away at about the same time and remained on the scene giving fixes until the crew were rescued. Compared with the situation in 1940, when baling out over the Channel more often than not resulted in a 'Missing on Air Operations' report, by the spring of 1944 the situation had turned round completely. Coming down by parachute over land carried more risk by landing in trees, on rough ground, hitting buildings in built-up areas, being shot by ground-based small-arms fire whether by friend or foe, or capture and imprisonment if over enemy territory. Baling out over the English Channel, most of which was now under aerial surveillance by dedicated patrols of Spitfires constantly looking for downed pilots, and within the range of the RAF's or RN's high-speed rescue boats – of which there were now many more – and amphibious aircraft was now a much safer option.

On 5 May, 144 Wing, composed of three RCAF squadrons led by Wing Commander 'Johnnie' Johnson, was returning from a sweep south of Charleroi when they saw five Fw190s in the Mons area. Johnson gave chase and downed one of them and two others fell to the guns of his squadron but one of his pilots, Pilot Officer McLachlan, was hit and was seen to crash. On the same day, Mustang IIIs of 122 Wing destroyed a Ju88, an He129 and two Ju88s on the ground northwest of Aalborg, Denmark, for the loss of Flying Officer Germain. 127 Wing was again in the news two days later when on a bomber escort sortie the Spitfires approached the point of no return on their fuel. Turning back, 403 (RCAF) Squadron were bounced among cloud near Mons by four Fw190s; the Canadians damaged two and a third was seen to crash and blow up, but after this combat one of the Spitfires ran out of fuel over the Channel and its pilot was forced to bale out, being rescued immediately. Other wings attacked goods trains, acted as escorts, and did the usual defensive patrols in the course of which two more Fw190s were damaged and another destroyed for the loss of four of our pilots. On 9 May, no fewer than 730 sorties – the highest number in a single day since the Dieppe Raid – were flown by the pilots of the Tangmere Sector Wings, and another 24 by the Typhoons of the Middle Wallop Sector, but no enemy aircraft were reported to have offered resistance.

No. 421 (RCAF) Squadron of 127 Wing, while on a Ranger to the Beauvais area at 06.30 on the 12th, spotted and attacked a convoy of road vehicles reported to be 10 miles long on the Paris-Rouen road travelling north. It contained tanks, armoured cars, trucks, and staff cars. At least eight vehicles were claimed hit and damaged, with casualties to personnel. Later in the morning an unsuccessful attempt was made to locate this road convoy again but at 11.30 am 12 Typhoons of 266 Squadron bombed and shot up about ten vehicles in the same area. Three days later, another long convoy of road vehicles was seen moving northwest between Montdidier and Amiens in the direction of Pas de Calais. A few enemy aircraft had been seen in this area in the last few days. No. 421 Squadron had destroyed one Me110 in the air and a Ju88 on the ground at Montdidier airfield on the 8th. A couple of days later Flight Lieutenant Hamilton of 401 (RCAF) Squadron destroyed an Fw190 as it was taxiing on the aerodrome, but during his attack he was hit by flak and baled out unhurt. No. 602 Squadron, on their third posting to Sussex since 1940 and now being accommodated at Ford airfield, shot down one Fw190 and probably destroyed another on the 10th. From the squadron's ORB:

10.5.44
Ramrod 859. The squadron acted as close escort to 36 Marauders whose duty was to bomb the marshalling yards at Criel. Rendezvous at Beachy Head, and crossing in at Le Treport proceeded south to a point

SE of Paris. The bombing was good. One Marauder was shot up by flak and the crew were seen to bale out. This proved to be a more exciting trip than has been usual in the last few days, as on the way out the fun started. The squadron were engaged by 10 Fw190s, and a general dog-fight ensued. The CO, S/L R.A. Sutherland DFC, claimed one destroyed and one probable. F/L F. G. Woolley DFC, F/O A. P. Robson RCAF, and P/O J.W. Kelly also fired but the range was so great they made no claims. On the return to base, it was found that one aircraft was overdue, and it is with great regret we have to post popular F/O M.W. Frith, Missing from Air Operations.

On the 16th, a formation of between 30 and 50 enemy aircraft came over the south coast and dropped two bombs just to the north of RAF Tangmere, damaging nearby cottages. Two of the enemy were shot down. A week later, during the early hours of the morning, about 30 hostile aircraft attacked Portsmouth; two of the attacking Ju88s were destroyed by the Mosquito night fighters of 456 (RAAF) Squadron, scrambled from Ford to intercept them. The night-fighter Australians of 456 Squadron would destroy two more Luftwaffe intruders, both Ju88s, during the month, but lose one of their Mosquitoes and its two-man crew. Over the following five days, Tangmere Sector's squadrons flew the usual bomber escort sorties and bombing attacks on Noball and other tactical targets in the course of which a mixed bag of enemy aircraft were destroyed, including four Ju88s, two JuW34s, one Me109, one He177, and two Fw190s with another four enemy aircraft probably destroyed or damaged. Allied losses were five pilots missing, one known killed in operations over enemy-occupied territory, and two Mustangs IIIs of 122 Wing were lost in a mid-air collision over Horsham which resulted in the death of one of the pilots. Worse was to come; on the 21st, the Tangmere Sector lost 19 aircraft in a single day. According to the station ORB:

21.5.44
This has been a very busy day with hundreds of our fighters attacking trains from Cherbourg to Bologne. Unfortunately owing to low cloud they were forced to fly at low altitude through heavily flak-defended areas, as a consequence of which this sector lost 19 aircraft. During these sweeps five locomotives were destroyed and 28 damaged, one

aircraft was destroyed on the ground, 20 lorries, four staff cars and three other vehicles were shot up. Four barges, two tugs and 24 trucks were damaged.

Shoreham Airport, which had been transferred to RAF Tangmere as a forward satellite in March, was occupied by 277 Squadron ADGB on air-sea rescue duties, equipped with Lysanders (for dinghy-dropping) and Spitfires (for spotting patrols) and amphibious Walruses and Sea Otters for picking up aircrew. Two weeks before the Normandy landings, 277 Squadron was involved in a particularly poignant rescue, as recounted by Graham Pitchfork in his book, *Shot Down and in the Drink*:

Eight Typhoons of 440 (RCAF) Squadron took off from Hurn at 4 pm on 22 May to attack the radar site at Arromanches, which overlooked one of the beaches to be used by the British Army two weeks later. Piloting Typhoon MN583 was Flying Officer Allen Watkins. As the fighters strafed the site with cannons and rockets, Watkins's aircraft was hit by ground fire and the engine of his aircraft was damaged. He turned out over the sea but he was soon forced to bale out. His colleagues saw him land in the sea and board his dinghy just five miles off the French coast. A search by a Walrus and Spitfires failed to find him before darkness fell.

The following morning the search was continued. Four Typhoons took off at dawn and they were relieved later in the morning by a further flight of four. By the end of the day, he had not been located and the squadron diarist noted 'we assume that he has been rescued by the Huns'.

The Sea Otter crews of 277 Squadron were not prepared to give up the search and over the next few days they flew regular patrols, but all to no avail.

On 28 May, the Spitfires and Sea Otters of 277 Squadron were busy checking numerous reports of aircraft ditchings and the sinking of a small vessel. At 9.30 am Warrant Officers W. Gadd and A. T. Bartels were airborne in their Spitfires, searching over a faded radar track 15 miles north of Fécamp, when they sighted a fighter pilot in a 'K' dinghy. Also airborne were Flight Lieutenant C. G. Robertson and his crew in a Sea Otter who were conducting a search nearer to their base at Shoreham. They immediately homed towards the circling Spitfires when the navigator, Flying Officer Len Healey, spotted the dinghy eight miles west of Fécamp. Robertson immediately alighted and taxied towards the survivor.

As the Sea Otter came alongside, the survivor fell from his dinghy, but the Sea Otter crew managed to get him on board and discovered that it was Watkins, the man they had been searching for over the past week. He was in a very bad way, having had virtually no water or food and having been exposed to the sun and glare, which had made him virtually blind. He was covered in sores from his long exposure to the sea and sun, and the crew gently stripped him and wrapped him in Healey's uniform. They gave him just small sips of water.

Two Spitfires from 277 Squadron were scrambled to escort the Sea Otter, but whilst doing so they were vectored 75 miles southeast of Shoreham where a Spitfire was reported to be down. They found the pilot and orbited the position until relieved by two more who remained overhead until a Walrus arrived and picked up the Belgian pilot, Flying Officer Ester. He suffered no ill effects from his experience, which was his second ditching – he had been picked up off Margate a year earlier.

In the meantime, Robertson was heading for Shoreham where Watkins was handed over to the medical staff. He had suffered a terrible ordeal.

On the first night he had seen rescue aircraft being fired at by the shore batteries, but he was reluctant to use his flares. During the night he drifted into the Seine estuary on the tide. A southerly wind carried him clear and he erected the sail and made his way north, but overnight he drifted back to the Seine. His efforts to sail and paddle away from the coast were constantly thwarted by the tides and fickle wind and he remained a few miles off Le Havre for the next two days. Remarkably, he was not seen from the coast, or perhaps no attempt was made to rescue him.

On 27 May he was too weak to paddle further and the dinghy started to drift northeast towards Fécamp. He was 8 miles off the coast when he saw two Spitfires – 30 minutes later the Sea Otter landed and picked him up.

This rescue illustrates the skill and perseverance of the air-sea rescue crews and it brought 277 Squadron's total of lives saved to 505. The two Spitfire pilots had been tasked to search for the wreckage of a bomber, but they spotted the tiny dinghy in the meantime. The Sea Otter crew made a quick approach and rescue just a few miles off the enemy coast and other Spitfires were quickly scrambled to escort the rescue aircraft. But the most noteworthy aspect of this episode is the determination and courage of Watkins, who never gave up hope of rescue.

On the same day that Flying Officer Watkins baled out, eventually to be rescued by 277 Squadron, an extraordinary thing happened at Tangmere. Flight Lieutenant 'Bud' Bowker, a 412 (RCAF) Squadron pilot being 'rested' and temporarily assigned to 410 Repair and Salvage Unit, climbed into a recently-overhauled and fully-armed Spitfire and took off on his own for a routine air test. Later the same day, he was interviewed by a Canadian war correspondent at Tangmere. A few hours later, the Canadian Press (CP) news agency released the following story to newspapers across Canada:

Canadian Pilots Blow Up Trains, Destroy 5 Germans in 5 Minutes

With a Canadian Fighter Wing in Britain, 22 May 1944 – (CP) – Piling the Canadian score higher all through the day in the sustained, aerial offensive, pilots of the City of Oshawa Spitfire Squadron late today added five more trains damaged to their earlier bag of five enemy planes destroyed and six enemy trains shot up in a foray over the Cherbourg Peninsula.

Their bag of 11 trains today raised to 24 the number they have attacked since yesterday morning and gave Canadian squadrons operating from this British 2nd Tactical Air Force airfield a total of 31 trains shot up in the same period.

The Canadians' total bag of planes for the day was brought to seven by F.O. Bud Bowker of Granby, Que., who shot two Fw190s into the English Channel while on a gun-testing flight in a Spitfire. Putting in his operational rest period between tours as a pilot with a Canadian repair and salvage unit, Bowker took off from this base today to test the guns of a Spitfire. He bumped into two Focke-Wulf 190s over the English Channel and sent them both crashing into the sea.

It was the first time this stocky flier, who had been "getting so darn sick of doing nothing," had taken off with guns loaded since he came off operations last February. The double victory brought his score to seven enemy aircraft destroyed.

Standing beside a mobile hangar around which Spitfires were being overhauled, Bowker, in battle dress and wearing flying boots, pushed his cap back on his head and told the story of his victory, achieved in a matter of seconds.

He was flying in the direction of St. Valerie and about a quarter of the way across the Channel he sighted the Fw190s, flying in line abreast in a northeasterly direction. Bowker said the enemy planes were carrying bombs or rockets.

"I crawled up behind them and went after one and they broke toward the French coast," he related. "I let one have a 20-degree shot and he blew up. The exploding aircraft swerved to one side and the other just barely bounced off it, went up 100 feet and then crashed into the sea."

In his Personal Combat Report on the incident for Air Intelligence, Bud Bowker wrote:

At 700 feet, south of Selsey Bill, I sighted two Fw190s on bearing of 250-260 degrees magnetic at literally zero feet, below and slightly in front. I dived and turned starboard to 300 yards astern. The E/A were flying in very close formation, line abreast. They pulled up to about 30 feet and turned slowly to port, closing in even more. I fired a long burst with 15 degrees deflection, hitting port wing of port aircraft, midway along, where a bulge which I thought to be a bomb, rocket or tank, had previously been observed. An explosion occurred and the aircraft was blown to starboard with right wing down. The second aircraft flew into the first, which exploded and hit the deck. I expended the remainder of my ammunition on the second which had a buckled port mainplane and fuselage. Two strikes were observed – on tail and starboard wing tip. Aircraft was now out of control and hit the deck almost vertically. I orbited position and gave fixes, but saw only a few pieces of wreckage.

Trains, marshalling yards, and airfields continued to be heavily targeted. On 24 May, fourteen Douglas Dakotas touched down at RAF Tangmere 'for an exercise with the wings' – dry-runs to test the arrangements for loading the wings' personnel onto the Dakotas for airlifting across the Channel. Another operational exercise involved 127 Wing based at Tangmere taking off for Deanland ALG and while there to be bombed-up and refuelled, while Deanland's Spitfire Wing flew to Tangmere likewise to be re-armed and refuelled. This was to simulate the plan to supply the wings with fuel and stores on the French side of the Channel just as soon as the Servicing Commando Units (SCUs) were established. Six SCUs (3205-3210) had been formed in April 1943 and had been allocated to 2TAF; four would go ashore on D-Day+1 along with the Airfield Construction Companies of the Royal Engineers. Army transport units would carry lorry-loads of petrol, oil, glycol, bombs, ammunition, and other consumables to supply the SCUs, which would begin to function as 'filling stations' the moment the last roll of wire-mesh runway carpet had been laid by the engineers, days before the wings arrived with their own servicing echelons.

The month of May 1944, after a spell of very fine and hot weather, ended with cloud reported to be 10/10ths from the deck to 30,000 feet. On the following pages of this chapter, the station Operations Record Book takes up the story from the first to last day of June in the words of Flying Officer R. H. Miller, whose duty it was to make an accurate historical record of events under the authority of the OC RAF Tangmere, Wing Commander P. R. 'Johnnie' Walker DSO DFC. These ORB entries are reproduced in full; nothing has been left out. The words of Ed Prizer, a flying officer with 412 (RCAF) Squadron, whose personal diary entry for 6 June 1944 was quoted at the beginning of this chapter, are also reproduced below: Ed's unit was part of 2TAF's 126 Wing, based at RAF Tangmere, awaiting their jumping-off to France; their turn would come on 18 June, D-Day+12. Ed made notes in his diary every few days, as he found the time. He was a good typist, after the war becoming a professional journalist; his diary entries appear below under the date-headings he gave them in a typewriter font similar to the one he used to distinguish his words clearly from the ORB entries. RAF Tangmere's resident 2TAF Wings at this moment were 126 (401, 411, and 412 Squadrons) and 127 (403, 416, and 421 Squadrons), all Canadian, and all flying Spitfire LF Mk IXs. From the station ORB:

1.6.44

There was very little activity during the first four days of the month largely owing to very poor weather. On the 1st the weather was completely non-operational until the evening when 127 Wing did one shipping recco.

2.6.44

Again on 2 June the weather was non-operational until the afternoon and then both 126 and 127 Wings were on sweeps.

3.6.44

Things looked a bit better on the 3rd and both wings went on a Ramrod but the weather was still not too good and 416 Squadron were prevented from bombing because of it. Three Lightnings and two Thunderbolts landed at Tangmere from operations and one of the Lightnings had put up a particularly good show having come from the Reims area on one engine and making a successful and very good landing on arrival. A pilot of 401 Squadron baled out over the Channel but, unfortunately, his parachute failed to open.

An instruction has been received that all aircraft of the 126 and 127 Wings are to be painted with special black and white stripes recognition markings and all aircraft are to be screened.

4.6.44

On 4 June the two wings at Tangmere made routine patrols and there was a scramble of one section. Five sections from Friston and Horne landed here after a convoy patrol.

During the early evening a large number of Liberators were seen going out in comparatively fine weather with high cloud, but later the weather clamped down badly and four Liberators were landed here at 22.00 hours.

5.6.44

Nos. 266, 257, 197, and 193 Squadrons went out on a dive-bombing attack in the Abbeville area, but apart from this, one weather patrol to Cherbourg and the shipping patrol to Le Havre, operations consisted almost entirely of convoy patrols.

No. 442 Squadron patrolled a convoy off the Isle of Wight from 11.00 to 13.00 hours and reported them to be sailing firstly in a southwest and later in a SE direction. 44, 310, 312, and 313 Squadrons maintained a patrol over a convoy from 06.25 hours having a section of four Spitfires at a time over the convoy for 50 minutes. 340 and 412 Squadrons were patrolling other convoys up to 15.00 hours. Later in the afternoon 442 Squadron were patrolling and reported a large concentration of ships 25 miles south of the Isle of Wight moving slowly in a south direction with many ships in two main columns moving from the Needles and joining the large concentration. At 16.00 hours 126 and 127 Wings were on a patrol and it was rumoured on their return that the convoy was moving in the direction of Cherbourg. At 22.00 hours 411 Squadron went on a shipping recco to Le Havre. Meanwhile rumours were flying round the station and the tempo of work increased in the Intelligence Section culminating in the arrival of high ranking officers who proceeded to open large sealed envelopes. Briefing started at 23.30 and carried on until 01.00 hours, or in other words …

6.6.44

The day for which everyone has waited so long and yet in some ways it seemed rather an anti-climax. Everything seemed rather quiet and there was little noticeable excitement, probably due in this case to a desire not to be unduly optimistic. Everyone tried to be near a radio for the hourly news bulletin but apart from that it might almost have been a normal day. The order of battle in the Tangmere Sector on the morning of D-Day was as follows:-

Wing	Squadron	Type		Location
122	19, 65, 122	Day fighters	Must.	Funtington
133	129, 306, 31		Must.	Coolham
125	132, 433, 602		Spitfire 9	Ford
126	401, 411, 412		Spitfire 9	Tangmere
127	403, 416, 421		Spitfire 9	Tangmere
132	66, 331, 332		Spitfire 9	Bognor
131	302, 300, 317		Spitfire 9	Chailey
134	310, 311, 312		Spitfire 9	Apuldram
135	222, 349, 485		Spitfire 9	Selsey

Wing	Squadron	Type		Location
144	441, 442, 443		Spitfire 9	Ford
145	329, 340, 341		Spitfire 9	Merston
Horne	130, 303, 402		Spitfire 5	Horne
Deanland	64, 234, 611		Spitfire 5	Deanland
Friston	350, 501		Spitfire 5	Friston
Shoreham	345		Spitfire 5	Shoreham
184	184	Fighter Bombers	Typhoon RP	Westhampnett
34	16	Fighter Recce	Spitfire 11	Northolt
34	140		Mosquito	Northolt
34	69		Well.	Northolt
39	169, 430, 414		Must.	Odiham
39	400, 414		Spitfire 11	Odiham
Lee	26, 63, 414		Spitfire 5	Lee-on-Solent
3 Naval	808, 885, 414		Seafire	Lee-on-Solent
3 Naval	886, 897		Seafire	Lee-on-Solent
	456	Night fighters	Mosq. 30	Ford
	264		Mosq. 13	Hartford Bridge

The night had been filled with the roar of heavy aircraft going out and some were so low that it was possible to pick out gliders and troop-carrying planes. In the early hours of the morning two Albemarles, a Stirling and one Dakota landed at Ford reporting that they had dropped paratroops and towed gliders over France.

The operations for the day consisted almost entirely of patrols over the assault beaches and the pilots brought back many interesting reports. 126 and 127 Wings did four beach cover patrols each during the day and met no enemy opposition. They reported that Allied troops set foot on the beaches at 6.30 hours between Cherbourg and Le Havre and that the operation continued all the morning. 126 Wing did the last patrol of the day from Tangmere and reported that a tremendous number of airborne troops had landed and that they were heavily engaged soon after landing.

No. 134 Wing after patrolling from 07.50 to 08.40 hours reported that return fire from the enemy coastal batteries had virtually ceased and mixed vehicles including tanks were to be seen to be making their way inland.

Many other bits of information came in including the penetration of AFVs [armoured fighting vehicles] as far as Caen and that the town was being heavily shelled by heavy artillery. Ducks [DUKWs, amphibious vehicles] were seen as far in as Bayeux.

Very few enemy aircraft were seen during the day but while 135 Wing were patrolling the East Sector they sighted some which they chased to Caen and during the ensuing combat they succeeded in destroying four Ju88s and damaging three others. F/S Van Molkot of 349 is missing. 129 Squadron also destroyed one Fw190. Although one or two other squadrons saw an occasional enemy aircraft they were too far away to be caught.

At 21.00 hours 234 and 345 Squadrons acted as escort to Dakotas towing Horsas – all the gliders landed safely. Other operations for the day consisted of bombing of a defended area at Cabourg by Typhoons of 184 Squadron, while 245 Squadron on a Ramrod destroyed two armoured cars, damaged two others and a light car, and bombed and damaged the railway bridge and cut the track south of Caen.

The 'Tangmere Bulletin' made its first appearance today. This bulletin is being issued for the purpose of giving the most up-to-date 'gen' possible for the members of the station and, judging by the reception it has been given by the airmen, it is 'just what the doctor ordered'.

7.6.44

During the night of 6-7 June patrols found it difficult to observe anything because it was extremely dark and some patrols returned early as they found it impossible to see anything at all. By 04.30 hours the visibility improved and there was 10/10ths cloud at 4,000 ft.

Mustangs of 133 Wing went on a Ramrod and destroyed two Fw190s. F/S Moravec was killed when he crash landed on return. 139 Squadron damaged one Me109G.

Despite the weather this has been a great day for 126 Wing, who while on patrol of the eastern beach met a mixed bunch of Ju88s, Fw190s and Me109s and in the ensuing combat destroyed eight Ju88s, three Fw190s and one Me109. Also they damaged one Ju88 and two Fw190s all without loss. W/C Keefer destroyed one of these Ju88s. W/C Crawford-Compton commanding 145 Wing destroyed one Ju88.

No. 306 Squadron had an excellent day. In the morning while on a Ramrod with 315, the two squadrons met 30 mixed Me109s and Fw190s, destroyed nine Fw190s and probably destroyed four Me109s, and then later in the day 306 Squadron on a Ramrod in the Argentan-Dreux area met 10 Me109s, destroyed five, probably destroyed one and damaged three others. Three pilots of 306 are missing. 315 Squadron while on the show mentioned above got four direct hits on a train when they dropped 24 500-lb bombs on the marshalling yard at Dreux. The other squadron of the wing, 129, attacked approximately 80 stationary vehicles, destroyed nine and damaged 20 after getting four direct hits on an intersection of a road and railway on the Falaise-Argentan road. Later in the day the same squadron destroyed 11 lorries and four motor cycles and damaged 18 lorries and 10 trucks. Apart from those mentioned above our losses were F/O Drope, 421 Squadron, whose parachute failed to open when he baled out. F/O Sans of 349 Squadron was hit by flak and crashed west of Caen.

During the day reports were received that more gliders had been seen landing, and at 10.20 hours a landing strip was already down but was marked 'do not land here'. At 20.00 hours disembarking was still proceeding.

Aircraft from various other squadrons landed at Tangmere during the day, all bringing reports of activity at the beachheads. Two Spitfire IX Squadrons from Lympne arrived in the night. They had to be off early in the morning to act as escort to Stirlings dropping equipment to airborne troops.

8.6.44

The weather was fine and clear in the morning but it clouded over towards midday and by 16.00 hours there was thick cloud and slight drizzle. It cleared slightly by 16.30 but then clouded over again and we had more rain.

The first patrol of the day was off at 04.40 and the two Lympne squadrons were briefed at 04.30 and took off at 04.50. While 501 Squadron were on low cover over [the] eastern area they were attacked by six Me109s offshore at Cabourg. The squadron destroyed one, probably destroyed another and damaged a third. F/L Fairbanks who was responsible for one destroyed and one damaged, crashed on the beach. Other successes during the day were obtained by 65 Squadron who shot down three Fw190s when they were attacked by 18 mixed Fw190s and Me109s. During this combat F/S Gheyssens baled out and was believed to have landed near Cabourg. 134 Wing led by W/C Cermak destroyed three Fw190s and damaged five, with the W/C getting one destroyed and one damaged. This was out of 12 enemy aircraft seen.

Incidentally the report handed in on this action commented upon the fact that there were so many of our own aircraft about that it was difficult to attack the enemy. 135 Wing attacked 12 Fw190s and 12 Me109s, and shot down four FWs and three MEs and damaged four FWs and three MEs. Apart from the above 442 Squadron endeavoured to engage eight-plus Fw190s which they saw near Cucerhan but were unable to do so owing to intense ack-ack from our beachhead which was seen to destroy two enemy aircraft. The remainder climbed through cloud and disappeared. During other operations direct hits were obtained on marshalling yards, tracks and buildings at Domfront by 122 Squadron. 306 Squadron dive-bombed 15 groups of 30 wagons, each of the bombs falling on the wagons. No. 129 Squadron also destroyed a number of trucks east of Falaise and 306 Squadron obtained direct hits on a train when they bombed a railway station. 602 Squadron scrambled on rendezvous with 12 Stirlings over Littlehampton but as they did not meet the bombers they patrolled 10 miles off the coast between Le Havre and Cherbourg and then escorted five Stirlings home.

During the day we received reports of fighting in the streets of Caen and a number of pilots returned with the information that Jerry was marking his aircraft with black and white markings similar to our own.

From Ed Prizer's diary:

June 8

Yesterday I did one show which was almost uneventful. Huns
in the distance but we couldn't get near. Some inaccurate
flak. At 9.30 yesterday night I took off for the night
shift, lots of cloud around. We got over and began our
patrol. Lots of alarms, but all friendly aircraft,
occasional bursts of flak but all inaccurate. Great fires
and smoke below as it began to get dark. Flashes from
artillery all over the countryside. Some Typhoons attacked
a town below us with bombs. It was immediately a mass of
flames. Suddenly a shower of red tennis balls flew up
around us. We were engulfed by them, shooting up like
streams from great hoses. The sky all around us was
brightly lit. We broke but they followed us for thirty
seconds. Seemed a year. God knows how they could have
missed. Came back in cloud. Missed hitting a barrage
balloon by about twenty feet. Had wheel trouble in circuit.
Made my first night Spitfire landing. Today I sat around
dispersal. Got ready to go on show tonight but the ceiling
was down to 200 feet so it was cancelled.

9.6.44

The weather today has been extremely bad with low cloud and
miserable drizzle and rather cold. All operations cancelled and
everyone rather depressed with the thought of being unable to give
air cover over the beachheads, especially in intelligence was the
atmosphere depressing owing to a report received early in the
morning that the enemy had penetrated to the coast in two places
dividing the Americans in two and also splitting them from the British
and Canadians.

The weather cleared sufficiently in the evening to enable one
squadron of 127 Wing to do a beach cover patrol.

During the day a Sea Otter of 277 Squadron managed to pick up
a Mustang pilot but the sea was so rough that the Otter found it

impossible to take off and was towed back.

The weather recco was made by a section of 453 Squadron to Le Havre and although it showed signs of improvement about 15.00 hours it was not until 20.20 hours that 127 Wing took off on the above-mentioned patrol. Because of cloud they naturally had to fly low and were unable to do the patrol owing to opposition from the Royal Navy. F/O Williams was missing, believed to have crashed in the sea and F/O Kelly was slightly wounded.

During the night 456 Squadron shot down three He177s making a total of seven destroyed since D-Day.

Aircraft of 83 and 84 Groups under Tangmere Sector control have since the morning of D-Day destroyed 48, probably destroyed nine and damaged 29 for the loss of 30 aircraft and pilots. From D-Day till the night of 8 June inclusive, aircraft of ADGB, 83 and 84 Fighter Groups have made a total of 5,018 sorties, the very large majority of which were cover.

10.6.44

Improvement in the weather today. 126 Wing started off with an escort job to Stirlings and Halifaxes. During the day numerous MT were shot up and destroyed, 184 Squadron claiming some when they very successfully released 62 rockets all of which were seen to strike the target area when attacking a concentration of infantry and AFVs at St Contest.

Six Spitfires of 340 Squadron escorted three Stirlings, dropping supplies on the west side of the Caen Canal. 130 Squadron saw several Ju88s but could only make contact with one which F/Lt Mathewson shot down. About the same time 611 Squadron saw five Ju88s and destroyed two.

Other successes during the day were as follows: F/L Scott of 130 Squadron destroyed one Ju88 on beach cover patrol. 135 Wing: one FW destroyed northwest of Caen. Two Me109s were destroyed and one damaged out of four by 10 Wing.

Two interesting bits of information were brought in during the day. Firstly, 65 Squadron who destroyed one Me109 and damaged another, reported that they were attacked by from 12 to 20 aircraft identified as Me109Fs with RAF roundels on the wings and fuselage and black and white stripes and shaded wings. Later 485 Squadron reported that Red section were attacked on the port beam by two Spitfire 5s, one making a pass at Red 3 as he came in and fired a burst. Red 3 turned tightly to port and found the Spit following him round and opening fire, these bursts being seen by Yellow 2 and Red 4. Red 3 had by this time come to the conclusion that the Spit 5s were hostile, especially as no Spits had so far encountered flying in smaller formations than four. He got behind and opened fire from 400 yards without result. Red 3 finally concluded that it had hostile intent, manoeuvred into line astern and shot it down.

Four Spitfires of 411 Wing land on the R&R [refuelling and re-arming] strip near St Croix-sur-Mer and on their return reported that the strip was equipped for handling two squadrons and had facilities for re-arming 36 Typhoons. Another report was received to the effect that the Creron landing strip was ready and aircraft were already making use of it. Owing to low oil pressure W/C Scott-Malden landed, wheels down, on one of the emergency landing strips. Two others, W/O Thomas and P/O Pyle both of 129 made forced landings in France, the former on our beaches seven miles west of Bayeux and the latter in enemy territory. F/S Konvicka, 312 Squadron, who had been reported missing, has now returned and claims one Me109 probably destroyed. Following a collision with him in which the enemy aircraft sustained damage to its tail unit, F/S Konvicka ditched and was picked up by HSL [ASR high-speed launch] who confirmed that another aircraft had crashed at that place about the same time.

11.6.44

The weather was only passable first thing in the morning and deteriorated rapidly. Because of this activity had to be confined to patrols over the assault areas.

Prior to this 456 Squadron destroyed one He177 and one Ju88 and damaged one He177 and one Fw190.

June 11
Bad weather has kept us down a lot. US Navy hit seven

planes out of 127 Wing with flak. Jamieson crashed-landed in France yesterday. Fellows of our wing were among first to land and refuel in France. I took a walk through some country lanes last night. Beautiful farmland with breezes rustling through the groves of trees. Today I did an uneventful show in the morning and another in the afternoon on which Smitty and I shot up some transport. Garwood crashed in France. Lots of shelling from the navy ashore. Caen is burning brightly throughout. Dodged some light flak. Tonight I'm storing excess baggage and preparing for our move to our airfield in France. Looking forward to it expectantly. Reports say much anti-British feeling over there. Other day they shot a 17 year old French girl who was sniping. Surprisingly the country is very prosperous and the Germans popular. Our hospital is in a former brothel. Jerry has taken the girls with him. I'm packing this diary for storage now. It's a record of my initiation into battle, the happiest and most enlightening phase of my life so far. There is no fear of death. It's too damn insignificant. If I go, I go meritoriously, much preferable to a prolonged useless existence. If I live the peak of my life will have passed in the skies of France.

12.6.44

The weather showed considerable improvement today and operational duties consisted of low-cover patrols of the beaches, armed reconnaissance, escort duties and dive-bombing operations. There was comparatively little air combat but some very successful bombing of railways, railway rolling stock, roads and MT vehicles.

No. 322 Squadron acted as escort to five Dakotas towing gliders all of which landed successfully. A number of squadrons made use of the landing strips for re-arming and refuelling. Sgt Rinde of 322 who baled out yesterday has now returned and states that he was shot at while coming down, landed 200 yards north of Bronay which was occupied by the Germans but managed to get away.

As mentioned above there were very few aerial combats but 484

Squadron found two Me109s flying at zero feet apparently with bombs on, attacked them causing one to break up in the air and the other to crash.

Two Spits of 277 Wing searched for a bomber in trouble over the Channel and successfully directed a corvette which was seen picking up survivors. There was no trace of any dinghy on a further patrol, but 134 Wing successfully directed a destroyer to a dinghy containing four of a Mitchell crew.

During the night the first pilotless planes were sent over by the enemy. [This refers to V1 flying bombs, which henceforth would be called 'Doodlebugs' in the popular press and 'Divers' by the RAF].

13.6.44

In the early hours of the morning 456 Squadron shot down a fighter-bomber which crashed in flames in the sea and a Mosquito of 264 Squadron destroyed a Ju188 which was last seen burning on the ground.

Another Mosquito of 264 Squadron destroyed a further Ju88 which after receiving a one-second burst during which strikes were seen all over the fuselage and port engine, went straight on its back with the port engine on fire, explosions taking place in the cockpit. The enemy aircraft hit the ground and burst into flames. An officer of 315 Squadron destroyed an Fw190 which was painted in a similar manner to our own with black and white stripes.

The usual armed recces, dive-bombing and bombardment-spotting took place, but owing to poor weather few results could be observed.

It is with great regret that we learn today that on the last patrol W/C Chadburn [CO of 126 Wing] and F/L Clarke of 421 Squadron collided in mid-air and were both killed.

The advance party of 184 Squadron left Westhampnett today for Holmsley South.

14.6.44

Mosquitoes are still keeping up their excellent work and early this morning destroyed two He177s. Later in the day six Mustangs of 65 Squadron were returning with bombs on when they saw Me109s and

Fw190s. They jettisoned their bombs and engaged the enemy, destroyed one ME, and damaged two others and one Fw190.

No. 19 Squadron who were out to bomb a railway yard but were unable to do so owing to low cloud saw three Me109s in the Rambouillet area which they attacked and destroyed. On a low cover patrol of the east and west assault areas, 149 Wing led by their W/C destroyed two Me109s, probably destroyed another and damaged 7 more.

16 to 20 Me109s were seen by 611 Squadron when south of Caen and were engaged in a running fight in and out of cloud. Two were seen to crash and in all the other attacks strikes were seen.

No. 414 Squadron escorted five Stirlings which dropped supplies by parachute very successfully in the Benouville region.

15.6.44

The most important occurrence today has been the first transfer of airlifts overseas which took place when the airlift party of 144 Wing departed from Ford for B.3 landing ground at 11.25 hours. The party was accommodated in nine Dakotas and one additional Dakota went with them carrying medical supplies and WAAF nursing orderlies.

Airlift Party of 122 Wing, Funtington, moved to Ford occupying space thus vacated, leaving Funtington ALG empty apart from ADGB.

The weather has been fine until this evening when it started to rain and the day has been a very busy one. There has been considerably more activity on the enemy's side and very good results from our point of view, the two outstanding being by 132 Wing and 127 Wing. The former met 20-plus mixed enemy aircraft flying at 2,000 feet. They bounced them from 10,000 over Evreux airfield with the following results:

	Destroyed	Probable	Damaged
331 Sqn	2 Fw190s	–	1 Fw190
332 Sqn	2 Fw190s	1 Fw190	2 Fw190s
	1 Me109	–	2 Me109s
66 Sqn	3 Fw190s	–	3 Me109s

Later in the day 127 Wing, while on a show, came across 20-25 Me109s at 15,000 ft over the northeast outskirts of Caen. They destroyed nine, probably destroyed one and damaged another. This was for the loss of one pilot.

Apart from the above two outstanding performances:

    443 Sqn destroyed two Do217s
    332 Sqn damaged one Me410
    602 Sqn probably destroyed two Me109s, one He111 and damaged another He111.

    Earlier in the day a Mosquito of 264 Squadron shot down a Ju188 and 456 Squadron shot down an unidentified aircraft which they picked up on AI and got at 12,000 ft. After having given it a two-second burst they saw a large flash and much debris from the aircraft. Three of the crew were seen to bale out.

    During the day rolling stock was bombed as usual with some very successful results by 122 Wing.

    No. 322 Squadron provided an escort of three Spits to Dakota carrying VIPs and landed safely on one of the strips. There were also the usual sweeps and patrols including two successful ASRs.

16.6.44

In the morning the sky was still very overcast, but it cleared quite early and the weather remained fairly good all day.

    At about 11.00 hours 10 Dakotas landed to take ground personnel of 127 Wing to France. They should have taken off at 13.15 hours but owing to a report of a front coming up from the Channel they were delayed and actually took off at 15.14 hours escorted by 421 Squadron. This was the first airlift from Tangmere.

    During the day 411, 412, 403, 416, and 421 Squadrons acted as escort to a cruiser taking HM the King to France and back.

    Nos. 350, 501, and 401 Squadrons acted as close escort to Mitchells IIs. 421 Squadron escorted 10 Dakotas back from B.3 landing strip and 322 Squadron a further 11 Dakotas from France to

Selsey. 453 Squadron destroyed two Me109s, probably destroyed two and damaged a fifth. S/L Chase of 264 Squadron damaged a Ju88 over the French coast. When 349 and 485 Squadrons returned from acting as close escort to Lancasters bombing Boulogne they reported excellent bombing results and stated that they had seen one extremely large explosion.

Apart from the above there were the usual attacks on marshalling yards, rolling stock, MT vehicles, etc.

No. 122 Wing left Funtington today for Ford.

AVM Embry, AOC of 2 Group with Sector Commander G/C Crisham, and senior officers of 2 Group, visited Westhampnett to see if the airfield was suitable for Mosquitoes. The project was abandoned owing to the lack of lighting for night flying.

No. 184 Squadron left Westhampnett for Holmsley South today.

17.6.44

The enemy are sending over their pilotless planes in increasing numbers and a new operation, anti-Diver patrol, is in force. Many pilots are reporting having seen these Divers and their successes are increasing. They apparently seldom fly at more than 3,000 ft and their speed appears to vary to anything in the region of 400 mph. We are hoping that the number of kills will increase rapidly.

Our night-fighter squadrons were busy as usual and 410 and 264 both had successes shooting down a Ju88 and Ju188 respectively, the latter was claimed by S/L Trollope who was vectored on to his bandit by No. 21 Sector GCI. In his report he made special mention of the excellence of their control.

The weather was bad, at times in the morning to such an extent in fact that 315 Squadron was forced to return without carrying out a Ramrod attack. It was due to this weather that there was an unfortunate accident when 130 Squadron on beach cover was ordered to climb owing to low cloud and two aircraft collided. F/S Fergusson crashed into the sea and is believed killed, but the other pilot managed to crash land at Tangmere. S/L Ireson was picked up by a high speed launch after having been hit by flak. He baled out 10 miles south of the Isle of Wight.

There were few engagements with enemy aircraft but of these few 310 Squadron destroyed two Fw190s and 306 Squadron two Fw190s.

During the day reports were received that pilots had seen a number of Divers going into the sea.

Nos. 123 and 136 Wings and No. 20 Sector Ops arrived at Funtington today.

18.6.44

Reports received from night-fighter squadrons show that many Divers were sent across the Channel but our aircraft were unable to attack them because of our own ack-ack. No doubt the position will be cleared up in the near future as at the moment there seems to be some confusion.

Besides seeing six Divers while they were on patrol, 264 Squadron, with the use of AI, also saw some enemy aircraft and succeeded in destroying two Ju188s and one Fw190.

A Dakota landed at Tangmere in the evening with mechanical trouble. On board were a number of wounded from the battle front. They were cared for by Tangmere medical staff and taken by ambulances into Chichester Hospital.

No. 322 Dutch Squadron destroyed two Divers during the day and S/L Page and F/O Collins of 132 Squadron damaged an Fw190.

June 18

I've been averaging a show a day lately. Sometimes I get up at 3.30 am, rush by truck to the aircrew mess for ham and chips then down to dispersal. It's dark, chilly; there's a loud roar of planes running up and flashing ghostly blue exhaust flames. We get briefed, climb in, and take off into the dawn. We're not finding any Huns but there's lots of flak from below. Smitty has been hit, Love knocked down. Garwood and Jamieson have returned from their crashes in France. I took a good walk through the country the other night. Today I was on readiness. Suddenly word came to pack in half an hour. Rush and riot. Soon 10 Dakotas landed on the field. We assembled all baggage, had a hurried dinner,

then loaded the planes and climbed aboard. No fanfare, just
a few WAAFs waving goodbye and another bunch of fellows off
to the front. Hard to feel the significance. Feels like a
routine trip across the Channel. Once over we landed on a
sandy strip amid great orange clouds of dust that blinded
everything from view. As we taxied a shell burst on the
ground 20 feet away. Guns were booming all around. We had
landed on the wrong field so took off again in a cloud of
dust. Shortly we had engine trouble so force-landed on a
strip just behind the line. There was a constant roar from
the guns and planes overhead. Some curious French people
came up and entered in conversation with one of our fellows.
They showed no dislike for the Germans, only the war. Cows
grazed on the edge of the landing strip and there was little
sign of where the fighting had passed in the green fields.
Wheat grew all around the strip. There were occasional
shell holes and jagged hunks of shrapnel lying around.
George and I walked through the woods to a soldiers'
encampment. There's one in almost every field. We had tea
with the soldiers. All sorts of equipment is piled in the
open everywhere. Returned to the strip and took off, engine
having been repaired. After much trouble we landed at our
base, four miles from the front. Worst dust yet, impossible
to see ten feet ahead through clouds raised by planes. All
personnel are coated with it. Went to our tent encampment
in a field lined with high hedges behind an old battered
village church. The village is called Beny-sur-Mer. An
old, grey stone barn is in an adjoining field and on another
side is a big apple orchard. We got settled in a tent and
dug our slit trench. Looked for my baggage in the big pile
of junk but it was missing as usual. Heard about French
Canadians catching women snipers and slitting their bellies.
Many of the French, especially the girls, are unfriendly.
Boys on the field have been looting neighbouring farms. We
have an open-air bar set up. After a beer there we ate
supper of canned rations at the mess tent. Outside camp is

a road through a beautiful park of large trees bounded by ancient stone walls and homes. It's dark now. The last Spits have just landed -- there are voices all over the field as the fellows are getting themselves settled in their tents. The Doc next door is energetically digging a deep hole for his camp cot. There's an odd contrast of the incessant roar of guns and the church bells ringing for vespers. The shells going back and forth overhead are setting up quite a whistling. The Jerries have just come over to bomb the beach a couple of miles away. The sky was filled with hosing streams of red tennis balls and the clatter of the airfield Bofors guns was deafening. We all jumped into slit trenches.

19.6.44

Visibility has been poor today but there has been a fair amount of activity. F/O Cramerus, 322 Squadron, destroyed a Diver [while on] patrol from 17.35 to 19.25, and F/O Dekker, 322 Squadron, destroyed another by making two attacks from underneath it at 600 and 400 yards respectively. This Diver exploded in the air.

S/L Johnson and S/L Foster of 66 Squadron each destroyed a Diver, the former succeeded in exploding his in the air, while the second exploded on the ground.

The W/C Flying of 145 [Wing] with Sgt Chapman of 346 Squadron both attacked a Diver which was afterwards damaged by three other Spits; the Diver was seen to crash and blow up in a field.

The usual shipping cover, convoy patrols and Ramrods were operated during the day.

The ground crews of 130, 402 and 303 (Polish), together with 1025 Servicing Wing, 6130, 6303 and 6402 Servicing Echelons arrived at Westhampnett.

20.6.44

While on defensive patrol during the early hours, a Mosquito of 264 Squadron piloted by S/L Chase was vectored onto a Ju88 at 6,000 ft. The enemy aircraft was given a three-second burst which was found sufficient to cause it to crash.

No. 96 Squadron claims three Divers, two of which exploded on the sea and one on the ground near Beachy. 332 Squadron also destroyed one Diver.

Three pilots of 331 Squadron share an Me109 which they destroyed while acting as low cover on a shipping patrol.

We may have more news of a report received from 133 Wing today. This report states they saw what they described as 'an air object' which gave varying impressions: one to three feet square and which, in one instance, was seen to burst giving out glittering strips of some 6" to 10". It is thought to have been fired from the ground and was encountered at 700 ft and 7,000 ft.

When 19 Squadron was bounced by 16-plus Fw190s, they succeeded in destroying two Fw190s, probably destroying a third and damaging four others.

No. 133 Wing very successfully bombed a railway track on which they got six direct hits and four near misses on a railway bridge in the Chartres-Nogent area. While on this show they damaged one heavy tank, destroyed six MT vehicles and damaged three others.

Nos. 130, 402, and 303 (Polish) arrived at Westhampnett from Horne after they had done a show.

21.6.44

During the night a Mosquito of 96 Squadron on Diver patrol saw 15 Divers and were able to attack two. They obtained strikes on the first but it flew weaving to port. The second they attacked at a range of 12,000 ft and it exploded after being hit. Another Mosquito of the same squadron destroyed a further Diver which blew up on hitting the sea.

F/L Taylor and W/O Mitchel of 409 Squadron claim one Ju188 damaged after they had given it a short burst and seen an explosion and smoke from the enemy aircraft. It went down to 1,500 ft and disappeared into cloud.

W/C Crew destroyed a Diver over the sea and it was seen to spin in overland at Dungeness and burst on the ground.

S/L Bond of 91 Squadron shot one Diver down into the sea.

When 19 Squadron was on a recco in the Dreux-Chartres area they sighted 16 Me109s west of Evreux. Four of our aircraft jettisoned their bombs and attacked the enemy, destroying four Me109s and damaging one. During this combat F/L Hayward was slightly wounded.

Nos. 125, 131, 132 and 145 Wings all gave cover to heavy bombers attacking 11 targets.

Apart from the above, the usual patrols were carried out.

At 23.45 hours six aircraft of 303 Squadron were diverted here instead of landing at Westhampnett where there had been a prang.

22.6.44

At 05.00 hours this morning six aircraft of 303 Squadron took off on their daily patrol duty rendezvousing with the rest of their squadron over Westhampnett.

During the morning the Czechoslovakian and Norwegian (134 and 132 Wings) ground staff arrived at Tangmere from Apuldram and Bognor respectively, and the aircraft turned up during the afternoon from assault area low cover and shipping patrols.

The Detling Wing in process of transfer to Merston landed here and did one low cover and shipping patrol. They first landed at 16.30 and took off again for a second show at 21.25, both of these being uneventful.

Mosquitoes were again busy on Diver patrols during the hours of darkness. 96 Squadron claim two destroyed.

Nos. 303 and 317 Squadron acted as withdrawal cover to 100 Halifaxes bombing Noball targets.

The RAF is certainly having a crack at these Divers and no doubt successes will increase as the days go by.

Nos. 302 and 317 Squadrons escorted Dakotas to and from France successfully.

A Sea Otter of 277 Squadron picked up two American aircrew one-and-a-half miles southwest of Littlehampton and two more Americans were picked up by lifeboat, while another Sea Otter rescued a Polish pilot of 303 Squadron from a dinghy.

The operations for the Tangmere Squadrons consisted of cover for Lancasters bombing Noballs, patrols over the assault area and the usual shipping patrols. On one of these operations in the early part of the day 2nd Lieut. Aarflot of 132 Wing was hit by flak and called up on his RT saying he was landing at an ALG in France. By the evening he had returned to Tangmere, both he and his aircraft being OK.

Lord Monsell, region commissioner, with Air Vice-Marshal Barton visited the operations block and the station today and accompanied by the station commander witnessed the setting up of 134 Wing on its move here from Apuldram. They also paid a visit to the control tower where they saw 72 aircraft land in 20 minutes.

The majority of 145 Wing left Merston for Funtington today and were replaced by 274, 80 and 229 Squadrons from Detling.

Nos. 123 and 136 Wings with 20 Sector Ops left Funtington for Hurn today.

23.6.44

Our night fighters were on the job again during the night and they succeeded in destroying three Divers, probably destroying one Ju88 and damaging one Ju88.

Incidentally a report has been received that the enemy are sending off salvos of seven Divers at a time from the Dieppe area.

A Mosquito of 29 Squadron destroyed a Me110 when it was in the circuit at Coulommiers, while another probably destroyed a Ju188.

When 125 Wing engaged eight Me109s and four Fw190s over Caen they destroyed three MEs, two FWs and damaged another ME.

Nos. 80 and 229 Squadrons have been congratulated by group for their speed on a scramble; two minutes after receiving the order both squadrons were airborne – a very good show indeed.

24.6.44

While on shipping and assault area patrol 331 and 332 Squadrons bounced 12 MEs flying at 2,000 ft northwest of Caen. Besides one claim by Wing Commander Berg, three others were destroyed and one damaged without loss.

During the day four Spits of 132 Wing acted as destroyer escort. Other escort duties were carried out by 130, 229 and 274 and

80 Squadrons to Ansons, Dakotas and Lancasters.

Nos. 661 and 131 Squadrons from Culmhead landed here in the afternoon and went off on a sweep at 16.40. They returned at 18.10 after an uneventful trip except for meeting a lame Lancaster which they escorted back. Both squadrons took off again at 20.00 hours on a Rodeo, after which they landed back at their own base.

This afternoon there was a parade in Chichester to wind up the Salute the Soldier Week. RAF, RAF Regiment and WAAF personnel took part in the parade.

June 24

Weather has changed to very good. I've done two shows behind German lines shooting up trucks. The other night we got some nice flamers. We've been doing lots of readiness at the end of the runway, sitting in the sun and getting all the dust from the planes taking off. A German post 2,000 yds away from here was taken the day before we arrived so we've got all sorts of loot including a piano and refrigerator. They had a wonderful set-up underground. From the looks of the empty bottles and discarded women's clothing they must have lived the life of Reilly. The squadron has also scrounged some cavalry horses, motorcycles, bikes, rifles and an Oerlikon gun which we shoot off at German planes when they come over just for the fun of it. Every night Jerry crosses over and there's a nice display of fireworks. Last night we saw a Ju88 hit, burst into flames, do a perfect loop, and crash nearby. In the day the naval guns firing from the sea inland make terrible earth-shaking crashes. We watch the American bombers going over the lines in the daytime, getting plastered with flak -- some when hit turn back to our field and land. Often the crews bale out and are blown into German territory by the wind. I haven't gone off the camp yet except to the German post but many of the fellows have been out scrounging for wine and trophies up around the lines.

25.6.44

Very little of note happened today but there was one outstanding performance.

S/L Elwell with F/O Fergusson as radio navigator, of 264 Squadron, when investigating flashes and heavy flak to the east of Cherbourg saw bombs exploding in the sea and a moment later saw five enemy aircraft climbing steeply to the north about two miles away. S/L Elwell gave chase and closed to 1,000 yards when two of the enemy aircraft turned to port and the other three to starboard. They were recognised as five Fw190s silhouetted against the sunset and the S/L turned after the three who were now flying east in formation and climbing rapidly. The range had opened to 2,000 yards but the S/L gave maximum speed and closed to 300 yards firing short bursts at the FW on the port side of the formation. At 300 yards a brilliant orange flash was seen to cover the fuselage and the enemy aircraft dived steeply to port from 6,000 ft, and still on fire, disappeared from view under the nose of the Mosquito. S/L Elwell immediately swung his sights to the starboard FW which was nearest and turning to port. A short burst produced strikes on the starboard wing and further bursts caused a large explosion after which the enemy burst into flames, put its nose up and did a flick roll passing the Mosquito on the port side. Without pausing the S/L attacked a third FW which was turning hard to port. No strikes were seen and the ammunition ran out so he had to break off. The navigator then shouted to him that the enemy aircraft were on his tail so he peeled off in a very tight diving turn to starboard, pulled out at 800 feet heading north and came home.

Other Mosquitoes on their usual nightly patrol succeeded in destroying nine Divers, and that covers practically all operations carried out today apart from the usual patrols.

Three aircraft of 438 Squadron landed here after a weather recco and reported seeing 30 Me109s who showed complete lack of any desire to fight. They jettisoned their tanks and scuttled off quickly in the other direction.

Six Spitfires of 56 Squadron landed here after escorting Dakotas to France. They were to have gone off again to bring Dakotas back but the operation was cancelled at the last minute and they took off for their own base.

During the night, which was very bad from the weather point of view, we had two Divers pass over the station.

The vacancy left at Bognor ALG when 132 Wing went to Tangmere was filled today by 83 Group Support Unit under W/C Passey DFC.

To the delight of the RAF Regiment, 2723 Squadron at approximately 22.30 hours today, shot down a flying bomb.

26.6.44

Still weather is bad and as a consequence there has been very little doing. A number of Divers have been destroyed during the very early morning but apart from that there is nothing worth recording.

June 26

Yesterday I was pulled out of bed at 3.30 am. It was a dark, damp morning. We ate a greasy breakfast in a dark, smoke-filled tent and went off to briefing. We took off before dawn. You could hardly see with all the dust. We roamed around shooting up transport. The ground control vectored us to a Ju88 but the winco who was lone-wolfing found it first and shot it down, a beautiful flamer. I plastered a black truck which one of the fellows says was an ambulance. And we talk about the Germans failing to observe the rules of war. You just don't have time to debate over such things. The second show was a shambles. Our squadron got all separated and the sky was full of black flak puffs. Smitty was hit but got back all right. We were released in the afternoon so a crowd of us piled on a jeep and went into Bayeux, the only town untouched by the invasion. We found a place called the Ping-Pong, a clean little estaminet on the main cobblestone street. Here we had Calvados, the rough local brandy made out of apples and also cognac. We met some British nurses there, moved on to a couple of other places, had a row with a red-headed provost marshal and came back to camp. We got well rained on, and made poor progress

through the narrow rocky little road, jammed with transport
to the front. Both sides of the road were lined with
supplies, stacked in fields. What a lot of stuff! Played
crap at mess tent. Slept 'till 10.30 today, then hung
around dispersal till dinner-time.

We have a couple of tents and a parachute truck at
dispersal, that's all. Had the afternoon off so Art Seller
and I hitch-hiked up to the front. Piles of transport were
moving up the roads between shell-battered grey stone walls
to the front for a big push coming off soon. The orchards,
thatched peasant cottages, and centuries-old villages were
greatly busted up by shells. More rain and much mud. MPs
at all the cross-roads were frantically trying to direct the
traffic. We got a ride with a captain going up to a
battalion headquarters near the front at Sequeville. Mud
everywhere, thick and oozy. Soldiers looked miserable and
filthy in the wet and cold. We walked a way then got a ride
with a sergeant going up to a front-line artillery
emplacement. He let us off on a ridge 1,500 yds from the
German lines. We walked over to some ammunition trucks
parked by some trees where a group of Englishmen were
drinking tea. The big guns were going off all around the
field. The salvos of shells sounded like a dozen trains
rushing through a subway. You could almost see the air
split by them. Just as we were leaving Seller decided to go
back and ask the fellows about a Luger they'd mentioned to
him. Then swish. A crumph, an ear-splitting blast of air,
and Jerry shells began to fall in the field. I went flat in
the mud, making a helluva mess of my raincoat which I didn't
consider for a minute. I saw some men jumping in a slit
trench so I ran over with the shrapnel whining around and
crackling in the foliage of the trees. I went into the
trench head first on top of the other fellows, dropping my
helmet and revolver. My rear end and legs were still
dangling above ground and I felt like an ostrich. The
hundred pounders were whistling over and exploding around

the field incessantly. I managed to work my way completely into the trench. Suddenly a whistle grew agonisingly loud, there was a muffled thud that shook us, and a shell had landed in the embankment about two feet behind our trench. It was a dud so we all smiled at how we'd cheated fate. Two ammunition trucks were hit in rapid succession. They burst into flames and started popping off to add to the shrapnel. Amid it all medical corpsmen rushed around the field with stretchers picking up wounded, seeming oblivious to the hot flying metal. Three trucks right next to us were peppered by shells landing close by. When the shelling finally stopped the exploding ammunition from the trucks, all of which were hit by now, was flying around and kept us in our trench for an additional ten minutes. When I climbed out of the hole I found from one of the medical men that there had been ten casualties out of the fifty men in the field. Seller came running over with a terrified expression on his face. He had a piece of shrapnel that had bruised his rear end. We stopped a motorcyclist and climbed on behind him. Started off at a great rate until we ran into some deep mud, the bike slewed and we all went off. Not hurt, so we ran down to Sequeville, got a truck, then a jeep back to camp. Hundreds of tanks were moving up in columns through the fields for the big push tonight. It's getting dark now and the pounding of the guns is rapidly increasing. Sounds like a big battle. Went to bed after a few shots of cognac.

27.6.44

The early morning visit to France was cancelled as reports were received that the landing strips were in such a condition that only Sunderlands could be expected to land on them. Surely there has never been such a June from the weather point of view and just when the 'flaming' type would have been so welcome.

During the night the Intelligence Section had received 'gen' from 21 Army Group reporting the capture of Cherbourg with 45,000 prisoners including one general and one admiral. Great joy as this is the first time an army group has beaten the BBC or the daily press in the issue of up-to-date news. Unfortunately, the anti-climax came later when they admitted finger trouble and suggested the removal of the last 'nought' from the 45,000! There is also some doubt regarding the admiral, but we are assured that the general is with us!!

Nos. 41 and 610 Squadrons from West Malling landed here en route for Westhampnett and proceeded to be on a high state of anti-Diver readiness including standing patrols. The station is very glad to welcome 41 Squadron back again and it is a matter of regret that they are only here for a day at the outside.

The Merston Wing (80, 22, 9 and 274) landed en route for Gatwick and in the middle of everything 80 Squadron tried to escort Dakotas but were unable to see them owing to the weather. At 14.30 they took off to escort the Dakotas back but were recalled and sent off again at 15.30 when owing to a delay on the part of the Dakotas they did a sort of Cook's tour of the battle area.

During the day 414 Squadron did 28 sorties in their Spit 12s on anti-Diver patrols and 610 scrambled six Spit 14s on similar patrols all without seeing anything.

In the evening 132 and 134 Wing went on a sweep. 274, 80 and 229 Squadrons left Merston today for Gatwick. They were replaced by 303, 130 and 402 Squadrons from Westhampnett. 41 and 610 Squadrons together with their echelons moved into Westhampnett from West Malling.

28.6.44

Merston Wing escorted heavy bombers bombing Noball targets in fairly bad weather, but once more owing to poor weather little else happened.

No. 134 Wing landed in France to do a bombing show and stayed there. Gatwick Wing were rumoured to be going to Gatwick all day long but never took off.

A Mosquito of 264 Squadron destroyed one Ju188 which disintegrated and fell into the sea after receiving a one-second burst at 300 ft.

In order to celebrate the fifth anniversary of the WAAF, a parade and march-past were held in the afternoon at which the salute was taken by the station commander, Wing Commander P. R. Walker DSO DFC. In the evening an all-ranks dance was held in the station cinema. According to all reports it was an extremely successful evening, although from the dancing point of view it was, to say the least, slightly overcrowded.

29.6.44

The operational duties for the day consisted of intruder patrols, beachhead patrols, convoy patrols and low cover of the assault and shipping areas.

Nos. 331 and 66 Squadrons acted as escort to Ansons to B.2 and B.3 landing strips respectively.

No. 312 Squadron strafed railway wagons and a staff car, numerous strikes being seen.

No. 310 Squadron shot up a lorry, set a large truck and two lorries on fire at one spot and then went on to shoot up two armoured cars, one of which blew up. At another point they blew up a further lorry and set a number more on fire.

Later the same squadron, on another show, damaged two Tiger tanks and then chased a staff car into a ditch where it overturned, after which they shot up another Tiger and a smaller tank.

No. 145 Wing came back from escorting 100 Lancasters and reported that they had witnessed some excellent and concentrated bombing.

No. 66 Squadron acted as escort to Dakotas returning from B.8.

Wing Commander Crawford-Compton, leading 340 Squadron, destroyed two Fw190s and a further one was destroyed in the same way when they were in combat with eight Fw190 and Me109s with whom they came in contact while on sweeps in the Evreux area.

No. 131 Wing moved from Chailey to Apuldram today.

June 29

Day before yesterday I did two shows. One, a scramble, rated us nothing. We were in and out of cloud and everyone got separated. One flak barrage hit three out of the six of

us. Stan Pyne was peppered in his legs, force-landed, and
passed out. The Huns are beginning to show up in droves.
Other squadrons got about eight. Yesterday I was up for the
early show at 4 am, grabbed some sleep in the parachute
truck, lying on a shelf, between shows and readiness. The
second show we ran into flak all the way. Got lots of
transport. The CO and Linton were both hit but got back.
On the early show we passed six 190s flying above. Yellow
section went after them. Everybody was weaving and looking
around. Five minutes later we saw the Huns with
reinforcements turning in behind us. They began their dive,
coming in with guns blazing. We held till they were close,
then broke. They tried to cut around, shooting behind our
tails, then broke down. We got after the ones we could see.
I picked a nice juicy one and chased him into cloud. Banks
smacked one beautifully. It went down spinning and smoking
with pieces falling off. Fox got a damaged, then they were
gone. On the night show, Seller went down over enemy
territory. The other squadrons also lost several but downed
eleven Huns. 127 and 144 Wings got a lot too. Our boys are
mixing with anywhere from even to 10:1 odds against them and
licking the bastards every time. The Jerries must know it's
sure defeat to go after us. Still there's lots turning up
now. We had to do readiness at dispersal last night where
we shot crap till 11, I'm up at four again this morning.
My kite was U/S so I didn't get away on the show. I did an
early afternoon show. Kenway radioed us a Hun plot. We
climbed above cloud to 16,000. Someone called: "109s!"
They were directly above shining in the bright sun. We
turned and down they came. They looked beautiful as they
passed, hardly fifty yards away. Gleaming, lacquered metal,
long noses painted brilliant yellow. Two half-rolled 100 ft
from me down into cloud after firing short bursts. Dewey
and I chased five others but they got away. We were doing
over 500 mph. Tonight we did readiness till 9.30.

30.6.44

No. 145 Wing left Funtington today for Selsey.

A small but interesting piece of information from Bognor ALG is that they are carrying blood plasma over to the hospitals at our beachheads.

Another bit of Bognor news is that a number of Dakotas arrived today from France carrying wounded.

No. 135 Wing moved from Selsey to Coolham.

No. 145 Wing moved from Funtington to Selsey today.

	Totals for June		
Destroyed	**Probably**	**Destroyed**	**Damaged**
W/C Keefer	2		
W/C Berg	1		
349 Squadron	2.5	2	4
401	7.5	1	2
411	2.5	2	4
412	1	–	2
443	1	–	1
485	8	1	2
501	2	1	1
611	6	1	1
W/C Cermak	1	–	1
W/C Checketts	–	–	1
W/C Crawford-Compton	3	–	1
19 Squadron	6	–	1
65	7	1	9
129	1	–	–
122	3	–	1
130	2	–	–
132	–	–	2
222	4	–	5
264	12	1	1
306	12	4	3
310	3	–	–
312	2	–	–

Destroyed	Probably	Destroyed	Damaged
315	10	1	–

Flt/Off Emerson was promoted to squadron officer on 3 June and thus becomes the first WAAF squadron officer at Tangmere. S/O Coles was promoted to flt/officer on 9 June. She is the first WAAF officer to hold the position of flt/officer in the Tangmere Equipment Section. S/O Sheppard was promoted to flt/officer on 12 June to fill the vacancy caused by Squadron Officer Emerson's promotion.

A notice appeared in the *London Gazette* dated 8 June 1944 stating that the undermentioned had been Mentioned in Despatches:

S/L Cunningham-Jones (station medical officer)
F/O Boxall (station HQ)
Flt Off Bevan (ops)
W/O Pilling (equipment)
Sgt O'Hagan (officers' mess)

[For] P. R. Walker
Wing Commander, Commanding
RAF Station, Tangmere

Although it was not mentioned in the station ORB, the first confirmed RAF victory on D-Day, 6 June, was made by Squadron Leader Johnnie Houlton of 485 (RNZAF) Squadron, flying from Selsey in Spitfire IXB ML407 OU-V. From his book, *Spitfire Strikes*:

In mid-afternoon I led Blue Section during the third patrol of the day. South of Omaha Beach, below a shallow, broken layer of cumulus, I glimpsed a Ju88 above cloud, diving away fast to the south. Climbing at full throttle I saw the enemy aircraft enter a large isolated cloud above the main layer, and when it reappeared on the other side I was closing in rapidly.

I adjusted the gyro sight on to the target at 500 yds with a deflection angle of 45 degrees, positioned the aiming dot on the right-hand engine of the enemy aircraft, and fired a three-second burst. The engine disintegrated, fire broke out, two crew members baled out and the aircraft dived steeply to crash on a roadway, blowing apart on impact. Supreme Headquarters nominated the Ju88 as the first enemy aircraft to be shot down since the invasion began, putting 485 (NZ) Spitfire Squadron at the top of the scoreboard for D-Day.

5
Doodlebugs and Homecomings
1944 – 1945

During the night of 22-23 July 1944, the weather was too bad for anti-Diver patrols, but not too bad for the pilotless Divers themselves, one of which exploded at the intersection of the runways at RAF Tangmere at about 23.55 hours, fortunately causing neither damage nor casualties.

Intelligence had first identified the V1 threat in the spring of 1943 and by December a systematic attempt was being made to destroy the launch sites with Noball raids. By the end of May 1944, 140 sites had been destroyed, but the enemy was now constructing much better camouflaged, pre-fabricated sites faster than the Allies could find them and knock them out. Intelligence anticipated that, within a week of D-Day, the Allied invasion would trigger a response in the form of V1 attacks aimed at London. On 13 June 1944, the first V1s were launched, exactly as predicted. Ten flying bombs were sent over on this first day, four of which reached their target. On 16 June, 244 V1s were launched and by 21 June the 1,000th flying bomb had been sent over the Channel. The 2,000th was launched the following week. The V1s were now coming at a rate of about 200 a day, each carrying a 1,000 lb warhead.

The watch staff at the Tangmere Sector operations room at Bishop Otter College were working flat out as increasing numbers of V1s entered the sector. That the busiest period of coordinating and controlling aircraft before, during, and after D-Day was rapidly drawing to a close was overshadowed by the appearance of the new V1 menace. Otherwise, July saw a general winding-down in offensive operations in the Tangmere Sector as the 2TAF Wings continued to move across the Channel, and from their forward bases join battle under the control of vehicle-mounted mobile GCI radar and an operations room unit set up in France within days of the invasion. The summer proved to be unseasonably cloudy and wet, and as the 2TAF Wings that had massed in the Tangmere Sector left for France, other wings that had been assigned tented accommodation at muddy and cheerless temporary airfields pending their jumping-off across the Channel, were delighted when orders were received to move to other Tangmere Sector aerodromes. This offered the prospect of hot food and dry beds while they awaited their moves to France. Over the following weeks, the remaining squadrons kept up the usual defensive patrols, anti-Diver operations, and convoy cover sorties, weather permitting. Ramrods and Rodeos by the 2TAF squadrons still left in the sector continued with gradually decreasing frequency until the last of the squadrons had either crossed the Channel to airfields in France or were reassigned to other duties.

Before the month of June 1944 was out, some of the temporary airfields mentioned in the Order of Battle had already seen the departure of their last fighter wings. Horne, north of the Downs in Surrey, whose airfield commandant and intelligence officer had come to Tangmere on the 4th to receive their orders for D-Day, was abandoned on the 19th when it proved dangerously close to the track of the V1s falling on the southern outskirts of London. Horne's 142 Wing was brought down to Westhampnett. Bognor saw its last operations as a temporary day-fighter base on 21 June, and Chailey was left empty on the 28th when 131 Wing moved out. Bognor was pressed into service a few days later by 83 Group Support Unit as a ferry airfield and as a depot for replacement aircraft to be delivered to battlefront units across the Channel as needed; 83 GSU had moved to Bognor from Redhill, which was now under the track of the V1s, but the ALGs at Chailey and Horne would not be used again save on infrequent occasions as emergency landing grounds. At RAF Tangmere it was a much quieter month but Flying Officer R. H. Miller, who continued to keep the ORB, recorded two especially noteworthy events in July:

12.7.44

In the evening, eight Marauders landed at Tangmere from operations owing to bad weather. After considerable difficulty the crews were collected together and taken for a meal, and from there to bed at Westhampnett. Just as the job appeared to be finished, information was received that a further 100 American aircrew had landed at Selsey and that Selsey were unable to cope with them so they were coming to Tangmere by road. These crews were also supplied with food and beds and on the following morning were supplied with breakfast. The catering arrangements for the sudden influx of large numbers of aircrew are certainly excellent and the catering staff are to be congratulated.

14.7.44
Today has been a Red Letter Day in the history of Tangmere. His Majesty the King accompanied by Her Majesty the Queen visited the station. At 11.30 hours they were greeted outside the officers' mess by Group Captain W. J. Crisham [the sector commander]. Their Majesties then drove to the perimeter where numerous officers were decorated. After the investiture Their Majesties inspected RAF and WAAF personnel and then visited the dispersals. Lunch was taken in the officers' mess and the following Tangmere officers were presented to the King:-
W/Cdr Walker
W/Cdr Grice
W/Cdr Wiggins
Lt/Col Jones
S/Ldr Farbrother
The Royal party left the station at 14.00 hours.

From an operational point of view it was another very quiet day and there were no operations from Tangmere.

When the Canadians of 126 and 127 Wings left RAF Tangmere in June for deployment in France, they had been replaced by the Czechs and Norwegians of 132 and 134 Wings, and then by the Free French of 145 Wing and the Belgians and New Zealanders of 135 Wing, but fewer and fewer interceptions and intruder sorties were being made by Tangmere's squadrons. By 24 July, Flying Officer Miller was moved to write:

There is so little excitement that this diary is rapidly becoming a repetition of practically the same words day by day. Almost the only operational work carried out now is escort duty and it is days since any of the squadrons have seen enemy aircraft in the air. The only people who seem to be getting any excitement are the Mosquito squadrons on anti-Diver patrols.

Quiet though it may have been at Tangmere, there was plenty of excitement across the Channel. From Ed Prizer's diary:

July 14

Bastille Day. Weather has been so very bad we've done little flying, just stayed uncomfortably wet. Several days ago we were on readiness and had to patrol this area. The first patrol was at 4.30. It was dark and cloudy. Just by luck we missed hitting some of the balloons that are along the beach in the path of our take-off. I did six hours flying altogether that day. Another time we made a sweep inland and ran into two 109s. Chased them. One got away but Banks got the other which exploded beautifully in mid-air. Most of time we've just been sleeping or playing cards. The other night a gang of us went over to sick quarters tents where Doc Jones was on duty. He crowded all the patients into other tents till we had one clear, then we had a crap game. I dropped 3,000 Francs. Came back at one am and ate pears in Bud Rhodes's tent. The nights have been very cloudy lately. Regularly after midnight Jerry has been buzzing over to lob down bombs. They're usually not too close although a couple did land at the end of our strip. All hell breaks loose when the flak starts. One gun just behind our tent makes an ear-splitting crash and then the shells sizzle right over our tent like a great hot poker dipped in water. Day before yesterday ack-ack at the front shot down six MEs and again today they got one just off our airfield. It was a brilliant flamer. Yesterday Schwalm and I hitch-hiked into Caen. We got a jeep ride along a road through the fields where the big fighting for the city had been just three days back. The villages were terribly

shattered, not much more than rubble heaps. Those houses
not completely demolished had their walls blown out exposing
inside all the furniture and belongings of the occupants
mixed in a pile of rubbish. There were, in some, unmade
beds and tables still set -- the families must have left
everything as they heard the roar of battle getting close.
Some people had returned and you could see them trying to
establish themselves in the wall-less homes. It was hard to
believe the earnest destitution -- it seemed more like a
lark or something in the movies. Burnt-out tanks and guns
lay around the fields although much of the grain was
standing intact. The putrid odour of burnt and rotting
bodies was sickening as the wind carried it over us.
Occasionally we saw bits of a soldier in a ditch, and the
remains of a soldier hit directly by a shell. Crews were
working to gather the bodies and ship them back to
cemeteries. Signalmen along the way were busily repairing
ground lines amid the dust of the rushing traffic. At one
cross-roads we saw an ambulance picking wounded out of a
truck, just hit by a Jerry mortar shell. We saw now why
everything was going like hell down the road. The Jerries
seemed to be tossing shells here and there just for the fun
of it. Then we reached Caen. As we drove in every house
seemed to have been hit, some slightly, others completely
demolished. At a cross-roads we got out of the jeep in
which we were riding and met a soldier with a bottle of
wine. He pointed down a road and said, "It's free". We
needed no more encouragement. Around a bend we arrived at a
large winery, walked into the courtyard, and asked some
soldiers what it was all about. "The manager has just
returned and is giving us all we can carry away", they said.
Horse wagons with large barrels were drawn up below the vats
to be filled for civilian deliveries. Stacks of cases full
of bottles stood all around amid the sweet smell of
fermented grapes. Overhead shells whistled constantly, lots
going out and a few coming back. To save time the French

manager of the place took the hose from the vats and filled
a large tub to the top with frothy purple wine. We all
gathered around with bottles and dipped them in. Everyone
had filthy hands and the bottles were covered with dirt, but
it was wine. George and I drank some, then took a bottle
apiece, said "Merci" and walked into town. Some streets
were untouched by shells and bombs. But it was a sad sight
to see old people and children covered with dirt picking in
the rubble of the demolished houses, trying to recover a few
of their possessions. Inside many of the homes with walls
blown out you could see families tidying up or sitting down
to a meal. We saw the outskirts of the north section of
town which had received the bombing and was now a complete
pile of rubble. Approaching the centre of Caen we walked
down a beautiful tree-lined boulevard, littered with rubbish
and broken glass, toward the Abbey which stood in the centre
of town, untouched by a single shell. For a week during the
bombardment two thousand people had lived there, almost
starving, tending wounded and holding mass three times
daily. In front of the town hall on the main square crowds
of refugees, many with dirty bandages, waited to be
evacuated by trucks. The badly wounded were being treated
inside and several women were sobbing, probably mothers of
dead children or had husbands who had died. A jeep with
four flat tyres drove up as we were watching and parked. A
major got out with a blood-spattered soldier who had been
hit by the shrapnel of a shell that had landed beside the
jeep up the street. The soldier seemed calm as he walked
over to the first aid station. Almost all the shops in town
were closed although the streets were full of people in
spite of occasional shells coming in. An MP came up and
told us to get out of town so we walked out toward Bayeux.
We stopped at a field to wait for a ride. In the field
beyond was an artillery emplacement sending shells whistling
over us into the Jerry lines. The Huns were reciprocating.
His shells crashing a few hundred yards beyond us made me

nervous but a soldier calmly said we could trust Jerry to
maintain the correct range so there was no danger where we
were. George and I eventually despaired of getting a ride
and headed into town. We met another MP who took our wine
and got us a ride to Bretteville. Here, near the spot where
I had been shelled two weeks before, thousands of vehicles
were packed on the dusty road. The clamour of motors and
brakes was tremendous. We got a ride luckily on a jeep
straight back to camp. But even here we have a constant
reminder of the front. Just back of our camp is a graveyard
where all the bodies, buried earlier around the fields at
random, are brought after being dug up. Rows of corpses
wrapped in blankets, many dirty-brown from blood, are being
buried. Each day the long rows of small white crosses
increase. There was only a handful here when we first
arrived. Now there are thousands. It's real war, all
right. Today is Bastille Day -- lots of church bells.
150 years ago France was swathed in blood and it still
goes on.

July 22
Five days ago armies massed at the front for a big push.
All night tanks rolled along the roads, their tracks
clanking on the hard ground. The artillery shook the ground
as more and more guns were brought into action. All three
of our squadrons were wakened at four and briefed for a big
show. We had the usual breakfast, tasteless sausage, canned
bacon, hard tack, then into our planes and off. It was
beginning to get light. Our squadron was to patrol the
flank of a great stream of bombers coming in to bomb all the
area east of the Orne river running by Caen. The rising sun
flecked the scattered layers of cloud with rainbow colours
as we began our circuits at three miles height. We watched
the first bombers straggle in, barely visible in the dull
haze. Each one dropped a load of incendiaries over its
designated target. The bombs burst into flames a mile up

and lit everything from below, showering down on the
villages and setting them ablaze. Then the big waves of
Lancs and Halifaxes came in, weaving across the coast.
Above the fires black splotches appeared throughout the sky
as the air was speckled with flak. The first bomb loads hit
and each village seemed to erupt in its entirety, emitting a
mass of black smoke. Then more waves came in and poured
more bombs into the inferno that had been created by the
first ones. The Jerry flak was not ineffective. We saw
bombers explode in mid-air and dive to the ground like
flaming comets. As far as you could see now the earth below
was enveloped in the black smoke. Then the American heavies
started in, stooging along in close formation, their bare
metal surfaces reflecting the rays of a bright sun just
above the eastern horizon. They too got their share of
flak, and some went down in flames. Their escort of
Lightnings swarmed all around us but no Jerry kites showed
up. At the end of two hours we came in to land. Once down,
we could hear a continual roar, like a distant earthquake,
of the bombs, and the sharper sound of the guns of the
advancing army. It was the greatest concentrations of bombs
ever delivered in one area. And they laughed at air power.
That afternoon a pilot came in who had been shot down in the
morning behind Jerry lines. His 'chute had been riddled by
German ack-ack. On the ground he had been in the midst of
the falling bombs. He had been shelled by the British, and
then lain in a field as Jerry tanks retreated by him. When
finally in friendly hands he was shelled by the Hun. In
three instances men were blown up right beside him. Lucky
boy. For two days we did low-level patrols over the front,
hopping tree-tops and watching the guns and shells exploding
below. Then the rains came and the battle was bogged down
in mud. It is said now that Jerry casualties in that short
time were well over 100,000. Ours must've been darn high.
Night before last we had some beer brought over in a drop-
tank so we threw a squadron party. The stuff was flavored

with gasolene -- but that hindered no one. Randall had his guitar so we harmonized, off-key, drowning out the sound of bursting ack-ack overhead. For the last two days our strip has been U/S from rain so we've slept in till noon and played poker till midnight, games with wild betting and lots of debts but what other good is money?

July 31
Days have been passing by, with our armies rolling along, sometimes by yards and recently by miles. News comes in of rebellions in Germany and Rommel wounded by strafing. Perhaps the old boy was in a car our squadron attacked, perhaps one of mine. Probably never know . . .

It probably *was* Rommel's car he attacked, but he was, indeed, never to know. Edward L. Prizer died at the age of 80 in January 2003. Only in 2011 was it positively established on the basis of an examination of his log book, kept by his family, that Ed was Charley Fox's wingman on the 412 Squadron armed recce that took off from Bény-sur-Mer at 17.20 and returned at 18.35 local time on 17 July 1944. The time and place of their claim to have attacked a staff car, which appeared in both Charley's and Ed's log books and in the squadron ORB, correspond closely with the time and place of the attack on Rommel's car as now generally accepted by researchers who have looked into the matter. Although Charley knew during his lifetime of the possibility of his having strafed Rommel's car, and was interviewed about it, he had not known who his wingman was on that sortie, assuming it to have been Steve Randall, with whom he normally flew. By the time the squadron diary was consulted on this point in 2003, which showed that Randall had not flown that sortie at all but Ed Prizer had in fact been his wingman and had fired his guns at the same target with Fox, Ed had died. As far as Ed's family knew, he had never spoken of the incident and is unlikely ever to have suspected that the vehicle he attacked on that sortie with Charley Fox might have been Rommel's staff car. As a result of the attack, Rommel was badly injured and one of the Wehrmacht's most capable field commanders was removed from the Battle of Normandy at a critical moment, helping the Allies to break through the Axis defences and opening the way to their drive on Paris.

Back at Tangmere, the front line of battle moved steadily farther away as the Allied armies advanced into Normandy, and the 2TAF units still operating from the Tangmere Sector moved to France one-by-one as soon as forward airfield space became available. July and August saw the closure of Coolham, Apuldram, Funtington, and Selsey ALGs. Merston would see no further use after 8 August with the departure of 142 Wing.

Meanwhile, on 6 August, the three Free French squadrons of 145 Wing moved to Tangmere from Selsey, to be joined that day by 74 Squadron, the fourth squadron of the wing. Later in the evening, seven of 74's LF Mk IX Spitfires took off for Northolt to act as escort for a VVIP flight. The VVIP in question was not named in the ORB, but turns out to have been Prime Minister Winston Churchill, in a DC-3. First thing next morning, 74 sent six Spitfires to Thorney Island to escort another VVIP flight to France. Again, the identity of the VVIP was too secret to be mentioned, if indeed it was known to anyone at Tangmere, but was in fact General Eisenhower in B-25J 43-4030 'Sunflower', converted for his personal use with a sound-proofed and walnut-panelled cabin containing two seats and a writing-table at the aft end of the former bomb bay.

On 19 August, 145 Wing, with three Free French squadrons, to their great delight packed up and transferred across the Channel. From that day, the liberation of Paris began, with the Germans surrendering the city intact on the 25th. Only 135 Wing was left at Tangmere; it, too, left for France on 31 August. RAF Tangmere was, by now, far away from the front line of battle and became something of a backwater as the action moved even farther away. From Ed Prizer's diary:

August 22

Several days ago the army closed the pocket south of Falaise but the Germans are still retreating outside it. We've been doing hundreds of sorties and having a regular field day among the roads which are filled with flaming trucks. One day our wing accounted for 715 vehicles. But Jerry is also pulling back; our flak and our reception are sometimes rather hot. Symons was shot down and went straight in. The other squadrons have lost three this week. Jamieson was hit by a bullet in the leg and arm but it was only a graze.

Next day Jock Swan stopped some shrapnel but got back. We
have news of the Americans crossing the Seine with their
bomb line moving north as the British moves east, leaving us
an ever-decreasing pocket for strafing south of the Seine.
There are Huns up every day now in the air but they're very
elusive. Linton and Fox got two damaged not long ago --
that's the only contact our squadron has made. F/L Halcrow
who was shot down behind the lines returned with a story
about being picked up by Germans. He was given medical
treatment and spent two days drinking with the Huns. He says
conditions at the camp were terrible. Filthy and poor food.
The soldiers themselves, a motley crew with very few true
Germans, were the scruffiest bunch of men he'd ever seen.
They had little idea what was going on, carried 'Safe
Conduct' cards in their pockets for surrendering. What SS
troops he saw seemed to be brutal, arrogant youths, unliked
by the others. He talked with them in French, told them how
badly they were beaten. Some spoke English too. He lived
with them in their dug-out and had a great party, while the
Allies shelled them mercilessly. Then the Huns sent him
through the lines to arrange a surrender. The Canadian
officers were none too anxious to listen to him. They said
there were so many Jerries surrendering they didn't know
what to do with them. Halcrow didn't wait to see what was
done about it. We've had a couple of big rainstorms lately
creating slews of mud everywhere. It's equally as bad as
the dust.

September 2
The rain has been intermittent for two weeks, cutting down
our flying considerably. Poker-playing is becoming a
regular daily ritual. The old army scourge of dysentery is
making the rounds, spread by millions of flies and wasps. A
week ago we decided to break the monotony of things with a
party. All expert scroungers were organised and
preparations began. We added two more marquees to our mess

tent, built a bar and painted it a gaudy red and black,
working in indirect lighting and mirrors. Bob Hyndman
painted nude scenes around the walls of one tent. In the
end tent we constructed our ballroom, nailing together a
conglomeration of boards of all different sizes and
thicknesses and then covering the whole with coco matting.
The scheduled day was beautiful and warm. After a quick
supper we put last-minute touches on things. 100 nurses we
had invited from neighbouring hospitals arrived at eight,
the bar opened, the orchestra began to play and the party
was on. With Scotch, gin, cognac and wine at the bar, the
party soon became very lively. At 11 we had a buffet supper
that astounded everyone -- lobster, chicken, tomatoes,
salads, all beautifully prepared, and right out in this god-
forsaken wilderness. I ate a plate piled half a foot high.
Met a cute little nurse who made the evening perfect. Some
of the boys came back from Cabourg, just captured, with a
load of looted champagne and a big box of beautiful flowers
which were passed around to all the girls. Phillip was
plastered and amused us by eating a tremendous plate of
food, with salad, fish, cake, fruit, and meat all mixed at
random, with his hands. Next day we flew patrols and
prepared for moving to Evreux, a field taken a few days
before up near the Seine. On the scheduled morning we got
up early, packed everything in trucks, and sat around
waiting for the word to go. It rained, making things pretty
uncomfortable. We had to take shelter under trees. About
noon orders came that we wouldn't move that day. Much
profanity. Some of the fellows took a truck out and bought
some steaks which we cooked over an open fire, passing away
some of the time. They were delicious. Then we went down
to dispersal and set up our bed rolls in the tent there, the
only available shelter. It was some job crowding twenty-
five men and beds into one tent. Some of the fellows
established themselves in the trucks. After supper cooked
out in a field in the rain we came back and played poker in

the tent till dark. Next day some of the boys went out and
gathered mushrooms. I went with a group down to a field
near Caen where we found some corn. We picked a couple
hundred ears and brought them back. We filled tin cans with
sand and poured in gasolene, then fried the mushrooms and
boiled the corn. Used up several quarts of canned margarine.
It was a royal feast. That evening the G/C sent us down
some bottles of Scotch. We had some champagne too. These
served as refreshment for our poker game which went on by
lamplight till midnight. The betting got wild and I lost
heavily. Next morning we got prepared to go definitely,
this time to St Andre near Evreux. After dinner we took off
18 aircraft, flew over the old countryside we used to
strafe, and landed on a large cement runway at St Andre, a
real treat after the dusty strips we'd been using. There
were hundreds of aircraft on the field already, dispersed in
lines among bomb craters, made by the British raids when the
Jerries were here. Our bombs had blown the hangars to bits.
Walking around we saw amid the wreckage the remains of what
was once a wonderfully organised field. We were all
interested in pranged 109s, 110s, and 190s, our first chance
to examine enemy aircraft at first hand. Behind one of the
hangars was a great mass of bent and torn wreckage which
turned out to be the remains of two British Lancasters.
They must've crashed in mid-air during the bombing of the
field. I walked around with Smitty and Laubman, carefully
watching to avoid mines and booby traps, and looked over a
repair depot where the Germans had worked on aircraft
engines. That evening I hitch-hiked into the town of St
Andre with a bunch of fellows. We found the town almost
intact, a pleasant change from the ruins in Normandy. The
village was full of celebrating soldiers and happy
Frenchmen. A big banner said 'Welcome Liberators'. Finding
the cafes all sold out, we moved on to another village and
drank spiced wine, delicious stuff, at a small unlighted
estaminet. Returning, we got a ride on top of a water

truck. It was a beautiful clear evening, with a cool breeze
and across the grain fields a big harvest moon. The Germans
had retreated through here with almost no fighting. It was
a relief to be out in the fresh country away from the roar
of guns. Back at camp we found things in a great state of
congestion; so many squadrons came in they could not arrange
any accommodations. Our squadron trucks finally turned up
with our bed rolls which we laid on the floor of the mess
tent. Many of the others were sleeping out on the ground.
This morning I woke up to the sound of loud cursing and
looked out to see it raining heavily. Fellows were climbing
out of their soaking blankets and rushing for shelter. We
managed to get a scanty breakfast, then waited for the sky
to clear. At ten we got in our planes and took off for
Iliers, a grass field five miles away. As soon as our
trucks arrived we set up our tents in the grounds around a
large chateau that had been completely wrecked. 127 Wing
was already established here. After dinner we drew lots for
going to Paris. I was lucky, and consider this my greatest
single experience in France. Seven of us rode in a jeep,
and another bunch followed us in a Jerry Volkswagen. The
distance was about 130 miles along a very good road, lined
on both sides by tall evenly spaced trees. The amount of
traffic was tremendous, one constant line of military
vehicles of all descriptions. There were signs of light
fighting every so often but no great destruction. On the
sides of the road were thousands of burnt-out Jerry
vehicles, many that we had strafed ourselves and again a
vivid example of the potency of air power. In all the
villages townsfolk lined the roads, waving and making V-
signs at us, much different from the cool reception we
received in Normandy. Only five days ago the Germans had
been retreating through here. Just outside Paris we passed
through one village completely demolished by bombs, then we
entered Versailles. The palace and gardens were
magnificent. The Continental countryside atmosphere had

suddenly become metropolitan. There were crowds waving and
cheering and flags flying everywhere. The street became a
wide boulevard, paved with cobblestone but very smooth.
There were large modern stores, people moving along the
streets on foot and bicycle. Set in parks were the big
classical government buildings and hotels. Frenchmen were
leisurely sipping wine in the sidewalk cafes. As we came
nearer the Seine we saw occasional bombed buildings and
piles of sandbags where fighting had taken place. But
everywhere Paris seemed to be the gay city of peace-time
years, entirely different from the stodgy Victorian London
or the hurried business-like New York. And the women are
indescribable. Each seems to have found her own form of
glamour and perfected it. In spite of four years under
Germany their dress and make-up is a knock-out. They seem
to have a natural something that women of other nations
lack. Blonde or brunette they all have a sort of glowing,
mysterious charm. We arrived at the boulevard running along
the Seine, a combination of nature and man-made beauty that
surpasses anything I've ever seen. The gardens and parks
are in perfect condition, mingled with monuments, winding
roads, and great stone buildings. The water in the Seine is
calm and blue, a much smaller river than I'd expected. But
it seems to form the focal point of the surrounding
landscape, all of which harmonizes with it perfectly. The
first impression of the whole was the same as an imaginative
mind conceives classical Athens or Rome, but no doubt this
modern city greatly surpasses its predecessors. And the
sensation heightened as we drove by places that were
formerly just magical names: Eiffel tower, Champs Elysees,
Arc de Triomphe, Place de la Concorde. On some of the
streets burnt-out tanks or machine-gun-spattered cars were
still lying around. A few of the· buildings had shell holes
in the walls and quite a number were spattered with small-
arms fire. We stopped at The Scribe hotel and drank
champagne. Then we moved to a sidewalk cafe and drank white

wine as we watched the crowds going by. A drunken American
was haranguing the crowd from a jeep, much to the amusement
of everyone. The people were well-dressed and looked
extremely happy. It won't take France long to recover from
German occupation. We visited other sidewalk spots, still
scarcely able to believe we were in Paris. Then we went
into an ancient wine shop, centuries old, a small place on a
side-street, damp and dark inside with the smell of ages
floating up from the wine cellar below. They had lots of
champagne. We remained until it was pitch dark. The
Germans had destroyed the power plant so as yet Paris has
almost no night life. The party later broke up, I took a
girl to a club, then realised it was past time to get back
to the jeep. I made a rush but it was gone. So I resigned
myself to hitch-hiking. Strolled down the Seine boulevard
with a black American soldier singing and eventually got a
ride to a deserted spot fifteen miles out of the city. It
began to rain and I was getting desperate since we were
scheduled to move first thing in the morning. And then by a
miracle the boys in the Volkswagen came by. We drove back
at top speed and beat the jeep which had had a breakdown on
the way.

September 4
Yesterday morning we were up and ready to move again. I chose
to go by truck to get a good view of the countryside. We set
out to St Andre and then on to Evreux, a town badly smashed.
From here north to the Seine where we found our bridge was
blown up. We took a small road that wound around the hills
along the river bank to a pontoon bridge leading into Les
Andelys. Above this town up on a high cliff were the remains
of a large medieval castle. How impotent it would have been
against the modern army crowding the roads below. Once across
the Seine we were out of Normandy. The roads were jammed with
traffic. The one we took ran parallel to the river through
the hills. The country was very green and fertile, with many

grazing cattle. The towns were medieval, slightly reminiscent of Quebec. Everywhere people waved and threw flowers. We turned north and travelled through large grain fields. Occasional German armoured vehicles lay gutted where there had been a skirmish during the retreat. We took a back road for a while that wound among farms which might well have been back home in Moore County. At six we arrived in Poix, a town of about 10,000 which showed signs of old bombings. There was a steep hill on the other side of the city. As we climbed to the plateau beyond where our airfield lay we saw German equipment of all sorts along the roadside. They must've abandoned almost everything in their rush to get up the hill. Much of it seemed to be personal baggage. There were all sorts of uniforms and clothing, small arms, big guns, vehicles, and dead horses. Still a few bodies in the ditches. At the top we turned onto our field. It had been completely bombed, everything smashed. Only four days ago Jerry had been here. It has been put in good enough order for us to fly off already. Last night patrols around the woods were still scouring the district for stray German soldiers, left behind in the retreat. There are still lots, hopelessly dropped in the retreat. We had supper, pitched our tents, and went to bed. Today I slept till noon. So far we haven't any gasolene here for our planes so we're just sitting around waiting. We hear our soldiers are deep in Belgium and the Americans are in Luxembourg. It appears there'll either have to be an armistice or a final decisive battle soon.

For the first time since the arrival of 43 Squadron in December 1926, RAF Tangmere was now empty of resident squadrons. In a dispirited and plaintive tone unusual in normally terse and unemotional Operations Record Books, Flying Officer Miller wrote:

1 to 7 September 1944
The weather has been non-operational for the past seven days, not

that it would have made very much difference, as we have no operational aircraft here now, and there is, consequently, nothing to report.

It would appear that this diary will consist of something like the above for some time to come.

News was received of Operation Market Garden, the Arnhem airborne landings, on 17 September. Having no resident squadrons and being too far away from the battlefield to act as a staging point or forward base for other squadrons, Tangmere did not participate, and neighbouring RAF stations had only limited direct involvement. A one-off armed recce over the Netherlands, apparently chiefly for patriotic publicity purposes, was made the previous day by 322 (Dutch) Squadron flying from Deanland. Thorney Island's Mosquitoes of 138 and 140 Wings, of 2 Group, 2TAF, were still heavily involved in intruder work but owing to the aerial traffic congestion over the battle area and bad weather, the conditions were difficult and sorties had to be cancelled. While operations from RAF Tangmere had for the moment ceased, individual aircraft, flights, squadrons, and wings based elsewhere continued to visit the station on weather diversions, to re-group or re-fuel; Dakotas evacuating important civilians, military personnel, or injured troops from France put down at Tangmere; and emergency landings by lame, lost, or fuel-short bombers returning from sorties across the Channel still created occasional flurries of activity.

Active operations continued at Tangmere's satellites and other nearby aerodromes if not at RAF Tangmere itself. Ford, Shoreham, Thorney Island, Westhampnett, Deanland, and Friston were still sending up defensive patrols, and making interceptions and occasional intruder sorties. Deanland and Friston had, by chance, an extended lease on usefulness because they happened to lie under the flight path of the V1s as they crossed the English coast, and day-fighter squadrons were maintained there to intercept them until the last of the Diver launch sites targeting London were overrun by the Allied armies. While at Friston, the Merlin-engined Mustang IIIs of 316 (Polish) Squadron and the Spitfire 12s of 610 Squadron together accounted for around 100 V1s by the time 316's place was taken by 131 Squadron. At Deanland, 91 and 322 Squadrons, assigned solely to anti-Diver protection with Spitfire XIVs, between them destroyed nearly 300 Divers by the end of

August; they remained on station for another five weeks until early October, by which time it had become clear that the V1 threat was over.

Ford's night-fighter Mosquitoes of 96 and 456 Squadrons, ADGB, also played their part in countering the V1 menace. By the end of July, they had destroyed 138 V1s, and two more were knocked down by the P-61 Black Widow night fighters of the USAAF's 422nd Fighter Squadron flying from Ford. As a part of their contribution to the Allied Expeditionary Air Force, the USAAF had brought two Black Widow squadrons across the Atlantic in May. Coincidentally, the design of the P-61 owed much to the experience of the London Blitz. In late 1940, the British Purchasing Commission asked the American delegation for a high-altitude, high-speed aircraft capable of intercepting the Luftwaffe bombers attacking London. The aircraft were to patrol continuously over the capital during the night, requiring an endurance of at least eight hours. The aircraft would need to carry an early (and heavy) AI radar unit, and to mount their armament in turrets.

As it turned out, the Northrop Corporation of Hawthorne, California, was already a step ahead, working on plans for an aircraft along these lines. The British interest stimulated its further development. The project also found favour with the US Army Air Corps, which until then had not issued a formal specification for a purpose-built, radar-directed night fighter.

By the time the first prototype flew in February 1942 the RAF's need for such an aircraft had passed and none was ordered, although it was adopted by the USAAF as their standard night fighter with more than 700 eventually being built. The aeroplane had twin booms, a central gondola-type fuselage, a radome nose, and provision for a crew of three. The P-61A-5 two-seat variant sent to Britain dispensed with the rear gun turret, had four 20-mm forward-firing cannon, and was powered by two Pratt and Whitney R-2800-65 Double Wasp 18-cylinder radials of 2,250 hp each, as also used in the USAAF's Thunderbolts and Marauders. The aircraft was huge, with a 66-foot wingspan and a loaded weight of nearly 30,000 lbs, not far short of a B-25 Mitchell medium bomber at 67 ft and 33,000 lbs, as compared with an AI-equipped Mosquito at 54 ft wingspan and around 17,000 lbs loaded weight.

The P-61 was so big and heavy that it was not initially regarded as suitable by the general staff of Ninth Air Force, who believed its performance would be inferior to the de Havilland Mosquito, whose effectiveness under European conditions had been well proven by the RAF and which the 9thAF

bove: No. 412 (RCAF) Squadron at Airfield B4, [B]ény-sur-Mer, July 1944. The squadron deployed [h]ere from Tangmere on 18 June. Kneeling at the far [l]eft, front row, is Edward Prizer. Charley Fox, hat[le]ss, is kneeling fifth from the left just in front of the [lo]wer-left propeller blade. *Prizer Collection, TMAM.*
[Be]low: A week after D-Day, the enemy initiated a [fly]ing-bomb offensive aimed at London. The V1s [tr]avelled at around 350 mph, making them difficult to intercept by any but the RAF's fastest aircraft. Tempests, Mosquitoes, and Griffon-engined Spitfire XIVs proved the most effective in shooting down the V1s. Here, a Spitfire XIV of 610 Squadron on V1 interception duty is refuelled at Friston, near Beachy Head and directly under the V1s' flight path, in July 1944. The airfield was then a satellite of RAF Tangmere. *Imperial War Museum CH18184.*

Above: The Central Fighter Establishment relocated to Tangmere in January 1945. Its task was to prepare the fighter tactics for the planned invasion of the Japanese mainland, as well as to train the squadron and wing commanders who would be responsible. Group Captain 'Batchy' Atcherley, officer commanding, is in the middle wicker chair, front row; also in the picture are Kit North-Lewis, Bob Stanford Tuck, and Pete Brothers. *Museum Collection.*

Middle: Ju88R of CFE's Enemy Aircraft Flight, RAF serial PJ876. This aeroplane came to Tangmere in early 1945, and was left behind when CFE moved to West Raynham at the end of August. It was saved for preservation by the Air Historical Branch and is now displayed at the RAF Museum Hendon.

Left: Left to right: Neville Duke, Teddy Donaldson, Sir James Robb, and Bill Waterton. High Speed Flight, Tangmere, 1946. *Museum Collection.*

Above: No. 85, Tangmere's first postwar resident squadron, 1945-48. *Coombe Collection, TMAM.*

Right: The station cinema prepared for Christmas dinner, 1948. The building was formerly the Handley Page shed, about one-third of which remained after the wartime bombings. It was the last remnant of the aeroplane sheds built for the ASAEF in 1918. *Parnaby Collection, TMAM.*

Below: Officers' mess in snow, February 1947. *Coombe Collection, TMAM.*

Left: Major Robin Olds, USAF (CO of 1 Squadron), Air Vice-Marshal Stanley Vincent, and Wing Commander George Parnaby, AOC's annual inspection, 5 May 1949. *Parnaby Collection, TMAM.*

Below: Meteor NF11 at Tangmere. *Museum Collection.*

Right: On 24 April 1953, 1 Squadron was presented with its standard, the first RAF squadron to receive one. Presenting the standard is AVM Sir Charles Longcroft (the squadron's second CO, 1914) and the standard-bearer is Flying Officer Chandler. Among those present were five former 1 Squadron commanding officers: ACM Sir Philip Joubert de la Ferté KCB DSO (Western Front, 1915), Group Captain Eustace Grenfell MC DFC AFC (Tangmere, 1928-31), Air Commodore R. W. Chappell MC (Tangmere, 1933-34), AVM Theodore McEvoy OBE (Tangmere, 1936), and Wing Commander H. R. Allen DFC (Tangmere, 1946). *Cooper Collection, TMAM.*

Below: Neville Duke in Hawker Hunter WB188, in which he set a World Air Speed Record flying from Tangmere over the same course used by the High Speed Flight in 1946, at Dunsfold in 1953. This aeroplane is now displayed at the Tangmere Military Aviation Museum. *Duke Collection, TMAM.*

Above: Nos. 1 and 34 Squadron from Tangmere on operational detachment to Cyprus during the Suez Crisis, 1956. *Museum Collection.*

Left: No. 34 Squadron Hunter Mk 5, looking north through the end hangar at Tangmere, 1957. *Davis Collection, TMAM.*

Below: Inside one of Tangmere's post war T2 hangars, 1960. Two Canberras of 245 Squadron and two Varsities of 115 Squadron, Signals Command, can be seen in the picture. *Dansie Collection, TMAM.*

Above: RAF Tangmere 'At Home' Day, 1962. It was an extraordinarily busy day in the control tower, with dozens of RAF and USAF aircraft of all types visiting the station for static display or to perform flypasts and aerobatics. *Estall Collection, TMAM.*

Below: Whirlwind of 22 Squadron and 115 Squadron Varsities, 1962. The ASR detachment was the last flying unit to remain stationed on the aerodrome, until May 1964. *Estall Collection, TMAM.*

Above: **16 October 1970.** At sunset, the ceremony to mark the closure of Royal Air Force Station Tangmere approaches its conclusion. The Queen's Colour Squadron salutes while the Ensign is lowered to the tune of the Last Post played by the Central Band of the Royal Air Force and a lone Spitfire passes overhead. *Museum Collection.*

Below: Control tower, 1975. *Estall Collection, TMA.*

had planned to use in a specialised night-fighter role to cover Operation Overlord and the subsequent drive on Berlin. It was only after having been evaluated in comparative trials with Mosquitoes that the Black Widow was accepted as agile and fast enough to be deployed operationally, but there were only two squadrons of them in England and neither was ready until July. For about six weeks in July and August, the 422nd and 425th flew from Ford to gain operational experience alongside the Mosquitoes of 96 and 456 Squadrons. The 422nd transferred to France on 25 July, and the 425th on 18 August.

During August, another 57 Divers were destroyed by Ford's ADGB night-fighter squadrons, the Black Widows accounting for three of them. By September, the Pas de Calais area was in Allied hands and very few V1s now came over the Tangmere Sector. Ford sent up continuous anti-Diver patrols, weather permitting, but only one V1 was sighted and claimed destroyed by 96 Squadron on the 16th; no other significant enemy activity was reported in Ford's patrol sector that month. September saw the return to Ford of the Fighter Interception Unit (FIU), which had been moved to Wittering temporarily with the general shifting-about of 2TAF and ADGB units in preparation for Operation Overlord. While at Wittering, the FIU was instrumental in developing the tactics of V1 night interception. Jeremy Howard-Williams was there, and later wrote:

At peak strength we only numbered eight or nine crews, including the CO, the flight commander and a post called squadron leader ops (largely responsible for coordinating reports), and we were fairly well committed to the intruder programme before the arrival of the first Divers, as flying bombs were code-named before they started coming over on 13 June, 1944. It quickly became evident to the powers-that-be that there was a problem at night. Even stripped out and using 150-octane fuel, the Mosquito was hardly fast enough. By flying well above the average height of the flying bomb's approach, Mosquitoes could overtake by diving, but this caused the aircraft to exceed its flight envelope, and firing the guns at 370+ mph tended to cause the plywood laminations of the forward fuselage to start breaking up. Hundreds of squadron pilots did it, but about the only aircraft which could catch the little fellows with any ease was the Tempest. However, not only were the Tempest boys heavily committed by day, but they were not in the best of instrument flying practice, so had their work cut out in all but the clearest weather after dark. We were accordingly ordered to find out whether it would be easier to convert twin-engine night-fighter pilots to the Tempest, or Tempest pilots to night flying.

A secondary problem which manifested itself at night was estimation of range. Glare from the V1's jet pipe progressively blinded the fighter pilot's view of the missile's wings as the range was closed, so it was hard to tell how far away it was. Mosquitoes didn't have this trouble because they had AI, but the single-seaters were handicapped, and TRE [the Telecommunications Research Establishment] were asked whether they could come up with a crude but quick (above all, quick) solution in the form of an elementary radar for the Tempest. The answer was provided by the physicist Sir Thomas Merton, who devised a simple spectroscope consisting of a three-inch-square glass plate containing a refracting system incorporating a graticule. Glued to the inside of the fighter's windscreen, this produced two images of the target's single exhaust flame, which merged as the range closed to 200 yards.

Squadron Leader Daniel took Flight Lieutenants Joe Berry and 'Timber' Woods with him to form a Tempest detachment at a small grass airstrip called Newchurch on top of Beachy Head; this left me, as deputy flight commander, to continue the intruder programme with four crews from Wittering.

Joe Berry was the 'find' of these Doodlebug trials. A small, unassuming man who had earned the DFC night-fighting in North Africa, he took to the flying bomb like a duck to water. Despite losing Teddy Daniel early on to a V1 explosion in the air, and Timber Woods who flew into the ground at high speed in poor visibility (the static vent of the Tempest's pitot head was found to cause over-reading of the altimeter above 300 mph due to local airflow irregularities, and it had to be re-sited — but not before we had lost Woods and his replacement), Joe went on to score over 50 V1s shot down, while others were still struggling to break their ducks (he twice got seven in one night). Further pilots were posted in from outside FIU, and

Joe was eventually promoted and given command of 501 Squadron, where he quickly increased that unit's kill rate ten-fold, finishing with a personal score of 60½ (he resolutely refused to accept the half, which was a shared kill with the AA, because he said that they never touched it and that it only went down when he attacked it after the AA had stopped firing. "If they're that hard up for victories, let 'em have the whole thing"). You'll find Joe in the record books as having made his score with 501 Squadron – but he got more than 50 of them with FIU.

The ramp-launched Diver campaign stuttered to a halt as the Allied armies overran the launching sites, so Joe was turned into a day-fighter pilot at the head of his squadron. In October 1944, while leading a section on a dawn sweep over Holland, he was hit by flak, rolled onto his back, called up on the RT and calmly announced, "Carry on chaps, I've had it", before diving straight into the ground. A waste of a first-class night-fighter pilot, whom we could have very much used back at FIU (though we couldn't have kept his acting rank for him, we would probably have saved his life). Chris Hartley had tried his best to get him proper recognition – he deserved a DSO for leading our detachment in the face of relatively heavy casualties, as he pioneered the night defence against V1s. By the time each gong recommendation reached the powers-that-be, Joe had added another ten or a dozen victories to his total, so that I sometimes wonder whether he didn't score too quickly – the tendency being to hold back an award until things settled down. Besides which, Chris Hartley was not able to push hard enough, because he was in hospital, having baled out after colliding with a Mosquito as they both dived on the same V1 on a dark night. Squadron Leader Joe Berry received a bar to his DFC after he had passed 50 destroyed, and a second bar later which was not gazetted until after he had died – in fact, I believe it was after the war; certainly most of FIU never even knew that he had got it.

Amazingly, 277 Squadron's semi-obsolescent Spitfire Mk Vs managed to shoot down the odd V1 in addition to their ASR-spotting duties, despite not having enough speed to overhaul a Diver in straight and level flight. From

195

March, 277 Squadron had been stationed at Shoreham when it became a satellite of RAF Tangmere to serve as an air-sea rescue base, but the establishment of forward airfields in France within a week of D-Day had made it possible for pilots to make emergency landings on both sides of the Channel, when earlier they might well have been forced to bale out over the sea. RAF HSLs, Royal Navy rescue launches, and US Navy and US Coast Guard vessels had been patrolling sectors off the invasion beaches and in mid-Channel; aircrew baling out were often more quickly reached by surface vessels than by scrambling a Walrus or Sea Otter. By September most of the excitement was over, and in October the ASR base at Shoreham was closed down and the squadron moved to Hawkinge.

At Westhampnett, RAF Tangmere's main satellite airfield, a succession of squadrons came and went, often staying only brief periods. Notable among them were 41 Squadron with Spitfire XIVs and 610 with Spitfire XIIs, brought in to cover Portsmouth and Southampton when they came under V1 attack. Both squadrons were old friends, having been stationed at Tangmere, Merston, or Westhampnett on more than one occasion previously, including stints with the Bader wing in the summer of 1941. Other squadrons followed them as the V1 threat declined, resuming routine escort work until the end of September, when operations from Westhampnett came to an end. For a month or so, the airfield was reduced to care and maintenance status but came to life again on 4 November when 83 Group Support Unit moved in from Bognor ALG. Bognor, in turn, was now vacated by the RAF, the next-to-last ALG in Sussex to have survived; Deanland would carry on for another month or so on V1 protection duties. 83 GSU would remain at Westhampnett into February 1945, ferrying Spitfires and Mustangs to and from 2TAF airfields across the Channel.

Air Defence Great Britain (ADGB) was renamed Fighter Command once again in October 1944. Tangmere had by now been without a resident squadron of any kind since the end of August, a circumstance which at last seemed to come to the notice of the powers-that-be, perhaps through the influence of Group Captain W. J. 'Paddy' Crisham, posted to an important job at 11 Group on 19 September, having been Tangmere Sector commander through the testing days of Operation Overlord. At any rate, soon after, the station ORB noted:

4.10.44

Early in the month rumours started going round the station to the effect that 26 Squadron would be coming to the station to be re-equipped with Mustangs, and this became more than a rumour on 7 October when we were advised that 6026 [Servicing] Echelon would be coming in within the next few days. Actually they arrived on 9 October when the marching-in parade was held. The echelon are being accommodated on No. 2 site.

The squadron arrived the same day, and once again the officers' mess was crowded, and it seems quite like old times, except that the squadron is not, of course, operational.

At this moment the only 2TAF fighting unit remaining in the Tangmere Sector was Mosquito-equipped 140 Wing, 2 Group, based at Thorney Island. On the last day of October, two dozen Mosquitoes, escorted by eight Mustangs and led by Group Captain P. G. Wykeham-Barnes DSO DFC, took off to bomb the Gestapo's headquarters at Aarhus, Denmark, in a daring daylight raid. The weather cleared just in time, and a precision attack was made. One Mosquito was lost to flak, one hit the ground, two were struck by a bomb blast, and two brought down by bird strikes. It was one of the longest flights made by the wing, covering 1,235 miles and taking five-and-a-half hours. Night-intruder sorties in support of the Ardennes offensive continued, weather permitting, and two V1s were shot down over the following weeks.

Landings by Dakotas and other transport aircraft with passengers from the Continent continued; this was now an almost-daily occurrence and Tangmere was assuming some of the functions of a civil airport. Although no one could have known it at the time, this would continue until the end of the war and beyond. Because of its benign climate and geographical position, there were occasions when Tangmere was one of only a couple of airfields in the United Kingdom still open that were capable of accepting four-engined transports. Transit and final-destination passengers had to be fed, found overnight accommodation if needed, and arrangements made for their onward journeys including the issue of railway warrants and ration cards or their handing-over to the police, hospitals, or other military or civil authorities. On the 12th, 15 fully-loaded Dakotas landed and on the 21st a large number of wounded American servicemen were brought to Tangmere from hospitals in the locality and airlifted to Ramsbury. The number of passengers alighting from flights from and taking off for the Continent was growing and causing concern to the Intelligence Section on the station, responsible for clearing them, who were at times unable to cope. People arriving without passports or indeed any identity documents at all had to be interrogated individually, causing long delays. Officials of HM Customs and Excise and the Immigration Service from Newhaven visited the station to assess the arrangements and advise the Intelligence Section and Pay and Accounts staff on how best to deal with floods of passengers who tended to arrive all at once. But amid this, there was more welcome news, too:

> 1.11.44
> It now appears certain that the Central Fighter Establishment will be coming to Tangmere within the next eight to ten weeks but everything is still very much in the air.

By the end of the month, personnel of the Central Fighter Establishment (CFE) were, indeed, beginning to arrive. A week later, on the afternoon of 6 December, Air Commodore R. L. R. 'Batchy' Atcherley OBE AFC, commandant of the Fighter Leaders' School and commandant-designate of CFE who would be taking over on its move to Tangmere, visited to confer with the station's commanding officer, Group Captain Duncan Somerville, and to discuss what facilities would be needed.

Early in the new year, the station began once more to fill up with people and aeroplanes. The Central Fighter Establishment completed its move from Wittering to Tangmere in January. At the same time, it was considerably expanded as a number of formerly dispersed units were moved to Tangmere and absorbed into CFE's command structure. On the 15th RAF Ford was formally transferred to CFE as a satellite station to accommodate its Night Wing, the Day Wing being located at Tangmere itself.

The Central Fighter Establishment was the RAF's academy of air fighting, undertaking comparative trials of fighter aircraft performance under service conditions, the testing and delivery of fighter-borne weapons, the practical application of innovations in fighter instrumentation and guidance, and in fighter tactics and operations. Many famous pilots who had made their names in the war were posted to the unit sooner or later during its time at

Tangmere: Frank Carey became head of the tactics branch; Bob Stanford Tuck, head of combat; Robin Johnston, dive-bombing; and Kit North-Lewis, close support. Frank Carey, then a group captain, later wrote in his autobiography of his time at CFE:

> It had an extremely high-powered staff. Regular courses were run for experienced fliers from various countries. It meant world tours, and discussing with my small team of experts the events of the European war. Lessons had to be learnt. In Indonesia, a small war was still rumbling on between the RAF, the Indonesians and the Dutch, many elements of which were far from accepting that the big war was over.
>
> It was a most attractive post and I enjoyed every minute of it and could have stayed there forever.

Important parts of CFE were the Fighter Leaders' Schools. There were two: a Day Fighter Leaders' School (DFLS), and a Night Fighter Leaders' School (NFLS), whose purpose was to ensure that those who passed out successfully were 'fitted in every way' to command a squadron or wing. The students of DFLS were put through intensive seven-week courses in groups of 36. The students were divided in three flights; on No. 2 Day Fighters Course, which started in May, two flights flew Spitfires and one flew Typhoons. The syllabus included tactical control of formations engaged in patrolling, escorting, strafing, air-to-air firing, dive-bombing, and rocketry attacks, and a programme of 28 tactical exercises. The student was expected:

> . . . to be capable of a high degree of accuracy in the use of the appropriate weapon and in manoeuvre bring it successfully to combat. He must, also, know his aircraft so well that he can exploit its maximum performance yet appreciate exactly those limitations which prevent a formation achieving single aircraft flexibility. Equally, he must appreciate his formation's maximum capability so that only the minimum concession in pace, climb and manoeuvre is made to maintain cohesion.
>
> — FLS Syllabus, No. 2 Course, Tangmere, 6.5.45-27.6.45

All students had two flying periods a day, weather permitting, from 10.00 to

12.00 and 14.30 to 16.00 with briefings and de-briefings before and after each flying period. At 17.30 there was a daily lecture session, which in addition to internal lectures on weapons and tactics included external talks given by experts (most of whom were attached to CFE, or were visitors to it) on topics such as airborne operations, local maintenance and engine handling, current military operations, interrogation of PoWs, meteorology, principles of briefing, pilot navigation, tactical formations, night flying for day fighters, squadron administration in the field, deck landings, physiological aspects of flying, photographic interpretation, and the work of the FIU and the development of radar, among many other topics of both specialised and general interest. In June, Group Captain Douglas Bader arrived back at Tangmere to command DFLS. However, Bader's experience was mostly of air-to-air combat up to the point of his capture and imprisonment by the Germans in August 1941; he had no experience of the kinds of tactical ground support conducted by fighters from 1943 onwards. It was soon realised that his knowledge of fighter tactics was woefully out-of-date and he was quickly posted away to command the North Weald Sector.

While at Tangmere, CFE not only encompassed the Fighter Leaders' Schools but also absorbed the Fighter Interception Unit, re-named the Fighter Interception Development Unit (FIDU) and shortly thereafter re-named again as the Fighter Interception Development Squadron (FIDS), still based at Ford. Jeremy Howard-Williams remembers:

Chris Hartley was promoted to group captain in charge of the Night Wing, which comprised FIDS (now led by Bill Maguire, who had been promoted from being sqn ldr ops, where I replaced him, Bill was sadly killed while slow rolling a Mosquito low down, in order to test a supposedly untopplable aircraft attitude indicator, after he and I had experimented with landing at Tangmere in a concentration of tear gas, to see whether our standard oxygen mask gave adequate protection should the enemy resort to using gas), the Navigator Leaders' School, and the Fighter Experimental Flight. The second of these three trained what were originally called observers, then radio operators, and finally navigators-radio. The third [the Fighter Experimental Flight] was a newly-formed unit, which flew Mosquitoes Mk VI, mostly on daylight Rangers, operating far and wide over enemy territory, usually in pairs.

A couple of their sorties deserve highlighting.

On 16 February 1945, Roy Compton and 'Tiny' Panter flew in daylight to Bad Aibling (south of Munich) where they beat up an airfield before returning via Landau (west of Stuttgart). Between them they destroyed six aircraft, probably destroyed another two and damaged a ninth. Tiny Panter was shot down over Landau, with his navigator so badly wounded that Tiny (a big man, as may be imagined from his nickname) had to clip on his parachute for him and push him out of the door while holding onto his rip cord (all this while at low level in a disabled Mosquito, never the best of aircraft to escape from); he fractured his ankle doing this, as his leg thrashed in the slipstream against the fuselage. Tiny was later able to watch, from his prison cell, the funerals of Me109 pilots he had helped to shoot down, and he eventually figured on the front cover of *Picture Post* magazine, hobbling on crutches in his plaster cast to greet the liberating Americans. Sadly his navigator did not survive.

I have tended to concentrate on the more glamorous side of our affairs. No mention has been made, for instance, of routine development of radar beacons and homing equipment for night fighters (Lucero and Rebecca), or of AI Mk VI (pilot-operated with windscreen projection in a Typhoon), of AI Mk IX (centrimetric with lock-follow, windscreen projection and so-called blind-firing), of windscreen projection itself (now known as 'head-up display', and then incorporating various combinations of artificial horizon, AI echo, air speed, and gyro compass indications), of early flights with what we then called GCF (ground controlled flying) and which eventually became better known as GCA (ground controlled approach), of night flying trials on such aircraft as the Westland Welkin (too slow and not high enough), Me410 (more like a Beaufighter than a Mosquito), the P-61 Black Widow (a cow), the Mustang (a delight; in July 1944 our aircraft was borrowed by Flight Lieutenant 'Togs' Mellersh – later air vice-marshal – one of our pilots who had gone on to 96 Squadron, where he used it to help notch up his score of 40 V1s destroyed at night), or the Meteor (it lacked both acceleration and deceleration). There were other trials on the naval aircraft and, still obeying the C-in-C's original instructions, there were always two of our crews on the station's defensive readiness state while we were at Ford. Life was certainly crowded and interesting.

The Central Fighter Establishment additionally included other units: the Air Fighting Development Squadron (AFDS), and the Fighter Support Development Squadron (FSDS), commanded by wing commanders; and the Tactics Branch under a group captain, broken down into Fighter-Bombers, Fighter Tactics, Rocket Projectile, and Army Support; each also under a wing commander. The purpose of these units was not only to evaluate new aircraft, armament and equipment under service conditions, but also to visit front-line squadrons to keep them up to date on fighter tactics.

On its move to Tangmere in January, CFE absorbed 787 Squadron, Fleet Air Arm, which thereupon became the Air Support Development Section of the Naval Air Fighting Development Unit (NAFDU). The unit trialled and demonstrated a number of types of ship-borne naval fighters and fighter-bombers, both British and American, and during its time at Tangmere flew Seafires, Barracudas, Avengers, Wildcats, Hellcats, Fireflies, Corsairs and, briefly, a Grumman Tigercat. Until March, a 'touring' flight was maintained in Northern England, Scotland and Northern Ireland; Rebecca radar trials were carried out at Odiham by a detachment of three Hellcats from March to June; and from April a detachment of five Fireflies was maintained at Ford for trials of AI Mk XV radar with horizontal scanning (code-named ASH in the Royal Navy). From June, a detachment would begin to prepare to relocate to the Pacific Theatre, but in the event the war in the Far East came to an end before they did so.

Attached to CFE during its time at Tangmere was perhaps the most interesting unit of all: the Enemy Aircraft Flight. No. 1426 (Enemy Aircraft) Flight was formed at Duxford in November 1941 to demonstrate ex-Luftwaffe aircraft at various places round the country to familiarise Allied personnel with their recognition features, performance, and capabilities. At first these visits were restricted to RAF and USAAF airfields; later they were extended to ground-defence organisations, such as anti-aircraft and Observer Corps units. Accurate identification of aircraft was vital in the earlier stages of the war before reliable IFF units in aircraft, GCI coverage, and radar control of AA guns had developed very far, if at all. The flight was initially staffed by RAF pilots who had previously been test pilots with maintenance units, and to an extent they still were, since few spare parts for these aircraft were available and consequently they suffered more than their share of mechanical and structural problems. Their pilots became experts in dealing with the unforeseen in the air and if at all possible getting these aeroplanes back on the ground in one piece. No. 1426 (Enemy Aircraft) Flight was taken over by CFE after its move to Tangmere, and the following eleven aircraft, now assigned RAF serials or Air Ministry numbers and wearing roundels, arrived on the station in March and April:

AX772 Messerschmitt Me110C
EE205 Junkers Ju88A
NF754 Focke Wulf Fw190A
NF755 Focke Wulf Fw190A
NF756 Henschel Hs129B
NN644 Messerschmitt Me109B
PJ876 Junkers Ju88R
PN999 Focke Wulf Fw190A
RN228 Messerschmitt Me109G
TS472 Junkers Ju88S
VD364 Messerschmitt Me109G

And, in addition, a dozen more were eventually received at Tangmere from other sources:

TF209 Messerschmitt 210A
TP190 Junkers Ju88G
VD358 Messerschmitt Me109G
VF204 Fiat G55 Centauro
VK888 Junkers Ju88G
AM 1 Junkers Ju88G
AM 2 Junkers Ju88G
AM 14 Junkers Ju88G
AM 15 Messerschmitt Me109G
AM 16 Junkers Ju88G
AM 32 Junkers Ju88G
AM 43 Heinkel He219A

AM 44 Heinkel He219A
AM 46 Siebel Si204D
AM 50 Messerschmitt Me262B
AM 86 Messerschmitt Me110G

Those that were safe for novices to fly were in great demand by CFE, FLS, and Ford's FIDS pilots who wanted to take them up for 'type experience' and add them to their log books. According to the station ORB, during April and May one or another of them was being flown almost every day when the weather was fine. AX772, an Me110C-5, was flown at Tangmere in demonstration mock combat against a Mosquito FB V1 on 3 May. On 17 May, two pilots were giving a demonstration of an Fw190 and an Me109 when the 109 made a hard landing on the concrete runway that wrecked the aeroplane; the pilot was unhurt. In July, Flying Officer Hodgen of FIDS, making his first solo flight in AM 16, a Ju88G, was unable to lower the undercarriage, was without RT, and made a successful belly landing on the grass alongside the runway. In September 1945, when CFE moved to its post-war base at West Raynham, most of the enemy aircraft were left behind at Tangmere or Ford, some in a fairly sorry state with blown cylinder heads or unserviceable hydraulics. In March and April 1946, those remaining were surveyed by the Air Historical Branch for possible preservation. Some flown at Tangmere have survived as museum exhibits, such as the Me109G-2 and the Ju88R-1 at the RAF Museum Hendon.

In April, the first Allied prisoners-of-war and internees to be repatriated by airlift began to arrive at Ford. Two Dakotas carrying 36 PoWs arrived on the 17th, three Stirlings carrying 70 arrived the next day, and on the 20th two Dakotas with 39 landed. Seven Stirlings with 192 arrived on the 21st, and the next day five Stirlings and four Dakotas brought in 241. More PoWs or wounded personnel had landed at Ford by the end of the month, bringing the total to 647 souls. An appendix to the Ford ORB for April explains:

On 8 April, 1945, F/L Jones, from Movements RTO Branch, arrived to take up his duties and his experience has been of considerable assistance in arranging the despatch of prisoners-of-war to their reception centres.

On the following day the first batch of prisoners-of-war arrived, consisting of five officers and twelve other ranks of various services. This was the first time the scheme operated, and the small quantity received enabled us to see various points in the organisation that could be improved upon. In the light of this experience a general directive on the whole scheme was prepared by the Senior Administrative Officer and issued to all concerned. By then sufficient staff had arrived to cope with larger numbers and the organisation has stood up well to the test and is now ready to deal with the numbers expected to arrive in the near future.

The commandant of the West Sussex Red Cross, Miss Blount, has given valuable help in organising voluntary assistance, as also has Lady Gregory with the Women's Voluntary Service. The Red Cross provided lady helpers throughout the day in serving the meals and free gifts of cigarettes and sweets etc., whilst the WVS are providing helpers for preparing and serving the meals. A continuous shift of voluntary helpers is kept up from 09.00 hours to 18.00 hours daily, and arrangements have been made to extend the voluntary help beyond this period as and when required. In the meantime, after 18.00 hours, a skeleton of the complete organisation of serving personnel is kept going on a 24-hour basis. This has proved essential, as unexpected aircraft containing both wounded and repatriated prisoners-of-war have arrived late at night and in the early hours of the morning.

Ford's station staff and volunteers coped magnificently in receiving and attending to these precious passengers, many of whom had come straight from prison camps and had not had the chance to build up their strength; many were sick and frail. As a result of this experience at Ford, and at receiving stations elsewhere (of which Odiham was one), these mercy flights were reduced for the time being in order to allow ex-PoWs weakened by the conditions of their captivity to receive medical attention and become better able to travel by air.

At the beginning of May, Ed Prizer, now stationed at a transit camp in Warrington having completed his overseas tour of duty and awaiting his repatriation to Canada and eventual release from the RCAF, wrote in his diary:

May 5

Still hanging around. Have had one interview here. I've
taken the train into Manchester several nights to see plays.
During the day I've spent a lot of time in the camp library,
reading books. At night I prepare for sleep by walking
around some of the country roads. The situation in Germany
seems to be crumbling like a house of cards, and these cold,
cloudy commonplace days here have been witness to one of the
most momentous periods in history. Yesterday the Italian
front collapsed, today northern Germany, Holland and
Denmark. Tomorrow we expect it to be Norway and probably
the southern redoubt shortly afterwards. Tonight I wandered
down to a local pub in the village and joined the folks in
an evening of singing. V-day to them was a question of what
are we going to do to celebrate? And I wonder if it's
anything more to me. How much we live in the immediate
present, confined to our locality and condition, and
observing everything completely subjectively. Probably the
pub-keeper is trying to forecast V-day in an effort to get
an extra beer supply in at the right time. There's
certainly none of the romance of history in day-to-day
existence, but what a shock to the future generations if
they only knew the simple selfish sentiments of most of us
on the eve of the climax of a six-year struggle that has
rocked the world.

And, from the Tangmere ORB:

8.5.45

This is the news that the world has been waiting to hear. Today is
officially declared as 'VICTORY IN EUROPE DAY' and in accordance
with the policy adopted throughout the country a stand-down of 48
hours has been declared. The station administration staff have worked
out a programme of sport and general jollification for today and
tomorrow. A highly successful dance was held in the station cinema
which was well attended by all ranks.

On the 10th, the nation and the RAF went back to work. From the Ford ORB:

10.5.45
Home based a/c carried out local flying. Visitors: 58 a/c including 44 Lancasters & two Hudsons, carrying 1,079 Ps. of W.

11.5.45
Home based a/c carried out local flying. Visitors: 110 including 78 Lancasters, 14 Fortresses & one Dakota carrying 2,329 ex- Ps. of W.

12.5.45
Home based a/c carried out local flying. Visitors: 66 including 22 Lancasters, three Hudsons, 25 Fortresses, carrying Ps. of W. Afternoon:- 17 Fortresses carrying Ps. of W, last one landed at 04.42 hrs. Total number of prisoners during day 1,606.

13.5.45
Home based a/c carried out local flying. Visitors: 77 including 42 Lancasters, 22 Fortresses, carrying 1,628 ex-P.O.W.

14.5.45
Home based a/c carried out local flying. Visitors: 115 a/c including 71 Lancasters, 21 Dakotas, 12 Fortresses, carrying 2,631 Ps. of W. Three Lancasters and seven Dakotas remained overnight, 44 aircrew accommodated.

Tangmere also received the former internees and PoWs. The first mercy flights, all Lancasters, arrived on the evening of the 10th. Ninety-five Lancasters arrived during the afternoon of the 11th, and more on the 12th, 13th, and 14th, necessitating the grounding of all other aircraft on the aerodrome and the cancellation of the Fighter Leaders' Schools' afternoon flying sessions and late-afternoon lectures, releasing the students to join the other staff of the station and the voluntary services to assist with receiving the ex-PoWs and helping them on their way to their various reception centres for repatriation. At Ford, the rate at which these mercy flights arrived declined sharply after the 14th, but continued at reduced levels until the end of the month; at Tangmere no more were reported in the ORB after the 14th. Neither the number of aircraft nor passengers arriving at Tangmere was recorded in the ORB except for the second day, when 95 Lancasters arrived. Each Lancaster had a capacity of 25 passengers, making a total of up to 2,375 people received on that day alone. While it is certain that several thousand ex-PoWs touched down at Tangmere, probably the exact number will never be known; it could well have been anything between 5,000 and 10,000. At Ford a careful day-by-day tally was kept. By the end of May, exactly 11,700 prisoners-of-war and internees had landed there, a huge humanitarian effort and an extraordinary feat of organisation for a station of its modest size and establishment. Hundreds of volunteers both military and civilian had unstintingly given their help to speed these men home.

List and Summary of Repatriated Prisoners-of-War Received at Ford Airfield in the Month of May 1945 (as given in Ford ORB)

Unit	Officers	Other Ranks	Total
British Army	52	6,610	6,662
Canadian Army	2	146	148
Australian Army	1	318	319
South African Army (white)	35	501	536
South African Army (non-white)	–	72	72
Indian Army	–	1,264	1,264
New Zealand Army	1	352	353
United States Army	7	18	25
Polish Army	4	21	25
Norwegian Army	–	3	3
Palestinian Army	–	66	66
Cypriot Army	–	86	86
Maltese Army	–	1	1
Mauritian Army	–	1	1
Belgian Army	–	1	1
Royal Navy	18	66	84
Royal Marines	1	60	61
Fleet Air Arm	4	1	5

Unit	Officers	Other Ranks	Total
Greek Navy	–	13	13
Greek Army	–	5	5
Dutch Fleet Air Arm	4	1	5
Merchant Navy	6	290	296
Chinese Merchant Navy	–	18	18
Dutch Air Force	–	1	1
Royal Air Force	460	586	1,046
United States Air Force	5	7	12
New Zealand Air Force	31	14	46
Australian Air Force	79	33	112
Canadian Air Force	261	105	366
South African Air Force	15	2	17
Rhodesian Air Force	5	5	11
Norwegian Air Force	6	–	6
Polish Air Force	6	2	8
Czech Air Force	6	–	6
Czech Army	–	1	1
French Air Force	4	11	15
Belgian Air Force	1	–	1
Totals	**1,017**	**10,683**	**11,700**

The war in Europe had ended, but in the Far East it was still in progress. At this moment, few people knew about the Manhattan Project; even so, it was far from certain that there would be a Japanese surrender without another D-Day and a costly, full-scale Allied invasion of the Home Islands. The Air Ministry was already preparing to transfer a 'Tiger Force' of around 30 of Bomber Command's heavy-bomber squadrons to Okinawa to augment the USAAF's Twentieth Air Force then flying B-29 Superfortresses from the Marianas. The South East Asia Air Command and the Air Arm of the British Pacific Fleet were still engaged in an air war and undoubtedly would be involved in the Allied air support of an invasion if there was to be one; hence CFE's work on aircraft evaluation, weaponry, and tactics continued to be carried out under the exigencies of war. Many of its findings and recommendations were directly applicable to air warfare as it was still being planned and fought.

On 6 June, CFE's Tactics Branch held a half-day general meeting at Tangmere to which external speakers and participants were invited, including Air Marshal Sir Roderick Hill, Air Marshal Sir James Robb, and the chief designers and test pilots for Rolls-Royce, Bristol, de Havilland, Supermarine, and Hawker's. The aim of the meeting was to inform the audience of the situation in the Far East, and how it differed from the war just fought in Europe as far as the design and deployment of day fighters were concerned. It consisted of briefing sessions, static displays, and aerial demonstrations. Nine briefings were scheduled: all were concerned with different aspects of the tactical air war in the Far East, and were given by external speakers who were serving Fleet Air Arm, army, and RAF officers with first-hand experience.

Immediately following the briefings, a flying programme was scheduled with a running commentary given over the station's tannoy system. The first was a comparative display of a Meteor III versus a Tempest V. According to the programme, both were to fly full-throttle at maximum speed over the station and climb to 8,000 ft in formation, come down again and do a zoom climb opening up to full throttle from pull-out. The Meteor was then to break away and fly over the aerodrome at 2,000 ft to be bounced by the Tempest, then the roles were reversed with the Meteor bouncing the Tempest. This display was scheduled to be followed by solo displays by a Fury, a Spiteful, and a Vampire.

Six static displays were listed on the programme: guns, ammunition, rocket projectile equipment, sights, cameras, and a static presentation of aircraft displaying a variety of stores and armament. The following plan of the aircraft available for inspection was included in the programme notes handed to the participants; no further detail such as serial numbers was given and it is not certain that all of them actually arrived on the station in time to be put on show:

Front Row	M.B.5	Vampire	Meteor III	Fury	Spiteful (if available)
Second Row	Hornet (if available)	Spitfire 21 with contra-rotating propellers	Me109	Fw190	Tempest II

Third Row	Tempest V with British Mark VIII zero rails	Spitfire XVI with British Mark VIII zero rails	P.47 with American zero rails	Tempest V with Mk VIIIA installation	Mustang III with Mk V installation
Fourth Row	Mustang VI with 70-gallon fuselage tank + 2 x 62½-gallon drop tank	Spitfire XVI with 75-gallon fuselage tank + 50-gallon drop tank	Tempest II with A.I.B.R. and 1 x 45-gallon tank + 1 x 1,000 lb. bomb	Mustang IV with American zero rails and bomb racks	Tempest V with 60 mm Motley projector
Fifth Row	Barracuda with Cuda floats	Fiesler Storch	Gadfly I	Miles 38	Miles Aerovan
Sixth Row	Corsair	Firefly	Hellcat	Seafire XV	Avenger

A note given on this plan stated that an Arado 234 would be included in the display, and it was hoped that a Messerschmitt 262 would arrive from Germany in time to be included. The aircraft on display ranged from army co-operation or communications aircraft such as the Miles Messenger or the Storch, to the latest single seaters such as the highly regarded but unique Martin-Baker MB5 experimental prototype. Powered by a Griffon 83 engine producing 2,340 hp driving two three-bladed contra-rotating propellers, the MB5 was said to be capable of a near-record-breaking (for a piston-engined aircraft) 460 mph – the world record then stood at 469.22 mph – in level flight. There was also a Meteor III on display. Other jets, Meteors and at least one Vampire, were present on the station as well as an array of night fighters. Some of the aircraft on display had been brought in especially for the occasion but many, including the Meteors, were already at Tangmere being regularly flown on development and evaluation trials by CFE's pilots.

Toward the end of June and into July, the ORB mentions four important Luftwaffe prisoners as having been brought to Tangmere to be interrogated by the Tactics Branch: Hans-Ulrich Rudel, who is reputed to have flown 2,530 combat sorties, mostly in Ju87s and Fw190s, and was the Luftwaffe's most highly-decorated pilot. Rudel is reported to have been 'especially talkative' about ground-attack tactics. Another was Günther Rall, who survived the war as the third-highest-scoring fighter ace of all time, credited with 275 victories. Rall re-joined the Luftwaffe as a major in January 1956, after its reactivation the previous July. He underwent refresher training, first in Germany, and later at Luke Air Force Base, Arizona, where he trained on the Republic F-84 Thunderjet; he served a period as inspector-general of the post-war Luftwaffe and retired as a Generalleutnant in October 1975. The other Luftwaffe prisoners to be interrogated at Tangmere were Generalmajor Hubertus Hitschhold and Gerhard Lindner, a civilian who had been for a time Messerschmitt's assistant chief test pilot.

On 9 July, some unwelcome news arrived less than a week before the No. 3 courses of the Fighter Leaders' Schools were due to begin, too late to postpone or cancel them, since the students had received their movement orders and some were already on their way from bases in Germany, the Far East, and elsewhere. A hectic round of planning meetings with departmental heads followed at station headquarters, whose result was released to everyone on the 13th. From the ORB:

13.7.45
It is announced that the Admiralty is to take over Ford Station with effect from 1 August. Since this is an undesirable date from the CFE point of view, all units of the establishment at present at Ford will evacuate the aerodrome within the next three days. To cope with the increase in personnel at Tangmere, NAFDU and the Air Firing Flight are moving to Westhampnett. The Night Fighter Leaders' School is moving to the dispersal vacated by one of these units and the Fighter Interception Development Squadron will move into the dispersal vacated by the other. The Fighter Experimental Flight has been disbanded and its officers absorbed into the NFLS and the FIDS. The maintenance and administration of all incoming units will be quartered at Westhampnett and all flying will be done from Tangmere. The mess at Shopwyke House has been re-opened to cope with this mighty influx.

On 26 July, the United States, Britain, and China released the Potsdam

Declaration outlining the terms for Japan's unconditional surrender. There was no Japanese response. A week later, the first atom bomb was dropped on Hiroshima. A month later, on 2 September, the Imperial Japanese government signed the formal instrument of surrender aboard the USS *Missouri*. The war in the Far East was over. There would be no invasion of the Japanese Home Islands, and the urgency of CFE's work in helping to develop the equipment and air-support tactics for such a contingency came to an unexpectedly sudden halt. At the end of August, the No. 3 courses of the Fighter Leaders' Schools finished. There would not be any further intakes of FLS students at Tangmere. During September the core units of CFE packed up and by the end of the month had left, a reduced peace-time establishment taking up residence at West Raynham.

At Ford, the move to Tangmere was started on 13 July and was largely completed by the 16th so as not to interfere with the start of the No. 3 FLS courses. A rear party was left at Ford with a nucleus of flying control, signals, and messing staff pending the hand-over to the Admiralty on 1 August. Left behind were at least three unserviceable aircraft of CFE's Enemy Aircraft Flight, the Me262, AM 16, and AM 43. Squadron Leader A. B. Carter, the station's senior administrative officer, appended the following valediction to the last page of RAF Ford's ORB:

BRIEF OUTLINE OF THE HISTORY OF THE STATION
FROM 1.10.40 – 31.7.45

In October 1940, the Royal Air Force took over Ford airfield from the Royal Navy, then operating Naval Observer and Photographic Schools. The Observer School did not remain, but the Royal Navy Photographic School, with the exception of a short period before D-Day, continued to operate from Ford airfield. At this time the airfield had no runways, but was operating one squadron of Bostons as intruders.

Wing Commander G. C. Maxwell MC DFC AFC took command of the station on 2 June 1941 and continued in this until May 1945. 11 Group decided to enlarge the airfield and construct runways. The work was commenced in October 1941 and completed on 22 May 1942. From August 1942, two squadrons of Bostons were operating, along with the Fighter Interception Unit. The Boston squadrons later converted to Beaufighters and were used for night-fighter defence. It was during this month that the first direct attack by enemy aircraft was experienced on the airfield (high explosives and machine gunning). During the Dieppe Raid, which also took place in the month of August, Ford airfield was used for Boston aircraft which carried out bombing movements in support of the raiding forces.

S/Ldr A. B. Carter took over duties of senior administrative officer on 19 November 1942, and remained till the station was closed on 1 August 1945. March/April 1943 saw the two Beaufighter squadrons replaced by two Mosquito squadrons, bringing the total of home-based units to four – two night-fighter squadrons, one intruder squadron, and the Fighter Interception Unit. Day-fighter squadrons were using Ford airfield as a forward base for refuelling and re-arming. Wings of USAAF Thunderbolts also started operating from Ford as did one squadron of Searchlight Co-operation Oxfords, assisting in the training in the defences of the London and Portsmouth areas. On 15 May 1943, the station started its Wings for Victory Week. The attractions arranged included dances, a fair on the lawns of Tortington Hall, the band of the Canadian Scottish, etc. The magnificent sum of £115,150 was subscribed in War Loan.

As the bombing of Germany progressed and became more vital, it was consequently necessary to provide more airfields for diversions. Once again, the location of Ford was an invaluable asset, especially as general weather conditions were well above average. Here also, Durrington GCI provided a very great assistance. Although no contact was normally made (except 'Darky') the distressed plot could be followed and the canopy exposed when necessary. Before 'Sandra' was installed, the army searchlights were relied upon to produce the canopy. The total number of Bomber Command aircraft diverted to Ford was 1,679.

Early one morning in the summer of 1943, two aircraft were scrambled to intercept one enemy aircraft approaching the coast. It turned out to be a Me108, which eventually crash-landed on the airfield. The pilot and passenger, both Huns, were killed. They had arrived to give themselves up. Two attacks with butterfly bombs were experienced in September and October respectively. On the first occasion a total of 96 were dropped, causing very minor damage.

April 1944 saw big changes all round. Two 2TAF Wings arrived. Detachments of Mosquito squadrons, besides two resident squadrons, operated from here. Many American aircraft were handled, due to the installation of USAAF Eighth and Ninth Air Force homer beacons. Wings of Typhoons were being refuelled and re-armed. Heavy and light aircraft diversions were becoming more numerous. It was during April that an enemy aircraft was destroyed over the airfield, the pilot of same baled out landed on the South West Intersection – unfortunately for himself, his parachute failed to open.

With the invasion imminent, the air movements increased to colossal proportions. Day Wings were doing three sorties per day, night fighters on patrol all night and innumerable aircraft of all types requiring assistance. As we were in a direct line with Beachy Head, we were able to assist many aircraft. The following figures might prove interesting: June, crash-landings, 86 of all types; total movements 12,000 approx. Out of the 86 crash-landings, there was only one fatality. With the admirable co-operation of the chief technical officer, Wing Commander Walster, the airfield was kept serviceable during this time.

When the position on the beach head became somewhat acute, the Day Wings were patrolling till dusk and arriving back at the base after dark, in many cases short of fuel. At first it was not too easy, due to lack of night-flying practice on the part of the pilots, but after a while with accurate timing, stacking and displacement from Control, it was found possible to land a wing by sections in 14 minutes (average). Bomber and Mosquito diversions continued. Two additional Mosquito squadrons operated during the 'Diver' activity, also two flights of Black Widows.

Once again, the location of Ford was a great asset to American and Royal Air Force transport aircraft carrying freight and wounded. An organisation was established by station headquarters for handling American and British wounded who arrived by air in large numbers and without warning. It was not before over 1,000 casualties had been dealt with that the assistance of the American Field Ambulance Service was called for. Work attending to wounded servicemen of all

Allied nations continued for some months. The highlight of the Dakota trade was the occasion when emergency landings were made by 116 aircraft on Christmas Day. All crews were given Christmas dinner, including roast turkey.

The remaining Mosquito squadrons departed on 1 January 1945, leaving NFDW, the night-fighter section of CFE.

To enable Ford to play its part in the acceptance of diverted aircraft of all kinds, an aircrew mess capable of feeding up to 1,000 additional personnel, and an aircrew sleeping site with accommodation for 500, were made available by the station headquarters staff. There is no accurate statement as to the number of visiting aircrew that used this accommodation, but it is on record that during the three-month peak period over 33,000 meals were served to visiting aircrew, apart from the 1,200 wounded who were all given a meal and hot drinks on their stretchers before removal to hospital. A reception centre for ex-prisoners-of-war was established. Over 1,000 aircraft were landed; they brought in 12,000 ex-prisoners-of-war, officers and other ranks, who passed through our hands.

So ends the story of RAF Station Ford, which, from October 1940 to the end of hostilities rose from an unimportant airfield with but few buildings and no runways, to one of the most important operational stations in Fighter Command. This building and reconstruction was accomplished whilst the station remained fully operational. It is a history that all who served there during this period can be justly proud.

(signed) A. B. Carter, S/L
RAF Ford

6

The Jet Age
and the Politics of Defence
1946 – 1970

From the station ORB:

22.1.46

Weather poor generally. Tangmere was the only airfield open in the south. At 12.00 hours a converted Fort of the Danish Air Line was diverted here; the 22 passengers were duly greeted by Customs and Immigration officers who had been warned of the diversion by the station security officer. At 12.40 hours a Dakota arrived from Gatow carrying M. Vishinsky, the leading Russian delegate to the UNO Conference, accompanied by his daughter Zenida and nine other members of the delegation. Passengers were greeted by M. Gusev, Soviet Ambassador in London, Air Commodore E. H. Fielden CVO DFC AFC representing C-in-C Transport Command, Colonel Roberts representing the Foreign Office and Wing Commander Hardiman DFC, officer commanding RAF Station, Tangmere. The visitors were entertained by Wing Commander Hardiman to lunch in the officers' mess after which they departed for London by road. A further diversion was an Irish air liner from Dublin.

The Dakota carrying the Russian diplomat and his retinue had come from RAF Gatow, Berlin, and should have landed at Northolt but for its diversion to Tangmere. On 10 January 1946, the first General Assembly of the United Nations Organisation, with 51 nations represented, had opened at Central Hall, Westminster. Andrey Januarevich Vyshinsky (to give a more orthodox transcription of his name from its Cyrillic spelling), Soviet Deputy Minister of Foreign Affairs, the Dakota's principal passenger, was on his way to attend the second meeting of the Security Council on the 25th, which decided as its Resolution No. 1 to set up a Military Staff Committee consisting of the chiefs of staff of the armed services of the five permanent Security Council members, the United States, Britain, France, China, and the Soviet Union. Among those on the ground to greet him at Tangmere, mis-described in the ORB as 'Colonel' Roberts of the Foreign Office, was Frank Roberts, British Chargé d'Affaires in Moscow. The two men knew each other well: Roberts had been at Churchill's side at the Yalta Conference which decided the fate of post-war Europe, as Vyshinsky had been at Stalin's. Also in attendance was 'Mouse' Fielden, formerly CO of 161 (Special Duties) Squadron, who in May would be re-forming the King's Flight, of which he had been captain from 1936 to 1942.

The Flying Fortress which had landed at Tangmere 40 minutes earlier belonged to the Danish airline Det Danske Luftfartselskab A/S (DDL). DDL had bought two second-hand converted USAAF B-17s from Sweden in late 1945, from among the eight interned there during the war of which seven were modified by Svenska Aeroplan Aktiebolaget to carry passengers for their original civil owner, Swedish Intercontinental Airlines, which later became part of SAS. One, subsequently registered in Denmark as OY-DFA, had flown 24 combat missions from Bassingbourne with the 91st Bomb Group. After its period of service as a commercial airliner with DDL, it was sold to the Danish air force. It then passed through the hands of the French Institut Géographique National which added the aeroplane to its fleet of B-17s that flew world-wide photographic and geophysical survey missions. Its French civil registration number was F-BGSP. It eventually ended up derelict, being cannibalised for parts. In 1972, the USAF Museum purchased the aeroplane and restored it to flying condition under its original serial 42-32076 and name 'Shoo Shoo Baby' after the Andrews Sisters song of 1943. The aircraft remains on display today at the National Museum of the United States Air Force at Wright-Patterson AFB, Dayton, Ohio. On the date in question, however, this aeroplane was being repaired after having made a wheels-up landing at Blackbushe in November 1945, and was not returned to DDL until the end of February 1946. The registration of the DDL Flying Fortress that landed at Tangmere was not recorded in the ORB, but since OY-DFA was out of action and DDL owned only two Fortresses it must therefore have been the other one, OY-DFE, formerly USAAF 42-107067. A week later, on 30 January 1946, OY-DFE was wrecked on the ground, fortunately without fire or fatality, in a serious taxiway collision with RAF Dakota KG427 at Kastrup Airport, Copenhagen; the aeroplane was written off and scrapped.

When the Central Fighter Establishment left for West Raynham in September 1945, RAF Tangmere was not immediately repopulated with people and aeroplanes. Construction crews moved in, and refurbishment work began on the airfield. Three all-steel T2 hangars were built on the foundations of the brick-and-wood Belfast-truss hangars constructed in 1918 and destroyed during the bombing of the airfield in August 1940. The blister hangars which had been placed around the airfield during the war were removed. The main NE/SW runway was extended westwards in preparation for the new generation of jet aircraft and new concrete walls erected at the aircraft dispersals to deaden the sound of jet engines.

It would be some months before the jets would arrive, however. The first post-war squadron to take up residence at Tangmere, in October 1945, was Mosquito-equipped 85, a squadron with a long and illustrious history. It had been commanded by Billy Bishop and Mick Mannock on the Western Front in the First World War, and during the Second World War by Peter Townsend, formerly of 43 Squadron at Tangmere, and by John 'Cat's Eyes' Cunningham, who had just left the RAF to take up a position as a test pilot with the de Havilland Aircraft Company. During the latter part of the war, 85 Squadron had flown Mosquito night fighters, and had brought their Mk30s with them to Tangmere, to be replaced by new NF36s equipped with AI Mk X radar beginning in January 1946. As the station's sole resident squadron for the time being, 85 Squadron's pilots flew both day and night sorties; generally these were flights of four to seven aircraft intended mainly to keep up the pilots' flying hours and maintain the squadron at operational readiness. The daily routine was enlivened by gunnery practice and frequent tactical exercises with other squadrons.

At the end of March, 85 Squadron was joined by 164 (Argentine British) Squadron. Tangmere once again had both a day-fighter and a night-fighter squadron in residence. No. 164 were no strangers to the locality, having been stationed with their Typhoons at Thorney Island as a part of 2TAF's 136 Wing from March to June 1944, sharing the aerodrome with 123 Wing commanded by Desmond Scott. They then moved across the Channel where they remained until the following summer. On their return to the UK, 164 were equipped with well-worn Spitfire Mk IXs, which they now flew from Tangmere when, that is, the aeroplanes were not grounded by serviceability problems as they frequently were. Nonetheless the squadron was lucky to have survived when so many well-known squadrons that had given great service during the war were unceremoniously disbanded where they stood at the war's end, their personnel shipped home for demobilisation or re-assignment. No. 164 Squadron was not to remain at Tangmere for very long, however; on 28 April, it moved to Middle Wallop, to be re-equipped with Spitfire XVIs.

Two days later, on 30 April, Squadron Leader H. R. 'Dizzy' Allen arrived with 1 Squadron, returning to their ancestral home where they would remain for the next twelve years. Since leaving for France in September 1939, the squadron had spent only a year or so at Tangmere, flying Hurricanes as night fighters in 1941-42. It is unlikely that any of the pilots now arriving had been stationed at Tangmere previously or were familiar with the locality. Those who had gone to France with the BEF had since scattered to the winds and had been replaced several times over. The squadron had lost forty-five pilots killed up to VE Day, and some of those now arriving at Tangmere were recently trained and had had no wartime operational experience. The squadron brought with them nine Spitfire 21s, four Spitfire Mk IXs, and a Harvard.

Dizzy Allen found the squadron's offices, workshops, and accommodation in a very shabby state after years of hard use and little maintenance. His first task was to set all ranks to work with gardening tools, brooms, paint brushes, screwdrivers, and a borrowed electric floor-sander to bring their new home up to a presentable peace-time standard. Meanwhile, a limited flying programme was maintained with the squadron's Griffon-engined Spitfire 21s. On 17 May, Allen took the whole squadron up on a navigational exercise to familiarise his pilots with the territory covered by 11 Group, from Land's End and mid-Wales and across to Suffolk, and pointing out local landmarks in case of poor visibility including the Arundel Gap, just as useful as it ever was. Then began two weeks of intensive working-up for the Victory Celebration Flypast, scheduled for 8 June. Maximum hours in formation practice were flown on days of decent flying weather.

The powers-that-be had decided that 1 Squadron was to have the leading role; its place in the flypast was to lay contrails high overhead to herald the massed formations of other aircraft to follow. The trouble with this idea was that no one knew when contrails formed or why; during the war, they were regarded as a menace to be avoided and no one had sought to make them deliberately. Allen started a series of experiments, and found that in the right conditions persistent contrails formed at around 30,000 feet, but there was a great deal of variation from one day to the next and there could be no guarantee that the atmospheric conditions would be conducive to contrails on the day of the flypast.

On 30 May, flying was suspended so that the squadron's nine Spitfire 21s could be gone over thoroughly; maximum serviceability was required, and no one wanted last-minute problems on the ground or aircraft being forced to drop out of formation once in the air. On 2 June, 85 Squadron's Mosquitoes, six of which would also be taking part in the flypast independently, were joined at Tangmere by Mosquitoes of 151 Squadron to make up a flight of ten. No. 1 Squadron's nine Spitfire 21s were joined on the morning of the 3rd by the Spitfire Mk XVIs of 65, 587, and 691 Squadrons to make up a formation of thirty. Allen and three other pilots did a 'contrail test' over London at 35,000 feet on the 5th with disappointing results; the contrails were said to have been poor, and two of the pilots had oxygen trouble provoking a thorough re-inspection of the oxygen systems on all nine Mk 21s once back at Tangmere. On the 6th, all nine of 1 Squadron's Spitfire 21s performed a dress rehearsal over London, but despite their best efforts for more than an hour no useful contrails could be made at any reasonable altitude.

On the 8th, day of the flypast, the capricious English summer weather was so unpromising that in the opinion of some the whole effort ought to have been cancelled. An occluded front was almost stationary over London and the southeast, with cloud, rain, and drizzle. At Tangmere, the cloud base was at 600 ft. Nonetheless, 30 Spitfires and 10 Mosquitoes took off, orbiting at 400 ft to form up. They climbed through cloud and levelled off at 30,000 feet over Canterbury. The cloud was so black above that Allen reckoned that it went up beyond 40,000 feet. There was absolutely no chance that high-altitude contrails could be seen from the ground over London, assuming contrails would form at all in these conditions. Allen took the decision to return to base. The radar station at RAF Heathrow, feeding through local GCI units, talked him through the descent over the South Downs in thick cloud, and through the Arundel Gap on instruments at 800 feet. Leading the formation, Allen descended further and turned right when the coast came into sight, dropping down almost to sea level. Another right turn at Selsey Bill brought the aircraft over Chichester beneath the cloud base, which Allen said was below the weather vane of the Cathedral's 270-foot spire. Twenty-seven Spitfires and six Mosquitoes made a safe landing at Tangmere moments before a blinding thunderstorm broke, the other aircraft having diverted elsewhere also making safe landings. In London, the flypast was a wash-out. *Flight* magazine's correspondent, from his vantage point in the Mall, complained that the new de Havilland Vampires, meant to be among the stars of the show, passed overhead completely unseen. That the event was not marred by mid-air collisions was miraculous, and due in no small part to the skill of the operating staff at RAF Heathrow who were responsible for local control of the V-Day flypast.

On 17 June, 85 Squadron left on two-weeks' detachment to Lubeck and 1 Squadron proceeded to Acklington on a fortnight's gunnery course; in both cases to be followed by two-weeks' annual leave, a pre-war custom re-instituted for the first time since 1939. The reason for clearing the station of its resident squadrons – if, indeed, this was not merely a coincidence – became evident four days later with the arrival of the first Meteor of Fighter Command's High Speed Flight, piloted by Group Captain E. M. 'Teddy' Donaldson DSO DFC. Only a month earlier, Donaldson had been given the job of organising an attempt on the World Air Speed Record. The work was urgent, and to be kept secret for as long as possible. The Americans were known to be preparing a trio of P-80 Shooting Stars to exceed 1,000 km/h, or 623 mph, and thus set both a milestone record and improve upon the official world title set the previous year on 7 November 1945 by Group Captain Hugh J. 'Willie' Wilson AFC, the commandant of the Empire Test Pilots' School at Cranfield, with a speed of 606 mph in a modified Meteor.

As Britain then held all three official world speed records, on land, sea, and air, maintaining them was a matter of national dignity and Donaldson was told that he could have whatever resources he needed to do it, within reason, but that it must be done between 1 August and 7 September to have a chance of stealing a march on the Americans. The target was 1,000 km/h. The aircraft would have to be Meteors, a pair of them, to be specially prepared; there was no time for developing any radically new, unproven designs. Donaldson set to work with the engineers to see what could be done, and then turned his mind to choosing his fellow pilots and the course for the record attempt. In choosing the course, which for practical reasons would need to be over water, Donaldson studied the RAF's meteorological records for the previous 50 years, looking for a place with high mean summer temperatures and suitable wind force and direction. To get the best performance from the aircraft at the low level at which they would be flying, he wanted a day that was hot and still with smooth air, calm sea, and light cloud. He chose Littlehampton, between Worthing and Bognor Regis, and RAF Tangmere as the flight's base. As his fellow pilots, he chose Squadron Leader Bill Waterton and Flight Lieutenant Neville Duke.

Unsurprisingly, the cloak of secrecy could not be maintained for very long. Soon after Teddy Donaldson's arrival on 21 June, word got out that an attempt on the World Air Speed Record was going to be made at Tangmere. Once work began on the laying-out of the course off Littlehampton, the intention became obvious. On 12 July the Air Ministry held a press conference at Tangmere, to which around 60 newspaper correspondents were invited. The press were informed officially about the record attempt and what was involved in it, introduced to Donaldson, Waterton, and Duke, told about the main modifications to the Meteors and their engines, and given lunch in the officers' mess. They were also told – or inferred from what was said – that the attempt would be made in approximately a month's time, on or about 14 August. From then on, the High Speed Flight was well and truly in the limelight, and there was the pressure of British public expectation to meet. The middle-of-August date turned out to be optimistic. The first specially prepared 'Star' Meteor, EE549, arrived only on 7 August. The second Star Meteor, EE550, arrived at Tangmere on the 10th from Gloster's works at Moreton Valence. Working-up on both Star Meteors now proceeded, and dignitaries and newspaper correspondents began to arrive in anticipation of the record runs, along with the witnessing Mosquito NF36s of 29 Squadron. For a day or two the weather held. Full-scale practice runs were made on the 13th, and by the next day the airfield was said to be 'seething with movie cameramen and gentlemen of the press' as well as distinguished RAF officers among whom, a few days earlier, had been Group

Captain Leonard Cheshire VC, one of Britain's most famous and highly-decorated airmen. From the station ORB:

14.8.46
At 12.39 hours, Group Captain Donaldson was airborne in Meteor 549 (No. 2 Star Job) but landed again immediately with some trouble. The aircraft stopped on the runway and had to be towed back to dispersal. Air Marshal Sir J. Robb tested one of the High Speed jet aircraft at 14.37 hrs, flying for about 10 minutes. Group Captain Donaldson gave an excellent flying exhibition in Meteor 549. A masterly, smooth show of airmanship, everyone getting a 'real thrill'.

There would be no record attempt that day, as the crowds gathered at the aerodrome and on the beaches had hoped. Obviously something was wrong with EE549, but at least the crowds enjoyed the impromptu shows put on by Sir James Robb and Teddy Donaldson. Neither Star Meteor flew again until the 20th, when both did extensive trials over the course for two days. On the 23rd, both were flown to Moreton Valence for some work by Gloster's, returning a day or two later. On the 26th, everyone was keyed up: the weather had improved with light breezes and visibility was good to very good. Everything looked set for an attempt that afternoon, but the ORB noted that to everyone's disappointment it had to be postponed; no reason was given. Then the weather clamped down for a week with moderate to heavy showers, thunderstorms, and winds gusting up to gale force; at times parts of the airfield were waterlogged.

Neville Duke described these weeks of practice, waiting, and anticipation in his autobiography, *Test Pilot*:

Tremendous organisation went into the preparation for making the new record. The course had to be marked out with balloons and buoys – some 200 buoys were used, tons of apparatus, and four mooring vessels. The length of the course was 72 kilometres or 45 miles. The record attempts had to be made under the regulations of the Fédération Aéronautique Internationale, and they included the stipulation that the aircraft were not to fly above 75 metres or 246 feet during the timed run over three kilometres, or during the 500 metres immediately preceding the timed run. Two photographic methods were used for measuring the speed of the aircraft …

Throughout July and August we flew round the course in new Meteor 4s. I went round it about 180 times. During these training flights we worked up speeds of about 595 miles per hour or about Mach Number 0.8 and we had a number of bumpy rides. These bumps could be caused either by the weather or, if the tide was out, from heat waves or thermals rising from the rocks and sand under the heat of the sun. At times you felt as though you were sitting at the top of a flight of stairs with your legs stuck out straight in front of you; and then somebody grasped your legs and pulled you all the way downstairs.

This was rather uncomfortable, and so was the occasion when one of the Rolls-Royce Derwent engines failed. I was flying along at between 120 and 150 feet at some 580 miles per hour when the revolutions of the port engine fell, with the result that the aircraft swung and rolled sharply to one side; and, with the controls heavy while flying at speed, it needed some effort to keep the machine straight. I was fortunately able to cut out the port engine altogether and to fly back on the other.

One of our bogeys was the shortage of fuel capacity or to run short of fuel at any part of the course; we felt, however, that even if this did occur with the Meteors flying at round about 600 miles per hour, we should have sufficient speed to glide back to Tangmere with both engines dead. To check this theory we cut both throttles back while flying at high speed on the run down the course away from Tangmere, and found that we did have enough speed to glide back.

Towards the end of August two new Meteors were delivered for the record attempt. They had no wireless equipment, no radio mast, and no armament; extra fuel was carried in three tanks to cope with the high fuel consumption. Each also had a special cockpit hood reinforced with metal; this was in case air passing over the windscreen at high speed should heat and soften the Perspex, causing bad distortion and possibly failure. When an aircraft is flying at between speeds of 600 and 640 miles per hour a rise in temperature, due to friction of the air, of between 35 to 40 degrees Centigrade can be expected. The bad weather continued, but Donaldson reached a true air speed of 626 miles per hour during one three-minute level speed test at 3,000 feet in cold, unfavourable conditions. I also remember that day, for Air Marshal Sir James Robb, who was then AOC Fighter Command, decided that Donaldson and Waterton should make the official attempts on the record, and that I should remain as reserve pilot. I was naturally disappointed but the decision had to be taken.

Donaldson was among the RAF's leading pilots. He had been one of the pre-war aerobatic Fury team which won a competition at Zürich. He excelled at air gunnery and his marksmanship was most valuable when he led a Hurricane squadron during the early days of the war. He is a most cheerful, noisy personality. Bill Waterton had a distinguished record on fighters during the war and had aided the development of fighter tactics at the Central Fighter Establishment. Steady, conscientious, he is a first-class pilot and is now chief test pilot for Gloster Aircraft.

I did get an opportunity to raise the record. One day Donaldson said:

"When Bill comes down, jump in and have a go yourself."

After Bill had landed I waited for about half an hour while the Meteor was refuelled and a few rivets were checked.

I made several flights round the course and managed to work up 625 miles per hour for one run. I started the runs at 1,000 feet over Worthing and put the nose of the aircraft down to reach 120 feet before beginning the measured section of the course. When I opened the throttle I could feel the seat pushing into my back. The needle of the air speed indicator swung quickly over to 550 miles per hour, and then seemed to creep to 600 miles per hour. The cockpit got hotter and hotter due to the friction of the air on the hood and I began to perspire freely. Compressibility developed and I found the aircraft beginning to shudder and vibrate quite violently; the nose began to drop and the port wing to dip. I had to use both hands firmly on the control column and to prop my left shoulder against the side of the cockpit to help keep the Meteor straight on the course.

Looking out, I could see the line of marker buoys flashing past almost like a blur, while an air-sea rescue flying boat on patrol out at sea appeared to be standing still. The marked vibration or buffet continued until, on passing beyond the buoys marking the end of the measured three kilometres, I eased back the throttles. The nose and the wing came up and I was able to fly with one hand again. My main impressions of the flight were of terrific noise from the air rushing past the fuselage and from the engines; of the sudden increase of heat in the cockpit; and of a feeling of exhilaration at flying so fast so near the sea. My average speed was 614 miles per hour.

On 7 September, with the weather improving but still far from ideal, Sir James Robb decided to let Donaldson and Waterton go for it. The newspaper correspondents and film cameramen still waiting in the locality for something to happen went wild when the attempt was announced, and according to the ORB the BBC's reporters even tried to force their way into the control tower as the runs were in progress. There was a tense six-hour wait for the results to be analysed by the National Physics Laboratory at Teddington, and nothing was certain until the small hours of the morning. There was uproar on the station when the result came through. They had done it.

In Teddy Donaldson's own words, from his biography by Nick Thomas:

Okay this is it. Climb in; strap myself in; am in shirtsleeves rolled up and have no helmet as there is no radio. Start the engines. They start instantly. Chocks away. Open throttles to the position of normal full power. Let go the brakes. That terrific push in the back and we are accelerating down the runway. We are in the air at 1,000 yards and have got about 280 mph on the clock by the end of the runway. I keep her low, flying due west in the same direction as take-off. Somewhere just south of Chichester start a turn to the left, straightening out just over Pagham Harbour, flying due east at just less than 1,000 ft. Start to lose height.

I have to be just as close as I dare to the water to get the best speed.

Soon I was at 10 feet above the sea with 600 mph on the speedo. Nine miles to run. Full throttle.

Ye Gods what a mess! The plane shakes like hell. Blurring vision.

Controls solid. Centre of lift shot back. Two hands on the stick and pull for all you bloody well can to keep her nose up.

Lined up with the buoys already and woooooooooosssssh through the measured course marked at each end with the barrage balloons.

Throttle straight back; control resumed; get off the sea quick.

Christ, what a picnic. A right turn with a constant 4½ G force; then left turn with 4½ G round towards Brighton and on to a westerly heading.

Down to sea level in the mist and rain. Shake, shake, shake, through the course with both arms pulling with all their might. Course complete. Jam throttles.

Throttles closed; turn right, and do the whole damned thing again both ways.

Finally through the course for the last time. Keep throttles shut; 600 mph plus to get rid of. I could have climbed to 10,000 ft with that speed without the engines. But I am not allowed by the regulations to break the 1,000 ft mark. Back to Tangmere in a minute. Round the airfield to lose speed, no airbrakes or flaps to help slowing down. After several circuits I have lost sufficient speed to lower the wheels and land. I am wringing wet with sweat. Am surprised to see the rain has not removed any paint from the machine.

Donaldson's official average speed over the required four runs to FIA rules was 615.78 mph, a new World Air Speed Record. Waterton's runs averaged only slightly less at 614 mph. Neville Duke remarked:

When Donaldson put up the new record the temperature was 14 degrees Centigrade – we had hoped for 30 degrees – and rain drops were falling although it was not raining hard. Conditions were bumpy, and when Bill Waterton made his runs, the first was a wash-out after he struck a bad bump at the start which threw him off course. He did an extra run to make up for this and his times were only slightly lower than Donaldson's.

Not only had Teddy Donaldson taken the record based on the average speed over four runs, but one of his runs had been timed at 623.45 mph, or

1,003.31 km/h. Although speeds of over 623 mph had been recorded unofficially in practice runs, this was the first time a speed of over 1,000 km/h had been officially authenticated by the FIA. Donaldson was later awarded a special certificate to this effect by the Fédération Aéronautique Internationale, a distinction that could never be taken away from him no matter how many times his World Air Speed Record might be improved upon in future.

Two weeks later, after the gap between record attempts required by the FIA, the High Speed Flight got back to work. Pleasing as it was to have broken the record at 616 mph, their ultimate goal was still to be achieved: a World Air Speed Record of 1,000 km/h, or 623 mph. On 21 September, some practice runs were done over the course. On the 24th, the weather was set fair for a concerted attack on the 1,000 km/h record. The first Meteor took off at 07.30 hours and record-attempt flights continued until 15.00. Twenty-nine runs were made by all three pilots. Duke's best average was 613 mph, Waterton's 610, and Donaldson's 614. Had the weather been warmer, approaching the 30°C that they had hoped for originally, Donaldson calculated that they could have reached 626 mph. But the summer was now over, the weather was not going to get warmer, and the Star Meteors were never intended to last for more than 12 or 13 hours' flying time at the levels of stress required of them. The risks of catastrophic airframe or engine failure were increasing as the hours accumulated on the aeroplanes. On the 26th, Sir James Robb, reluctant to allow the team to push their luck any further, announced his decision to disband the High Speed Flight. Neville Duke summed it up:

In many ways, the results of Donaldson's High Speed Flight were disappointing. It is true that Donaldson increased the world's record by ten miles an hour, with a figure of 616 miles per hour, or Mach 0.81, but we had hoped to do much better. One of the main reasons was that the weather was against us. We wanted a hot sunny day, a high tide and no bumps. We got the worst summer in England for several years and plenty of bumps; when Donaldson put up the new record, the weather was cold, the sky was overcast and light rain was falling ...

If there was a rather negative side to the work of this High Speed

Flight, there was also a positive result too: the conventional type of aircraft form was shown to have reached the limit of its development for flying at speed. In the past the problem had been to provide an engine to fly an aircraft at high speed; from 1946 onwards it was accepted that, with the development of the turbo-jet engine, the problem would be to design an aircraft to make the fullest use of the greater engine power now available. In other words, while at Tangmere the flight could, and did occasionally, fly at 626 miles per hour, the limit of the Meteor had been reached. The era of swept-back wings and delta wings was approaching.

Meanwhile, Tangmere's resident squadrons, 1 and 85, had returned to the station. On 27 August, No. 1 began rehearsals for the first Battle of Britain Memorial Flypast scheduled for Sunday, 14 September. No. 1's Spitfires were to fly with the Duxford Wing, which would be led by Group Captain Douglas Bader. On the 9th, 1 Squadron flew to Duxford for their final run-throughs. From the squadron ORB:

14.9.46
To commemorate the Battle of Britain, a flypast of about 300 aircraft took place over London this morning. 1 Squadron, together with 41 and 91 Squadrons, all flying Spitfire 21s, formed the leading wing of the first fighter stream. Eleven of our aircraft were airborne, nine flew in our own formation, one spare filled a gap in 91 Squadron and our second spare broke away when we reached the outskirts of London. The weather was poor with some low cloud but the flypast was achieved on time. 1 Squadron afterwards broke away from the Duxford Wing and returned to Tangmere.

Just as 1 Squadron left Tangmere to fly to Duxford on the 9th, an unrecorded number of P-47 Thunderbolts of the USAAF's 79th Fighter Group arrived at Tangmere from their base in Austria and took up temporary residence in No. 1's now-vacant accommodation. The 79th FG's Thunderbolts were one of three USAAF contingents – the others were comprised of Mustangs – due to take part in the Battle of Britain flypast along with the RAF and Commonwealth air forces. On the 11th, the Thunderbolts put on a dress rehearsal with 85 Squadron's Mosquitoes at Tangmere, a highly-disciplined display which was described in the station ORB as 'a very successful show'. They were joined by 151 Squadron's Mosquitoes on the 13th who would again be augmenting 85 Squadron's, as in June. The weather had been cloudy since the 79th's arrival and did not improve. On the morning of the flypast, rain or drizzle and poor visibility set in at 10.40 hours. The station ORB noted:

14.9.46
The day of the flypast over London opened with the weather being very poor, and by 12.00 hours cloud base was down to 400'. Mosquitoes of 85 and 151 Squadrons and the Thunderbolts were airborne at 09.45. At one period there were 10 squadrons orbiting Tangmere in and out of cloud. The Mosquitoes of 85 Squadron returned to base because of bad weather and took no further part in the flypast; the Thunderbolts pressed on. The Spits of 1 Squadron and the Thunderbolts returned to base about the same time. The Spits were short of fuel and given priority to land. The weather was deteriorating rapidly and despite the fact that the Thunderbolts were near base they had trouble finding it. With the aid of the D/F they were brought back to base and landed safely. The D/F operator did an excellent job of work and is to be commended.

A week later, 1 Squadron received the news that they were to be re-equipped with Meteors. The plan was that when 222 Squadron arrived at Tangmere from Weston Zoyland at the beginning of October, 1 Squadron would take over half their Meteors. Less welcome was the news that when this happened, the squadron would be reduced to half its present strength, the squadron ORB noted, 'in accordance with the so-called "cadre" policy of Fighter Command'. The news about the Meteors was not much of compensation; in the opinion of some pilots, apart from their somewhat greater top speed the second-hand Meteor Mk 3s they were being given offered few, if any, advantages over their Spitfire 21s. Dizzy Allen had serious doubts about them:

... In my experience, having flown more than a hundred different types of aircraft, if an aeroplane looks good to a skilled eye, it usually is good. But the Meteor looked like nothing on earth. It had twin engines, each widely spaced from the cockpit, indicating that it would be hell to handle if either engine flamed out. The wing roots were thick so that the main spars were big enough to accept the weight of the engines. Twin-engined fighters were rare. True, the Luftwaffe introduced the Messerschmitt 262 towards the end of the war, and it bore a certain resemblance to the Meteor. It caught the long-range USAAF with its trousers down simply because it was much faster than conventional fighters; but I didn't believe the Meteor had much speed advantage over the Spitfire Mk 21, and it certainly lacked its manoeuvrability.

In my estimation a Spitfire Mk 21 in the hands of a capable pilot could have shot down five Meteors for the loss of one Spitfire. However, only a limited number of the Mk 21 was produced and it would not have been cost-effective to retain the breed. Ironically, today there is a school of thought inclined to the view that souped-up Spitfires should be re-introduced for battlefield purposes. Some of the advantages are ease of maintenance, the ability to take off from autobahns and land back again using improvised servicing facilities, outstanding manoeuvrability, and comparatively high speed at low level. Modern jet fighters are stressed essentially for top speed at high level in rarefied air; they would break up if full power was used at low level. Above all, modern ground-to-air defence systems rely on heat-seeking missiles, and jet engines produce an awful lot of heat, but they would be unable to home onto the heat produced from exhaust stubs. The Air Staff have always been notoriously short-sighted in their planning, but I suppose it is difficult to point the finger of blame at them for not foreseeing such possibilities in 1946/47.

The first Meteor Mk 3 was ferried into Tangmere, and before the pilot removed one of my precious Spitfires, I asked him how to fly the bloody thing. He said he didn't know, save for the rudiments, he was just a sodding ferry pilot. He did show me how to start the engines, and pointed out that if the jet efflux temperature gauges went off the clock, that meant that the engines had caught fire. I had sent teams of skilled fitters to the factory on courses to learn how to service the engine and airframes and they were instructing the mechanics what to do. When a jet engine is started, a turbine begins to rotate which sucks air to the intakes. Kerosene fuels jets and they stink of paraffin oil. By pressing the starter button, having first opened the fuel cocks, a large sparking plug glows white-hot and the turbines, powered either by electricity from starter batteries, or later by explosive cartridges, turn. Fuel jets spurt kerosene over the spark plug and this is ignited; and hot air is sucked in by the turbine, accelerated, expanded and spouted from the efflux. By opening the throttle more kerosene is pumped into the furnace, increasing the rotation of the turbine which draws more and more air into the engine and hurls it out. There are many variations on the theme but that should suffice. A jet cannot function in space for there is insufficient oxygen for the burning process, but a rocket engine can because it carries its own liquid oxygen.

I climbed into the Meteor to find for myself how to fly it, and was immediately impressed by the forward vision, being perched high above a tricycle undercarriage – no big engine cowling to obscure my forward vision. The smell of kerosene abated when I clipped on my oxygen mask. I started the engines and gingerly opened the throttles; if I had given full throttle the burnt air would have blown down the dispersal huts. I moved onto the taxi track and found that I could steer either by using the brakes or by giving more power to one of the engines. The engines responded sluggishly to the throttles, but I worked out the solution to that when I was lined up on the runway. I applied full brakes, gently gave both engines full power and then released the brakes, whereupon she began to trundle up the runway like a lame cart-horse, but gathered speed as more and more air was sucked in by her forward movement. She took longer than a Spitfire to gather take-off speed. I eased back on the stick and lifted her off the ground. I had applied 15 degrees of flap for take-off, and I retracted the undercart and the flaps after getting airborne. I eased back the throttles from full take-off power, waited until we had arrived at an air speed of 270 knots and put her into a climb, maintaining that speed. (Not long after the war the RAF rejected miles per hour as a measure of speed and used knots instead.)

What was most welcome was the absence of noise in the sealed, pressurised cockpit and the lack of vibration; the Merlin engine in the Spitfire had to turn an enormous airscrew, but although the jet turbines were rotating at 14,500 revs per minute, the Meteor ran like a sewing machine. I climbed to 35,000 feet, straightened her up and gave her full throttle. Jets give their best performance at height, for although the air is thin it is also very cold, which proportionally increases the mass of air turning the turbines. Furthermore, much less fuel is used at height – flying flat out at ground level would exhaust the fuel supply in about half an hour, but at height the endurance would be approximately one-and-a-half hours. Tactically this was unsound and presupposed that intruding enemy aircraft would fly at great height, which was not necessarily so. It didn't matter a damn in a Spitfire whether one made an interception high or low from a fuel consumption aspect, apart from the use of petrol on the climb.

I put her into a dive and she quickly gained speed since she had no propeller to create drag. Then I hauled her up into a loop to which she easily responded, having plenty of speed for the purpose. The aileron control was sluggish compared with the quick reactions of the Spitfire, which presented another tactical defect. Then I reduced speed, throttled one engine back to idling revs and opened the other throttle wide. Without the slightest warning she flicked onto her back and tried to fall in an incipient spin. I hastily throttled back the other engine, rolled her out and dived to gain speed before opening both throttles. Although my reaction was immediate, I noted that I lost 3,000 feet in height during all this. I don't like spinning aeroplanes for they are out of control, and the pilot has to work hard to correct them. It was fun in the old biplanes, but not in monoplanes. Sometimes aircraft refuse to come out of a spin for no apparent reason, and it is often impossible to bale out as the pilot is hurled from one side of the cockpit to the other. The introduction of rocket ejection seats helps in such conditions, but when I went up in one my back was permanently injured. Jet engines occasionally flame out, possibly because of dirt affecting the fuel filters, and there is a relighting drill. The fuel cock must be closed down, speed reduced, an emergency button pressed which causes a stand-by sparking plug to glow, the throttle opened slightly, then the fuel cock is opened. But the system was by no means infallible. I have been president of three Boards of Enquiry enquiring into how Meteor pilots were killed. They were all caused by failure of the relighting system, combined with the pilots' inability to control a Meteor on one engine. Yet the Canberra bomber, a blown-up version of the Meteor, is perfectly safe on one engine unless the pilot is suffering from delirium tremens.

As I thought about descending to land I noticed a lever by the throttle quadrant which nobody had told me about. It wasn't marked red for danger so I pulled it to see what happened, whereupon the aircraft shuddered like a maiden aunt about to be raped. It didn't seem to be a bale-out situation and I looked out of the canopy and saw an aerofoil with holes in it at an angle of ninety degrees extended from the wing surface. There was another one on the other wing and when I pushed the lever they both retracted leaving clean wing surfaces. I then saw that the Meteor had lost a lot of speed in short time, clearly due to these aerofoils. I racked my brain and it was clear that they were intended to decelerate the aircraft, and they had spoiled the airflow over the wing surfaces thus creating drag. I soon found out the reason for their existence when I turned her on her back, hauled back the stick to put her into a vertical dive. I throttled back and eased her out of the dive, but she continued to dive without much reduction of speed. It then occurred to me that there was nothing to check her since she had no propeller to create drag. I extended the airflow spoilers, or dive brakes as they are termed, and she quickly lost speed to the extent that I had to give her engine power to maintain my angle of descent.

I arrived at 1,500 feet three miles east of the runway, retracted the dive brakes and gave her full throttle aiming at the squadron dispersal huts. We passed over them at fifty feet making a lot of noise. I hauled her up in a vertical climb, performed four upward charlies and stall-turned as she ran out of flying speed. Then I sidled back and joined the circuit. The short runway was in use even though the wind was light, and I had to approach over the Goodwood Downs which didn't give me much room to lose height to ground level. I touched down just beyond the runway threshold on the main wheels and let the nose-wheel drop. She roared along the runway showing little inclination to slow down, but I didn't want to use the brakes until she had slowed down for in all probability they would have begun to burn from excess friction. I put out the dive brakes but they didn't help because they were only effective when flying reasonably fast. As we devoured more and more of the runway, something dramatic had to be done about it, so I gave her short blasts of brake, sponging them on and off in an attempt to ensure that they didn't get red-hot. I began to run out of runway and in desperation applied full brakes, which brought her to a halt just ahead of ploughland. I turned off the runway steering by applying power to one engine, and stayed put for a quarter of an hour with the brakes off. They were white hot, and, if anyone had thrown a bucket of water over them they would have exploded. Then, steering by engines I taxied back to the dispersal. The pilots ganged up and asked me what they were like to fly. I said it was a piece of cake.

By the end of the year 222 Squadron had indeed arrived as planned to form a new Tangmere Wing. The Air Ministry's new 'cadre' policy meant that both squadrons were being cut down by half to a minimum peace-time Home Service establishment in accordance with the government's directive to reduce the size and expense of the armed forces. Ten of 1 Squadron's Spitfire 21s were ferried out in the first week of October, and by the 11th the squadron's full complement of eight Meteors — one flight of six aircraft and two spares — had arrived. At the end of the month, Dizzy Allen was posted away, to be replaced by Squadron Leader Colin Macfie DFC, who had flown with 611 Squadron during the Battle of Britain and had been shot down over France and captured in July 1941 while with 616 Squadron, then part of the Bader Wing flying from Tangmere.

On 1 February 1947, King George VI and Queen Elizabeth, accompanied by Princesses Elizabeth and Margaret, left Portsmouth on the battleship HMS *Vanguard* en route for their tour of South Africa. If all had gone as planned, there would have been a ceremonial flypast to mark the occasion. Tangmere had been chosen as the base for Operation Vanguard, involving all three resident squadrons, 1, 85, and 222 as well as the aircraft of six other squadrons that were scheduled to take part; by the third week in January the preparations were well in hand. On the 24th, it began to snow and continued to for the next four days. On the 29th, all station personnel, aircrew included, were mobilised to clear the runway to enable the aircraft of four of the visiting squadrons to land. Once they were down safely, it began to snow heavily again. Two days later, the Vanguard exercise was cancelled. Snow continued to fall in one of the worst winters in living memory, closing the entire southern sector for ten days. Snow blanketed Tangmere for four weeks. No. 65 Squadron's de Havilland Hornets remained stuck in the snow at Tangmere until 24 February.

March was another month of poor flying weather. In mid-April, 85 Squadron, which had been at Tangmere since October 1945, said goodbye and moved to West Malling, to be replaced on the same day by 266 (Rhodesia) Squadron, which had flown Typhoons with 146 Wing, 2TAF, and were now equipped with Meteor day fighters. There were now three day-fighter squadrons on the station, but this was not to last. In August, much to 1 Squadron's dismay, the squadron ceased to be a fighter squadron and was reformed as 11 Group's Instrument Flying Training Unit, initially with three Harvards and one Oxford, eventually becoming eight of each. Although this was generally regarded as a come-down, it was also a back-handed compliment: pilots were posted out and in, and now became instrument rating examiners responsible for teaching others to fly on instruments and hence gain their 'green cards' which qualified them to fly in all conditions. Over the next nine months the squadron took in twelve intakes of student pilots, over 150 in all, who successfully passed out as rated pilots under the RAF's new Instrument Rating Scheme.

On 1 June 1948, this interlude came to an end, and 1 Squadron was once again redesignated as a fighter squadron. From the 7th to the 17th, the majority of the squadron went on leave. Four pilots of the former Instrument Flying Team and a skeleton crew remained to carry out acceptance tests on new Meteor Mk 4s. Eight Mk 4s and two Mk 3s were allotted to the squadron, which gained eight new pilots posted in as against three posted out and one released from service. The strength of the squadron as at the end of June stood at nine officers and 78 other ranks, but went down to six officers and around 60 other ranks through November, and then down to just five commissioned pilots in December, January, and February, a number which now included Major Robin Olds, who had joined the squadron in October under the RAF-USAF exchange scheme, as well as Squadron Leader Burne, the CO, leaving only three other commissioned pilots. During December, nearly all of the squadron's other-ranks staff were transferred from 1 Squadron's establishment to the station's establishment, leaving only five officers and five other ranks – ten people all told – on the squadron's strength. This was 1 Squadron's lowest point since the RAF's post-war retrenchments of 1919-1920.

On 1 June 1948, Air Vice-Marshal Stanley Vincent had become AOC 11 Group. Vincent had himself survived the RAF's retrenchments of 1919-1920, and had joined 1 Squadron at Tangmere in 1928. When he visited the station on 23 August he renewed his acquaintance with 'Vincent's Folly', a grove of poplar trees near the officers' mess that he had planted in 1930 while he was mess president. That summer also saw the return to Tangmere of newly re-formed auxiliary squadrons – now the Royal Auxiliary Air Force – for their summer camps for the first time since 1939: Nos. 602, 603, 605, and 610, all of which had had either pre-war or wartime associations with the aerodrome, in most cases both, and were now flying late-marque Spitfires.

AVM Vincent returned to Tangmere in February 1949 to attend the ceremonial revival of 43 Squadron. On that day, 245 (Northern Rhodesia) Squadron was 'linked' to 266, already at Tangmere, and the combined 245/266 Squadron was renumbered as 43. The ceremony was held with all due military formality following a programme timed to the minute, as follows:

11.00   By this time all the guests were in position flanking the parade ground and the station warrant officer, W/O L. Flint, called for the markers.

11.33   The 'Advance' was sounded by trumpeters of the Royal Air Force Central Band, under the command of Wing Commander A. E. Sims MBE.

11.35   The squadrons marched on the markers. 1 Squadron was commanded by Squadron Leader L. J. Menness, 2 Squadron by Squadron Leader D. L. Harvey, 3 Squadron (245 Squadron from Horsham St Faith) by Squadron Leader E. Wootten DFC, and 4 Squadron by Squadron Leader G. W. Utting.

	Simultaneously, the Guard of Honour marched on under the command of Flight Lieutenant A. W. G. Brown.
11.39	The officer commanding, RAF Tangmere, Wing Commander G. S. A. Parnaby OBE, took command of the parade from the adjutant, Flight Lieutenant N. A. Horlock.
11.44	Arrival of the official party who took their places on the dais.
11.46	Arrival of Marshal of the Royal Air Force The Lord Douglas of Kirtleside GCB MC DFC. The Guard of Honour presented arms for the General Salute and was then inspected by Lord Douglas.
11.50	The Guard of Honour then marched off, the salute being taken by Lord Douglas.
11.53	The commanding officers of 266 and 245 Squadrons took up their posts in front of the dais.
11.55	The commander-in-chief of Fighter Command, Air Marshal Sir William Elliot KBE CB DFC gave an address, at the end of which, at:
11.59	He presented the 43 Squadron Crest to Squadron Leader D. L. Harvey.
12.00	The commander-in-chief of Fighter Command presented the 266 Squadron Crest to Squadron Leader E. Wootten DFC.
12.01	An address was then given by Marshal of the Royal Air Force the Lord Douglas of Kirtleside GCB MC DFC.
12.08	An address was given by Mr. Goodenough, the High Commissioner for Southern Rhodesia.
12.10	An address by Sir John Waddington (the Governor of Northern Rhodesia from 1941 to 1947), who presented a shield to Squadron Leader Wootten for the purposes of internal competition in 245 Squadron.
12.20	The ceremony was now completed, and the parade, led by the RAF Central Band, marched past, the salute being taken by Marshal of the Royal Air Force Lord Douglas.
12.30	The Meteor aircraft of 43 Squadron, which had been in position on the edge of the perimeter track, were then started up by their attendant ground-crews.

12.34	The first aircraft taxied out on to the perimeter track, and at 12.38 the first aircraft became airborne.
12.39	Flight Lieutenant Clayton's aircraft became airborne. Flight Lieutenant Clayton then proceeded to give a very skilful aerobatic display, during which time aircraft of 43 Squadron appeared in low formation runs across the airfield.
12.49	Aircraft of 43 Squadron then broke formation and peeled off to land.
12.51	The first aircraft touched down on the runway.
13.00	The visitors then proceeded to the station cinema for lunch.

In his address of dedication, Marshal of the Royal Air Force the Lord (Sholto) Douglas of Kirtleside spoke the following words:

It is a very great pleasure indeed to be present here at the resurrection of my old squadron, No. 43. But before I talk about 43 Squadron, I would like to say a word of sympathy for the personnel of 266 Squadron. I am well aware of the affection and regard in which the officers and men of a squadron hold their squadron, as expressed in the squadron number plate; and I can quite understand that it is with mixed feelings that the personnel of 266 Squadron find themselves losing their old number and being given another number, however distinguished the latter may be.

I was the original founder member of 43 Squadron, when as a young flight commander, I was sent off to Stirling on 1 April, 1916, to form 43 Squadron. My one and only flight commander then was Air Marshal Sir Alan Lees, who is with us today. It is a long time ago, and much water has flowed under the bridge since, including a second world war.

I took 43 Squadron to France in January, 1917, where we had a very tough time for several months, owing to the fact that we were equipped with obsolescent types of aircraft, which were outclassed by the German fighters. I was lucky enough then to have as one of my flight commanders one Captain Harold Balfour who is now the Lord Balfour of Inchrye, and an ex-under secretary of state for air, who is here on the dais with me to-day. Unfortunately or perhaps fortunately for me, in May, 1917, I hit a plough horse taking off on patrol from Trezennes airfield, and disappeared from the squadron via hospital. Shortly afterwards the squadron was equipped with Sopwith Snipes, a far superior type of aircraft, and continued to cover themselves with even greater glory.

The achievements of 43 Squadron in the Second World War will be fresh in your memories. It fought with distinction in the Battle of Britain, and later in North Africa, Malta and Italy.

You will note from the booklet on the ceremony that, in the two world wars, 43 Squadron destroyed no less than 269 enemy aircraft, a record of which any fighter squadron might well be proud.

Between the world wars, 43 Squadron was stationed continuously here at Tangmere alongside its old friend, 1 Squadron.

It is sometimes puzzling not only to members of the general public, but to me also, how an aura of tradition can attach itself to a number. 43 Squadron has always had a fine tradition, and has always maintained the affection and regard of its members. We hear nowadays a certain amount of talk about the morale of the RAF – some of it is misguided talk. There is no doubt in my mind that one of the main factors in building up and maintaining the morale of the RAF is the tradition of courage, efficiency, humour and chivalry which is associated with the most famous of the old squadrons of the RAF. I am sure that the new members of 43 Squadron will carry the torch and will maintain the high tradition of this fine squadron. On my part I wish 43 Squadron all possible success whatever the future may bring forth.

The great majority of the roughly 800 personnel on the station who formed the bulk of Lord Douglas's audience were National Servicemen who were not directly involved in flying and mostly only indirectly in aircraft maintenance. The costs of fighting the war now had to be paid, with interest, by the Exchequer. The national economic situation was so grave that without National Service, nearly all of these young men would have been unemployed. These had been bleak years for the country, for the RAF, for Tangmere, and for its squadrons. A casual observer of the 43 Squadron dedication ceremony would not have realised that no people or aircraft from 245 Squadron, apart from its former CO, actually came to Tangmere; the so-called 'link' was a paper exercise. No. 266 Squadron, for a few moments both 245 and 266 and now No. 43, was no better off than No. 1, having – all told – just six officers and five senior NCOs on its strength when this ceremony was carried out. How a squadron's worth of Meteors in 43's colours – or even half a squadron's worth of serviceable aeroplanes – was conjured up for the occasion is a mystery.

The station and squadron ORBs complained continually of a shortage of spare parts for the Meteors, causing aeroplanes to be grounded. At times, either or both squadrons were down to just one or two serviceable Meteors and had to borrow each other's to put up a flight of four. Due to 'our parlous shortage of aircraft' the participation of either or both squadrons in exercises that summer frequently had to be curtailed. It required a maximum effort on the part of the station's engineering staff to ensure the availability of eight aircraft, four from each squadron, for the Battle of Britain Memorial events on 15 September. Six aircraft from both 1 and 43 Squadrons took part in the main flypast over London, headed that year by AVM Vincent in his personal Hurricane LF363, thought at that time to be the last serviceable Hurricane on the RAF's strength and now part of the Battle of Britain Memorial Flight. Four Meteor Mk 4s of 1 Squadron took part in the local flypast at Hendon that afternoon, and the four Meteors of 43 flew at Biggin Hill.

Tragedy struck 43 Squadron on 25 November. During a snake formation descending through cloud, pilots Lancey and Jeffries collided in mid-air and crashed in the Downs eight miles northwest of the aerodrome. Both were killed. 1950 saw two more fatal accidents. In the first, the four-man 1 Squadron team were practising over the airfield for the annual Fighter Command Championship when two of the Meteors collided, the wreckage of one of the aircraft crashing near the control tower; the pilot, Flight Lieutenant Speller, was killed. A month later, another Meteor pilot was killed while carrying out a practice asymmetric overshoot with one engine closed down.

Otherwise, 1950 was a brighter year. Tangmere's squadrons carried out regular affiliations and practice interceptions with USAF B-29s and B-50s and RAF Lincolns and Washingtons, amongst other exercises and routine practice flying. 11 Group's new AOC, Air Vice-Marshal T. G. Pike, like Stanley Vincent a great friend of Tangmere, made monthly visits to the station; Tom Pike had been at Tangmere during the war, commanding 219 (Night-Fighter) Squadron from March to June 1941. Another USAF-RAF exchange officer, Major Donovan Smith, arrived in January in succession to Robin Olds and was immediately appointed CO of 1 Squadron, introducing to the station two memorable trans-Atlantic customs: softball games and 'sundowners', or summer cookouts of hot dogs in buns and ice-cold canned beer. Just as Don Smith relinquished command and returned to the States, 1 Squadron re-equipped with Meteor 8s, receiving their first on 19 August and by the end of the month had received ten. No. 43 received theirs in September. After many months of squadron strengths of 10 to 12 men, more pilots were at last posted in and again it became possible to split the squadrons into two flights each. Both squadrons rehearsed formations of nine aircraft for the Battle of Britain Memorial Flypast in September but the capricious English weather once more intervened and their participation had to be cancelled.

During the course of the year, a decision was taken by Fighter Command that all their home stations should consist of one day-fighter squadron and one of night fighters. In November, 43 Squadron was moved to Leuchars, until then a Coastal Command base that initially was not well equipped for fighters, and 29 Squadron completed its move to Tangmere from West Malling by the end of the month. Initially, 29 Squadron was equipped with Mosquito NF36s. In July of the following year they converted to the new Meteor NF11s, the first RAF squadron to receive them. The Meteor NF11 had been developed as a two-seat night fighter from the Meteor T7 training aircraft. Development and production had been undertaken by Armstrong-Whitworth at Baginton, Coventry, the first production NF11 flying in May 1950. This Meteor variant differed externally from the Meteor T7 by having a lengthened nose to accommodate the AI Mk 10 radar.

Little other than by-now routine peace-time events and annual exercises occurred on the aerodrome during 1951 and 1952. In neither year did Tangmere's squadrons take part in the Battle of Britain memorial flypasts. The next year, 1953, saw more construction on the airfield. Operational readiness platforms were built at the ends of the main NE/SW runway (07/25) and a large hard-standing was laid in front of the hangars.

In the early summer, Tangmere once again hosted an air speed record attempt. The Hawker Aircraft Company believed that its swept-wing Hunter jet fighter was capable of setting a new World Air Speed Record. As it was Coronation year it was felt that, in spite of the climatic disadvantages, the record attempt should be made in Britain. The prototype Hunter Mk 3, WB188, was chosen for the attempt. It was fitted with an afterburning version of the Rolls-Royce Avon engine and the aircraft was modified with a pointed nose, a curved windscreen, and an airbrake along each side of the rear fuselage, then painted a polished gloss red to assist the photographic time-keepers. Neville Duke, now Hawker's chief test pilot, would fly it.

The course to be used was that previously surveyed for the 1946 High Speed Flight. The support aircraft would again be provided by 29 Squadron: in 1946 it had been Mosquitoes; in 1953 it was to be Meteor night fighters. In 1946 the course had been fully marked out. In 1953 the three-kilometre measured course had marker buoys only at either end. A fully marked-out course was not needed; Neville Duke had, as he later said, 'flown the course a couple of hundred times already'. Since the attempt would involve only one aeroplane, the necessary engineering support was to be provided by Hawker's.

All was ready by the end of the month and on 30 August Neville Duke took off from Tangmere for the first record attempt. Unfortunately, on the last of four practice runs, the aircraft's engine began to run intermittently and the attempt was abandoned. The problem was solved and for the next attempt on 1 September it was decided to take off at dawn when calmer weather conditions were likely to be present. At first light next morning Tangmere was fogbound, but then the fog cleared sufficiently for take-off at about 07.00 hours. Neville Duke later described that flight:

> I took off from Tangmere on to course, dropping the nose to build up speed rapidly. Coming down first from 1,000 feet I lined up on the marker flares seven miles away. I caught a glimpse of Bognor Pier and my indicated airspeed was registering 550 knots. I switched in reheat. There was a surge of acceleration, followed by a loud bang. The Hunter flipped over in a vicious roll to starboard, and a force of six-and-a-half G crushed down on my ribs and nearly blacked me out. Beach and sea had swum into the place of the sky and were coming closer every second. I cut off the reheat, thrust over the stick, and came out of the roll, right way up, at about 200 feet.

I looked out at the wing and saw part of the undercarriage leg sticking through a jagged hole in the wing surface. The aerodynamic stresses and strains of the high speed had sucked out the undercarriage leg and smashed it through the wing like a cannon shell. I flew back to Dunsfold (Hawker's airfield) and circled around burning up fuel so that the landing on one leg would be as light as possible. Below on the aerodrome I could see the red fire engines at readiness. At last with the tanks reading 'zero', I put the Hunter on final approach, keeping up the wing by the aileron, holding off as long as possible, and gently brushing the one wheel on to the runway. As the speed fell, the wing dropped and the Hunter swung round in a circle on the port wingtip and the starboard wheel. All things considered, I had survived the disaster very well. If the undercarriage leg had come out seconds later we should both, the Hunter and me, have flipped straight into the sea. We managed to land, too, with the minimum of damage that could be expected in the circumstances. A lot of hard work followed and I marvelled at the way the ground crew had the repairs done and the Hunter recellulosed, looking like new and ready for another attempt within a week.

After the attempt of 1 September the actual record-breaking run was somewhat of an anti-climax. On 7 September Neville Duke was back on the tarmac at Tangmere after fifteen minutes having achieved a mean average over the four runs of 727.63 mph. He was proclaimed in next day's papers as 'The Fastest Man on Earth!'

1953 was such an eventful year that it was the first and only occasion a separate appendix summing up the previous twelve months' activities was added to the station's ORB:

Summary of the Events of the Year 1953

General

The year 1953 has been perhaps the busiest ever experienced by the Royal Air Force with the exception of the war years. This has certainly been true in the case of Tangmere. Early in the year arrangements were made for 1 Squadron to take part in the Coronation Flypast. This necessitated a considerable amount of practice on the part of the squadron which was 'winged' with 41 at Biggin Hill.

Further upset was caused by the selection of RAF Station Odiham as the site for Her Majesty's Review of the Royal Air Force in the month of July. In order to accommodate the great number of officers and men and to assemble some 700 aircraft it became necessary to detach the Odiham Wing to Tangmere. This, in turn, meant moving 1 Squadron to Biggin Hill and 29 Squadron to West Malling. This situation lasted for just over three months. Whilst here the Odiham Wing took part in numerous practices for the Coronation Flypast and later in those for the Royal Review.

Owing to its geographical position in relation to Odiham, Tangmere was chosen for the debriefing of the leaders of the various formations taking part in the Royal Review Flypast. These conferences, where all the participants arrived by air, made imperative a considerable amount of organisation and split-second timing as the majority of the jet aircraft were short of fuel and it was necessary to land some 42 aircraft of which 22 were jet fighters, in addition to the wing of 24 jet aircraft, in a very short space of time. Once on the ground all these aircraft, plus the piston-engined machines, had to be marshalled and the fighters refuelled. This threw a very heavy load on the Technical Wing but everything went off very smoothly on every occasion except the first when the pilots disregarded their instructions for take-off and the subsequent scene was rather reminiscent of a rat race. One senior officer, in fact, knocked over a fire extinguisher and then took off down wind!

The air traffic control organisation was sorely tried on these occasions and it is to their great credit that they were able to bring in aircraft varying from Chipmunks to Washingtons within the hour and only on one occasion was an aircraft damaged and that was an RCAF Sabre which made a very heavy landing indeed, the blame for which can hardly be laid at the door of air traffic.

A further complication during this period of intensive flying was the presence of three auxiliary squadrons who succeeded one another at Tangmere for their summer camp. Each squadron remained for a period of two weeks at the end of which time it was relieved by the succeeding one. The first squadron to arrive was 501 followed by 608 and finally 602 (City of Glasgow) Squadron. All were equipped with Vampires and as they usually commenced operations at an early hour the local populace were none too pleased! In this they had the sincere sympathy of the regular inhabitants of Tangmere as sleep became well nigh impossible after 6 am when the first Vampires started up their banshee wail.

Shortly after the Royal Review and after the Odiham Wing had left and 1 and 29 Squadron returned, the annual exercise 'Momentum' was upon us. Quite a considerable amount of useful experience was obtained although our squadrons were not kept as busy as they would have liked. In the first phase of the exercise, 1 Squadron was unfortunate in losing two pilots and their aircraft in a collision whilst attacking a Lincoln at 19,000 feet off the coast of France. A large explosion followed the impact and the aircraft completely disintegrated and fell into the sea leaving a long trail of black smoke in the sky. Although they fell near a yacht which spent a considerable time searching, no trace of the pilots was found.

At the beginning of September, Tangmere was chosen as the base from which the Hawker High Speed detachment would make an attempt upon the World Speed Record. The aircraft, a Hunter fitted with re-heat and a special nose and windscreen, was flown by Squadron Leader Neville Duke DSO OBE DFC AFC, Hawker's chief test pilot. After an initial set-back due to undercarriage trouble which necessitated hurried repairs to the aircraft, Squadron Leader Duke was successful in establishing a new World Air Speed Record of 727 mph. The course over which the runs were flown extended from Bognor Regis to near Brighton. This splendid effort was eclipsed, however, very shortly afterwards by Lt. Commander Lithgow in the Supermarine Swift and later by an American pilot.

The original arrangements for the Hawker team were made on the assumption that only about a dozen people would be involved. The publicity departments of the press, however, had not been reckoned with and the station was invaded by some 85 press reporters and photographers. A considerable amount of trouble was taken to make them comfortable during their several days' wait which was well worthwhile as they all co-operated most willingly with the station and gave no trouble at all. As a result of the station's efforts, the prestige of the RAF was considerably enhanced amongst this particular section of the press.

At the same time as the Hawker team was at Tangmere, some 200 officers of the three services of several Allied nations arrived to take part in a large escape exercise. During this period, the station was very crowded indeed and the administrative organisation was very severely taxed. Fortunately, this terrific overloading lasted for only a few days and so it was just possible to cope.

On 19 September, the station was open to the public in commemoration of the Battle of Britain. Some 15,000 members of the public attended although it was rather a cold day. The static and flying displays were quite successful, and one particular event which was most popular was the bursting of balloons by, apparently, the passenger of a Tiger Moth picking them off with a shotgun. Having burst three, he missed the fourth twice, whereupon the airman who had been hidden behind the screen came out in desperation and openly burst it with his pin on a stick!

Two days after the open day, the squadrons moved off to their annual armament practice camp at Acklington, where they remained until the latter part of October. Upon their return, activity began to die down and the result of the year's exertions began to become apparent in a marked decrease in serviceability of the aircraft.

Visitors

The station was visited by a number of high-ranking officers during the year in connection with the Coronation and Review Flypast, the summer exercise, the auxiliary squadrons and, in a number of instances, as a result of diversions. Tangmere was particularly honoured by several visits by His Royal Highness the Duke of Edinburgh. On his first visit he arrived in a Harvard to inspect 29 Squadron at that time commanded by his equerry, Squadron Leader Horsley AFC. After having lunch in the officers' mess, he departed for White Waltham. His second visit was on the occasion of a polo match at Cowdray, in which he was taking part; this time he flew from Scotland in an Oxford. From his forcibly expressed opinion, it would appear that this is not his favourite type of aircraft.

During Goodwood Week, Her Majesty and His Royal Highness stayed with the Duke and Duchess of Richmond at Goodwood Park. During this period, Prince Philip paid several visits to Tangmere to fly his Devon which was positioned here. On one occasion he took as passenger the Duke of Richmond and his two sons.

Amongst other notable visitors was His Grace the Duke of Hamilton who came to pay a visit to 602 Squadron, of which he is honorary air commodore. It was particularly appropriate that we should receive at this time a visit from the first man to fly over Mt Everest such a short while after Hilary and Tensing had at last managed to reach the top on foot. In December, the deposed Kabaka of Buganda landed at Tangmere and was taken on into London by car. As he had only his tropical clothing and the weather was cool, he departed dressed in a warrant officer's greatcoat which seemed to cause him some amusement.

AOC's Inspection

The annual inspection by the AOC 11 Group took place on 14 April, and was carried out by Air Vice-Marshal the Earl of Bandon CB DSO. The AOC was entertained to lunch in the officers' mess after the inspection and the station commander succeeded in winning a half-crown wager on the identity of one of the silver models of aircraft with which 29 Squadron had at one time been equipped. The AOC claimed it was a Bulldog, whereas in fact it was a Siskin!

Presentations

The first squadron in the Royal Air Force to receive its Standard was, appropriately enough, 1 Squadron based at Tangmere. The presentation of this took place on 24 April and was made by Air Vice-Marshal Longcroft, the first CO of the squadron after it had been re-equipped with aeroplanes in place of balloons in 1914. Many distinguished officers and guests attended the presentation including the AOC-in-C Fighter Command, Air Marshal Sir Dermot Boyle KBE CB AFC, the AOC 11 Group, Air Vice-Marshal the Earl of Bandon CB DSO, and numerous ex-members of the squadron.

The parade was commanded by Squadron Leader Morison DFC, the squadron commander, and a most impressive march-past was carried out as the Standard was paraded after its presentation. The Standard itself is beautifully embroidered and incorporates the squadron crest on a pale blue background with scrolls commemorating the principal battles in which the squadron took part during both world wars.

Although one of the oldest and best-known of the fighter stations, it is strange that Tangmere only received its official station badge this year. This was presented by the AOC 11 Group, Air Vice-Marshal H. L. Patch CB CBE on the 2nd December, 1953. The badge was accepted on behalf of the station by the commanding officer, Group Captain J. A. Kent DFC AFC, who commanded the parade. Following the presentation, a cocktail party was held and a buffet lunch served in the officers' mess which was attended by the AOC and the official guests.

Changes of Command

Several changes of command took place during the year which affected the station. In April, Air Marshal Sir Basil Embry KCB KBE DSO DFC AFC relinquished command of Fighter Command and was succeeded by Air Marshal Sir Dermot Boyle KBE CB AFC. In October, Air Vice-Marshal the Earl of Bandon CVO CB DSO handed over command of 11 Group to Air Vice-Marshal H. L. Patch CB CBE. Earlier in the year, in March, Group Captain S. C. Elworthy CBE DSO DFC AFC, as senior station commander in Fighter Command, left Tangmere and assumed command of RAF Station Odiham, which had been selected as the site of the Royal Review. The officer commanding RAF Station Odiham, Group Captain J. A. Kent DFC AFC, then assumed command of Tangmere.

Casualties

As previously mentioned, two pilots of 1 Squadron, Flying Officer Gisborne and Pilot Officer Anthonisz, were killed as a result of a collision during Exercise Momentum. One aircraft of 29 Squadron was lost in the Channel as a result of the crew becoming uncertain of their position and running out of fuel. In this case both the pilot and navigator were saved. The air-sea rescue service did remarkably well on this occasion and the naval helicopter from Ford piloted by Lt Commander Sproule, on his first rescue mission, picked up the crew of the Meteor NF11 within eight minutes of their having ditched about five miles south of Littlehampton. An interesting sidelight on the case is the fact that the rescued pilot, Flying Officer Sneddon, had himself but recently been recommended for his second Royal Humane Society Certificate for saving drowning people. He himself is not a very good swimmer!

Social Functions

The main social event of the year was the station's summer ball which took place on 7 August. The committee in charge of the arrangements did a magnificent job of organising the ball, and the results were most satisfactory. The station cinema, which is the sole remaining pre-war hangar, was chosen as the most suitable place to hold this function and large tents were erected outside as ante-rooms for the buffet. The entrance was decorated with plants and flowers and a covered way was constructed of bunting. Inside the main building, a false ceiling was constructed of strips of different coloured bunting giving the impression of being inside a large marquee.

The centre-piece was a large crown from which balloons cascaded at midnight. On either side of the stage, on which the band was located, large coloured portraits of Her Majesty and the Duke of Edinburgh were projected from behind onto ground glass screens let into frames, whenever the music started up.

The first three rows of cinema seats were removed and a false floor built in. On this were placed tables, chairs, and settees for the use of the special guests, of which there were a good number. Principal amongst the official guests were Marshal of the Royal Air Force the Viscount and Viscountess Portal of Hungerford and the Hon. Miss Rosemary Portal, Air Marshal Sir Dermot and Lady Boyle, Air Vice-Marshal and Mrs Fraser, Air Vice-Marshal and Mrs Constantine, the Mayor and Mayoress of Chichester, Air Vice-Marshal Sir George and Lady MacFarlane Reid, Sqn Ldr and

Mrs Neville Duke, and Colonel and Mrs Pike, Mrs Pike being better known to the RAF as Olive Snell, the artist who painted so many portraits of outstanding RAF personalities during the war.

Sports

The station's teams acquitted themselves well in their various fixtures throughout the year, particularly the cross-country and soccer teams. The former won the 11 Group Inter-Station Challenge Cup for the second time while the latter reached the final for the Headquarters Fighter Command Cup in addition to winning the 11 Group Inter-Station Challenge Cup, the Mid-Week Sussex League Cup, the Littlehampton Hospitals Charity Cup and the Broadwater Bowl, altogether a most praiseworthy effort.

(signed) J. A. Kent
Group Captain Commanding RAF Station Tangmere, Sussex

The fanfare of 1953 had obscured some uncomfortable facts. Nowhere in Group Captain Kent's review of the year were the hostilities in Korea mentioned, or that an uneasy cease-fire had come to prevail in 1953. Although the RAF had not sent any squadrons to Korea in support of the United Nations intervention, RAF pilots had flown operations under officer exchange schemes and 77 Squadron RAAF had been supplied with Gloster Meteor Mk 8s. The Meteors proved to be woefully inferior to the swept-wing Soviet MiG-15s they encountered in air-to-air combat, and neither did the Meteors' performance compare at all favourably with the USAF's F-86 Sabres. Korea had shifted the geopolitical balance: it demonstrated conclusively, if anyone was still in doubt, that the Soviets had acquired the capacity to produce technologically-advanced and highly-effective military aircraft in their thousands.

Between December 1952 and December 1953, the RAF received 438 Canadair CL-13 Sabres (North American F-86Es built under licence) on loan under the NATO Mutual Defence Aid Programme. The purpose of this allocation was to compensate for the lack of a credible British opponent to the MiG-15 and MiG-17, the Meteor's obsolescence having been exposed for all the world to see in Korea. As a stop-gap measure, the Sabres equipped ten RAF squadrons stationed in the British occupation zone in Germany with

NATO's Second Tactical Air Force and two Home Defence squadrons at Linton-on-Ouse, North Yorkshire, pending the arrival of sufficient numbers of British-built, second-generation jet fighters. Many more Home Defence squadrons might well have deployed Sabres but for the political sensitivities which prevented all but a handful from being stationed in the UK. Indeed, enough Sabres had been allocated to the RAF to suggest that this was the intention, but only about half were put into service, the rest being held in reserve.

In the meantime, 34 Squadron was reformed at Tangmere with Meteor F8s in August 1954 and joined 1 Squadron in the day-fighter role, 29 Squadron still being present on the airfield with Meteor night fighters. By the autumn of 1954, not only was it evident that the Meteor day fighter was completely outclassed by more modern fighters in air-to-air combat, but the new English Electric Canberra bomber which had entered squadron service could fly higher, and was very nearly as fast. In the early part of 1955, 1 Squadron's flight commanders, Flight Lieutenants Harry Irving and Freddie Pickard, were sent on a Day Fighter Leaders' Course at West Raynham to fly the Hawker Hunter Mk 1. Back at Tangmere the squadron received its first Hunter, a Mk 2, for the ground staff to familiarise themselves with the type. In June 1955 the first of the Sapphire-engined Hunter Mk 5s arrived and the 1 Squadron pilots began their conversion on to this new fighter aircraft. The Hunter Mk 5 had an uprated engine, was supersonic in the dive, and had the provision to carry under-wing stores. The squadron's new aircraft were proudly displayed to the public during September 1955 at the SBAC Farnborough air show and at RAF Tangmere's 'At Home' Day. Late in 1955, the other Meteor day-fighter squadron on the airfield, 34, also converted to the Sapphire-engined Hunter Mk 5.

During the winter of 1955-56 the squadrons familiarised themselves with their new aircraft and in doing so found a number of serious technical faults with the Hunter Mk 5. In October, one of the aircraft suffered an undercarriage failure when landing at Tangmere, the aircraft narrowly missing the ground control approach caravan on the airfield. Another accident occurred due to malfunction of the tailplane control system, the pilot having to eject from the aircraft. However, during the first half of 1956 these deficiencies were gradually overcome.

During that year, in response to a specification from the Ministry of

Supply for an aircraft to investigate flight and control at transonic and supersonic speeds, the Fairey Aviation Company had developed the Delta 2, a mid-wing tail-less monoplane, with a circular cross-section fuselage and engine air inlets in the wing roots. The engine was a Rolls-Royce Avon RA.14R with an afterburner. The aircraft had a long tapering nose which obscured forward vision during landing, take-off and taxiing on the ground; the problem was resolved by a drooping nose design later used on Concorde.

Two aircraft were built, the first, WG774, made its maiden flight on 6 October 1954, flown by Fairey's test pilot Lieutenant Commander Peter Twiss DSC and Bar, who during the war had been involved in developing night-fighter tactics with the FIU and had flown long-range intruder operations over Germany from RAF Ford. On 28 October 1955, the FD2 achieved supersonic flight and following this success, despite a cool reaction from the Ministry of Supply, Fairey Aviation announced their intention to challenge the World Air Speed Record set in 1955 by an American F-100 Super Sabre. By January 1956 all obstructions had been cleared for the bid. The FAI rules had changed since 1953 and no longer required the aircraft to be flown at a low level. The new regulations for a World Air Speed Record attempt at a non-restricted altitude required the aircraft to fly over a 15-25 kilometre course once in either direction in level flight.

Fairey decided not to use RAF Tangmere as on the previous two UK attempts but to base the aircraft at Boscombe Down and make the attempt at 38,000 feet over a course between Chichester and Ford, in much the same place as used in 1946 and 1953. To time the aircraft, a camera-chronometer method was used. In this, the aircraft had to be photographed on each timed run, at the beginning and end of the course by two cameras, the time interval between the two photographs being recorded by an electronic chronometer. Obtaining the photographs required visual identification of the aircraft by the camera operators on the ground. RAF radar units assisted in this but it still proved difficult to achieve with a fast-moving small jet aircraft at 38,000 feet. The solution was to fly the aircraft at an altitude that produced a condensation trail. As in Neville Duke's record attempt three years earlier, Tangmere's 29 Squadron Meteor night fighters were again utilised, this time to determine each morning the best contrail-making altitude. Camera sites were set up away from the public gaze at RNAS Ford and at Apuldram sewage works, near Chichester. By the beginning of March 1956 all was ready for the attempt.

On Saturday, 10 March, a flight was conducted at eight o'clock but tracking system faults thwarted Fairey's. Later that morning, another attempt was made; Twiss took off at 11.22 hours; all seemed to go well and he landed back at Boscombe at 11.45 hours, after deviating in height over the course by only 98 feet. After the photographic plates had been developed, it was found that the Apuldram camera showed the start of the contrail but not the aircraft! However, the judges agreed that the attempt was a record and this was announced the next day.

Not everyone was pleased with this success; market gardeners across the south complained about the sonic boom breaking the glass windows in their greenhouses; one even threatened to sue Twiss for £16,000. Peter Twiss had broken the record with an average speed of 1,132 mph. He had also become the first pilot officially to exceed the milestone of 1,000 mph in level fight, just as Teddy Donaldson had been the first officially to exceed 1,000 km/h ten years earlier along the same stretch of England's south coast.

On 7 August 1956, 1 and 34 Squadrons were deployed to RAF Akrotiri, Cyprus, to provide fighter cover in the event of British military intervention if Egypt's Colonel Nasser carried out his threat to nationalise the Suez Canal. On 1 September the Tangmere Wing was moved to Nicosia airfield. On 5 November, when the British and French offensive against Egypt began, both squadrons were tasked with providing fighter cover for the paratroop drop on Gamil airfield. The RAF Valleta and Hastings aircraft were covered by relays of four Hunters from both squadrons throughout the unopposed drop. During the next two days the wing conducted high-level fighter sweeps over the Nile Delta but due to fuel limitations could only spend about ten minutes over the target area. Because of these difficulties, the wing was withdrawn from offensive operations and was reassigned to provide fighter cover over the Cyprus bases. After both squadrons returned in late 1956, life at Tangmere returned to much as it had been before Suez with flying devoted mainly to high-level formation interceptions and air-to-air combat exercises.

No. 29 Squadron, the night-fighter unit on the airfield that had been at Tangmere since 1950, moved to Acklington on 14 January 1957. Following their departure there was an eight-month gap until 25 Squadron arrived on 30 September with a mixed batch of NF12 and NF14 aircraft. The NF12 was a progressive development of the NF11 with a 17-inch longer nose to improve the aerodynamic shape and accommodate the US-built APS 21 AI radar. The NF14 was the last production version of the Meteor and externally differed from the NF12 in having a clear 'bubble' cockpit canopy. The night-fighter presence at RAF Tangmere was not to last much longer, however, and finally ended when 25 Squadron was disbanded on 1 July 1958.

The beginning of 1958 had brought some very unwelcome news, as Michael Shaw explains in his history of 1 Squadron:

> Little had been done in recent years to maintain the links between 1 Squadron and the people of Brighton. This was remedied on 28 October when the mayor and representatives of the local press visited Tangmere. In a lunchtime speech Alderman Charles Tyson recalled the close ties that had existed in the past and of the pride with which Brighton had regarded its squadron in war-time years. To help revive those ties he invited 'Brighton's Own' to take part in a week-end of friendship during the following January.
>
> Shortly before Christmas, 1 Squadron sent eight Hunters to Holland for another squadron exchange visit, this time with 327 Squadron RNAF at Soesterberg. A good week of flying and parties took place in Holland and the Hunter pilots were particularly glad to get their Christmas shopping done in Amsterdam.
>
> The friendship week-end in Brighton was a great success. As well as an ice show on 25 January and a church parade on the following morning, the pilots attended a ball in their honour at the Metropole on the Monday night. It was unfortunate that the Air Ministry should have chosen that morning to announce the forthcoming closure of Tangmere as a fighter station. This shattering news rather took the edge off what was otherwise an excellent party, but Squadron Leader Kingsford went to some pains to point out that No. 1, wherever it was posted, would never forget its links with the townspeople of Brighton.
>
> The impending demise of England's finest fighter station was one of the many unfortunate results of the Defence White Paper of 1957 known throughout the RAF as the 'Sandys Axe'. In this White Paper, the Secretary of State, Mr Duncan Sandys, foretold the widespread

introduction of guided weapon technology. The last manned fighter, he said, was with us already. As a result of this policy statement over 30 fighter squadrons both at home and in Germany were disbanded or reformed for other tasks.

It seemed that those squadrons flying the early marks of Hunter would be among the first to go and this, coupled with the impending closure of Tangmere as a fighter station, was ominous news for No. 1. The situation looked even blacker at the end of January when 34 Squadron was disbanded and suffered the ignominy of being reformed with Beverleys!

Eventually the news arrived that 1 Squadron itself was to be disbanded.

Fortunately it was to be simultaneously reformed at Stradishall by renumbering 263 Squadron which had recently re-equipped with the Avon-powered Hunter F Mk 6.

Poor old 253 was to be disbanded totally. This squadron had a fine history of its own, operating Gladiators from frozen lakes in Norway and using the Whirlwind and Typhoon to great effect during the latter stages of World War II.

The current pilots and ground crew of 1 Squadron were to be dispersed when disbandment occurred. To maintain continuity two pilots, Flg Offs Pete Highton and Bob Turner, were to be transferred to the 'new' No. 1 at Stradishall. The date of the hand-over was set at 23 June.

The members of the 'old' Squadron at Tangmere made the best of that last spring and summer at No. 1's ancestral airfield. Tangmere, with its beaches and pubs, its fine flying and sea air, would soon be just another memory for the greatest of its old squadrons.

The final month at Tangmere, with all its parties and festivities, was marred by a tragic accident when Flt Lt Michael Paxton and Fg Off John Turner failed to return from a sortie at the end of May. It was thought that they had been involved in a mid-air collision. A memorial service, the last of so many at Tangmere, was held in the station church on 29 May.

The squadron threw a number of parties before they finally left Sussex. A dinner dance in Brighton on 13 July was attended by many familiar faces who had served with No. 1 during the past three years. The all-ranks dance at Chichester was a great success as was Squadron Leader Kingsford's barbecue held on the 19th. During the barbecue a series of shattering explosions was heard close overhead: someone had tied a number of 'thunderflashes' to a met. balloon and sent it drifting over the party.

They paraded the Standard at Tangmere on 23 June. The salute was taken by Air Chief Marshal Sir Thomas Pike as twelve aircraft of 1 and 25 Squadron flew past in immaculate formation. Fg Off Pete Highton then handed the Standard of 1 Squadron to Fg Off Anthony Mumford of 263.

The handover of the colour symbolised the end of an era.

Tangmere, with all its nostalgia and history, would never more echo to that evocative blue note of Meteors and Hunters running home to break and land. Never again would the bars of the Old Ship, the Spotted Cow or the Red Lion at Pagham echo to the merry laughs and bawdy stories of fighter pilots. It was a sad day for Sussex and for 1 Squadron.

The news that Fighter Command had decided to withdraw from RAF Tangmere may have come as a shock to the officers and men of 1 Squadron when it was officially announced in January 1958, and it is clear that they blamed the 'Sandys Axe', but the possibility of the closure of RAF Tangmere as a Fighter Command station had been known since the end of 1956 when it was first mentioned in the station ORB: this was before Mr Sandys was appointed Minister of Defence in January 1957 and initiated the defence review that resulted in the infamous White Paper later that year.

A document appended to the January 1957 pages of station ORB, entitled 'Minutes of a Meeting Held at Royal Air Force Tangmere on 9 January 1957, to Discuss the Possible Future Deployment of an Operational Conversion Unit at Tangmere' gave a detailed account of the station's facilities in answer to a query from Fighter Command. The twelve officers who sat on the committee were to determine the suitability of RAF Tangmere as a Hunter conversion unit, initially with intakes of 17 students per four weeks for an eight-week course, with 34 students on course at any one time (Plan A); or 10 students per three weeks for an 'all through' course of 12 weeks to include gunnery training with 40 students on course at any given time (Plan B).

In either case accommodation for 30 to 40 students, 20 or more instructors and administrative officers, and 56 Hunter aircraft (or, in the case of Plan B, with an additional 10 Vampires and four Meteors) would be required. These numbers were no greater than the aerodrome had accommodated when it was occupied by the Central Fighter Establishment in 1945 and had been the site of the Fighter Leaders' Schools. Indeed, the overall numbers now being considered were fewer than in 1945, since as a whole CFE had many additional functions not at issue here. Yet the committee were insistent on the need for a new station headquarters building, a new flying wing headquarters building, a new control tower, a new engine preparation centre, and a new sick quarters building; while accepting that the residential accommodation, messing arrangements, hangarage, Technical Wing support, workshop spaces, and the airfield and its navigational aids were satisfactory for the purpose envisaged. Inexplicably, there was not a single word of welcome for, or interest in, the idea of using Tangmere as an OCU in the committee's report. Not surprisingly, Fighter Command chose to locate the OCU elsewhere.

The Sandys Defence White Paper was a coincidence; it was not the cause of RAF Tangmere's eventual closure. Its cause was the Cold War. Tangmere was in the wrong place to counter a threat coming from the east. By the mid-1950s the aerodrome was no longer regarded by Fighter Command as having a future as a front-line interceptor station, hence the query about whether it would be suitable as an OCU. When the last of the Canadair Sabres were returned to NATO in June 1956, replaced by new British-built Hawker Hunters, it was inevitable that the Hunters and any other new-generation fighter aircraft would be concentrated, sooner or later, on the east coast where they would be most effective. Tangmere's last chance of remaining an active Fighter Command station, as an OCU, had now vanished.

Tangmere's 'At Home' Day for 1957, held during the Battle of Britain Week celebrations on Saturday 14 September, would be the last time the station's resident fighter squadrons would put on a major public aerobatic display over the airfield. It was a swan song for 1 Squadron, soon to end its 30-year association with Tangmere. Following the disbandment of Tangmere's three fighter squadrons in the summer of 1958, the station was released from Fighter Command and transferred to Signals Command's 90 (Signals) Group. Two new squadrons moved in: a Ground Radio Calibration Flight of 245 Squadron operating Canberras, and 115 Squadron with Varsities. The Canberras carried out daily checks on Britain's early warning radars and the Varsities were used to calibrate navigation and approach aids.

On 5 May 1960, RAF Tangmere received the Freedom of the City of Chichester with a scroll and silver-and-enamel image of the city's arms presented to the officers' mess. In the following year, 'B' Flight of 22 Squadron arrived with its yellow-painted air-sea rescue Whirlwind helicopters. There was still the occasional drama: on 11 April 1962, an 81st Tactical Wing F-101 Voodoo of the US Air Force crashed on landing, scattering its undercarriage all over the airfield and beyond; a wheel was later found by St Andrew's Church, Oving, to the southwest of the airfield. At the end of October, the station's fire crews were again in action when a Hawker P1127 (the experimental prototype of the VSTOL Harrier) made an emergency landing after a total engine failure. Flown by test pilot Hugh Merewether, it was damaged beyond economic repair. The year also saw the runway used by Donald Campbell for early trials of his Bluebird-Proteus CN7 jet-engined car, which later raised the World Land Speed Record to 403.10 mph at Lake Eyre, Australia.

No. 245 Squadron was renumbered as No. 98 on 19 April 1963, and moved, together with 115 Squadron, to Watton on 1 October as the station was transferred from Signals Command to 38 Group, Transport Command. This change of role brought no new flying units and when, in May 1964, the air-sea rescue Whirlwinds of 22 Squadron moved to Thorney Island, the only unit left at Tangmere was 623 (Volunteer) Gliding School with Slingsby T21 gliders, used to give flying experience to Air Training Corps cadets. In yet another reorganisation of the RAF, Transport Command became Air Support Command on 1 August 1967; nine months later, on 30 April 1968, Fighter Command and Bomber Command would be merged as Strike Command. As it turned out, the last air officer commander-in-chief of Fighter Command would be Air Marshal Sir Frederick Rosier, who had started his career with 43 Squadron at Tangmere in 1936.

For a while, Air Support Command used Tangmere's runways to practice supply drops by Lockheed Hercules aircraft of 242 OCU based at Thorney Island. Tangmere was also used as a relief landing ground. Having long since lost its status as a master diversion airfield, Tangmere's still-serviceable runways were now used increasingly infrequently by powered aircraft, but on 4 April 1968, almost ten years after the squadron had left Tangmere, five of 1 Squadron's Hunter FG9s landed at the aerodrome after completing the RAF's 50th Anniversary Flypast over Brighton and Chichester. That evening, the squadron's pilots were entertained by local dignitaries and the following morning they took off from Tangmere to return to their base at West Raynham.

On the way back, Flight Lieutenant Alan Pollock (one of the flight commanders) broke away from the formation and flew down the River Thames at low level to make a protest about the continuing retrenchment in the RAF and the Wilson government's refusal to allow a flypast over London to mark the RAF's 50th anniversary. Pollock proceeded to put on his own show, circling the Houses of Parliament three times, dipping his wings over the Royal Air Force Memorial on the Embankment and flying under the top span of Tower Bridge. He beat up three airfields in inverted flight at an altitude of about 200 feet en route to West Raynham, where, within the hour, he was formally arrested. Alan Pollock successfully achieved the publicity he sought, but at the cost of bringing his RAF career to a premature end.

Epilogue

The end for RAF Tangmere came following a ceremonial closing-down parade on 16 October 1970. Even as some limited use by 623 Gliding School continued, consideration was being given to possible future uses of the aerodrome. The procedures specified by the Ministry of Defence for its disposal required that decisions be made by the county and district authorities about the new uses to which the aerodrome's land and buildings were to be put before it could be released from Crown ownership.

Thus between 1970 and 1975, while the airfield was reduced to care-and-maintenance status, lying dormant and largely unoccupied except for the gliding school, behind-the-scenes consultations and discussions were proceeding involving the Property Services Agency (acting for the Crown), the West Sussex County Council, the Chichester District Council, Tangmere Parish Council, and Oving Parish Council. It was eventually agreed by all parties that no flying activity would be permitted on any part of the airfield; that the landing ground would be returned to agricultural uses; and that the 50-acre domestic site and all the buildings, hangars, runways, aprons, and perimeter tracks would be purchased by the county and district councils so that their future development could be planned and managed in ways that would be in keeping with the semi-rural character of the locality. This proposal for a 'managed' approach under the direct control of the local authorities was contrasted with the fate of RNAS Ford, closed in 1959, which had been subdivided and sold off to a number of private purchasers with, from the planners' point of view, chaotic results. The Tangmere proposal was accepted by the Property Services Agency, and accordingly in 1975 steps began to be taken to transfer the ownership of the site to the county and district councils. The flying ban thereupon came into force, the gliding school having already disbanded. The airfield would never again be used for flying.

The final passing of the aerodrome was deeply felt by many, both inside and outside the RAF. In its time, Tangmere had been one of Britain's best-known – and within the RAF, best-loved – fighter stations. At the suggestion of local residents, Tangmere Parish Council erected a memorial stone on the village green at the end of the road leading to St Andrew's Church, commemorating RAF Tangmere and serving to remind future generations about the role played by the aerodrome in the defence of the nation. The memorial was unveiled by Group Captain Sir Douglas Bader in December 1976. Earlier that year, the Wealden Aviation Archaeological Group (WAAG), whose president Group Captain J. A. Kent was a former RAF Tangmere station commander, wrote to the West Sussex County Council asking if it would be possible to set up a museum in one of the buildings on the airfield. Nothing immediately materialised from the WAAG initiative, however.

Four years later, a meeting was called by former 1 and 43 Squadron pilot Alan Pollock to look, once again, into the possibility of setting up a museum. The meeting was held in the Spitfire Club (the former station NAAFI building) in September 1980. Many well-known people attended including Lord Balfour of Inchrye who, as Captain Harold Balfour MC and Bar, had been a pilot with 43 Squadron during the First World War and had shot down seven enemy aircraft; Lord Balfour had served as an MP from 1929, and while under secretary of state for air during the Second World War had visited Tangmere on several occasions. The outcome of the meeting was to set up a working group that included local people and RAF veterans to find premises for a museum that would be a fitting tribute to the role played by Tangmere in British history, both in peace and in war. Leading the working group was Jim Beedle, who had served with the RAF at Tangmere during the dark days of 1940 including being present during the Luftwaffe's main raid on the airfield on 16 August. Jim had served with 43 Squadron throughout the war, participating in the desperate defence of Malta, in the victorious North African desert campaign, and in the long and arduous Italian campaign. He had left the RAF in 1949, but continued to take an interest in the affairs of the 43 Squadron Association, of which he was secretary, and had also written a book about the squadron.

In 1981, Len Jepps (chairman of the local parish council) joined Jim

Beedle's group and arranged for the council to donate to the museum two large Uni-Seco prefabricated huts which had been built on the airfield in the late 1940s and served as a radio repair workshop. These huts, constructed of wood framing and asbestos-cement panels with steel-framed windows, were in very poor condition. The buildings were derelict, vandalised, and covered with bramble. Although work had not even started on converting one of the huts into a display hall (later called the Tangmere Hall) until late 1981, Jim Beedle set an opening date of 6 June 1982: many thought this to be an impossible target. The creation of the museum faced many difficulties and obstacles and Jim, who often travelled down daily from his home at Harpenden, Hertfordshire, some eighty miles away, and sometimes worked and slept in the building for days on end, kept the project moving forward. He was described by many who knew him during this time as being 'Churchillian' in manner. 'He could demolish your best ideas and suggestions in about ten seconds flat, leaving you rather deflated, but this was never through any sense of superiority, but simply what he thought was best for the museum at that time', as one of his colleagues was later to say. During this period the museum's display collection was being gathered. A large selection of aircraft parts and wartime remains were brought to the museum and artefacts and equipment were donated by enthusiasts and well-wishers from all parts of the country.

On 6 June 1982 the Tangmere Military Aviation Museum opened its doors to the public for the first time with Jim Beedle as its chairman. From the outset the museum was staffed entirely by volunteers, with no paid employees, and was completely self-supporting without any local authority financial help, and has remained an all-volunteer, independent effort ever since. The financial situation for the first two years was difficult, however. Most of the income from admissions was swallowed up by capital cost projects such as providing hot water and in funding the construction of the museum's exhibitions and displays. An information sheet sent round to the staff in July 1984 reported that the museum's first two years had been successful, with 'visitors mightily impressed by what they see here, the style of the museum and that the personalised and intimate approach in displaying the exhibits provides an atmosphere which they find moving and appealing'. It also reported that during the eight months of opening in 1983, 28,000 visitors came to see the museum and its first aircraft acquisition, an ex-

Danish Hawker Hunter Mk 51, from British Aerospace, Dunsfold. During 1983, the museum volunteers were delighted to hear that Squadron Leader Neville Duke had accepted the invitation to be the museum's honorary president, a responsibility he enthusiastically carried out with the support of his wife Gwen for the next 24 years until his death in April 2007.

Further exhibits were acquired in 1984, including a hydraulically-operated Pickett-Hamilton Fort, which was a machine-gun post placed alongside runways from late 1940. Manned by two or three men, these pillboxes were designed to be lowered to ground level when aircraft were operating so as not to present a hazard to the aircraft; it could also rise out of the ground to surprise attacking enemy paratroopers landing on the airfield. Tangmere's fort had been recovered from its satellite Merston by Royal Engineers and moved to the museum in the autumn. A second aircraft arrived when an American T33A, the two-seat jet trainer version of the Lockheed P-80/F-80 Shooting Star, was loaned by the US Air Force to the museum; this example had been allocated to the French air force as part of a military aid development plan but was later reclaimed by the USAF and placed in storage after France left NATO in 1966. Other acquisitions during the year were a superb original oil painting by Robert Taylor of James Nicolson's engagement with the enemy over Romsey, Hampshire, when he was awarded the only Fighter Command Victoria Cross of the Second World War, and Neville Duke's flying suit and helmet he wore on his famous World Air Speed Record flight on 7 September 1953. This year also saw a second successful 'aeromart' (an aeronautical flea market) at the museum which attracted some 1,200 visitors. This was the first of several annual aeromarts to be held at the museum.

By the end of 1986, the number of volunteer staff had risen to about 45 and in an information sheet produced by Jim Beedle it was reported that during the year annual visitor numbers continued to be a consistent 28,000 which compared favourably with other small independent museums. In this information sheet there is also first mention of a museum shop and of a Spitfire simulator, designed and built for children by Ken Murch, a former wartime RAF flight lieutenant, instrument specialist, and Chichester High School teacher. Apparently, the simulator had been a fascinating draw to both boys and girls and had been serviceable for most of the year but had a wayward rudder control which could be surprising to the would-be pilot!

Also reported was that the Danish Hunter, exhibited outside, was now resplendent in RAF 43 Squadron markings.

A major change to the museum's organisation took place during 1987 when the limited-liability Tangmere Military Aviation Museum Trust Company was formed. This new entity took over all the assets of the Tangmere Memorial Company, the main aim being to enable the museum to apply for charitable status – which it did, successfully – and to receive the advantages that thereby accrue, such as reduction in rates and relief from Corporation Tax. During the closed period (to the public) at the beginning of the year, a new display hall – to be called the Middle Hall – was erected to the side of the Battle of Britain Hall at a cost of £7,000 and fitted out and filled with new exhibits. The hall was officially opened by Bob Symes, presenter of the BBC television programme *Tomorrow's World*, at the end of February just before the museum opened for the 1987 season. During the year the museum accessioned over 500 objects into the collection, varying from a single postcard to a Mk 14 bombsight computer and a Second World War searchlight. Sadly, during 1989, the museum lost its inspirational chairman when Jim Beedle died, aged 79. In an address given at the service of thanksgiving to Jim's life and work, Dr W. J. Guild said that up to the day he died he 'worked on 43 Squadron business and on museum business, delegating work and responsibilities for others to carry forward in the future'.

By the early 1990s the museum was financially secure, established as a charitable trust and limited company, and a major Sussex visitor attraction with a strong, enthusiastic volunteer workforce. The museum's new chairman was another charismatic figure, the former wartime Spitfire, Hurricane, and Walrus pilot, Nick Berryman. As well as numerous important artefacts, the museum now had many interactive exhibits mostly constructed by Ken Murch. Examples, in addition to the Spitfire simulator that had now 'flown' over 700 hours and raised over £2,000 for The Save the Children's Fund, were helicopter and bombsight simulators, a cut-away Derwent jet engine, and a Mark VIII automatic pilot that controlled a large Lancaster model.

In an information sheet written by Nick Berryman to the staff, there is the first mention of a possible loan to the museum of Neville Duke's record-breaking Hawker Hunter and Teddy Donaldson's Gloster Meteor from the RAF Museum, and the loan of a replica of the prototype Spitfire K5054 owned by the Spitfire Society. During June 1992, the museum hosted a visit of former members and the families of the US Army Air Force's 31st Fighter Group which operated from Merston and Westhampnett in 1942. During the year, construction of a large new aircraft display hall, to be called the Merston Hall, was completed and in a trustees' meeting in August, it was decided to officially open the hall in 1993. Ken Murch used the empty hall to give presentations to visitors of some of his flying models. This was also the year that Ken met the Princess Royal when she visited the museum to accept on behalf of the Save the Children's Fund the sum of £2,500 donated by visitors to 'fly' Ken's simulators.

On Saturday, 20 March 1993, the Merston Hall was officially opened by former Battle of Britain pilot and Tangmere Wing leader, Air Commodore Pete Brothers CBE DSO DFC. Over 350 people attended. The year also saw the start of the creation of a memorial garden to remember the courage of the young men and women of the military services together with those of the civilian services who preserved our liberty during both world wars and since. The museum attempted during the year to acquire Tangmere's former Spitfire gate guardian (TE311) on loan from the RAF but the MoD declined the request. However, negotiations were in progress with the family of a Danish Spitfire pilot who flew with the RAF's 234 Squadron during the Second World War. On 24 April 1942, 234 Squadron, then part of the Ibsley Wing along with 118 and 501 Squadrons, put down at Tangmere to join forces with the Tangmere Wing for a show over occupied France. Later that day, Pilot Officer Axel Svendsen was shot down in Spitfire Mk V (BL924) over Berck-sur-Mer, Pas de Calais. His aeroplane, named 'Valdemar Atterdag' after a king of the Middle Ages credited with making Denmark a powerful country, was a 'presentation Spitfire', a gift of the free Danes in Britain. Axel Svendsen was one of very few Danes to serve as a fighter pilot in the RAF. The family, keen to have a memorial to him, instructed the museum to purchase a full-size replica of his aeroplane.

As well as the Danish replica Spitfire, which arrived in 1994, the museum acquired a full-sized replica Hawker Hurricane Mk 1 painted in the colours of the aircraft flown by Flying Officer Paul Richey when he served with 1 Squadron during the Battle of France. The replica was fitted with a Rover V-8 car engine turning a two-bladed propeller, making suitably loud, gruff noises and enabling the aircraft to be taxied. During one taxiing demonstration it is reported that the pilot, the museum's chairman Nick Berryman, enthusiastic as ever, almost got airborne! In September 1994 the completed memorial garden was officially opened by the museum's patron, the Duke of Richmond and Gordon. Also that year, the museum obtained on loan from the RAF Museum a rare Supermarine Swift. Lieutenant Commander Mike Lithgow, Supermarine's chief test pilot, had set the absolute World Air Speed Record in Libya in 1953 in a Mk 4 Swift, and although the new acquisition was a photo reconnaissance version, the aircraft was considered to be an excellent addition to the museum's growing collection of speed-record aircraft. Ken Murch, as well as managing the simulators, continued during the year his education programme for children in which he taught the principles of flight. Since 1991, when he had started the programme, he had taught over 2,400 schoolchildren how aeroplanes fly.

Air Commodore David Lawrence, keeper of aircraft and exhibits at the RAF Museum Hendon, visited Tangmere in 1995 and was impressed with the quality and layout of the exhibits. After inspecting the aircraft on loan, he declared that he was satisfied with the standard reached by the museum. He commented that Hendon gets a number of requests from museums to loan exhibits and stated that in future he would say to those making such requests, 'Go to Tangmere and if you can reach their high standard, then I will consider your application'. The museum took charge during the year of another important loaned aircraft with the arrival of the prototype Spitfire replica K5054, then owned by the Spitfire Society.

The museum's Society of Friends was formed in 1993 and by 1997 had enrolled some 430 members. Apart from assisting in the planting of the memorial garden, the Society of Friends had purchased a number of original paintings. During 1999, museum volunteer and aviation archaeologist Keith Arnold brought to the museum the parts of Dennis Noble's Hurricane Mk 1 he had dug out of the ground three years before from the crash site at Hove, Sussex. Twenty-year-old Sergeant Dennis Noble had joined 43 Squadron at Tangmere in early August 1940, during the Battle of Britain, but was shot down over Brighton on 30 August. The aircraft remains had lain in the ground for more than 50 years until Keith obtained the necessary authority to extract them.

During 2000, a Sea Vixen FAW2 was donated to the museum by the Sea Vixen Society. The aircraft had previously spent many years displayed outside the former de Havilland aircraft factory at Christchurch, Dorset, and restoration work started immediately after its arrival in June to prepare the aircraft for the winter months. The aircraft was an important airframe as it had been the first production conversion from FAW1 to FAW2 and, after twenty years of service life, was the last Sea Vixen to fly operationally in Royal Navy markings. In June 2002, the museum received a generous donation when Meryl and Raymond Hansed gifted two classic British jet fighter aircraft; a Hawker Hunter F5 and an English Electric Lightning F53. In November 1994, the couple had purchased the Hunter F5 (WP190) at a MOD auction at Sotheby's. It had been a gate guardian at RAF Stanbridge, Bedfordshire, for many years and Raymond moved it initially to the Gloucestershire Aviation Collection premises at Brockworth and then, with the assistance of Air Commodore Graham Pitchfork (archivist of the Air Crew Association), to a rented building at RAF Quedgeley, Gloucestershire. Raymond, with the help of Sandy Mullen, John Holder and Syd Griffith, formed the Hunter Restoration Flight and work began in earnest on the aircraft. Grit-blasting removed layers of old paint, revealing traces of a 1 Squadron badge on the nose, prior to corrosion treatment and the painstaking work of reconditioning the cockpit, undercarriage and equipment bays. Many firms and individuals were generous with sponsorship and support. Finally WP190 was given an immaculate paint finish to represent her time with Tangmere-based 1 Squadron during the Suez campaign with the characteristic black and yellow recognition stripes.

In 1996 Raymond Hansed heard of the closure of the Wales Aircraft Museum, Cardiff, and grasped the opportunity to fulfil another ambition, to own a Lightning. English Electric Lightning F53 53-670 was delivered to the Royal Saudi Air Force in November 1968, but returned to British Aerospace at Warton, Lancashire in January 1986 and was then allocated to the Cardiff museum. The Hunter Restoration Flight moved the aircraft by low-loader to Quedgeley in August 1996. Upon arrival, access panels and ventral fuel tanks were removed and internal corrosion treatment carried out to secure the aircraft's long-term future. Hydraulic lines were repaired so the canopy could be raised on a hand pump, enabling the cockpit to be refurbished more easily. Considerable surface corrosion was present and doubts were expressed over the planned return to a polished aluminium finish. However, an aluminium cleaner, supplied courtesy of the manufacturer, produced excellent results on all but the very severely corroded wing undersurfaces, the decision being made to paint the latter silver. The choice of paint scheme was that of a 23 Squadron Lightning F6 XR753, flown by Wing Commander Ian Thomson when he was squadron CO in 1975 at Leuchars, prior to the squadron re-equipping with McDonnell-Douglas Phantoms.

Meryl and Raymond Hansed dedicated Hunter WP190 to the Air Crew Association, but with the impending closure of Quedgeley a museum had to be found in which to display both aircraft. Tangmere was eventually chosen, the aircraft being gifted to the museum in June 2002. The Lightning arrived and was initially displayed outside whilst the Hunter was put into storage until covered accommodation could be provided. A new aircraft hall adjacent to the Merston Hall was constructed in early 2005 to accommodate the two Cold War jets. Sadly, Meryl Hansed did not live to see them displayed together but the museum's Trust Council decided to honour her memory by naming the new aircraft hall the Meryl Hansed Memorial Hall. The Hunter, which had been stored since 2002 in a local farmer's barn, was reassembled by members of the Hunter Flying Club based at Exeter and was manhandled into the new building by willing museum volunteers. The much heavier Lightning was winched into position a few days later with only inches to spare.

In November 2005, a McDonnell-Douglas Phantom FGR2, XV408, was acquired on loan by the museum courtesy of the trustees of the RAF Museum. The aircraft had served with 6, 19, 23, and 29 Squadrons and on retirement from service had been displayed on the parade ground at RAF Halton. The aircraft was moved to RAF Fairford in 2003 to be included in the static display of an airshow celebrating '100 Years of Flight' and was then abandoned in a corner of the airfield. She was on the list for scrapping but efforts to save her resulted in the aircraft being allocated to the RAF Museum and loaned to Tangmere. Another aircraft also was accepted during the year when a Royal Navy Westland Wessex HU5 (XS511) was delivered for safe-keeping at the museum. The commando support helicopter had been allocated to the Storrington, West Sussex, Air Training Corps squadron.

In May 2006, Group Captain David Baron OBE took up the post of museum chairman. In his service career he had been a Hunter, Jaguar, Gnat, and Phantom pilot. By a happy coincidence, the museum's Phantom XV408 was in his log book as one of the aircraft he had flown. The year continued to be an extremely busy one for the museum with the official opening of the Meryl Hansed Memorial Hall by the museum's patron, the Duke of Richmond and Gordon, on 1 April in the presence of some 80 guests, including many relations and friends of the Hanseds. Another major achievement during the first half of the year was the introduction of a completely new museum website. Other physical developments during the year included the arrival on-site of a prefabricated building generously gifted by the West Sussex County Council to be used as an education room. The main open day during the year was a highly successful 'Meteor Day' to mark the 60th anniversary of Group Captain Teddy Donaldson's world-record-breaking flight from RAF Tangmere in Meteor EE549. The museum hosted some 30 members of the Donaldson family and approximately 40 ex-Meteor pilots in addition to a large number of visitors. A major achievement for the museum during 2006 was successful accreditation by the Museums, Libraries and Archives Council (MLA), the national body overseeing museum standards. The chairman of the MLA wrote to the museum thus: 'Being awarded accreditation is an impressive achievement. It recognises the high standard and service the Tangmere Military Aviation Museum provides and acknowledges the hard work of the staff. Many congratulations.'

The museum lost a great friend and supporter when our honorary president Squadron Leader Neville Duke died on 7 April 2007. He was flying his own aircraft with his wife Gwen by his side when he was taken ill but managed to land at Popham airfield, Hampshire, where he collapsed and was rushed to hospital. He died in Chertsey Hospital just before midnight. Later that year, the museum's Trust Council invited Duncan Simpson, like Neville a previous Hawker chief test pilot, to become our honorary president which he accepted. On 16 and 17 June 2007, the museum celebrated the 25th anniversary of its opening. On the second day, a Sunday, Duncan Simpson officially opened our new education facility, called the Neville Duke Hall in honour of our past president.

During the next five years up to the museum's 30th Anniversary in 2012, the staff made great efforts to improve the professionalism of the museum to ensure it could continue to compete with other museums and visitor attractions in the area. It was thought that more interactive exhibits should be made available for our visitors and the museum's director (a new post introduced in 2007), Alan Bower, encouraged the introduction of aircraft cockpit simulators and touchscreens. The museum was now fortunate in having the skills within its all-volunteer workforce to design and build both simulators and touchscreens in-house. New efforts were also made by the the curatorial staff to improve the quality and consistency of the presentation of our artefacts, and their labelling and interpretation. Many new information boards, short films, and video presentations were produced in-house. That year the museum's twice-yearly magazine, funded by the Society of Friends, was re-launched as *The Tangmere Logbook*, now a serious journal registered with the British Library and sent to subscribers as far away as Australia, New Zealand, Canada, the USA, and South Africa.

The museum staff also concentrated during this period on the conservation and preservation of our aircraft and artefacts. In addition to continuing preservation work on the aircraft, a particularly challenging task on those displayed outside, conservation work was undertaken on the museum's uniform collection, medals, and documents. The museum's impressive library of more than 4,000 aviation books was reorganised and the books re-catalogued. In furtherance of our accreditation status with the MLA, a new collection management database was designed in-house and introduced to manage the 30,000-plus artefacts, ranging from complete aeroplanes to airmen's service and release books, that the museum now had in its collection.

Three new aircraft were accessioned into our collection between 2007 and 2012: a Sea Harrier FRS2 prototype and a Canberra B2 cockpit were accepted on loan, and a Vampire T11 was accepted as a gift. In addition, on the engineering side, an RAF Regiment Daimler scout car which had been displayed at the front of the museum for over twenty years was taken in hand and totally refurbished to running condition. In education, the museum developed two new programmes for school visits, now running at about 45 a year, and several of the museum's volunteers, including Dudley Hooley who took over from Alan Bower as director in 2011, provided talks on topics connected with the museum to outside groups.

By the time the museum reached its 30th anniversary in 2012, it had become a successful, well-established visitor attraction and a nationally accredited centre for the care and conservation of historic artefacts pertaining to military aviation. Its original buildings have been extended again and again to accommodate its growing collections of aircraft and memorabilia. At the outset, the museum was completely self-supporting. It has remained an all-volunteer, independent effort ever since. Over the years, hundreds of people from all walks of life, mostly retired, have freely given their time to keep the museum going, and thousands of people have generously donated artefacts ranging from complete aeroplanes to medals and photographs. The millionth visitor will soon pass through its doors, and will read this dedication outside the main entrance:

TANGMERE MEMORIAL
FOR ALL AIR FORCE PERSONNEL
OF ALL NATIONS WHO FOUGHT
AND DIED IN THE CAUSE OF
PEACE AND FREEDOM
THROUGHOUT THE WORLD
1939 – 1945

Appendix 1
Glossary of Terms and Acronyms

2TAF	Second Tactical Air Force (RAF)
9thAF	Ninth Air Force (USAAF)
AA	Anti-Aircraft
AAF	Auxiliary Air Force
AASF	Advanced Air Striking Force (RAF component of BEF, 1939-1940)
ACM	Air Chief Marshal
ADGB	Air Defence Great Britain
AFC	Air Force Cross
AI	Airborne Interception (radar)
ALG	Advanced Landing Ground
AOC	Air Officer Commanding
AOC-in-C	Air Officer Commander-in-Chief
ASAEF	Air Service of the American Expeditionary Forces (1917-1918)
ASR	Air-Sea Rescue
AVM	Air Vice-Marshal
Beat up	Fly over an airfield at low level
Beehive	Bomber formation closely escorted by fighters; see also Circus
BEF	British Expeditionary Force
BG	Bomb or Bombardment Group (USAAF)
CB	Companion of the Most Honourable Order of the Bath
CBE	Commander of the Most Excellent Order of the British Empire

CFE	Central Fighter Establishment
CH	Chain Home (radar station)
Circus	Short-range bombing attack on specific target closely escorted by fighters
CO	Commanding Officer
DFC	Distinguished Flying Cross
DFM	Distinguished Flying Medal
DI	Daily Inspection (aircraft maintenance)
Diver	Luftwaffe V1 rocket
Dogfight	Aerial combat between fighters
DSO	Distinguished Service Order
EA or E/A	Enemy aircraft
EGM	Empire Gallantry Medal (exchanged for George Cross 24.09.1940)
ELG	Emergency Landing Ground
FAA	Fleet Air Arm
FG	Fighter Group (USAAF)
FIDS	Fighter Interception Development Squadron
FIDU	Fighter Interception Development Unit
FIU	Fighter Interception Unit
Flak	Enemy anti-aircraft fire
Flamer	Aircraft or vehicle attacked and left burning
FLS	Fighter Leaders' School
FS	Fighter Squadron (USAAF)
GC	George Cross
GCA	Ground Controlled Approach radar
GCI	Ground Controlled Intercept radar
GSU	Group Support Unit
HSL	High Speed Launch
IFF	Identification Friend or Foe
KCB	Knight Commander of the Most Honourable Order of the Bath
Lucero	Airborne homing, beam approach and IFF interrogator
MBE	Member of the Most Excellent Order of the British Empire
MC	Military Cross
MFDF	Medium Frequency Direction Finding

MM	Military Medal
MP	Military Police
MT	Motor Transport, motorised vehicles
MU	Maintenance Unit
NAAFI	Navy, Army and Air Force Institutes
NAFDU	Naval Air Fighting Development Unit
NAS	Naval Air Squadron
NCO	Non-Commissioned Officer
Noball	Attack on a V1 rocket launch site
OBE	Officer of the Most Excellent Order of the British Empire
Oboe	Target marking system controlled from ground radar stations
OCU	Operational Conversion Unit
Ops	Operations
RAAF	Royal Australian Air Force
RAF	Royal Air Force (1.4.1918 – present); see also RFC
RAFVR	Royal Air Force Volunteer Reserve
Ramrod	Fighter-escorted daylight attack by medium or heavy bombers
Ranger	Large-scale fighter intrusion intended to find and destroy enemy aircraft
RCAF	Royal Canadian Air Force
RDF	Radio Direction Finding
RFC	Royal Flying Corps (13.4.1912 – 1.4.1918); see also RAF
Rebecca	Blind homing and approach aid for aircraft
Recce or Recco	Reconnaissance sortie; if armed, may include attacking targets of opportunity
Rhubarb	Small-scale, low-level fighter intrusion in search of targets of opportunity
RNZAF	Royal New Zealand Air Force
Roadstead	Attack on enemy shipping
Rodeo	Small-scale fighter intrusion intended to find and destroy enemy aircraft
RP	Rocket Projectile (airborne armament)
RT or R/T	Radio Telephony
Squadron	Operational unit consisting of (normally) 2 or 3 flights of 6 aircraft

SOE	Special Operations Executive
US or U/S	Unserviceable
USAAC	United States Army Air Corps (2.7.1926 – 9.3.1942)
USAAF	United States Army Air Force (9.3.1942 – 18.9.1947)
USAF	United States Air Force (18.9.1947 to present)
VC	Victoria Cross
Vector	To direct an aircraft in the air to a specific location or target
Vic	Arrowhead (V) formation of three or more aircraft
WAAF	Women's Auxiliary Air Force
Wing	A group of (normally) 2 to 4 squadrons under unified command
WT or W/T	Wireless Telegraphy

Appendix 2
Numerical List of Squadrons
Stationed at RAF Tangmere, its Satellites, and Tangmere Sector Airfields

Short stays on RAF stations were often incompletely mentioned, or not mentioned at all, in the Operations Record Books. Stays of three weeks or more during peace-time are noted below, but squadrons visiting on air exercises, summer camps, etc., are omitted. In wartime, stays of normally three days or more are listed below, but brief visits by squadrons en route elsewhere, or to regroup, refuel or re-arm are not included.

Squadron	Airfield	Dates from	to
1	Tangmere	01.02.1927	09.09.1939
	Tangmere	02.07.1940	01.08.1940
	Tangmere	01.07.1941	08.07.1942
	Tangmere	30.04.1946	01.07.1958
3	Shoreham	14.08.1942	21.08.1942
14	Tangmere	01.01.1919	04.02.1919
17	Tangmere	19.08.1940	02.09.1940
19	Bognor	26.06.1943	01.07.1943
	Ford	15.04.1944	12.05.1944
	Ford	15.06.1944	25.06.1944
21	Thorney Island	18.06.1944	06.02.1945
22 B Flight	Tangmere	01.06.1961	01.05.1964
23	Ford	12.09.1940	06.08.1942
23 Detachment	Tangmere	01.03.1941	01.06.1942
25	Tangmere	30.09.1957	01.07.1958
26	Tangmere	11.10.1944	01.11.1944
	Tangmere	04.11.1944	08.12.1944

Squadron	Airfield	Dates from	to
29	Ford	03.09.1943	01.03.1944
	Tangmere	25.11.1950	14.01.1957
32 Royal Squadron	Tangmere	05.03.1919	08.10.1919
33	Tangmere	03.07.1944	17.07.1944
	Funtington	17.07.1944	06.08.1944
	Selsey	06.08.1944	19.08.1944
34	Tangmere	01.08.1954	15.01.1958
40	Tangmere	13.02.1919	04.07.1919
41	Tangmere	10.02.1919	08.10.1919
	Merston	28.07.1941	16.12.1941
	Westhampnett	16.12.1941	01.04.1942
	Merston	01.04.1942	15.06.1942
	Westhampnett	19.06.1943	04.10.1943
	Westhampnett	28.06.1944	02.07.1944
	Friston	02.07.1944	11.07.1944
42 Detachment	Tangmere	01.03.1938	01.09.1938
43	Tangmere	12.12.1926	18.11.1939
	Tangmere	31.05.1940	08.09.1940
	Tangmere	16.06.1942	01.09.1942
	Tangmere	11.02.1949	09.11.1950
56 Detachment Punjab	Tangmere	01.05.1942	01.06.1942
64	Deanland	29.04.1944	26.06.1944
65 East India	Tangmere	29.11.1940	26.02.1941
	Westhampnett	07.10.1941	22.12.1941
	Selsey	31.05.1943	01.07.1943
	Ford	15.04.1944	14.05.1944
	Funtington	14.05.1944	15.06.1944
66	Tangmere	03.07.1942	07.07.1942
	Tangmere	16.08.1942	20.08.1942
	Bognor	31.03.1944	22.04.1944
	Bognor	25.04.1944	08.05.1944
	Bognor	14.05.1944	22.06.1944
	Tangmere	22.06.1944	06.08.1944
	Funtington	06.08.1944	12.08.1944
	Ford	12.08.1944	20.08.1944

Squadron	Airfield	Dates from	to
69	Tangmere	19.04.1947	16.05.1947
72 Basutoland	Tangmere	22.02.1937	01.06.1937
74 Trinidad	Tangmere	03.07.1944	17.07.1944
	Selsey	17.07.1944	24.07.1944
	Tangmere	01.07.1950	08.07.1950
80	Merston	22.06.1944	05.07.1944
82 United Provinces	Tangmere	01.05.1919	04.07.1919
84	Tangmere	12.08.1919	08.10.1919
85	Tangmere	09.10.1945	16.04.1947
87 United Provinces	Tangmere	15.03.1937	07.06.1937
91 Training	Tangmere	15.03.1918	17.08.1918
91 Nigeria	Westhampnett	28.06.1943	04.10.1943
	Tangmere	04.10.1943	08.02.1944
	Tangmere	20.02.1944	29.02.1944
	Deanland	21.07.1944	07.10.1944
92 Training	Tangmere	17.03.1918	Unknown
92 East India	Tangmere	10.10.1939	30.12.1939
93 Training	Tangmere	19.03.1918	17.08.1918
96 Detachment A	Tangmere	01.09.1942	01.06.1943
96 Detachment B	Tangmere	01.10.1942	01.08.1943
	Ford	20.06.1944	24.09.1944
98	Tangmere	19.04.1963	01.10.1963
115	Tangmere	25.08.1958	01.10.1963
118	Tangmere	03.07.1942	07.07.1942
	Tangmere	16.08.1942	24.08.1942
	Westhampnett	15.08.1943	24.08.1943
	Merston	24.08.1943	20.09.1943
122 Bombay	Funtington	15.09.1943	06.10.1943
	Ford	15.04.1944	14.05.1944
	Funtington	14.05.1944	20.05.1944
124 Baroda	Tangmere	25.09.1942	29.10.1942
	Westhampnett	29.10.1942	07.11.1942
127	Tangmere	04.07.1944	12.07.1944
	Tangmere	23.07.1944	06.08.1944
	Funtington	06.08.1944	12.08.1944

Squadron	Airfield	Dates from	to
127	Ford	12.08.1944	20.08.1944
129 Mysore	Westhampnett	29.08.1941	23.12.1941
	Thorney Island	30.07.1942	23.09.1942
	Tangmere	28.02.1943	13.03.1943
	Coolham	03.04.1944	22.06.1944
	Ford	24.06.1944	08.07.1944
130 Punjab	Horne	30.04.1944	18.06.1944
	Westhampnett	19.06.1944	27.06.1944
	Merston	27.06.1944	03.08.1944
	Tangmere	03.08.1944	11.08.1944
131 County of Kent	Merston	16.05.1942	24.08.1942
	Tangmere	31.08.1942	24.09.1942
	Westhampnett	07.11.1942	18.01.1943
	Friston	28.08.1944	05.02.1945
132 City of Bombay	Ford	18.04.1944	25.06.1944
141	Tangmere	23.06.1942	10.08.1942
	Ford	10.08.1942	18.02.1943
145	Tangmere	10.05.1940	23.07.1940
	Westhampnett	31.07.1940	14.08.1940
	Tangmere	09.10.1940	07.05.1941
	Merston	07.05.1941	28.07.1941
148	Tangmere	17.02.1919	04.07.1919
161 Detachment	Tangmere	01.04.1942	01.09.1943
164 Argentine British	Tangmere	02.10.1942	11.10.1942
	Thorney Island	15.03.1944	17.06.1944
	Funtington	17.06.1944	21.06.1944
	Tangmere	25.03.1946	26.04.1946
165 Ceylon	Tangmere	01.08.1942	02.11.1942
	Tangmere	02.11.1942	09.03.1943
165 Detachment Ceylon	Tangmere	23.03.1943	29.03.1943
168 Detachment	Tangmere	01.07.1942	01.11.1942
170 Detachment	Tangmere	01.06.1943	01.09.1943
174 Mauritius	Merston	12.06.1943	01.07.1943
	Westhampnett	10.10.1943	21.01.1944
	Westhampnett	04.02.1944	01.04.1944

Squadron	Airfield	Dates from	to
175	Apuldram	02.06.1943	01.07.1943
	Westhampnett	09.10.1943	24.02.1944
	Westhampnett	08.03.1944	01.04.1944
181	Apuldram	02.06.1943	02.07.1943
	Merston	08.10.1943	31.12.1943
	Merston	13.01.1944	06.02.1944
	Merston	21.02.1944	01.04.1944
182	Apuldram	02.06.1943	02.07.1943
	Merston	12.10.1943	31.12.1943
	Merston	21.01.1944	01.04.1944
183	Tangmere	04.08.1943	18.09.1943
	Funtington	03.04.1944	20.04.1944
	Thorney Island	21.04.1944	18.06.1944
	Funtington	18.06.1944	22.06.1944
184	Merston	31.05.1943	12.06.1943
	Westhampnett	23.04.1944	13.05.1944
	Westhampnett	20.05.1944	17.06.1944
193	Thorney Island	15.03.1944	06.04.1944
197	Tangmere	28.03.1943	15.03.1944
	Tangmere	01.04.1944	10.04.1944
198	Tangmere	16.03.1944	30.03.1944
	Thorney Island	06.04.1944	18.06.1944
	Funtington	18.06.1944	22.06.1944
207	Tangmere	22.08.1919	08.10.1919
208 Detachment	Tangmere	01.01.1958	01.03.1958
213	Tangmere	07.09.1940	29.11.1940
217	Tangmere	07.06.1937	16.08.1937
	Tangmere	13.09.1937	28.09.1938
	Tangmere	10.10.1938	25.08.1939
219	Tangmere	10.12.1940	23.06.1942
222 Natal	Selsey	11.04.1944	30.06.1944
	Coolham	30.06.1944	04.07.1944
	Funtington	04.07.1944	06.08.1944
	Tangmere	19.08.1944	31.08.1944
	Tangmere	02.10.1946	28.04.1947

Squadron	Airfield	Dates from	to
222 Natal	Tangmere	16.06.1947	01.05.1948
229	Tangmere	22.06.1944	24.06.1944
	Merston	24.06.1944	27.06.1944
232	Merston	25.06.1942	08.07.1942
234 Madras Presidency	Deanland	29.04.1944	19.06.1944
238	Tangmere	16.05.1940	20.06.1940
245	Selsey	01.06.1943	30.06.1943
245	Westhampnett	10.10.1943	01.04.1944
	Tangmere	25.08.1958	19.04.1963
247 China-British	Merston	11.10.1943	31.12.1943
	Merston	13.01.1944	01.04.1944
253 Hyderabad State	Shoreham	24.05.1942	30.05.1942
256	Ford	24.04.1943	25.08.1943
257 Burma	Tangmere	03.02.1944	10.04.1944
266 Rhodesia	Tangmere	09.08.1940	12.08.1940
	Tangmere	16.04.1947	11.02.1949
268 Detachment	Tangmere	01.07.1943	01.09.1943
274	Merston	22.06.1944	28.06.1944
277 Detachment	Shoreham	22.12.1941	07.10.1944
302 Polish *Poznański*	Westhampnett	23.11.1940	07.04.1941
	Tangmere	18.09.1943	21.09.1943
	Deanland	01.04.1944	26.04.1944
	Chailey	26.04.1944	28.06.1944
	Apuldram	28.06.1944	16.07.1944
	Ford	16.07.1944	04.08.1944
303 Polish *Kościuszki*	Horne	30.04.1944	18.06.1944
	Westhampnett	18.06.1944	26.06.1944
	Merston	26.06.1944	09.08.1944
	Westhampnett	09.08.1944	25.09.1944
306 Polish *Toruński*	Coolham	01.04.1944	27.06.1944
	Ford	22.06.1944	08.07.1944
308 Polish *Krakowski*	Deanland	01.04.1944	26.04.1944
	Chailey	26.04.1944	28.06.1944
	Apuldram	28.06.1944	16.07.1944
	Ford	16.07.1944	04.08.1944

Squadron	Airfield	Dates from	to
310 Czech	Apuldram	04.04.1944	22.06.1944
	Tangmere	22.06.1944	27.06.1944
	Tangmere	29.06.1944	03.07.1944
312 Czech	Apuldram	04.04.1944	22.06.1944
	Tangmere	22.06.1944	28.06.1944
	Tangmere	30.06.1944	04.07.1944
313 Czech	Apuldram	04.04.1944	22.06.1944
	Tangmere	22.06.1944	28.06.1944
	Tangmere	30.06.1944	04.07.1944
315 Polish *Deblinski*	Coolham	01.04.1944	22.06.1944
	Ford	25.06.1944	10.07.1944
316 Polish *Warszawski*	Friston	11.07.1944	27.08.1944
317 Polish *Wileński*	Deanland	01.04.1944	26.04.1944
	Chailey	26.04.1944	28.06.1944
	Apuldram	28.06.1944	16.07.1944
	Ford	16.07.1944	04.08.1944
322 Dutch	Deanland	21.07.1944	10.10.1944
329 French *Cigognes*	Merston	17.04.1944	19.05.1944
	Merston	23.05.1944	22.06.1944
	Funtington	22.06.1944	01.07.1944
	Selsey	01.07.1944	06.08.1944
	Tangmere	06.08.1944	19.08.1944
331 Norwegian	Bognor	31.03.1944	22.06.1944
	Tangmere	22.06.1944	06.08.1944
	Funtington	06.08.1944	12.08.1944
	Ford	13.08.1944	30.08.1944
332 Norwegian	Bognor	31.03.1944	21.06.1944
	Tangmere	22.06.1944	06.08.1944
	Funtington	06.08.1944	12.08.1944
	Ford	12.08.1944	20.08.1944
340 French *Ile de France*	Westhampnett	07.04.1942	20.07.1942
	Westhampnett	26.07.1942	28.07.1942
	Merston	17.04.1944	15.05.1944
	Merston	18.05.1944	22.06.1944
	Funtington	22.06.1944	01.07.1944

Squadron	Airfield	Dates from	to
340 French *Ile de France*	Selsey	01.07.1944	14.08.1944
	Tangmere	14.08.1944	19.08.1944
341 French *Alsace*	Merston	17.04.1944	22.06.1944
	Funtington	22.06.1944	01.07.1944
	Selsey	01.07.1944	06.08.1944
	Tangmere	06.08.1944	19.08.1944
345 French *Berry*	Shoreham	26.04.1944	16.08.1944
	Deanland	16.08.1944	10.10.1944
349 Belgian	Selsey	11.04.1944	30.06.1944
	Coolham	30.06.1944	04.07.1944
	Funtington	04.07.1944	06.08.1944
	Tangmere	19.08.1944	26.08.1944
350 Belgian	Friston	25.04.1944	04.07.1944
	Westhampnett	04.07.1944	08.08.1944
401 RCAF Ram	Tangmere	17.04.1944	17.06.1944
402 RCAF City of Winnipeg	Merston	07.08.1943	19.09.1943
	Horne	30.04.1944	18.06.1944
	Westhampnett	19.06.1944	27.06.1944
	Merston	27.06.1944	08.08.1944
403 RCAF Wolf	Tangmere	18.04.1944	16.06.1944
411 RCAF Grizzly Bear	Tangmere	15.04.1944	17.04.1944
	Tangmere	22.04.1944	18.06.1944
412 RCAF Falcon	Merston	18.06.1942	10.08.1942
	Merston	14.08.1942	23.08.1942
	Tangmere	23.08.1942	23.09.1942
	Tangmere	15.04.1944	18.06.1944
416 RCAF City of Oshawa	Westhampnett	25.06.1942	08.07.1942
	Merston	09.08.1943	19.09.1943
418 RCAF City of Edmonton	Ford	15.03.1943	08.04.1944
421 RCAF Red Indian	Tangmere	18.04.1944	16.06.1944
422 Flight RCAF Flying Yachtsman	Shoreham	14.10.1940	18.12.1940
438 RCAF Wildcat	Funtington	03.04.1944	20.04.1944
439 RCAF Westmount	Funtington	02.04.1944	19.04.1944
440 RCAF City of Ottawa	Funtington	02.04.1944	19.04.1944
441 RCAF Silver Fox	Westhampnett	01.04.1944	12.04.1944

Squadron	Airfield	Dates from	to
441 RCAF Silver Fox	Funtington	23.04.1944	14.05.1944
	Ford	14.05.1944	15.06.1944
442 RCAF Caribou	Westhampnett	01.04.1944	22.04.1944
	Funtington	30.04.1944	14.05.1944
	Ford	15.05.1944	15.06.1944
442 Flight RCAF Caribou	Shoreham	14.10.1940	18.12.1940
443 RCAF Hornet	Westhampnett	01.04.1944	22.04.1944
	Funtington	22.04.1944	14.05.1944
	Ford	14.05.1944	15.06.1944
453 RAAF	Ford	18.04.1944	25.06.1944
456 RAAF	Ford	29.02.1944	31.12.1944
464 RAAF	Thorney Island	18.06.1944	05.02.1945
485 RNZAF	Westhampnett	02.01.1943	15.02.1943
	Westhampnett	22.02.1943	21.05.1943
	Merston	21.05.1943	16.06.1943
	Selsey	07.04.1944	30.06.1944
	Coolham	30.06.1944	04.07.1944
	Funtington	04.07.1944	07.08.1944
	Tangmere	19.08.1944	31.08.1944
486 RNZAF	Tangmere	29.10.1942	31.01.1944
487 RNZAF	Thorney Island	18.06.1944	02.02.1945
501 County of Gloucester	Tangmere	28.11.1939	10.05.1940
	Tangmere	03.07.1942	07.07.1942
	Westhampnett	30.04.1943	17.05.1943
	Westhampnett	12.06.1943	21.06.1943
	Friston	30.04.1944	02.07.1944
	Westhampnett	02.07.1944	02.08.1944
	Tangmere	05.09.1951	08.10.1951
534 from 1455 Turbinlite Flight	Tangmere	02.09.1942	25.01.1943
601 County of London	Tangmere	30.12.1939	17.05.1940
	Tangmere	17.06.1940	19.08.1940
	Tangmere	02.09.1940	07.09.1940
602 City of Glasgow	Westhampnett	13.08.1940	17.12.1940
	Bognor	01.06.1943	01.07.1943

Squadron	Airfield	Dates from	to
602 City of Glasgow	Ford	18.04.1944	25.06.1944
604 County of Middlesex	Ford	18.02.1943	24.03.1943
605 County Of Warwick	Tangmere	27.08.1939	11.02.1940
	Ford	07.06.1942	15.03.1943
607 County of Durham	Tangmere	01.09.1940	10.10.1940
609 West Riding	Tangmere	16.03.1944	21.03.1944
	Thorney Island	01.04.1944	18.06.1944
610 County of Chester	Westhampnett	19.12.1940	28.08.1941
	Westhampnett	23.01.1943	30.04.1943
	Friston	02.07.1944	12.09.1944
611 West Lancashire	Deanland	29.04.1944	24.06.1944
614 Detachment County of	Tangmere	01.06.1940	01.03.1941
Glamorgan	Tangmere	01.09.1942	01.01.1943
616 South Yorkshire	Tangmere	26.02.1941	09.05.1941
	Westhampnett	09.05.1941	06.10.1941
	Tangmere	02.09.1942	29.10.1942
	Westhampnett	29.10.1942	02.01.1943
720 NAS	Ford	Dec 1940	Apr 1944
	Ford	Oct 1944	Aug 1945
	Tangmere	18.07.1947	25.08.1947
746 NAS	Ford	01.12.1942	03.04.1944
771 NAS Detachment	Tangmere	12.08.1948	Dec 1948
787 NAS	Tangmere	17.01.1945	12.07.1945
	Ford	29.04.1945	12.07.1945
	Westhampnett	12.07.1945	27.10.1945
	Tangmere	27.10.1945	05.11.1945
801 NAS	Tangmere	28.07.1947	23.08.1947
823 NAS	Tangmere	25.09.1942	01.01.1943
	Tangmere	22.03.1943	31.05.1943
841 NAS Detachment	Tangmere	31.05.1943	07.10.1943
1310 Flight	Bognor	23.06.1944	26.09.1944
1426 Flight	Tangmere	17.01.1945	31.12.1945
1455 Flight	Tangmere	07.07.1941	02.09.1942
92nd Aero Squadron,	Ford	Unknown	17.11.1918
ASAEF	Tangmere	17.11.1918	21.12.1918

Squadron	Airfield	Dates from	to
48th/49th FS, 14th FG, USAAF	Westhampnett	01.10.1942	15.10.1942
307th FS, 31st FG, USAAF	Merston	22.08.1942	30.09.1942
308th FS, 31st FG, USAAF	Westhampnett	29.08.1942	30.09.1942
309th FS, 31st FG, USAAF	Westhampnett	30.07.1942	30.09.1942
422nd FS, 9thAF, USAAF	Ford	Unknown	25.07.1944
425th FS, 9thAF, USAAF	Ford	Unknown	18.08.1944
Central Fighter Establishment	Tangmere	15.01.1945	01.10.1945
Fighter Interception Unit	Tangmere	18.04.1940	20.08.1940
	Shoreham	20.08.1940	01.01.1941
	Ford	01.02.1941	01.04.1944
	Ford	23.08.1944	01.07.1945
83 Group Support Unit	Bognor	23.06.1944	26.09.1944
	Thorney Island	26.09.1944	04.11.1944
	Westhampnett	04.11.1944	22.02.1945

Appendix 3
Chronological Squadron Arrivals and Departures, RAF Tangmere and Tangmere Sector Airfields

Apuldram (ALG 1943-1944)

Situated 2.5 miles SW of Chichester alongside the A286 and 5.5 miles WSW of Tangmere. Surveyed June 1942, work commenced February '43 and was completed in May. Occupied from the beginning of June 1943 by 2TAF Wings. Apuldram was an extremely busy ALG until a few weeks after D-Day. Flying ceased in late July. Derequisitioned 06.11.1944. Two flights of No. 5027 Works Unit removed the Sommerfeld tracking and Blister hangars immediately thereafter.

Squadron	Dates from	to	Aircraft	Code	Task	Remarks
175	02.06.1943	01.07.1943	Typhoon IB	HH	Ramrods	
181	02.06.1943	02.07.1943	Typhoon IB	EL	Ramrods	
182	02.06.1943	02.07.1943	Typhoon IB	XM	Ramrods	
						Airfield reverted to standby status. Four Extra Over Blister hangars and metal track hardstandings added
310 Czech	04.04.1944	22.06.1944	Spitfire IX	NN	Ramrods, Rodeos	
312 Czech	04.04.1944	22.06.1944	Spitfire IX	DU	Ramrods, Rodeos	
313 Czech	04.04.1944	22.06.1944	Spitfire IX	RY	Ramrods, Rodeos	
302 Polish *Poznański*	28.06.1944	16.07.1944	Spitfire IX	WX	Ramrods (army direction)	
308 Polish *Krakowski*	28.06.1944	16.07.1944	Spitfire IX	ZF	Ramrods (army direction)	
317 Polish *Wileński*	28.06.1944	16.07.1944	Spitfire IX	JH	Ramrods (army direction)	

Bognor (ALG 1943-1944)

Situated 1.5 miles NW of Bognor Regis to the north of Chalcraft Lane. In 1928 it was the proposed site for a municipal airport. Bognor ALG was approved in December 1942 and work commenced in January '43 and opened 1 June. 2TAF's 122 Airfield was the first occupant until July, it was then closed for upgrading and reopened 1944 when 132 Airfield of 84 Group arrived; its squadrons were busy until late June when it was replaced by 83 GSU. Flying ceased late September when 83 Group moved to Thorney Island.

Squadron	Dates		Aircraft	Code	Task	Remarks
	from	to				
122 Bombay	01.06.1943	01.07.1943	Spitfire VB, VC	MT	Circuses and ground attack training	
602 City of Glasgow	01.06.1943	01.07.1943	Spitfire VB, VC	LO	Circuses and ground attack training	
19	26.06.1943	01.07.1943	Spitfire VB, VC	QV	Circuses and ground attack training	
						Deserted from July until autumn when taxi track and additional hard-standings laid. Extra Over Blisters increased from 2 to 4.
331 Norwegian	31.03.1944	22.06.1944	Spitfire IX	FN	Circuses, Rodeos	
332 Norwegian	31.03.1944	21.06.1944	Spitfire IX	AH	Circuses, Rodeos	
66	31.03.1944	22.04.1944	Spitfire IXB	LZ	Circuses, Rodeos	
66	25.04.1944	08.05.1944	Spitfire IXB	LZ	Circuses, Rodeos	
66	14.05.1944	22.06.1944	Spitfire IXB	LZ	Circuses, Rodeos	
83 GSU	23.06.1944	26.09.1944	Spitfires, Mustangs, Typhoons, etc.		Replacement aircraft for operational squadrons	
1310 Flight	23.06.1944	26.09.1944	Anson		Air ambulance duties until end July then communications	

Chailey (ALG 1944)

Situated 3.75 miles E of Burgess Hill. Built amongst woodland with the runway intersection close to the road between Plumpton Green and Godley's Green. Surveyed in 1942, work commenced early '43. As with many ALGs, 4 Blister hangars were erected over winter '43-'44. Arriving from Deanland in April '44 were the Polish Sqns of 131 Airfield of 84 Group, 2TAF. Became 131 Wing in May and on D-Day the wing supplied low-level cover for the beachhead. 131 moved to Apuldram 28 June. Derequisitioned January 1945.

Squadron	Dates		Aircraft	Code	Task	Remarks
	from	to				
302 Polish *Poznański*	26.04.1944	28.06.1944	Spitfire IX, IXE	WX	Rangers, Rhubarbs	
308 Polish *Krakowski*	26.04.1944	28.06.1944	Spitfire IX	ZF	Rangers, Rhubarbs	
317 Polish *Wileński*	26.04.1944	28.06.1944	Spitfire IX	JH	Rangers, Rhubarbs	
						161 Sqn Lysander crashed 18.10.1944

Coolham (ALG 1944-1945)

Situated 6 miles SW of Horsham close to the village of Coolham. Surveyed late 1942, work started at the end of January '43 with two Sommerfeld Track runways but the airfield was left unused until spring '44. The Polish sqns of 133 Airfield moved in from Heston. The Mustangs dive-bombed the beachhead area on D-Day and later escorted gliders. 133 Wing moved to Holmsley South at the end of June. 135 Wing moved in with Spitfire IXs for a very brief stay departing 4 July, ending RAF flying at Coolham. In January '45 a USAAF Liberator made an emergency landing, flying out 26 January after repairs. The runway tracking was then lifted and the airfield again became agricultural.

Squadron	Dates		Aircraft	Code	Task	Remarks
	from	to				
306 Polish *Toruński*	01.04.1944	22.06.1944	Mustang III	UZ	Ramrods, Rangers, dive-bombing	
315 Polish *Dębliński*	01.04.1944	22.06.1944	Mustang III	PK	Ramrods, Rangers, dive-bombing	
129 Mysore	03.04.1944	22.06.1944	Mustang III	DV	Conversion to type then Ramrods, Rangers	
222 Natal	30.06.1944	04.07.1944	Spitfire IXB	ZD	Ramrods, Rangers	
349 Belgian	30.06.1944	04.07.1944	Spitfire IXB	GE	Ramrods, Rangers	
485 RNZAF	30.06.1944	04.07.1944	Spitfire IXB	OU	Ramrods, Rangers	

Deanland (ALG 1944-1945)

Situated about 5 miles NW of Hailsham. As with other ALGs in the area it was surveyed in late 1942 and built mid '43. Before it was officially opened, two aircraft used it for emergencies, a Spitfire and a B-17. The airfield opened April '44 with the arrival of 131 Airfield for intensive training with some escort work, moving to Chailey late April. 149 Airfield moved in for bomber escort work. The squadrons of 149 Wing (re-designated as such mid-May) in addition to bombing escorted tugs and gliders. 149 Wing moved for re-equipment late June. In July Spitfire XIVs moved in on anti-Diver work. Together with a Free French sqn they moved out in October and the airfield closed in November. The Sommerfeld Track runways were lifted and the site released in January '45.

Squadron	Dates from	to	Aircraft	Code	Task	Remarks
						Fortress B-17F 306 BG crashed 06.09.43
302 Polish *Poznański*	01.04.1944	26.04.1944	Spitfire IX	WX	Circuses, Rangers, dive-bombing training	
308 Polish *Krakowski*	01.04.1944	26.04.1944	Spitfire IX	ZF	Circuses, Rangers, dive-bombing training	
317 Polish *Wileński*	01.04.1944	26.04.1944	Spitfire IX	JH	Circuses, Rangers, dive-bombing training	
64	29.04.1944	26.06.1944	Spitfire VC	SH	Circuses	
611 West Lancashire	29.04.1944	24.06.1944	Spitfire VB	FY	Circuses	
234 Madras Presidency	29.04.1944	19.06.1944	Spitfire VB	AZ	Circuses	
91 Nigeria	21.07.1944	07.10.1944	Spitfire IXB, XIV	DL		Anti-Diver ops
322 Dutch	21.07.1944	10.10.1944	Spitfire IXE, XIV	VL, 3W		Anti-Diver ops
345 French *Berry*	16.08.1944	10.10.1944	Spitfire VB, IX	2Y	Rodeos	
						Released 12.01.1945 but road closure order not revoked until 1947

APPENDIX 3

Ford (RFC/ASAEF station 1917-1920, RAF station 1937-1939 and 1940-1945, RAF Tangmere satellite 1945)

Situated 2.5 miles W of Littlehampton. Originally named Ford Junction. Construction began as RFC aerodrome in 1917; from January 1918 financed by the American government and intended as a training depot for Handley Page 0/400 night bombing squadrons of the Air Service of the American Expeditionary Forces. Opened under ASAEF control 01.08.1918, possibly earlier. Vacated by ASAEF mid-November 1918 but buildings (including 6 100' x 170' Belfast-truss hangars and a Handley Page shed as at Tangmere) remained under American ownership. Thought to have been used for a time by the US Navy in 1919; also used by the RAF for squadron disbandment. Closed January 1920. The Ford Motor Company planned to use the aerodrome as an assembly plant for their Trimotor civil airliners but project was abandoned; it was then used by Rollason Aircraft followed by Alan Cobham's Flight Refuelling Ltd. Reopened as a military airfield in December 1937 for use by RAF Coastal Command, transferring in May '39 to the Royal Navy as HMS Peregrine for training and squadron work-up. Relinquished by Royal Navy and transferred to RAF in late 1940 with 23 Sqn as the first occupant. Became a satellite of RAF Tangmere 15.01.1945 to accommodate CFE's Night Fighter Leaders' Schools, naval and night-fighter development units, etc. Vacated by RAF and returned to Admiralty 01.08.1945. Data below for RAF Ford, 1940-1945 only.

Squadron	Dates		Aircraft	Code	Task	Remarks
	from	to				
23	12.09.1940	06.08.1942	Blenheim IF, Havoc, Boston III, Hurricane	YP	Night-fighter and night-intruder ops	Detachment of 23 Sqn, later 1455 Flight, maintained at Tangmere from March 1941 to September 1942, thereupon becoming 534 Sqn
720 NAS Detachment	Dec 1940	Apr 1944	Anson I		Photographic flight	Supported Naval Photographic School, which remained on the aerodrome

Squadron	Dates from	to	Aircraft	Code	Task	Remarks
Fighter Interception Unit	01.02.1941	03.04.1944	Blenheim IF, Hurricane, Mosquito II	None	Night-fighter development, night-fighter and night-intruder ops	From Tangmere (where formed) via Shoreham to whence FIU was evacuated following bombing of Tangmere 16.08.1940
605 County of Warwick	07.06.1942	14.03.1943	Boston III	UP	Intruder ops	
141	10.08.1942	18.02.1943	Beaufighter I	TW	Defensive night-fighter ops	
746 NAS	01.12.1942	03.04.1944	Fulmar IINF Firefly NFI, NFII		Naval night development and operations	Naval Night Fighter Interception Unit, then Naval Night Fighter Development Squadron
604 County of Middlesex	18.02.1943	24.04.1943	Beaufighter VI	NG	Defensive and night-intruder ops	
170	26.02.1943	13.03.1943	Mustang I	TL	Fighter reconnaissance	
418 RCAF City of Edmonton	14.03.1943	02.04.1944	Mosquito II, VI	TH	Night-bomber support, day intruder, Noballs	
256	24.04.1943	02.07.1943	Mosquito XII, XIII	JT	Defensive night-fighter ops	
29	03.09.1943	29.02.1944	Mosquito XII	RO	Defensive night-fighter ops	
456 RAAF	29.02.1944	30.12.1944	Mosquito XVII	RX	Defensive patrols for Coastal Command, Noballs, night-intruder ops	
65 East India	15.04.1944	14.05.1944	Mustang III	YT	Fighter bombers	
122 Bombay	15.04.1944	14.05.1944	Mustang III	MT	Circuses	
132 City of Bombay	18.04.1944	25.06.1944	Spitfire IXE	FF	Rodeos	
453 RAAF	18.04.1944	25.06.1944	Spitfire IXE	FU	Circuses, Rodeos	
602 City of Glasgow	18.04.1944	26.06.1944	Spitfire IX	LO	Rhubarbs	
441 RCAF Silver Fox	14.05.1944	15.06.1944	Spitfire IX	9G	Rodeos, shipping cover	
442 RCAF Caribou	14.05.1944	15.06.1944	Spitfire IX	YZ	Rodeos, shipping cover	
443 RCAF Hornet	14.05.1944	15.06.1944	Spitfire IX	2I	Rodeos, shipping cover	
19	20.05.1944	15.06.1944	Mustang III	QV	Long-range escort	

Squadron	Dates		Aircraft	Code	Task	Remarks
	from	to				
96	20.06.1944	24.09.1944	Mosquito XII, XIII	ZJ	Night-fighter cover over beaches	
315 Polish Dębliński	26.06.1944	10.07.1944	Mustang III	PK	Circuses, Noballs	
306 Polish Toruński	27.06.1944	09.07.1944	Mustang III	UZ	Circuses, Noballs	
302 Polish Poznański	16.07.1944	03.08.1944	Spitfire IX	WX	Rhubarbs	
308 Polish Krakowski	16.07.1944	03.08.1944	Spitfire IX	ZF	Circuses, Rodeos	
317 Polish Wileński	16.07.1944	03.08.1944	Spitfire IX	JH	Rodeos, beach cover	
422nd Night Fighter Sqn, 9thAF, USAAF	Not known	25.07.1944	P-61 Black Widow	Not known	Operational experience, anti-Diver ops	Date of arrival not recorded; may have stayed 2 or 3 weeks
425th Night Fighter Sqn, 9th AF, USAAF	Not known	18.08.1944	P-61 Black Widow	Not known	Operational experience, anti-Diver ops	Date of arrival not recorded; may have stayed 2 or 3 weeks
66	12.08.1944	20.08.1944	Spitfire IX	LZ	Fighter bombers	
127	12.08.1944	20.08.1944	Spitfire IX	9N	Circuses, Rhubarbs	
331 Norwegian	12.08.1944	20.08.1944	Spitfire IX	FN	Rodeos	
332 Norwegian	12.08.1944	20.08.1944	Spitfire IX	AH	Rodeos	
Fighter Interception Unit	15.09.1944	31.07.1945	Mosquito NF13, Welkin NFII, Wellington	ZQ	Development work, defensive and intruder ops to 08.05.1945, then development work only	Absorbed into CFE as Fighter Interception Development Unit (FIDU), later Fighter Interception Development Squadron (FIDS)
720 NAS Detachment	Oct 1944	01.08.1945	Anson I		Photographic flight	
						Aerodrome reassigned as satellite to RAF Tangmere for Night Fighter Leaders' Schools, FIDS, naval and night-fighter development units, 15.01.1945

Squadron	Dates		Aircraft	Code	Task	Remarks
	from	to				
Central Fighter Establishment	15.01.1945	31.07.1945	Various		Various	
787 NAS Detachment	29.04.1945	12.07.1945	Firefly I		Radar Trials	Detached from NAFDU at Tangmere Aerodrome vacated by RAF and returned to Admiralty, 01.08.1945

Friston (RAF Tangmere satellite 1944-1945 and 1946)

Situated 4.5 miles W of Eastbourne, near Beachy Head. Grass field known pre-war as Gayles or East Dean; used occasionally for AAF camps and formally as ELG summer '40. Used by various squadrons under Kenley control until April '44 when it came under the control of Tangmere with the arrival of 350 and 501 Squadrons. Operations were conducted over the D-Day beaches. With the arrival of 610, 41 and 316, anti-Diver operations were the priority. During its hectic months of '44 Friston was frequently used as an emergency landing ground for aircraft returning from operations over France. Finally 666 undertook training at the airfield. Reduced to C & M in May '45; parenting was transferred to Dunsfold in June and to Tangmere again in February '46 before being derequisitioned early April of the same year. Only usage by Tangmere is shown below.

Squadron	Dates		Aircraft	Code	Task	Remarks
	from	to				
350 Belgian	25.04.1944	04.07.1944	Spitfire IX	MN	Roadsteads, Rodeos, beachhead cover	
501 County of Gloucester	30.04.1944	02.07.1944	Spitfire IX	SD	Roadsteads, Rodeos, beachhead cover	
610 County of Chester	02.07.1944	12.09.1944	Spitfire XIV	DW	Anti-Diver ops	
41	02.07.1944	11.07.1944	Spitfire XII	EB	Anti-Diver ops	
316 Polish *Warszawski*	11.07.1944	27.08.1944	Mustang III	SZ	Anti-Diver ops	
131 County of Kent	28.08.1944	05.02.1945	Spitfire VII	NX	Circuses	
666 (AOP) RCAF	18.04.1945	28.05.1945	Auster V	No Code	Air Observation Post	

Funtington (ALG 1943-1944)

Situated 5 miles W of Chichester. Requisitioned late 1942 and building started late February '43 with two Sommerfeld Track runways. First occupant in September was 130 Airfield which returned to Odiham early October and over-winter improvements, including taxiways and 4 Over Blister hangars, were completed. Reopened 1 April with 143 Airfield HQ and its squadrons, to be replaced by 122 Wing in May which was in action until it departed late June when replaced by 123 and 136 Wings. Five days later they were replaced by 145 French Wing from Merston. Short stays were the norm and 145 went to Selsey 1 July to be replaced by 135 Wing from Coolham to undertake bomber escort work. The final occupant was 132 Wing from Tangmere. After its departure to France via Ford, the airfield closed and was de-requisitioned mid December '44 returning to agriculture early '45.

Squadron	Dates		Aircraft	Code	Task	Remarks
	from	to				
268	15.09.1943	08.10.1943	Mustang I, IA	NM	Tactical reconnaissance	
4	15.09.1943	06.10.1943	Mustang I	No code	Reconnaissance and defensive patrols	
						Closed for improvements addition of hard-standings and 4 Extra Over Blisters; handed over 1 April 1944 for use by 2nd TAF
122 Bombay	15.09.1943	06.10.1943	Mustang I	No code	Reconnaissance and defensive patrols	
439 RCAF Westmount	02.04.1944	19.04.1944	Typhoon IB	5V	Dive-bombing Noball sites	
440 RCAF City of Ottawa	02.04.1944	19.04.1944	Typhoon IB	I8	Dive-bombing Noball sites	
438 RCAF Wildcat	03.04.1944	20.04.1944	Typhoon IB	F3	Dive-bombing Noball sites	
183	03.04.1944	20.04.1944	Typhoon IB		Dive-bombing Noball sites	
329 French Cigognes	22.04.1944	24.04.1944	Spitfire IX	Y2	Circuses, Roadsteads, Rodeos, Ramrods, Rangers	
441 RCAF Silver Fox	23.04.1944	14.05.1944	Spitfire IX	9G	Circuses	
442 RCAF Caribou	22.04.1944	24.04.1944	Spitfire IX	Y2	Circuses	
443 RCAF Hornet	22.04.1944	14.05.1944	Spitfire IX	2I	Circuses	
442 RCAF Caribou	30.04.1944	14.05.1944	Spitfire IX	2I	Circuses	
65 East India	14.05.1944	15.06.1944	Mustang III	YT	Circuses, Roadsteads, Rodeos, Ramrods, Rangers	

Squadron	Dates from	to	Aircraft	Code	Task	Remarks
122 Bombay	14.05.1944	20.05.1944	Mustang III	MT	Circuses, Roadsteads, Rodeos, Ramrods, Rangers	
19	20.05.1944	15.06.1944	Mustang III	QV	Circuses, Roadsteads, Rodeos, Ramrods, Rangers	
122 Bombay	28.05.1944	15.06.1944	Mustang III	MT	Circuses, Roadsteads, Rodeos, Ramrods, Rangers	
485 RNZAF	17.06.1944	21.06.1944	Typhoon IB	OU	Preparation for transfer to France	
164 Argentine British	17.06.1944	21.06.1944	Typhoon IB	FJ	Preparation for transfer to France	
198	18.06.1944	22.06.1944	Typhoon IB	TP	Preparation for transfer to France	
183	18.06.1944	22.06.1944	Typhoon IB	HF	Preparation for transfer to France	
329 French *Cigognes*	22.06.1944	01.07.1944	Spitfire IX	5A	Circuses, Rodeos	
340 French *Ile de France*	22.06.1944	01.07.1944	Spitfire IXB	GW	Circuses, Rodeos	
341 French *Alsace*	22.06.1944	01.07.1944	Spitfire IX	NL	Circuses, Rodeos	
222 Natal	04.07.1944	06.08.1944	Spitfire IX	ZD	Circuses	
349 Belgian	04.07.1944	06.08.1944	Spitfire IX	GE	Circuses	
485 RNZAF	04.07.1944	07.08.1944	Spitfire IX	OU	Circuses	
33	17.07.1944	06.08.1944	Spitfire IXE	5R	Circuses	
66	06.08.1944	12.08.1944	Spitfire IX	LZ	Circuses, Rhubarbs	
127	06.08.1944	12.08.1944	Spitfire IXB	9N	Circuses, Rhubarbs	
331 Norwegian	06.08.1944	12.08.1944	Spitfire IX	FN	Circuses, Rhubarbs	
332 Norwegian	06.08.1944	12.08.1944	Spitfire IX	AH	Circuses, Rhubarbs	

Horne (ALG 1944)

Situated further N than other ALGs, about 5 miles ENE of Gatwick. This all-grass field accommodated three sqns from the end of April for just 6 weeks, probably the shortest-lived of any of the ALGs. It reverted to agriculture immediately after the sqns' departures.

Squadron	Dates from	to	Aircraft	Code	Task	Remarks
130 Punjab	30.04.1944	18.06.1944	Spitfire IX	AP	Rodeos	
303 Polish *Kościuszki*	30.04.1944	18.06.1944	Spitfire IX	RF	Rodeos	
402 RCAF City of Winnipeg	30.04.1944	18.06.1944	Spitfire IX	AE	Rodeos	

Merston (RAF Tangmere satellite 1941-1945, USAAF station 1942)

Situated 2.5 miles SW of Tangmere. The site was requisitioned July 1939 and building undertaken to create semi-permanent domestic and technical quarters; the rectangular grass airfield was surrounded by a 30 foot perimeter track. The wet ground affected completion which took until early 1941. First occupants were 145 Sqn in May of that year. The waterlogging affected operation and it was closed between December '41 and April '42. It became a two-squadron base but immediately after the Dieppe raid the 307th Fighter Squadron USAAF moved in, the airfield then being temporarily redesignated as USAAF Station 356. When the 307th moved out to support Operation Torch, the airfield was closed over winter with Sommerfeld Track runways and 20 hard-standings being added before reopening in May '43. The incoming squadrons were involved in Circuses, Roadsteads and Rhubarb operations; training using rockets was undertaken both with Hurricanes and Typhoons. The airfield was continually busy in the lead-up to and shortly after D-Day by 2TAF, but from late June '44 was briefly used by 80, 229 and 247 squadrons ADGB and finally 142 Wing 2TAF flying support for 2 Group bombers. Flying ceased the second week of August '44. ATC facilities removed and the airfield reduced to care and maintenance. In March 1945 it was used by 103 Wing SHAEF to house men of the Air Disarmament Units for a few weeks. In November '45 it was used by the Admiralty for storage of surplus equipment and later returned to agriculture.

Squadron	Dates from	to	Aircraft	Code	Task	Remarks
145	07.05.1941	27.07.1941	Spitfire IIB	SO	Rhubarbs	Cannon-equipped Spitfire IIBs
41	28.07.1941	16.12.1941	Spitfire IIB, VB	EB	Rhubarbs	
						Airfield waterlogged
41	01.04.1942	15.06.1942	Spitfire VB	EB	Rhubarbs	
131 County of Kent	16.05.1942	24.08.1942	Spitfire VB, VC	NX	Circuses	
412 RCAF Falcon	18.06.1942	10.08.1942	Spitfire VB	VZ	Circuses	
232	25.06.1942	08.07.1942	Spitfire VB	EF	Circuses	
412 RCAF Falcon	14.08.1942	23.08.1942	Spitfire VB	VZ	Circuses	
307th FS, 31st FG USAAF	24.08.1942	01.09.1942	Spitfire VB	MX	Ramrods	Temporarily became USAAF Station 356 between these dates Closed
485 RNZAF	21.05.1943	16.06.1943	Spitfire VB	OU	Circuses	
184	31.05.1943	12.06.1943	Hurricane IV	BR	Rocket-firing training	
174 Mauritius	12.06.1943	01.07.1943	Typhoon IB	XP	Rocket-firing training	

Squadron	Dates		Aircraft	Code	Task	Remarks
	from	to				
402 RCAF City of Winnipeg	07.08.1943	19.09.1943	Spitfire IX	AE	Roadsteads	
416 RCAF City of Oshawa	09.08.1943	19.09.1943	Spitfire IX	DN	Roadsteads	
118	24.08.1943	20.09.1943	Spitfire VB	NK	Circuses	
181	08.10.1943	31.12.1943	Typhoon IB	EL	Ramrods	
247 China-British	11.10.1943	31.12.1943	Typhoon IB	ZY	Ramrods	
182	12.10.1943	31.12.1943	Typhoon IB	XM	Ramrods	
181	13.01.1944	06.02.1944	Typhoon IB	EL	Ramrods, Circuses	
247 China-British	13.01.1944	01.04.1944	Typhoon IB	ZY	Ramrods, Circuses	
182	21.01.1944	01.04.1944	Typhoon IB	XM	Ramrods, Circuses	
181	21.02.1944	01.04.1944	Typhoon IB	EL	Ramrods, Circuses	
329 French *Cigognes*	17.04.1944	19.05.1944	Spitfire IX	5A	Rodeos, Circuses	
340 French *Ile de France*	17.04.1944	15.05.1944	Spitfire IXB	GW	Rodeos, Circuses	
341 French *Alsace*	17.04.1944	22.06.1944	Spitfire IXB	NL	Rodeos, Circuses	
340 French *Ile de France*	18.05.1944	22.06.1944	Spitfire IXB	GW	Rodeos, Circuses	
329 French *Cigognes*	23.05.1944	22.06.1944	Spitfire IX	5A	Rodeos, Circuses	
80	22.06.1944	05.07.1944	Spitfire IX	EY	ADGB	
274	22.06.1944	28.06.1944	Spitfire IX	JJ	ADGB	
229	24.06.1944	27.06.1944	Spitfire IX	9R	ADGB	
303 Polish *Kościuszki*	26.06.1944	09.08.1944	Spitfire IX	RF	Circuses	
130 Punjab	27.06.1944	03.08.1944	Spitfire VA, VB, VC	PJ	Circuses	
402 RCAF City of Winnipeg	27.06.1944	08.08.1944	Spitfire IX	AE	Circuses	

Selsey (ALG 1943-1944)

Situated 5 miles S of Chichester. Originally used for private flying in the '30s, it was surveyed early 1942, requisitioned in July and the site plan issued February '43. 65 and 245 sqns arrived at the end of May leaving a month later. The addition of 4 Extra Over Blister hangars and hard-standings prepared the site for the April '44 re-opening. 135 Airfield's sqns arrived early April and were busy dive-bombing communication targets. D-Day saw the wing giving cover over the beaches. 135 moved from Selsey at the end of June being replaced by 145 Wing which undertook beachhead patrols and bomber escort operations, moving to Tangmere early August when 135 Wing returned until 19 August when flying from Selsey ceased. The site was de-requisitioned just after the war's end when the road into Church Norton which had been closed was again opened.

Squadron	Dates		Aircraft	Code	Task	Remarks
	from	to				
65 East India	31.05.1943	01.07.1943	Spitfire VB, VC	YT	Circuses	
245 Northern Rhodesia	01.06.1943	30.06.1943	Typhoon IB	MR	Air-firing, tactical training	
						Closed for improvements: addition of hard-standings and 4 Extra Over Blisters
485 RNZAF	07.04.1944	30.06.1944	Spitfire IXB	OU	Circuses, Roadsteads	
222 Natal	11.04.1944	30.06.1944	Spitfire IX	ZD	Circuses, Roadsteads	
349 Belgian	11.04.1944	30.06.1944	Spitfire IX	GE	Circuses, Roadsteads	
33	06.08.1944	19.08.1944	Spitfire IXE	5R	Circuses, Rodeos, Rhubarbs	
329 French *Cigognes*	01.07.1944	06.08.1944	Spitfire IXB	5A	Beachhead patrols, Circuses	
340 French *Ile de France*	01.07.1944	14.08.1944	Spitfire IX	GW	Beachhead patrols, Circuses	
341 French *Alsace*	01.07.1944	06.08.1944	Spitfire IX	NL	Beachhead patrols, Circuses	
74 Trinidad	14.07.1944	24.07.1944	Spitfire IXE	4D	Beachhead patrols, Circuses	

Shoreham (Occasional use by Tangmere squadrons 1940-1942 and RAF Tangmere satellite 1944)

Situated 1 mile NW of Shoreham-by-Sea. First opened in 1911 and used for various early air races. The world's first recorded cargo flight was made from Shoreham. Taken over by the War Office in August 1914 and used by the RFC throughout the First World War mainly for pilot training but several fighter squadrons were formed there. The airfield was closed in 1921, reopened in '33 and again used for pilot training until September '39. It was then used for civil flights transferred out of Gatwick until June '40 when it became an advance fighter field in the Kenley Sector. Shoreham was used to house FIU after the August bombing of Tangmere; accommodated one Tangmere Sector fighter sqn for a week in the summer of '42 for the Dieppe Raid; used as an ASR airfield and satellite to Ford in November '42; and lastly used by Tangmere as a forward satellite in March '44. In September '44 it was reduced to C&M and returned to civil use in 1946. Only usage by Tangmere shown below.

Squadron	Dates		Aircraft	Code	Task	Remarks
	from	to				
Fighter Interception Unit (FIU)	20.08.1940	01.01.1941	Beaufighter I Blenheim I	ZQ	Development, operations	
422 Flight RCAF Flying Yachtsman	14.10.1940	18.12.1940	Hurricane I	Not known	Night-fighter ops	Sqn reformed 02.04.1942 at Lough Erne as a flying-boat unit
277 (Detachment)	22.12.1941	07.10.1944	Walrus I, II Defiant I, IA Spitfire IIA, VB Sea Otter II	BA	Air-Sea rescue	
3	14.08.1942	21.08.1942	Hurricane IIC	QO	Ramrods, night-intruder ops	
345 French Berry	26.04.1944	16.08.1944	Spitfire VB	2Y	Rodeos, beachhead patrols	

Tangmere (RFC/ASAEF station 1917-1919 and RAF station 1925-1970)

Construction began as RFC aerodrome in 1917; from January 1918 financed by the American government and intended as a training depot for Handley Page 0/400 night bombing squadrons of the Air Service of the American Expeditionary Forces. Opened under ASAEF control 01.08.1918. Vacated by ASAEF at the end of 1918 but buildings (including 7 100' x 170' Belfast-truss hangars and a Handley Page shed) remained under American ownership. Used by the RAF as a disbandment depot during 1919. Purchased by the Crown in 1923 for use as an RAF air defence fighter station; opened as such 01.06.1925 but used as an aircraft storage depot pending the arrival of resident fighter squadrons (43 and 1) at the end of 1926 and beginning of 1927. Relinquished by Fighter Command in 1958, and closed in 1970.

Squadron	Dates		Aircraft	Code	Task	Remarks
	from	to				
						Aerodrome construction financed by US government as from January 1918; remained American-owned until 1923
91 (T)	15.03.1918	17.08.1918	Unknown	No code	Temporary lodger; training	
92 (T)	17.03.1918	Unknown	Unknown	No code	Temporary lodger; training	Remained after ASAEF personnel arrived and RAF's 91 and 93 training sqns had departed
93 (T)	19.03.1918	17.08.1918	Unknown	No code	Temporary lodger; training	Aerodrome opened under ASAEF control, 01.08.1918
ASAEF	01.08.1918	21.12.1918	Various types	No code	Flying training	RAF's 92 (T) Squadron provided flying instruction for ASAEF aircrew

Squadron	Dates from	to	Aircraft	Code	Task	Remarks
92nd Aero Squadron, ASAEF	17.11.1918	21.12.1918	Handley-Page 0/400 intended, various types flown	No code	Working-up for night-bombing on Western Front	Awaited Handley Page 0/400 aircraft did not arrive before Armistice on 11.11.1918
14	01.01.1919	04.02.1919	Unknown	No code	Temporary lodger	
41	10.02.1919	08.10.1919	S.E.5A	No code	Temporary lodger	
40	13.02.1919	04.07.1919	S.E.5A	No code	Temporary lodger	
148	17.02.1919	04.07.1919	F.E.2B, 2D	No code	Temporary lodger	
32 Royal Squadron	05.03.1919	08.10.1919	S.E.5A	No code	Temporary lodger	
82 United Provinces	01.05.1919	04.07.1919	F.K.8	No code	Temporary lodger	
84	12.08.1919	08.10.1919	S.E.5A	No code	Temporary lodger	
207	22.08.1919	08.10.1919	0/400	No code	Temporary lodger	
						Purchased by Crown in 1923 for use as an air defence fighter station. Opened 01.06.1925; used for aircraft storage until arrival of 43 and 1 Sqns
43	12.12.1926	18.11.1939	Gamecock I, Siskin IIIA, Fury I, Hurricane I	No code then NQ, FT	Home Defence fighter	
1	01.02.1927	09.09.1939	Gamecock I, Siskin IIIA, Fury I, Hurricane I	No code then NA, JX	Home Defence fighter	
72	22.02.1937	01.06.1937	Gladiator I	RN	Home Defence fighter	
87	15.03.1937	07.06.1937	Fury II	No code	Home Defence fighter	

Squadron	Dates		Aircraft	Code	Task	Remarks
	from	to				
217	07.06.1937	25.08.1939	Anson I	MW	General reconnaissance	
42 Detachment	01.03.1938	01.09.1938	Vildebeest III	No code	Torpedo bomber bomber	
605 County Of Warwick	27.08.1939	11.02.1940	Gladiator II, Hurricane I	HE	Home Defence fighter	
92 East India	10.10.1939	30.12.1939	Blenheim IF	GR	Home Defence fighter	
501 County of Gloucester	28.11.1939	10.05.1940	Hurricane I	SD	Home Defence fighter	
601 County of London	30.12.1939	17.05.1940	Blenheim IF, Hurricane I	UF	Home Defence fighter	
Fighter Interception Unit	18.04.1940	20.08.1940	Blenheim IF, Beaufighter I	No code	Night-fighter development	First RAF unit to receive Beaufighters, beginning 12.08.1940
145	10.05.1940	23.07.1940	Hurricane I	SO	Home Defence fighter	
238	16.05.1940	20.06.1940	Spitfire I	VK	Home Defence fighter	
43	31.05.1940	08.09.1940	Hurricane I	NQ	Home Defence fighter	
614 County of Glamorgan Detachment	01.06.1940	01.03.1941	Lysander II, III	LJ	Coastal patrol	
601 County of London	17.06.1940	19.08.1940	Hurricane I fighter	UF	Home Defence	
1	02.07.1940	01.08.1940	Hurricane I	JX	Home Defence fighter	
266 Rhodesia	09.08.1940	12.08.1940	Spitfire I	UO	Home Defence fighter	
17	19.08.1940	02.09.1940	Hurricane I	YB	Home Defence fighter	
607 County of Durham	01.09.1940	10.10.1940	Hurricane I	AF	Home Defence fighter	
601 County of London	02.09.1940	07.09.1940	Hurricane I	UF	Home Defence fighter	
213	07.09.1940	29.11.1940	Hurricane I	AK	Home Defence fighter	
145	09.10.1940	01.02.1941	Hurricane I	SO	Offensive sweeps	
65 East India	29.11.1940	26.02.1941	Spitfire I	FZ	Offensive sweeps	
219	10.12.1940	23.06.1942	Beaufighter IF	FK	Night-fighter ops	
145	01.02.1941	28.05.1941	Spitfire IIA, IIB	SO	Rhubarbs, Circuses	
616 South Yorkshire	26.02.1941	09.05.1941	Spitfire IIA, IIB	QJ	Rhubarbs, Circuses	
23 Detachment	01.03.1941	01.06.1942	Havoc I	YP	Intruder ops	
1	01.07.1941	08.07.1942	Hurricane IIB	JX	Night-fighter, intruder ops	

Squadron	Dates		Aircraft	Code	Task	Remarks
	from	to				
1455 Flight	07.07.1941	02.09.1942	Havoc I, II Boston II, III	No code	Turbinlite night-fighter development and ops	
161 Detachment	01.04.1942	01.09.1943	Lysander IIIA	MA	SOE ops	
56 Punjab Detachment	01.05.1942	01.06.1942	Typhoon IB	US	Anti-shipping patrols	
43	16.06.1942	01.09.1942	Hurricane IIC	FT	Night-fighter, intruder ops	
141	23.06.1942	10.08.1942	Beaufighter I	TW	Local defence, intruder ops	
168 Detachment	01.07.1942	01.11.1942	Tomahawk IIA	EK	Army co-operation	
66	03.07.1942	07.07.1942	Spitfire VA, VB, VC	LZ	Rhubarbs, Ramrods	
118	03.07.1942	07.07.1942	Spitfire VB	NK	Rhubarbs, Ramrods	
501 County of Gloucester	03.07.1942	07.07.1942	Spitfire VB, VC	SD	Rhubarbs, Ramrods	
165 Ceylon	01.08.1942	02.11.1942	Spitfire VB, VC	SK	Rhubarbs, Ramrods	
66	16.08.1942	20.08.1942	Spitfire VA, VB, VC	LZ	Dieppe Raid ops	
41	16.08.1942	20.08.1942	Spitfire VB	EB	Dieppe Raid ops	
118	16.08.1942	24.08.1942	Spitfire VB	NK	Dieppe Raid ops	
131 County of Kent	22.08.1942	24.08.1942	Spitfire VB, VC	NX	Ramrods, Roadsteads	
412 RCAF	23.08.1942	23.09.1942	Spitfire VB	VZ	Ramrods, Roadsteads	
131 County of Kent	31.08.1942	24.09.1942	Spitfire VB, VC	NX	Ramrods, Roadsteads	
614 Detachment	01.09.1942	01.01.1943	Spitfire VB	FJ	Ramrods, Roadsteads	
96 Detachment	01.09.1942	01.06.1943	Beaufighter VI	ZJ	Intruder ops	
534	02.09.1942	25.01.1943	Havoc I, II Boston I, III Hurricane IIB, IIC, X, XI, XII	No code	Defensive night-fighter operations	Formerly 1455 Flight. Operated Turbinlite Havocs and Bostons, Boston night fighters, and a dedicated Hurricane night-fighter flight
616 South Yorkshire	02.09.1942	29.10.1942	Spitfire VB	YQ	Ramrods, Rodeos	
124	25.09.1942	29.10.1942	Spitfire VB	ON	Ramrods, Rodeos	
823 NAS	25.09.1942	22.03.1943	Albacore I		Anti-shipping	Torpedo-bomber reconnaissance

Squadron	Dates		Aircraft	Code	Task	Remarks
	from	to				
96 Detachment	01.10.1942	01.08.1943	Beaufighter II	ZJ	Ramrods, Rodeos	
164 Argentine British	02.10.1942	11.10.1942	Spitfire VB	FJ	Ramrods, Rodeos	
486 RNZAF	29.10.1942	31.01.1944	Typhoon IB	SA	Low-level defensive ops	
165 Ceylon	02.11.1942	09.03.1943	Spitfire VB, VC	SK	Ramrods, Rodeos	
129 Mysore	28.02.1943	13.03.1943	Spitfire VB	DV	Ramrods, Rodeos	
823 NAS	22.03.1943	31.05.1943	Albacore I		Anti-shipping	
165 Ceylon Detachment	23.03.1943	29.03.1943	Spitfire VB, VC	SK	Ramrods, Rodeos	
197	28.03.1943	15.03.1944	Typhoon IB	OV	Rhubarbs, Ramrods	
841 NAS Detachment	31.05.1943	07.10.1943	Albacore I		Anti-shipping	
170 Detachment	01.06.1943	01.09.1943	Mustang I, IA	No code	Army co-operation, coastal defensive ops	
268 Detachment	01.07.1943	01.09.1943	Mustang I, IA	NM	Tactical reconnaissance	
183	04.08.1943	18.09.1943	Typhoon IB	HF	Roadsteads, Rhubarbs, Ramrods	
302 Polish *Poznański*	18.09.1943	21.09.1943	Spitfire IX	WX	Rodeos, Circuses	
91 Nigeria	04.10.1943	08.02.1944	Spitfire XII	DL	Rodeos, Circuses	
257 Burma	03.02.1944	10.04.1944	Typhoon IA, IB	FM	Rodeos, Circuses	
91 Nigeria	20.02.1944	29.02.1944	Spitfire XII	DL	Rodeos, Circuses	
198	16.03.1944	30.03.1944	Typhoon IA,	TP	Rhubarbs, Ramrods	
609 West Riding	16.03.1944	21.03.1944	Typhoon IA, IB	PR	Rhubarbs, Ramrods	
197	01.04.1944	10.04.1944	Typhoon IB	OV	Rangers, Noballs	
416 RCAF City of Oshawa	14.04.1944	16.06.1944	Spitfire IX	DN	Rangers, Noballs, beachhead ops	
411 RCAF Grizzly Bear	15.04.1944 17.04.1944	22.04.1944 18.06.1944	Spitfire IX	DB	Rangers, Noballs, beachhead ops	
412 RCAF Falcon	15.04.1944	18.06.1944	Spitfire IX	VZ	Rangers, Noballs, beachhead ops	
401 RCAF Ram	17.04.1944	17.06.1944	Spitfire IXB	YO	Rangers, Noballs, beachhead ops	
403 RCAF Wolf	18.04.1944	16.06.1944	Spitfire IX	KH	Rangers, Noballs, beachhead ops	
421 RCAF Red Indian	18.04.1944	16.06.1944	Spitfire IX	AU	Rangers, Noballs, beachhead ops	
66	22.06.1944	06.08.1944	Spitfire IX	LZ	Rodeos, Rangers, beachhead ops	
229	22.06.1944	24.06.1944	Spitfire IX	9R	Circuses	
310 Czech	22.06.1944	27.06.1944	Spitfire VC	NN	Beachhead cover	
312 Czech	22.06.1944	28.06.1944	Spitfire IX	DU	Beachhead cover	
313 Czech	22.06.1944	28.06.1944	Spitfire IX	RY	Beachhead cover	
331 Norwegian	22.06.1944	06.08.1944	Spitfire IX	FN	Rhubarbs	
332 Norwegian	22.06.1944	06.08.1944	Spitfire IX	AH	Rhubarbs	
610 County of Chester	27.06.1944	02.07.1944	Spitfire XIV	DW	Anti-Diver ops	

Squadron	Dates from	Dates to	Aircraft	Code	Task	Remarks
310 Czech	29.06.1944	03.07.1944	Spitfire VC	NN	AGDB, Anti-Diver ops	
312 Czech	30.06.1944	04.07.1944	Spitfire IX	DU	Beachhead cover, Rangers, then ADGB	
313 Czech	30.06.1944	04.07.1944	Spitfire IX	RY	Beachhead cover, Ramrods	
33	03.07.1944	17.07.1944	Spitfire IXE	5R	Beachhead cover, glider escort ops	
74 Trinidad	03.07.1944	17.07.1944	Spitfire IXE	ZP	Working up for fighter-bomber ops	
127	04.07.1944	12.07.1944	Spitfire IX	9N	Rhubarbs	
127	23.07.1944	06.08.1944	Spitfire IX	9N	Rhubarbs	
130 Punjab	03.08.1944	11.08.1944	Spitfire XIV	AP	Anti-Diver ops	
329 French *Cigognes*	06.08.1944	19.08.1944	Spitfire IX	5A	Ramrods	
340 French *Ile de France*	06.08.1944	19.08.1944	Spitfire IXB	GW	Beachhead cover and Circuses	
341 French *Alsace*	06.08.1944	19.06.1944	Spitfire IXB	NL	Beachhead cover and glider tug support	
222 Natal	19.08.1944	31.08.1944	Spitfire IX	ZD	Armed reconnaissance and dive bombing	
349 Belgian	19.08.1944	26.08.1944	Spitfire IX	GE	Ramrods	
485 RNZAF	19.08.1944	31.08.1944	Spitfire IXB	OU	Ramrods	
26	11.10.1944	01.11.1944	Spitfire VA, VB, VC, XI	RM, XC	Gun spotting for naval bombardment	Type conversion was almost continuous from Mustang I to Spit Vs to Spit XI and back to Mustangs
26	04.11.1944	08.12.1944	Mustang I, Spitfire IX	XC	Conversion to type, reconnaissance	
Central Fighter Establishment	15.01.1945	01.10.1945	Various		Testing, development training	Operated a wide variety of aircraft types
787 NAS	17.01.1945	12.07.1945	Various		Development	Absorbed into CFE as Naval Air Fighting Development Unit (NAFDU)

Squadron	Dates from	to	Aircraft	Code	Task	Remarks
1426 (Enemy Aircraft) Flight	17.01.1945	31.12.1945	Enemy Aircraft	EA	Demonstration	Absorbed into CFE on arrival at Tangmere
85	09.10.1945	16.04.1947	Mosquito 30, NF36	VY	Day- and night-fighter defence	
164 Argentine British	25.03.1946	26.04.1946	Spitfire IXE	FJ	Day-fighter defence	
1	30.04.1946	01.07.1958	Spitfire 21, Meteor 3, Harvard T2B, Meteor F4, Meteor F8, Hunter F5	JX	Day-fighter defence	Disbanded at Tangmere 01.07.1958, reformed at Stradishall by renumbering 263 Sqn
222 Natal	02.10.1946	28.04.1947	Meteor F3	ZD	Day-fighter defence	
266 Rhodesia	16.04.1947	11.02.1949	Meteor F3	FX	Day-fighter defence	Disbanded at Tangmere 11.02.1949, renumbered as 43 Sqn
69	19.04.1947	16.05.1947	Mosquito 16	No code	Temporary lodger	
222 Natal	16.06.1947	01.05.1948	Meteor F3	ZD	Day-fighter defence	
720 NAS	18.07.1947	25.08.1947	Anson I		Temporary lodger	
778 NAS	18.07.1947	28.05.1948	Sea Fury FBII Sea Hornet F20		Temporary lodger	
801 NAS	28.07.1947	23.08.1947	Sea Hornet F20		Temporary lodger	
771 NAS Detachment	12.08.1948	Dec 1948	Sea Mosquito TR33		Temporary lodger	
43	11.02.1949	09.11.1950	Meteor F4, F8	SW	Day-fighter defence	Reformed 11.02.1949 by renumbering 266 and 245 Sqns
29	25.11.1950	14.01.1957	Mosquito NF36, Meteor 4, NF11	RO	Night-fighter defence	
501 County of Gloucester	05.09.1951	08.10.1951	Vampire FB5	No code	Temporary lodger	
34	01.08.1954	15.01.1958	Meteor F8, Hunter F5	No code	Day-fighter defence	

Squadron	Dates		Aircraft	Code	Task	Remarks
	from	to				
25	30.09.1957	01.07.1958	Meteor NF12, NF14	ZK	Night-fighter defence	
208 Detachment	01.01.1958	01.03.1958	Hunter F5, F6	No code	Day-fighter defence	
						Aerodrome relinquished by Fighter Command and transferred to Signals Command, August 1958
115	25.08.1958	01.10.1963	Varsity T1	No code	Calibration of navigational and approach aids	
245 Northern Rhodesia	25.08.1958	19.04.1963	Canberra B2	No code	Calibration of early warning radars	Disbanded at Tangmere and renumbered as 98 Sqn 19.04.1963
22 B Flight	01.06.1961	May 1964	Whirlwind HAR.2, HAR.10	No code	Air-Sea rescue	Last RAF flying unit to remain at Tangmere into 1964
98	19.04.1963	01.10.1963	Canberra B2	No code	Calibration of early warning radars	Renumbered from 245 Sqn 19.04.1963
						Aerodrome relinquished by Signals Command and transferred to Transport Command, October 1963
38 (Air Support) Group	01.10.1963	16.10.1970	Non-flying unit		Equipment maintenance, storage	
						Aerodrome closed 16.10.1970

Thorney Island (Occasional use by Tangmere and 2TAF squadrons 1942 and 1944-1945)
Situated 2 miles S of Emsworth. Opened as a Coastal Command airfield in 1938 and was
used as such for most of its wartime operational life although also used by 2TAF during the
build-up to D-Day and following. During the summer of 1942, one Tangmere fighter squadron
was accommodated there while Westhampnett was occupied by the USAAF; two 2TAF
Typhoon Wings, 123 and 136, were resident from March to June '44; and from mid '44 to
early '45 there were three 2TAF Mosquito squadrons based at Thorney. Only Tangmere
Sector usage is shown below.

Squadron	Dates		Aircraft	Code	Task	Remarks
	from	to				
129 Mysore	30.07.1942	23.09.1942	Spitfire VB, VC	DV	Circuses, Rangers, Rhubarbs	
193	15.03.1944	06.04.1944	Typhoon 1B	DP	Armed recce, ground attack	
164 Argentine British	15.03.1944	17.06.1944	Typhoon IA, IB	FJ	Noballs, armed recce	
183	21.04.1944	18.06.1944	Typhoon IA, IB	HF	Ground attack, fighter interception	
609 West Riding	01.04.1944	18.06.1944	Typhoon 1B	PR	Ground attack	
198	06.04.1944	18.06.1944	Typhoon IA, IB	TP	Ground attack	
21	18.06.1944	06.02.1945	Mosquito FBVI	YH	Day precision bombing, night-bombing ops	
464 RAAF	18.06.1944	05.02.1945	Mosquito FBVI	SB	Night-intruder ops	
487 RNZAF	18.06.1944	02.02.1945	Mosquito FBVI	EG	Day precision bombing, night-intruder ops	
83 GSU	26.09.1944	04.11.1944	Spitfires, Mustangs, Typhoons, etc		Replacement aircraft for operational squadrons	

Westhampnett (RAF Tangmere satellite 1940-1946; USAAF station 1942)
Situated 2.5 miles NW of Tangmere. Land acquired from the Goodwood Estate late 1938 for use as an emergency landing ground. Upgraded to satellite status May '40, officially opened end July when 145 moved in from Tangmere. Continuously in use by 11 Group squadrons on Circuses and Ranger operations until it became USAAF Station 352 with the 31st Fighter Group flying Spitfires. In October Lockheed P-38 Lightnings of the 14th FG used the airfield. RAF squadrons returned in October '42. The airfield's squadrons were busy in the preparations for D-Day and giving beachhead cover to the landings and escorting 2 Group bomber operations. Westhampnett was quiet from late September until 83 GSU arrived in November. In February '45 the airfield was placed on care and maintenance status. On 1 March '45 it was transferred to Air Staff SHAEF and accommodated Air Disarmament Units. In July it became active again with the personnel of CFE's Naval Air Fighting Development Unit (787 NAS) and other CFE personnel moving in from Tangmere and Ford, although all flying was done from Tangmere. The last CFE personnel being accommodated on the aerodrome left at the end of November '45. It closed completely May 1946. From 1948 to 1965 the perimeter track was used as a motor racing circuit. Granted permission for use as a civil airfield and still in use today as Goodwood Airfield.

Squadron	Dates		Aircraft	Code	Task	Remarks
	from	to				
145	31.07.1940	14.08.1940	Hurricane I	SO	Fighter defence	
602 City of Glasgow	13.08.1940	17.12.1940	Spitfire I	LO	Fighter defence	
302 Polish *Poznański*	23.11.1940	07.04.1941	Hurricane I	WX	Coastal patrols, Circuses	
610 County of Chester	19.12.1940	28.08.1941	Spitfire I	DW	Circuses, Rangers, Rhubarbs	
616 South Yorkshire	09.05.1941	06.10.1941	Spitfire IIA, IIB	QJ	Circuses, Rangers, Rhubarbs	
129 Mysore	29.08.1941	23.12.1941	Spitfire VB	DV	Circuses, Rangers, Rhubarbs	
65 East India	07.10.1941	22.12.1941	Spitfire VB, VC	YT	Circuses, Rangers, Rhubarbs	
41	16.12.1941	01.04.1942	Spitfire VB	EB	Circuses, Rangers, Rhubarbs	
340 French *Ile de France*	07.04.1942	20.07.1942	Spitfire IXB	GW	Circuses, Rangers, Rhubarbs	
416 RCAF City of Oshawa	25.06.1942	08.07.1942	Spitfire VB	DN	Circuses, Rangers, Rhubarbs	
340 French *Ile de France*	26.07.1942	28.07.1942	Spitfire IXB	GW	Circuses, Rangers, Rhubarbs	
						Becomes USAAF Station 352
309th FS, 31st FG USAAF	30.07.1942	30.09.1942	Spitfire V	WZ	Convoy escort & Rodeos	
307th FS, 31st FG USAAF	22.08.1942	30.09.1942	Spitfire V	MX	Convoy escort & Rodeos	
308th FS, 31st FG USAAF	29.08.1942	30.09.1942	Spitfire V	HL	Convoy escort & Rodeos	

Squadron	Dates from	to	Aircraft	Code	Task	Remarks
48th/49th FS, 14th FG USAAF	01.10.1942	15.10.1942	P-38 Lightning	ES/QU	Operational experience	
						Reverts to RAF
124	29.10.1942	07.11.1942	Spitfire VI	ON	Circuses, Rangers, Rhubarbs	
616 South Yorkshire	29.10.1942	02.01.1943	Spitfire VI	YQ	Circuses, Rangers, Rhubarbs	
131 County of Kent	07.11.1942	18.01.1943	Spitfire VB, VC	NX	Circuses, Rangers, Rhubarbs	
485 RNZAF	02.01.1943	15.02.1943	Spitfire VB	OU	Circuses, Rangers, Rhubarbs	
610 County of Chester	23.01.1943	30.04.1943	Spitfire VB, VC	DW	Circuses, Rangers, Rhubarbs	
485 RNZAF	22.02.1943	21.05.1943	Spitfire VB	OU	Circuses, Rangers, Rhubarbs	
501 County of Gloucester	30.04.1943	17.05.1943	Spitfire VB, experience	SD	Circuses, Rangers, Rhubarbs	
501 County of Gloucester	12.06.1943	21.06.1943	Spitfire VB, experience	SD	Circuses, Rangers, Rhubarbs	
41	19.06.1943	04.10.1943	Spitfire XII	EB	Circuses, Rangers, Rhubarbs	
91 Nigeria	28.06.1943	04.10.1943	Spitfire XII	DL	Circuses, Rangers, Rhubarbs	
118	15.08.1943	24.08.1943	Spitfire VB	NK	Circuses, Rangers, Rhubarbs	
175	09.10.1943	24.02.1944	Typhoon IB	HH	Roadsteads, Ramrods, Noballs	
174	10.10.1943	21.01.1944	Typhoon IB	XP	Roadsteads, Ramrods, Noballs	
245 Northern Rhodesia	10.10.1943	01.04.1944	Typhoon IB	MR	Roadsteads, Ramrods, Noballs	
174	04.02.1944	01.04.1944	Typhoon IB	XP	Roadsteads, Ramrods, Noballs	
175	08.03.1944	01.04.1944	Typhoon IB	HH	Roadsteads, Ramrods, Noballs	
441 RCAF Silver Fox	01.04.1944	12.04.1944	Spitfire IX	9G	Circuses	
442 RCAF Caribou	01.04.1944	22.04.1944	Spitfire IX	Y2	Circuses	
443 RCAF Hornet	01.04.1944	22.04.1944	Spitfire IX	2I	Circuses, high-level fighter cover	
184	23.04.1944	13.05.1944	Typhoon IB	BR	Roadsteads, Ramrods, Noballs	
303 Polish *Kościuszki*	18.06.1944	26.06.1944	Spitfire IX	RF	Roadsteads, Ramrods, Noballs	
130 Punjab	19.06.1944	27.06.1944	Spitfire VA, VB, VC	PJ	Circuses, beachhead patrols	
402 RCAF City of Winnipeg	19.06.1944	27.06.1944	Spitfire IX	AE	Circuses, beachhead patrols	

Squadron	Dates from	to	Aircraft	Code	Task	Remarks
41	28.06.1944	02.07.1944	Spitfire XII	EB	Circuses, beachhead patrols	
501 County of Gloucester	02.07.1944	02.08.1944	Spitfire IX	SD	Circuses	
350 Belgian	04.07.1944	08.08.1944	Spitfire IX	MN	Circuses	
303 Polish Kościuszki	09.08.1944	25.09.1944	Spitfire IX	RF	Circuses	
83 GSU	04.11.1944	22.02.1945	Spitfires, Mustangs, Typhoons, etc	No code	Replacement aircraft for operational squadrons	
Central Fighter Establishment (NAFDU, Air Firing Flight, etc.)	13.07.1945	27.11.1945	All flying from Tangmere			NAFDU (787 NAS) personnel moved to Tangmere 27.10.1945 and thence to West Raynham 05.11.1945. Last CFE personnel left on 27.11.1945

References

Published works

ND = Date of publication or copyright not given

NP = Place of publication or copyright not given

Allen H. R. *Fighter Station Supreme: RAF Tangmere.* London: Panther, 1985.

Ashworth, Chris. *Action Stations 9: Military Airfields of the Central South and South-East.* Wellingborough: Patrick Stephens, 1985.

Beedle, J. *43 Squadron Royal Flying Corps, Royal Air Force: The History of the Fighting Cocks, 1916-1984.* London: Beaumont, 1985.

Bennett, John. *Fighter Nights: 456 Squadron RAAF.* Belconnen: Banner, 1995.

Bowyer, Michael J. F. *2 Group RAF, 1936-1945.* London: Faber and Faber, 1974.

Brooks, Robin. *Sussex Airfields in the Second World War.* Newbury: Countryside, 1993.

Bushell, G. D. 'A Letter from the Heat of the Battle,' *Military History Journal,* Vol. 5 (No. 1), June 1980.

Buss, Brian. *RAF Horne's D-Day Spitfires: The Story of a Small Surrey Airfield near Gatwick.* NP: privately published, 1994.

Butler, Phil. *War Prizes: An Illustrated Survey of German, Italian and Japanese Aircraft brought to Allied Countries during and after the Second World War.* Leicester: Midland Counties, 1994.

Cooksley, Peter G. *Flying Bomb.* London: Robert Hale, 1979.

Delve, Ken. *D-Day: The Air Battle.* London: Arms and Armour, 1994.

Duke, Neville. *Test Pilot.* London: Grub Street, 1992.

Endacott, Sylvia. *It Started with a Map: The Story of Bognor Regis Advanced Landing Ground, 1943-1944.* Bognor Regis: privately published, 2005.

Falconer, Jonathan. *RAF Fighter Airfields of World War 2.* Shepperton: Ian Allan, 1993.

Flintham, Vic and Andrew Thomas. *Combat Codes: A Full Explanation and Listing of British, Commonwealth and Allied Air Force Unit Codes since 1938.* Barnsley: Pen and Sword, 2008.

Franks, Norman. *Another Kind of Courage: Stories of the UK-based Walrus Air-Sea Rescue Squadrons.* NP: Patrick Stephens, 1994.

Franks, Norman. *Royal Air Force Fighter Command Losses of the Second World War. Operational Losses: Aircraft and Crews.* 3 Vols: 1939-1941, 1942-1943, 1944-1945. Earl Shilton (Leicestershire): Midland, 1997, 1998, 2000.

Franks, Norman. *Frank 'Chota' Carey: The Story of Group Captain Frank Carey, CBE, DFC, AFC, DFM.* London: Grub Street, 2006.

Franks, Norman and Mike O'Connor. *Number One in War and Peace: The History of No. 1 Squadron, 1912-2000.* London: Grub Street, 2000.

Halley, James J. *The Squadrons of the Royal Air Force and Commonwealth, 1918-1988.* Tonbridge: Air Britain, 1988.

Halpenny, Bruce Barrymore. *Action Stations 8: Military Airfields of Greater London.* Wellingborough: Patrick Stephens, 1984.

Hamlin, Paul and Ann Davies. *Coolham Airfield Remembered: Memories and Anecdotes of a Sussex D-Day Fighter Station and Village.* Horsham: privately published, 1996.

Hillier, Mark, Dieter Sinanan and Gregory Percival. *Westhampnett at War.* NP: privately published, 2010.

Houlton, Johnnie. *Spitfire Strikes: A New Zealand Fighter Pilot's Story.* London: John Murray, 1985.

Jacobs, Peter. *Airfields of the D-Day Invasion Air Force: 2nd Tactical Air Force in South-East England in WWII.* Barnsley: Pen and Sword, 2009.

Johnstone, Sandy. *Enemy in the Sky: My 1940 Diary.* London: William Kimber, 1976.

Kellett, J. P. and J. Davies. *A History of the RAF Servicing Commandos.* Shrewsbury: Airlife, 1989.

Mason, Francis K. *Battle over Britain.* London: McWhirter, 1969.

Matthews, Rupert. *Heroes of Fighter Command: Sussex.* Newbury: Countryside, 2007.

Maurer, Maurer, ed. *The U. S. Air Service in World War I. Volume I: The Final Report and a Tactical History.* Washington: Headquarters of the United States Air Force, 1978.

Moulson, Tom. *The Flying Sword: The Story of 601 Squadron.* London: Macdonald, 1964.

Olley, Daphne. 'The Moon Men and the Girl with the Golden Voice.' *The Tangmere Logbook,* Summer 2011.

Pitchfork, Graham. *Shot Down and in the Drink: RAF and Commonwealth Aircrews Saved from the Sea, 1939-1945.* London: National Archives, 2005.

Ramsey, Winston G. *The Battle of Britain Then and Now.* Fifth Edition. London: Battle of Britain Prints International, 1989.

Rawlings, John. *Fighter Squadrons of the RAF and their Aircraft.* London: Macdonald, 1969.

Rawnsley, C. F. and Robert Wright. *Night Fighter.* London: Collins, 1957.

Richey, Paul. *Fighter Pilot: A Personal Record of the Campaign in France, 1939-1940.* Revised edition. London: Cassell, 2001.

Rogers, Bogart. *A Yankee Ace in the RAF: The World War I Letters of Captain Bogart Rogers.* John H. Morrow Jr and Earl Rogers, eds. Lawrence: University Press of Kansas, 1996.

Rosier, Frederick with David Rosier. *Be Bold: Air Chief Marshal Sir Frederick Rosier, GCB, CBE, DSO.* London: Grub Street, 2011.

Shaw, Michael. *Twice Vertical: The History of No. 1 Squadron, Royal Air Force.* London: Macdonald, 1971.

Shores, Christopher F. *2nd TAF.* Reading: Osprey, 1970.

Shores, Christopher and Chris Thomas. *2nd Tactical Air Force: Volume 1, Spartan to Normandy, June 1943 to June 1944.* Hinckley: Classic, 2004.

Shores, Christopher and Chris Thomas. *2nd Tactical Air Force: Volume 2, Breakout to Bodenplatte, July 1944 to January 1945.* Hinckley: Classic, 2005.

Sturtivant, Ray. *The Squadrons of the Fleet Air Arm.* Tonbridge: Air-Britain, 1984.

Thomas, Nick. *RAF Top Gun: The Story of Battle of Britain Ace and World Air Speed Record Holder, Air Commodore E. M. 'Teddy' Donaldson, CB, CBE, DSO, AFC.* Barnsley: Pen and Sword, 2008.

Townsend, Peter. *Time and Chance: An Autobiography.* London: Collins, 1978.

Twiss, Peter. *Faster than the Sun.* London, Macdonald, 1963.

Vincent, S. F. *Flying Fever.* London: Jarrolds, 1972.

White, Ian. *Si vis pacem, para bellum: If You Want Peace, Prepare for War. A History of No. 604 (County of Middlesex) Squadron, RAuxAF, in Peace and War.* NP: 604 Squadron Association, 2005.

Wood, Derek, ed. *Overlord, 1944: Bracknell Paper No. 5, A Symposium on the Normandy Landings.* Bracknell: Royal Air Force Historical Society, 1994.

Wood, Derek, ed. *The RAF and the Far East War, 1941-1945.* NP: Royal Air Force Historical Society, 1995.

Wood, Derek, ed. *Defending Northern Skies 1915-1995.* NP: Royal Air Force Historical Society, 1996.

Verity, Hugh. *We Landed by Moonlight: Secret RAF Landings in France, 1940-44.* Revised edition. Manchester: Crécy Publishing, 2000.

Official documents and unpublished manuscripts

NA = National Archives
RAFM = Royal Air Force Museum
TMAM = Tangmere Military Aviation Museum
USAFHRO = United States Air Force Historical Research Office
WSRO = West Sussex Record Office

Air Ministry, Aerodrome Board. Reports on Training Depot Stations at Tangmere, Ford Junction, Goring-by-Sea, Rustington, and Southbourne. AIR 1/452, NA and MP 1704, WSRO.

Air Ministry, Air Historical Branch, Operations Record Books:

1 Squadron, 1926-40. AIR 27/1. NA.

1 Squadron, 1946-50. AIR 27/2388. NA.

1 Squadron, 1951-57. AIR 27/2688. NA.

1 Squadron, 1958-60. AIR 27/2724. NA.

41 Squadron, 1941-43. AIR 27/425. NA.

43 Squadron, 1925-39. AIR 27/440. NA.

43 Squadron, 1940. AIR 27/441. NA.

43 Squadron, 1949-50. AIR 27/2414. NA.

129 Squadron, 1942. AIR 27/934. NA.

145 Squadron, 1939-40. AIR 27/984. NA.

161 Squadron, 1942-45. AIR 27/1068. NA.

412 Squadron, 1944-46. AIR 27/1806. NA.

486 Squadron, 1942-45. AIR 27/1935. NA.

601 Squadron, 1940. AIR 27/2068. NA.

602 Squadron, 1927-42. AIR 27/2076. NA.

602 Squadron, 1943-45. AIR 27/2078. NA.

610 Squadron, 1940-41. AIR 27/2106. NA.

616 Squadron, 1940. AIR 27/2126. NA.

Fighter Interception Unit, 1940-44. AIR 29/27. NA.

RAF Ford, 1940-45. AIR 28/285. NA.

RAF Tangmere, 1925-44. AIR 28/815. NA.

RAF Tangmere, 1945 + CFE Reports. AIR 28/817. NA.

RAF Tangmere, 1946-50. AIR 28/1129. NA.

RAF Tangmere, 1951-55. AIR 28/1272. NA.

RAF Tangmere, 1956-60. AIR 28/1426. NA.

RAF Tangmere, 1961-65. AIR 28/1686. NA.

RAF Tangmere, Administrative and Operations Orders, 1949-59. AIR 28/1129. NA.

Air Ministry, Air Historical Branch. Purchase of Land and Buildings at Tangmere Aerodrome. AIR 2/240. NA.

Air Ministry, Works and Buildings Branch. Tangmere location plan revised to December 1927 and various photographic views. RAFM.

Central Fighter Establishment. Fighter Leaders' School, Syllabus No. 2 Course, 6.5.45 – 27.6.45. TMAM.

Correspondence and notes relating to the history of Tangmere RAF Station 1923-1985. Par 192/7/16. WSRO.

Gloster Aircraft Ltd and Rolls-Royce Ltd. World Air Speed Record press releases and technical notes on modifications to and performance of Meteor airframe and Derwent V engines, Mimeo., dated 1946. TMAM.

'History of the Night Bombardment Section in France' and related documents referring to Tangmere and Ford extracted from Gorrell's *History of the Air Service of the American Expeditionary Force in World War I*. USAFHRO.

Howard-Williams, Jeremy. 'The Fighter Interception Unit: The Operational Flying Club.' Typescript. TMAM.

Letters relating to the Mid-Lavant Wood Distillation Factory (with some references to the sale of Tangmere aerodrome site). Goodwood Mss 1316. WSRO.

Marsden, Eric. '145 Squadron, Tangmere 1940.' Typescript. TMAM.

Ordnance Survey maps relating to the establishment of Tangmere Airfield. Par 192/7/15. WSRO.

Plan of land at Tangmere and Boxgrove sold to the Air Ministry. WDC/LA 16/4. WSRO.

Plans of RFC airfields in the 20th century. MP1704. WSRO.

Prizer, Edward L. 'Overseas Diary.' Typescript. TMAM.

Selway, Sir Anthony. 'RAF Tangmere, 1929-1930.' Typescript. TMAM.

Title deeds of property in Tangmere now part of the site of Tangmere Airfield 1749-1901. Add Mss 29543-29568. WSRO.

Townsend, Charles. 'RAF Tangmere: The Goodwood Papers, December 1916 – September 1927.' Transcribed extracts from the Goodwood estate letter books. Typescript. TMAM.

Townsend, Charles. Untitled compendium of maps and statistics relating to RAF Tangmere 1916–1944. TMAM.

Index

People and Principal Places

Persons later knighted or ennobled are listed under the names or titles by which they were known at the time of their first appearance in the text. Refer to Appendices 2 and 3 for data on Tangmere Sector squadrons, airfields, and aircraft.